THE
"CUBAN CRISIS"
of 1962

Selected Documents and Chronology

❖ ❖ ❖ ❖ ❖ ❖ ❖

Edited by

David L. Larson

Tufts University

HOUGHTON MIFFLIN COMPANY · BOSTON

Under the editorship of

Dayton D. McKean

University of Colorado

❖ ❖ ❖ PREFACE

The "Cuban Crisis" of 1962 is but one in a long series of crises which has involved the United States and Cuba from the time of George Washington down to John Kennedy [1] These various Cuban crises manifest one or more of four recurrent and interdependent themes in the foreign policy of the United States throughout this long period. The first theme was the hegemony of the United States in the Western Hemisphere and was evidenced most popularly in the "Monroe Doctrine" The second theme was the physical expansion of the country from ocean to ocean and bay to bay, which was rationalized in the messianic phrase of "Manifest Destiny" A third theme of U.S. foreign policy was the acquisition and/or control of Cuba which reached its height in the "Ostend Manifesto" of 1854. The fourth theme of Yankee hemispheric policy was the construction and protection of an inter-oceanic canal, and was characterized by Teddy Roosevelt's overt declaration in 1911: "I took Panama"

The chronic crises between the United States and Spain over Cuba in the nineteenth century became known as the "Cuban Question." The Cuban Question and the gradual dissolution of the Spanish Empire was to the Western Hemisphere what the "Eastern Question" and the slow disintegration of the Ottoman Empire was to the Eastern Hemisphere. As these two formerly great empires began to contract, they attracted the Great Powers of Europe which began to maneuver for position, power and prestige. However, here the analogy begins to break down, for if the Eastern Question acted like a "vortex pulling all the Great Powers in," the Cuban Question aroused inter-American aspirations for independence and U.S. foreign policy acted more like a centrifuge throwing the Great Powers out.

One of the first indications of this centrifugal force in American politics was George Washington's "Farewell Address" in 1796. Although this statement has been variously construed, it is relatively clear that the spirit and intent of this message was to keep the United States disengaged from "permanent alliances" and European politics. Thomas Jefferson furthered this separateness through his Louisiana Purchase and his "non-transfer" principle of a colony in the Western Hemisphere from one European power to another. This general policy of the disengagement of American from European politics gradually grew and finally crystallized in the Monroe Doctrine.

The Monroe Doctrine was included in several passages of James

---

[1] Refer to Chronology for historical survey.

Monroe's annual message to Congress in 1823, and had some interesting motivations [2] The first and most generally recognized desire was to restrain the Holy Alliance from possible attempts to repossess the vanishing Spanish colonies in the Western Hemisphere. A second purpose may have been to steer an independent course from European politics and not be a "cock-boat in the wake of a British man-of-war." A third and less well known cause for the enunciation of the Monroe Doctrine was the extension of Russian claims down the West Coast of North America to San Francisco and out to sea for about three hundred miles. The physical presence of Russia on the North American continent and her expansive claims and holdings came into conflict with several themes of American foreign policy and were cause for concern down to the actual purchase of Alaska from Russia in 1867.

While the United States was attempting to fend off European interference in the Western Hemisphere, it was simultaneously expanding across the continent from ocean to ocean and struggling to assert its hegemony throughout the Hemisphere. Up to the Civil War, Cuba looked quite attractive primarily to the Southern slavery expansionists, but after the Civil War it was largely the Northern humanitarian imperialists who found Cuba a seductive lure. In the latter part of the nineteenth century the chronic internal troubles of Cuba invited interference on the part of the United States and other powers. To the North American imperialists Cuba held a special significance because of its strategic location commanding the entrances to the Gulf of Mexico as well as to the proposed canal routes in Nicaragua and Panama. Cuba in the hands of an unfriendly power was generally considered an impossible proposition, and Cuba in the hands of a declining Spain was a barely acceptable condition.

The pretexts for an American attack on Cuba developed in the 1890's, and the United States soon found itself in global conflict with Spain. The exact causes or motivations for this war with Spain are difficult to ascertain clearly; however, the underlying causes were undoubtedly intertwined with the four basic themes of United States foreign policy. The immediate causes may be attributed to the growing realization of American power and the bitter newspaper rivalry between the *New York World* and the *New York Journal* which distorted Cuban-American relations out of all proportion. The Spanish-American War was soon over, and by the Treaty of Paris, the United States received control over Cuba and exercised a direct protectorate for the next thirty-five years and an indirect protectorate for an indeterminate period.

From the Treaty of Havana in 1899 to the Treaty of Washington in 1934, the relationship between the United States and Cuba was very much that of sovereign and protectorate. The United States had to

---

[2] Refer to Appendix for text.

intervene directly in Cuban affairs several times prior to World War I, and a readily discernible anti-Yankee feeling began to emerge in Cuba and among the other Latin American states. The various attempts by the United States to manipulate Latin America and assert its hegemony throughout the Hemisphere caused considerable friction and concern among its hemispheric neighbors. The negative feelings of the Latin American states became even more apparent after World War I and Herbert Hoover attempted to remove the unilateral aspects of United States policy toward Latin America and substitute a policy of equality and equal dignity among all hemispheric states. This general program became known as the "good neighbor policy" and was quickly adopted and expanded by Franklin Roosevelt. One of the first things Roosevelt did was to terminate the Cuban protectorate in 1934 and eschew the U.S. policy of unilateral intervention for multilateral non-intervention. This became the pattern of United States-Latin American relations throughout the 1930's, but under the threat of international war in Europe and the Far East the Latin American states willingly exchanged these recent guarantees for the protection afforded by the "Colossus of the North."

Following World War II, multilateral non-intervention was exchanged by the Pan-American states for the more positive policy of collective security under the aegis of the United Nations and the Organization of American States. This system of international collective security and hemispheric solidarity worked reasonably well until the penetration of international communism into Cuba in 1959. This caused a great disruption and embarrassment in inter-American affairs and presented a real dilemma for the United States: intervention in the internal affairs of a sovereign state or the establishment of international communism in the Western Hemisphere. This dilemma cut squarely across the roots of United States foreign policy in the Western Hemisphere and caused the fruits of the Monroe Doctrine to wither on the branch or rot on the ground: hegemony in the Western Hemisphere was broken, expansion and influence had been checked, Cuba was controlled by a European political system, and the Panama Canal lay exposed.

It was in this general context that we saw the frustration of Dwight Eisenhower, the "failure" of the Bay of Pigs invasion, and the "Cuban Crisis" of 1962 developing and reaching a climax. It is still much too early to assess with any clarity or precision what effects this recent Cuban crisis will have on world politics, but it is reasonably safe to assume that the international climate and environment has changed — exactly to what degree and in which direction is a determination left to each individual and the later revelations of time.

❖   ❖   ❖

This collection of documents and the chronology are primarily designed as a case study for the student of international relations and

United States foreign policy. All documents and events were received and treated as they occurred and not edited with the benefit of hindsight. Most of the material included was derived from United States or United Nations sources, although every effort was made to be as objective and inclusive as possible.

The second purpose of this study is to provide as complete and comprehensive a collection of documents and chronology of events relating to the Cuban Crisis as is available at the moment, in order that the student or interested layman may have a concise history readily available. However, it should be made clear that this collection of documents and chronology is not definitive, largely because completeness is neither possible nor wholly necessary. For example, a literal text of Chairman Khrushchev's letter to President Kennedy of October 26th is not available, and yet this formed much of the substantive basis for the initial agreement. However, this lack should not inhibit or prevent us from examining the materials available and making a reasonable estimate of what the contents of the October 26th letter are. In fact, it is really incumbent upon all of us, students and citizens alike, to examine, evaluate, and collate the information available on this or any similar crisis, if we are to become informed and intelligent observers of the international scene.

One of the tasks of the decision-maker and the political scientist (a pseudo-decision-maker) is to determine the facts of a given situation as quickly and accurately as possible in order to arrive at a reasonable estimate upon which to base future action. In this regard the decision-maker and the political scientist are not totally different from the citizen at large, because an informed citizenry is one of the factors to be considered when evaluating a situation or planning an action.

The study is broken down into four basic sections: documents, appendix, chronology, and bibliography. The purpose of the documents section is to present a collection of contemporary statements, proclamations, and letters in some systematic and representative order which will unfold and reveal the essential characteristics of the Cuban Crisis as they occurred. The appendix is designed to expand and elaborate the contemporary documents with pertinent and historical statements or treaties The chronology is intended to provide some background and continuity to the documents, and is so constructed as to be more representative than complete. And finally the bibliography is developed both as a reference and as an indication of the sources consulted.

The development of this case study was made possible through a grant from the Tufts University Faculty Research Fund and with the encouragement of Professor Robert R. Robbins, Chairman of the Department of Government. The invaluable assistance of Miss Dorothy Fox and Mrs Rachel Lewis of the Edwin Ginn Library of the Fletcher School of Law and Diplomacy at Tufts University is appreciated, along

with the assistance of Mrs. Susan Bove of the library at the World
Peace Foundation in Boston. I would also like to acknowledge the
counsel and suggestions received from Professor Ruhl J. Bartlett of the
Fletcher School.

Of particular help and assistance was Mr. Irvin S. Taubkin, Program
Director of *The New York Times*, who cooperated in securing permission to reprint selected articles and statements from *The New York
Times*. The production of the manuscript fell upon the capable
shoulders of Mrs. Katharine Dempster, Mrs. Evelyn Howard and Miss
Florence Hill, who also made some constructive suggestions in form
as the study progressed. Mr. Richard N. Clark of the Houghton
Mifflin Company also made many helpful comments throughout the
development of the book from manuscript to printed word, and greatly
contributed to the balance and accuracy of the text. However, the
fundamental responsibility for the inclusion or exclusion of materials
rests entirely with the editor.

DAVID L. LARSON

Tufts University
Medford, Massachusetts
March, 1963

✧ ✧ ✧ CONTENTS

APPENDIX

DOCUMENTS

✧ ✧ ✧

✧ ✧ ✧ **1**

STATEMENT BY PRESIDENT JOHN F. KENNEDY ON CUBA, *September 4, 1962*

All Americans, as well as all of our friends in this Hemisphere, have been concerned over the recent moves of the Soviet Union to bolster the military power of the Castro regime in Cuba. Information has reached this Government in the last four days from a variety of sources which establishes without doubt that the Soviets have provided the Cuban Government with a number of anti-aircraft defense missiles with a slant range of twenty-five miles which are similar to early models of our Nike. Along with these missiles, the Soviets are apparently providing the extensive radar and other electronic equipment which is required for their operation. We can also confirm the presence of several Soviet-made motor torpedo boats carrying ship-to-ship guided missiles having a range of fifteen miles. The number of Soviet military technicians now known to be in Cuba or en route — approximately 3,500 — is consistent with assistance in setting up and learning to use this equipment. As I stated last week, we shall continue to make information available as fast as it is obtained and properly verified.

There is no evidence of any organized combat force in Cuba from any Soviet bloc country; of military bases provided to Russia; of a violation of the 1934 treaty relating to Guantanamo; of the presence of offensive ground-to-ground missiles; or of other significant offensive capability either in Cuban hands or under Soviet direction and guidance. Were it to be otherwise, the gravest issues would arise.

The Cuban question must be considered as a part of the worldwide challenge posed by Communist threats to the peace. It must be dealt with as a part of that larger issue as well as in the context of the special relationships which have long characterized the inter-American system.

It continues to be the policy of the United States that the Castro regime will not be allowed to export its aggressive purposes by force or the threat of force. It will be prevented by whatever means may be necessary from taking action against any part of the Western Hemisphere. The United States, in conjunction with other Hemisphere

3

countries, will make sure that while increased Cuban armaments will
be a heavy burden to the unhappy people of Cuba themselves, they
will be nothing more.

U.S., Department of State, *Bulletin,* Volume XLVII, No. 1213 (September
24, 1962), p. 450. (Read to news correspondents on September 4, by Pierre
Salinger, White House Press Secretary.)

✧ ✧ ✧ **2**

STATEMENT BY SENATOR EVERETT McKINLEY DIRKSEN, *September 7, 1962*

From 1823 until 1947 the nations of North and South America were
protected by the Monroe Doctrine, which declared that the United
States would consider the extension of any alien system of government "to any portions of this Hemisphere as dangerous to our peace
and safety."

In 1947 this doctrine was extended to embrace action by all American nations when the Inter-American Treaty of Reciprocal Assistance
was signed at Rio de Janeiro. In 1954, under the Caracas declaration,
this multilateral promise of action was specifically applied to communism.

The United States and its sister members of the Organization of
American States are now confronted by the existence of a Communist
Government in Cuba and delivery of Soviet arms and Soviet military
technicians to that Communist state, by the admission of the Soviet
Union itself. These facts constitute a deliberate challenge to the
Monroe Doctrine of 1823, the Rio de Janeiro treaty of 1947 and the
Caracas declaration of 1954.

Several courses of action have already been advanced. In view of
our treaty commitments, however, we believe:

(1) A course of action should be promptly fixed by the Organization of American States in concert, or

(2) As President Kennedy has already stated in his speech to
United States editors (April 20, 1961), "If the nations of this Hemisphere should fail to meet their commitments against outside Communist penetration," then the United States must act on its own.

Obviously the Congress of the United States has responsibility in the
matter. In 1955, when Communist China menaced Formosa [Taiwan]
and the Pescadores [Pengau], the Congress by joint resolution au-

thorized the President of the United States to employ our own armed forces as he deemed necessary to protect those Asiatic islands.

We, the members of the joint Senate-House Republican leadership, believe that the Congress should adopt a similar authorizing resolution to meet the Cuban problem and we shall invite our Democratic counterparts to join us in its drafting, its introduction and its passage by this Congress before it adjourns. We recommend that the measure be drawn up by the Foreign Relations Committee of the Senate and the Foreign Affairs Committee of the House, acting in consultation with the appropriate agencies of the Executive Branch.

This course of action by the Congress will reflect the determination and clear purpose of the American people and will demonstrate to the world the firmness of this nation in meeting this problem.

The New York Times, September 8, 1962, p. 2. Copyright by The New York Times. Reprinted by permission.

✧ ✧ ✧ **3**

STATEMENT BY REPRESENTATIVE CHARLES A. HALLECK, *September 7, 1962*

On September 1 the Soviet Union announced what this nation has long known — that Russia had agreed to supply "armaments" to Cuba and technical specialists "for training Cuban servicemen."

It is important to point out that the only thing new about Soviet military assistance to Cuba is the Kremlin's confirmation of it. Evidently forgotten is the fact that the Department of State on April 3, 1961 — nearly eighteen months ago — issued its white paper on Cuba, which contained the following facts:

As of eighteen months ago, 30,000 tons of arms had been shipped by Iron Curtain countries to Cuba, having an estimated value of $50,000,000.

Included as of eighteen months ago were Soviet JS–2 fifty-one-ton tanks, Soviet SU–100 assault guns, Soviet T–34 thirty-five-ton tanks, and Soviet field guns of 76 mm., 85 mm. and 122 mm. caliber.

Also included as of eighteen months ago were an unspecified number of Soviet and Communist Czechoslovakian military technicians sent to train a Cuban military establishment estimated at between 250,000 and 400,000 personnel, the largest in this Hemisphere except for our own military establishment.

This week, President Kennedy advised the American people these armaments have been increased since July by the Soviet Union through shipments of anti-aircraft missiles with a slant range of twenty-five miles, torpedo boats with guider-missile launchers having a range of fifteen miles, and 3,500 military technicians.

On the basis of official information from the State Department eighteen months ago and the President's statement only three days ago, it must be inescapably concluded that not only is the situation in Cuba serious but that it is getting worse from the point of view of our own vital interests and the security of this country.

Obviously there is no easy solution, but we believe it imperative for the Congress, the Executive Branch and the American people to unite in a calm, considered approach to meet this problem. The time is at hand for effective and decisive leadership in the Cuban situation. Our national security must be our first concern.

The New York Times, September 8, 1962, p. 2. Copyright by The New York Times. Reprinted by permission.

✧ ✧ ✧ **4**

REQUEST BY PRESIDENT KENNEDY TO CONGRESS FOR STANDBY AUTHORITY TO CALL UP RESERVES, *September 7, 1962*

I transmit herewith a draft of a proposed bill to authorize the President to order units and members in the Ready Reserve to active duty for not more than twelve months, and for other purposes.

In my judgment this renewed authorization is necessary to permit prompt and effective responses, as necessary, to challenges which may be presented in any part of the free world, and I hope that the Congress will give its prompt support of this authorization as it did, so effectively, a year ago.

Sincerely,
JOHN F. KENNEDY

A bill to authorize the President to order units and members in the Ready Reserve to active duty for more than twelve months, and for other purposes.

Section 1. Be it enacted by the Senate and House of Representatives of the United States of America in Congress assembled, that, notwithstanding any other provision of law, until February 28, 1963, the President may, without the consent of the persons concerned, order any unit, and any member not assigned to a unit organized to serve as a unit, in the Ready Reserve of an Armed Force to active duty not more than twelve consecutive months. However, not more than 150,-000 members of the Ready Reserve may be on active duty (other than for training), without their consent under this section at any one time.

Section 2. Notwithstanding any other provision of law, until February 28, 1963, the President may authorize the Secretary of Defense to extend enlistments, appointments, periods of active duty, periods of active duty for training, periods of obligated service or other military status, in any component of an Armed Force or in the National Guard that expire before February 28, 1963, for not more than twelve months. However, if the enlistment of a member of the Ready Reserve who is ordered to active duty under the first section of this act would expire after February 28, 1963, but before he has served the entire period for which he was so ordered to active duty, his enlistment may be extended until the last day of that period.

Section 3. No member of the Ready Reserve who was involuntarily ordered to active duty under the act of August 1, 1961, Public Law Law 87–117 (75 Stat. 242), may be involuntarily ordered to active duty under this act.

Section 4. This act becomes effective on the day after the Eighty-Seventh Congress adjourns sine die.

The New York Times, September 8, 1962, p. 2. Copyright by The New York Times. Reprinted by permission.

✧ ✧ ✧ **5**

STATEMENT BY SOVIET UNION THAT A U.S. ATTACK ON CUBA WOULD MEAN NUCLEAR WAR, *September 11, 1962*

The Soviet Government has stated more than once that, carrying through a policy of peaceful coexistence with all countries irrespective of their socio-political order, it has exerted and does exert all efforts to safeguard peace for all the peoples of the world, to secure agreement on general and complete disarmament under strict international control.

The Government of the U.S.S.R. deems it necessary to draw the attention of the governments of all countries and world opinion to the provocations the United States Government is now staging, provocations which might plunge the world into the disaster if a universal world war with the use of thermonuclear weapons.

Bellicose-minded reactionary elements of the United States have long since been conducting in the United States Congress and in the American press an unbridled propaganda campaign against the Cuban Republic, calling for an attack on Cuba, an attack on Soviet ships carrying the necessary commodities and food to the Cuban people, in one word, calling for war.

At first the Soviet Union did not pay special importance to this propaganda against peace, against humanity and humaneness, believing that this propaganda was conducted by irresponsible persons who do not represent or represent but do not heed the interests of the people and that all this provocative clamor was raised in the United States in connection with the preparation for the Congressional elections when the rival bourgeois parties, the Republicans and the Democrats, as usual in imperialist states, vie with each other in who can hurl more infamies against the peace forces. Unfortunately, there still are many people in the United States who were fooled by this vile propaganda. The United States monopoly capital owning the entire press of the country, radio and broadcasting, all means of influencing the minds of the peoples, keep the American people as captives of ignorance and take advantage of this in order to condition public opinion of the country in a direction that suits them. During the many years of coexistence with the United States we have already become accustomed to such kind of devil's Sabbath and therefore did not attach special importance to it.

Now, however, one cannot ignore this, because the President of the United States asked Congress to permit the call-up of 150,000 reservists to the armed forces of the United States. Motivating his request, the President said that the United States must have the possibility of rapidly and effectively reacting in case of need to a danger that might arise in any part of the free world, and that he was taking such a step in connection with the strengthening of the armed forces of Cuba, which, they say, aggravates tension and all but creates a threat to other countries.

Such a step by the United States Government cannot be assessed otherwise than a screen for aggressive plans and intentions of the United States itself and will inevitably lead to aggravating the international atmosphere. It is said that this step is allegedly designed to ease tension. But it has never been thought that a fire can be put out by kerosene or petrol. Each thoughtful person understands that such steps do not lead to the relaxation of tension, but on the contrary are a means of aggravating tension to the limit and creating such a situation when the disaster of a world thermonuclear war can be sparked off by some accident. Hence, this is a provocation against the peace, this is done in the interests of war, in the interests of aggression.

The United States leaders seek to explain this step by the aggravation of tension. But, compared with the situation a year or even two ago, no special change can be observed. Hence, such a step is not designed to ease tension, but on the contrary, this is done to aggravate tension in the international situation.

What then has now taken place which alarmed and impelled the United States Government to take such aggressive actions? Members of the United States Congress and the press are calling a spade a spade thus giving away the real inside story behind such United States steps.

The American imperialists have been alarmed by the failure of the United States-staged economic blockade of revolutionary Cuba. They would like to strangle the Cuban people, to make them their satellite to wipe out the achievements of the revolution, accomplished by the heroic people of Cuba. To attain these ends they refused to purchase Cuban sugar, refused to sell to her their goods including even medicine and food; they did not even stop at seeking to strangle children and old folk and adults by the raw-boned hand of starvation. And all this they call humaneness!

The Soviet Union, like the other Socialist countries, stretched out a hand of assistance to the Cuban people because we understand full well Cuba's situation. After the October Revolution, when the young Soviet state was in capitalist encirclement and the peoples of our country lived through tremendous difficulties caused by postwar destruction, the United States, instead of rendering assistance, staged armed intervention against the Soviet Republic. United States troops were landed in Murmansk, Archangel and in the Far East. British troops were landed at Archangel and occupied Baku. French troops were landed at Odessa and Japanese in the Primorye (Maritime) Territory. The imperialist powers set up counter-revolutionary armies under the leadership of Kolchak, Yudenich, Denikin, Vrangel, mobilized and armed the entire counter-revolutionary mob, this scum. The peoples of the Soviet Union firmly resolved to establish at home their own order which would accord with their aspirations, exerted many efforts and sacrificed many lives to smash internal counter-revolution and expel the foreign invaders from the country.

The Soviet Union, in spite of tremendous difficulties, not only held out in the struggle for its independence but also demonstrated to the whole world the superiority of the people's Socialist order in which all means of production belong to the people, when everything is being done for the sake of the people. The whole world knows that the Soviet Union is the first Socialist country, which made a tremendous progress in the advance of the economy, science and culture, the first,

that blazed a trail into outer space and successfully continues the ex-
ploration of outer space. The peaceful constructive labor of the Soviet
people is yielding rich fruit. The flight of two Soviet spacemen side
by side for three-four days and the simultaneous landing of their space
ships indeed overwhelmed the minds of all honest people who rejoice
in progress, rejoice in the successes of the Soviet Union, in the ex-
ploration of outer space for peaceful purposes. This has been a striking manifestation of the peace-loving policy of the Soviet Union, all
whose efforts are aimed at safeguarding peace and the progress of
mankind.

The United States now wants to repeat against little heroic Cuba
what they undertook at one time against our country. But one can
say confidently that such plans are doomed to failure.

The Soviet Union could not fail to take account of the situation in
which Cuba had found itself as a result of imperialist provocations and
threats, and it went fraternally to the Cuban people's assistance. This
is being done by the other Socialist countries, too, and also by other
peace-loving states which maintain trade relations with Cuba. Soviet
ships carry to Cuba the goods she needs and return with commodities
she has in abundance, particularly sugar, which the United States —
previously the main importer — has refused to buy in the hope of undermining the economy of the Cuban Republic. This is why the
Soviet Union and other Socialist countries are buying this sugar — to
support the economy of the Cuban state.

If one is honest and proceeds from the understanding of the need
of living in peace, declared by the United States President himself, i e.,
to safeguard peaceful coexistence between states irrespective of their
socio-political order, what could have alarmed the American leaders,
what is the reason for this devil's Sabbath raised in Congress and in
the American press around Cuba?

To this one can say: Gentlemen, you are evidently so frightened
that you are afraid of your own shadow and you do not believe in the
strength of your ideas and your capitalist order. You have been so
much frightened by the October Socialist Revolution and the success
of the Soviet Union, achieved and developed on the basis of this revolution, that it seems to you some hordes are supposedly moving to
Cuba when potatoes or oil, tractors, harvesters combines and other
farming and industrial machinery are carried to Cuba to maintain the
Cuban economy.

We can say to these people that these are our ships, and that what
we carry in them is no business of theirs. It is the internal affair of the
sides engaged in this commercial transaction. We can say, quoting the
popular saying. "Don't butt your noses where you oughtn't "

But we do not hide from the world public that we really are supplying Cuba with industrial equipment and goods which are helping
to strengthen her economy and raise the well-being of the Cuban
people.

At the request of the Cuban Government, we also send Soviet agronomists, machine-operators, tractor-drivers and livestock experts to Cuba to share their experience and knowledge with their Cuban friends in order to help them raise the country's economy. We also send rank-and-file state and collective farm workers to Cuba, and accept thousands of Cubans to the Soviet Union to exchange experience and teach them the more progressive methods of agriculture, to help them master the Soviet farm machinery which is being supplied to Cuba

It will be recalled that a certain amount of armaments is also being shipped from the Soviet Union to Cuba at the request of the Cuban Government in connection with the threats by aggressive imperialist circles. The Cuban statesmen also requested the Soviet Government to send to Cuba Soviet military specialists, technicians who would train the Cubans in handling up-to-date weapons, because up-to-date weapons now call for high skill and much knowledge. It is but natural that Cuba does not yet have such specialists That is why we considered this request. It must, however, be said that the number of Soviet military specialists sent to Cuba can in no way be compared to the number of workers in agriculture and industry sent there. The armaments and military equipment sent to Cuba are designed exclusively for defensive purposes and the President of the United States and the American military just as the military of any country know what means of defense are. How can these means threaten the United States?

No, gentlemen, it is not this that alarms you. You yourselves realize all the absurdity of your claims that there is some threat to the United States emerging on the part of Cuba. You have invented this threat yourselves, and you now want to persuade others of its existence. It is the revolutionary spirit that you fear, and not the military equipment received by the Cubans for their own defense. And why should this alarm you if the statement by the President of the United States that the U[nited] S[tates] is not preparing an aggression against Cuba, is not contemplating an attack against her, accords with the real intentions of the American Government? If this is an honest statement, and the Government of the United States abides by it in its policy, then the means of defense which Cuba is getting will not be used because the need to use them will arise only in the event of aggression against Cuba.

The Government of the Soviet Union also authorized *Tass* to state that there is no need for the Soviet Union to shift its weapons for the repulsion of aggression, for a retaliatory blow, to any other country, for instance Cuba. Our nuclear weapons are so powerful in their explosive force and the Soviet Union has so powerful rockets to carry these nuclear warheads, that there is no need to search for sites for them beyond the boundaries of the Soviet Union. We have said and we do repeat that if war is unleashed, if the aggressor makes an attack on one state or another and this state asks for assistance, the Soviet Union has the possibility from its own territory to render assistance to any peace-loving state and not only to Cuba. And let no one doubt that the Soviet Union will render such assistance just as it was ready in 1956 to render military assistance to Egypt at the time of the Anglo-French-Israeli aggression in the Suez Canal region.

We do not say this to frighten someone. Intimidation is alien to the foreign policy of the Soviet State. Threats and blackmail are an integral part of the imperialist states. The Soviet Union stands for peace and wants no war.

The Soviet Government calls the attention of the world public and the governments of all countries which stand on positions of peaceful coexistence to the fact that even now, when the United States of America is preparing an act of aggression and is increasing its armed forces for this purpose by calling up 150,000 reservists, into the army, when the President of the United States is asking Congress for permission to do this, the U.S.S.R. Minister of Defense, Marshal [Rodion Y.] Malinovsky, has ordered the discharge into reserve of the service men who have completed their term. Trained soldiers are being released from the armed forces of the U.S.S.R. and recruits are being called up to replenish the units. This alone is a clear enough indication of our peaceful intentions. No Government would take such a measure if it contemplated any action of a military nature. One must realize what it means when trained soldiers are being released from the army and recruits called up who must yet be trained — and this is not so easy to do considering the complex equipment of the army which requires a great amount of knowledge not only from the commander but also from every private. In taking this step we realize measures in our day-by-day life which confirm that the Soviet Union is following a policy of insuring peace and friendship with all peoples.

The Soviet Union will not take any similar retaliatory actions to the call-up of 150,000 reservists in the United States, the more so that this cannot be of any serious military importance, given up-to-date means of nuclear rocket warfare. If in the past the yardsticks for armies of the belligerents were mainly the number of soldiers, sabers and bayonets, in our time the might of these armies is determined by a different yardstick — nuclear rocket weapons.

But at a moment when the United States is taking measures to mobilize its armed forces and is preparing for aggression against Cuba and other peace-loving states, the Soviet Government would like to draw attention to the fact that one cannot now attack Cuba and expect that the aggressor will be free from punishment for this attack. If this attack is made, this will be the beginning of the unleashing of war.

How are the preparations for aggression against Cuba being motivated? By saying that Soviet merchant ships carry cargoes to Cuba, and the U[nited] S[tates] considers them to be military cargoes. But this is a purely internal matter of the states which send these cargoes and those which buy and receive them.

The whole world knows that the United States of America has ringed the Soviet Union and other Socialist countries with bases. What have they stationed there — tractors? Are they perhaps growing rice, wheat, potatoes, or some other farm crops there? No, they have brought armaments there in their ships, and these armaments, stationed along the frontiers of the Soviet Union — in Turkey, Iran, Greece, Italy, Britain, Holland, Pakistan and other countries belonging to the military blocs of NATO, CENTO and SEATO — are said to be there lawfully, by right. They consider this their right! But to others the U[nited] S[tates] does not permit this even for defense, and when measures are nevertheless taken to strengthen the defenses of this or that country the U[nited] S[tates] raises an outcry and declares that an attack, if you please, is being prepared against them. What conceit! The U[nited] S[tates] apparently believes that in the present conditions one can proceed to aggression with impunity.

Equal rights and equal opportunities must be recognized for all countries of the world. This is not only in conformity with the recognized standards of the international law which have already taken shape. This should be strictly adhered to in practical life and activity too. And what happens in fact? The United States, for instance, is now mobilizing allegedly because our merchant ships are proceeding to Cuba. At the same time United States ships, not merchant ships, it is not a question of merchant ships, but warships, the entire Sixth Fleet of the United States, are in the Mediterranean. How many kilometers, what distance is this from the United States? The Seventh United States Fleet is in the Taiwan Strait. By how many thousands of kilometers is this fleet separated from the shores of the United States? It is even said in the United States that they have the right to be there.

What are the aims of the presence of these fleets in the Mediterranean and in the Taiwan Strait? They are not peaceful aims. That much is certain. They are aggressive military aims. And can it conduce to normal relations when U[nited] S[tates] warships cruise off the shores of other states while American admirals and generals, as if competing with each other, prattle in the press and radio from time to time about the Sixth and Seventh Fleets being designed for attack, for destroying the Socialist countries?

So long as this madness continues, this policy will not contribute to the strengthening of peace but will, on the contrary, always be a source which might at any moment produce a military conflict with all attendant consequences.

A vile campaign against the Soviet Union is now being conducted in the United States. It is shouted from the housetops that since a merchant fleet is plying between the U.S.S.R. and Cuba, carrying freight, this gives the United States the right to attack Cuba and the

Soviet Union. But what purpose serves the stay of United States warships in Turkish ports, and by what right is their stay there regarded as lawful and normal? What do they want — to obtain for themselves some exclusion from the general rules? What is declared a violation of standards for one, is regarded as normal for others.

We warn that given present conditions the Socialist camp has no fewer forces and opportunities than the United States and its allies in war blocs. This must be taken into consideration. One must be guided by this in politics so that it does not prejudice one side or the other. Only under these conditions can one avoid a military conflict, safeguard peace. Resort to provocations, guided by the absurd expectation to frighten the other side, this means irresponsible playing with the destinies of the world. Such a policy can but lead to dismal results.

It should be remembered that the times have gone forever when the U[nited] S[tates] had the monopoly of nuclear weapons. Today the Soviet Union has these weapons in sufficient quantities and of a higher quality. It should be known therefore that he who starts a war, he who sows the winds, will reap a hurricane. In digging an abyss for its opponents an aggressor will inevitably fall into it himself. Only a madman can think now that a war started by him will be a calamity only for the people against which it is unleashed. No, already Hitler's experience should have taught something to those who contemplate aggression in our days. Hitler, who started war together with Mussolini, himself perished in it, and brought disaster to all the peoples of the world. A war now would be a hundredfold more terrible, and it would bring calamities to both the peoples against which the U[nited] S[tates] is preparing aggression now, and to the people of the United States itself, and probably bigger, not lesser calamities than this will be even truer of those states, allies of the U[nited] S[tates], who border on the Soviet Union, and also of its other Allies in Europe and Asia.

But those quarters that determine the policy of the United States do not take this into consideration, they set up military bases on territories of the United States allies, build up nuclear weapons stores there, install rockets, for instance, in Turkey, Italy and Japan. It is not difficult to understand what destiny they are preparing for these their allies in case of war. For all this is done to attack the Soviet Union, the People's Republic and other Socialist states. This is well understood by the people in those very countries where United States military bases are being established, for instance, in Japan whose people are resolutely protesting against these bases.

In the light of the latest events, in the light of the request of the United States President to Congress for the permission to call up 150,000 reservists, the Soviet Government also assesses differently the flight of the American U–2 reconnaissance plane over Soviet territory in the region of Sakhalin on August 30 this year. Reports have appeared to the effect that U–2 planes are being based in Britain, Japan, Turkey, the Federal Republic of Germany and are making flights from American bases in those countries. These flights are explained by alleging that they have peaceful purposes — they take samples of air, study cloud movements. But today it is still clearly visible what samples they are taking and for what purposes these flights are undertaken.

That is why the Soviet Government appeals to the peoples urging them to raise a voice of denouncing aggressive schemes, not to allow the American aggressors to unleash war, to safeguard world peace.

The Government of the U.S.S.R. appeals to the Soviet people urging them to continue working as successfully as they are working now. The Government of the Soviet Union will do its utmost to safeguard peace and peaceful coexistence with all countries. But this does not always depend on us. The Soviet Union did not want the second World War, but Hitler imposed it upon us and we were forced to wage war. That is why we must do everything to be prepared, to see to it that our armed forces — the strategic rocket forces and the ground forces, the anti-aircraft defense, the navy and especially the submarine fleet of the Soviet Union — be able to cope with their tasks If the aggressors unleash war our armed forces must be ready to strike a crushing retaliatory blow at the aggressor.

The Soviet Government will not follow the way of the U[nited] S[tates] which is calling up 150,000 reservists. If we repeated this action of the U[nited] S[tates] we would do what apparently is wanted by certain American circles — we would help them inflame the situation. But neither can we disregard the aggressive preparations of the United States. The Soviet Government considers it its duty in this situation to display vigilance and to instruct the Minister of Defense of the Soviet Union, the command of the Soviet Army, to take all measures to raise our armed forces to peak military preparedness.

But these are exclusively precautionary measures. We shall do everything on our part so that peace is not disturbed.

The Soviet Government appeals to the government of the United States urging it to display common sense, not to lose self-control and to soberly assess what its actions might lead to if it unleashes war.

Instead of aggravating the atmosphere by such actions as the mobilization of reservists, which is tantamount to the threat of starting war, it would be more sensible if the Government of the United States, displaying wisdom, would offer a kind gesture — would establish diplomatic and trade relations with Cuba The desirability of which has been recently declared by the Cuban Government. If the American Government displayed this wisdom, the peoples would assess this properly as a realistic contribution of the United States to the relaxation of international tension, the strengthening of world peace.

If normal diplomatic and trade relations were established between

the United States of America and Cuba, there would be no need for
Cuba to strengthen her defenses, her armed forces. For then nobody
would menace Cuba with war or other aggressive actions, and the
situation would become normal.

Thus stand matters now, such is the situation at the present moment.

The Soviet Government has declared more than once and declares
now: We are stretching out a hand of friendship to the people and
Government of the United States. We would like to pool our efforts
with the Governments of the United States and other countries to
solve all ripe international problems, to safeguard peace on earth. To
do so one must agree, above all, on the first step which might be a
solution of the problem of ending nuclear weapons tests. We are
ready to reach agreement on general and complete disarmament under
strict international control.

The Soviet Government expresses the hope that the Government
of the U[nited] S[tates] will at last draw sober conclusions concerning
the need for a peace treaty with Germany. There have been many
negotiations on this question, but no progress has thus far been made.
A pause has now been reached in the talks on a German peace treaty.
But the issue remains as sharp as ever before, and is felt even more
acutely now in view of the provocations by revanchists in West Berlin
against the German Democratic Republic. It is said that it is difficult
for the United States to negotiate on the German peace treaty now as
elections to the American Congress are due in November. Well, the
Soviet Government is prepared to reckon with this. But one cannot
link the solution of the question of a German peace treaty all the
time to elections in this or that country. Elections are held often —
now here, now there, and further delay in settling the question of a
German peace treaty can only produce fresh difficulties and fresh
dangers The Soviet Government, as before, stands for the earliest
conclusion of a German peace treaty and the adjustment of the situation in West Berlin on its basis.

This task must be accomplished and it will be accomplished. The
sovereignty of the German Democratic Republic must be protected
and it will be protected. The vestiges of World War II in Europe,
including the occupation regime in West Berlin, must be liquidated
and they will be liquidated. This accords not only with the interests
of the Soviet Union and the German Democratic Republic, it accords
with the vital interests of all states, all peoples.

The Soviet Union is stretching out a hand of friendship to all peoples of the world, in order to achieve by common effort the establishment of an enduring, inviolable peace on our planet. As regards
questions of the internal, socio-political order of states, they must
be settled by each people independently, without any outside intervention. Peace can be safeguarded only if one respects the inalienable

right of each people to independence, if one strictly observes the principle of non-intervention by some states in the domestic affairs of other states. That is precisely the meaning of peaceful coexistence, underlying the peaceable policy of the Soviet state.

The New York Times, September 12, 1962, p. 16. Copyright by The New York Times. Reprinted by permission.

✧ ✧ ✧ **6**

STATEMENT BY PRESIDENT KENNEDY
ON CUBA, *September 13, 1962*

There has been a great deal of talk on the situation in Cuba in recent days both in the Communist camp and in our own, and I would like to take this opportunity to set the matter in perspective.

In the first place it is Mr. Castro and his supporters who are in trouble. In the last year his regime has been increasingly isolated from this Hemisphere. His name no longer inspires the same fear or following in other Latin American countries. He has been condemned by the Organization of American States, excluded from the Inter-American Defense Board, and kept out of the (Latin American) Free Trade Association. By his own monumental economic mismanagement, supplemented by our refusal to trade with him, his economy has crumbled and his pledges for economic progress have been discarded, along with his pledges for political freedom. His industries are stagnating, his harvests are declining, his own followers are beginning to see that their revolution has been betrayed.

So it is not surprising that in a frantic effort to bolster his regime he should try to arouse the Cuban people by charges of an imminent American invasion and commit himself still further to a Soviet take-over in the hope of preventing his own collapse.

Ever since communism moved into Cuba in 1958, Soviet technical and military personnel have moved steadily onto the island in increasing numbers at the invitation of the Cuban government. Now that movement has been increased. It is under our most careful surveillance. But I will repeat the conclusion that I reported last week, these new shipments do not constitute a serious threat to any other part of this Hemisphere.

If the United States ever should find it necessary to take military action against communism in Cuba, all of Castro's Communist-supplied weapons and technicians would not change the result or significantly extend the time required to achieve that result.

However, unilateral military intervention on the part of the United States cannot currently be either required or justified, and it is regrettable that loose talk about such action in this country might serve to give a thin color of legitimacy to the Communist pretense that such a threat exists. But let me make this clear once again: If at any time the Communist build-up in Cuba were to endanger or interfere with our security in any way, including our base at Guantanamo, our passage to the Panama Canal, our missile and space activities at Cape Canaveral, or the lives of American citizens in this country, or if Cuba should ever attempt to export its aggressive purposes by force or the threat of force against any nation in this hemisphere, or become an offensive military base of significant capacity for the Soviet Union, then this country will do whatever must be done to protect its own security and that of its allies.

We shall be alert to, and fully capable of dealing swiftly with, any such development. As President and Commander in Chief I have full authority now to take such action, and I have asked the Congress to authorize me to call up reserve forces should this or any other crisis make it necessary.

In the meantime we intend to do everything within our power to prevent such a threat from coming into existence. Our friends in Latin America must realize the consequences such developments hold out for their own peace and freedom, and we shall be making further proposals to them. Our friends in NATO must realize the implications of their ships' engaging in the Cuban trade.

We shall continue to work with Cuban refugee leaders who are dedicated as we are to that nation's future return to freedom. We shall continue to keep the American people and the Congress fully informed. We shall increase our surveillance of the whole Caribbean area. We shall neither initiate nor permit aggression in this Hemisphere.

With this in mind, while I recognize that rash talk is cheap, particularly on the part of those who did not have the responsibility, I would hope that the future record will show that the only people talking about a war and invasion at this time are the Communist spokesmen in Moscow and Habana, and that the American people, defending as we do so much of the free world, will in this nuclear age, as they have in the past, keep both their nerve and their head.

U.S., Department of State, *Bulletin*, Volume XLVII, No. 1214 (October 1, 1962), pp. 481–482. (Read by the President at the press conference on September 13.)

❖ ❖ ❖ **7**

JOINT RESOLUTION OF CONGRESS ON CUBA, *September 20/26, 1962*

WHEREAS President James Monroe, announcing the Monroe Doctrine in 1823, declared that the United States would consider any attempt on the part of European powers "To extend their system to any portion of this Hemisphere as dangerous to our peace and safety"; and

WHEREAS in the Rio Treaty of 1947 the parties agreed that "an armed attack by any State against an American State shall be considered as an attack against all the American States, and, consequently, each one of the said contracting parties undertakes to assist in meeting the attack in the exercise of the inherent right of individual or collective self-defense recognized by article 51 of the Charter of the United Nations"; and

WHEREAS the Foreign Ministers of the Organization of American States at Punta del Este in January 1962 declared: "The present Government of Cuba has identified itself with the principles of Marxist-Leninist ideology, has established a political, economic, and social system based on that doctrine, and accepts military assistance from extracontinental Communist powers, including even the threat of military intervention in America on the part of the Soviet Union"; and Whereas the international Communist movement has increasingly extended into Cuba, its political, economic, and military sphere of influence; Now, therefore, be it

RESOLVED by the Senate and House of Representatives of the United States of America in Congress assembled, That the United States is determined

(a) to prevent by whatever means may be necessary, including the use of arms, the Marxist-Leninist regime in Cuba from extending, by force or the threat of force, its aggressive or subversive activities to any part of this hemisphere;

(b) to prevent in Cuba the creation or use of an externally supported military capability endangering the security of the United States; and

(c) to work with the Organization of American States and with freedom-loving Cubans to support the aspirations of the Cuban people for self-determination.

U.S., Congress, *Congressional Record,* 87th Congress, 2nd Session, Vol. 108, No. 170, September 20, 1962, pp. 18892–18951.
U.S. Congress, *Congressional Record,* 87th Congress, 2nd Session, Vol. 108, No. 174, September 26, 1962, pp. 19702–19753. (The resolution passed the Senate on September 20 by a vote of 86 to 1 and passed the House of Representatives on September 26 by a vote of 384 to 7.)

EXCERPT FROM STATEMENT BY SOVIET FOREIGN MINISTER ANDREI A. GROMYKO, *September 21, 1962*

The United Nations would not be justifying the hopes of the peoples if it were to repeat the sad experience and mistakes of its predecessor, the League of Nations, which, like the United Nations, was designed to combat aggression and the arms race, and to strive for the strengthening of the peace and security of states.

It is a matter of common knowledge that the League of Nations fell apart, like a metal structure eaten away by rust, because it was undermined and crippled by the aggressive forces. They frustrated the adoption of proposals for disarmament and for the halting of aggression and international provocations which were put forward by the Soviet Union and by other peace-loving countries, and thereby they prevented the League of Nations from becoming a genuine peace-keeping instrument.

The present situation in the United Nations cannot fail to cause alarm among those who espouse peace and peaceful coexistence.

Particular concern among the members of the United Nations who have assembled for the 17th session of the General Assembly should be provoked by the statement which was made in regard to Cuba by Mr. Kennedy, the President of the United States, at his news conference on September 13 of this year.

The United States is a founder member of the United Nations and a permanent member of the Security Council, and economically and militarily it is the most powerful of the capitalist states. It would appear that such a country, and its statesmen, by virtue of the responsibility that devolves on the United States as a great power should display particular respect for the United Nations Charter and should conduct their policies accordingly. This particular statement by President Kennedy, however, bespeaks exactly the opposite.

The Soviet Government has, of course, noted that the statement of the United States President also contains some sound appraisals which attest to a realistic understanding of certain aspects of the Cuban question and of the [resultant] situation. Note cannot fail to be made of the fact that the United States Government has publicly divorced itself from those bellicose American circles which are calling for immediate armed aggression against Cuba. But it is blatant threats, not these sober remarks, that are the keynote, and this in effect erases whatever positive points this statement contained.

It follows from the President's remarks that the United States is at liberty to mount military action against Cuba and that it will itself decide when to deem it necessary to start an invasion. The President declared that the United States Government would go on cooperating with Cuban counterrevolutionary leaders who have found refuge in the United States.

It is also stated that the United States will be prepared to attack Cuba if it believes that Cuba is building up her forces to such a degree that she can pose a threat to the United States, or to the passage of the United States to the Panama Canal, or else a threat to any state of the Western Hemisphere.

Any sober-minded man knows that Cuba is not pursuing either the first, or the second or third, of these goals. This is fully realized by American statesmen, too. They know full well that the aid rendered by the Soviet [Union does not advance] these goals either, since they are alien to our policy.

One may well ask what kind of policy this is. Surely this is a policy of aggression, a policy of international depredation. What underlies this policy? Quite evidently the notion, inherited from the time of barbarity, that if you are strong, strangle one who is not as strong, and the more so one who is weak. But such laws are common among animals where the strong devour the weak. That goes for animals — surely humans should differ from animals.

Can the United Nations reconcile itself with a situation when one of its members loudly declares itself entitled to attack another country which is also a member of the United Nations? And all this is done because the internal order in that country contradicts the way of thinking of the United States Government, and is not to its liking.

No, such statements cannot be disregarded. This is indeed subversion of the sole foundation on which the United Nations can rest, which is non-interference in the internal affairs of other States and respect for their system and way of life. It appears that countries belonging to the capitalist system consider it possible, in order to insure the domination of that system throughout the world, to attack a state with a different, namely Socialist, social system. But such a policy passes the death sentence on the United Nations since this organization can exist only on condition that all countries, regardless of their socio-political systems, respect each other's independence and sovereignty and make no attempt to interfere in the affairs of others.

Were we to agree with the principles laid down by the President of the United States in his statement on Cuba this would lead straight to the disintegration of the United Nations. This is a policy that can kill the United Nations and the United Nations will be killed if this policy prevails.

If one state member of the United Nations makes so bold as to declare and practice a policy that endangers the independence and security of its neighbors, other United Nations member states will obviously no longer be able to rely on the United Nations and they will be compelled to seek other means in order to repel the arrogant imperialist encroachments of those who want to dominate the world by force of arms.

In our day of mastery over outer space, states possess rocket nuclear weapons with all their monstrous destructive power. Today, only a madman can pursue a policy "from positions of strength" and at that believe such a policy can yield any success and enable him to impose his ideology, and his form of political structure, on other states.

The Soviet Union and the Socialist countries possess, at the least, the same means as the capitalist countries. Today, therefore, questions at issue must be resolved by way of seeking reasonable arguments and elaborating decisions that would strengthen the peace and security of all nations, and not by way of rattling the saber or by way of threats.

For this reason, the Soviet Government believes it necessary to raise its voice in warning, and to draw the attention of members of the United Nations to the grave consequences which the policy practiced by the United States in regard to the Republic of Cuba can have for the cause of peace. If the states here represented want to preserve the United Nations, and to make it an effective instrument for the preservation and consolidation of peace, this policy and such actions must be resolutely condemned.

In our day — and this concerns particularly a big power — one must not lose common sense and composure, and display such a flippant attitude to questions bearing on war and peace, as is being displayed by some United States political leaders in regard to the situation that has taken shape in connection with Cuba. An attack on Cuba would have implications about which the Soviet Government warned the whole world in the well-known statement issued on September 11, 1962.

Those who have mustered aggressive military groupings and enmeshed the whole world with a web of their military bases to serve as springboards for aggression, those who impede the elimination of the vestiges of World War II will hardly be expected to come to this rostrum and say: yes, we are sponsors of, and participants in, preparations for war. It is a fact that wars have almost always been prepared under a veil of assurances of dedication to peace. Such is the bitter truth. And the alarm must be sounded today, not after the fatal event.

There is just one reliable way to prevent a new world war from coming to a head, and this is the destruction of material machinery of war. General and complete disarmament is the program of action, and it is now being advocated by no less than three-quarters of the countries of the world. This program will become reality all the sooner if fewer people remain in the grasp of notions that the arms race and war are inevitable, and if they fight with greater resolve and unity for disarmament as an urgent and feasible task.

The United Nations has been addressing itself to the disarmament

problem for over sixteen years. It may well be said that the problem
has become a United Nations sputnik. No small number of diverse
commissions, committees and sub-committees have been placed in
orbit around this problem.

Unfortunately, they too have had to experience a state akin to
weightlessness for, translated into realistic language, for the decisions
they took actually carry no weight at all. Again, today, the eighteen-
nation committee which was charged with working out an agreement
on general and complete disarmament under effective international
control cannot gladden the General Assembly by success in the fulfillment of the task it was set.

The Soviet Government submitted to the committee a complete
draft treaty on general and complete disarmament in three stages to
last four years. As early as after the completion of the first stage the
world would be radically different from the one in which we are living
today — it would differ in that the danger of nuclear attack by one
state on another would have vanished.

Indeed, in accordance with the Soviet draft, all nuclear weapons
delivery vehicles would have been destroyed, military bases in foreign
territories dismantled, and foreign troops withdrawn to within their
national frontiers in the first stage. This means that nuclear weapons
would already have been rendered harmless and would have become
dead ballast in depots. The implementation of second stage measures
would result in nuclear weapons being destroyed and in the disappear-
ance of the very term "nuclear power." By the end of the third stage
the elimination of all armed forces and armaments would have been
completed.

If to this day it has still not proved possible to move disarmament
out of the rut, as if it were frozen in a block of age-old ice, the
blame rests with the NATO powers, and with them alone. The proposals which the Western powers brought to Geneva are stuffed with
everything under the sun, but they lack the crucial item, namely readiness to scrap the military establishment of states.

The fact that the Western powers are now couching their demands
on control in different terms does not change their substance at all.
We are invited to turn the territories of states into something like a
chess board by dividing them into zones, and then to play a game of
control on that board. But the moves in this game will be made with
the same goal in mind, which is to obtain intelligence information in
which only a potential aggressor can be interested.

At the talks in Geneva the United States Government categorically
objected to the elimination, at the first stage of disarmament, of all
nuclear weapons delivery vehicles declaring that states embarking on
disarmament would for some time allegedly need some sort of "pro-
tective umbrella." We do not believe such arguments to be justified.
But in order to make a genuine move forward we are ready to make
yet another effort.

Taking account of the stand of the Western powers, the Soviet Government agrees that in the process of destroying nuclear weapons delivery vehicles at the first stage exception be made for a strictly limited and agreed number of global (intercontinental) missiles, anti-missile missiles, and anti-aircraft missiles of the ground-to-air type which would remain at the disposal of the U.S.S.R. and the United States alone. Thus for a definite period the means of defense would remain in case someone, as certain Western representatives fear, ventured to violate the treaty and conceal missiles or combat aircraft.

The Soviet Government is introducing the appropriate amendments to its draft Treaty on General and Complete Disarmament under Strict International Control which we are submitting for consideration by this session of the General Assembly of the United Nations.

The diversion of funds spent on armaments to the development of a peaceful economy and to the elevation of the living standards and culture of the nations is a great and noble task which requires most serious consideration. That is why the Soviet Government is proposing the inclusion of the question entitled "Economic Program of Disarmament" in the agenda of the General Assembly as a separate item.

The Soviet Government is submitting to the General Assembly the draft of a "Declaration on the Conversion to Peaceful Uses of the Means and Resources Released as a Result of Disarmament." The Soviet Government believes that the United Nations should [agree on this proposal] here and now, without waiting for the completion of negotiations on general international program for the peaceful uses of means and resources that are presently being diverted to military uses.

This session of the General Assembly is due to have its say on the problem of ending nuclear tests.

The stand of the Soviet Union is well-known — we are in favor of banning all nuclear tests without exception — in the atmosphere, in space, underground or underwater — immediately and unconditionally.

It is common knowledge that it was not the Soviet Union that initiated nuclear tests and the race of nuclear armaments — this was done by the United States. All experimental nuclear explosions that have ever been conducted by our country were but a reply to the actions of the United States and its NATO allies, Britain and France. The United States was the first to start nuclear tests, and the United States with its allies should be the first to stop them. The Soviet Union has every reason to end nuclear tests last.

A day or two ago the Soviet Government proposed an agreement to ban nuclear tests in the atmosphere, under water and in outer space, and to formalize therein a provision that countries should continue negotiations on the discontinuance of underground tests. Needless to say, while the negotiations are in progress, and until an agreement on the discontinuance of underground nuclear tests is reached, such tests should not be conducted.

We believe this proposal provides a good basis for an agreement. The key to the solution of the problem is in the hands of the Western powers.

In the present international situation the normalization of international trade has assumed tremendous — and I would say extreme — importance. Here there are some very abnormal developments which became specially aggravated with the establishment of the "Common Market."

The United Nations is witnessing a spectacle of groups of industrially advanced countries using discriminatory restrictions in trade to board up the doors of their markets and adapt external economic ties to the interests of the NATO military bloc.

Whatever the publicity attire in which the initiators of the "Common Market" would dress their policy, they will not dispel the impression that this exclusive economic grouping is used above all with a view to intensifying the arms race and strengthening the West German revenge-seeking forces. At the same time a stake is laid on binding the economy of still less-developed States to the economy of imperialist powers, on preserving in the emergent states the one-sided economic structure which they inherited from colonialism and to handicap those states in the achievement of genuine independence.

The Soviet Government is submitting to the General Assembly of the United Nations as a separate item of the agenda a proposal to convene in 1963 an International Conference on Trade Problems. It is convinced that such a conference and the setting up of an international trade organization, besides creating a sound basis for the development of economic intercourse between states, could facilitate the development of an atmosphere of trust in their relations and the lessening of international tensions.

Those who bear responsibility for the present situation in the Congo attempt to demand that the Soviet Union and other states should pay for the operations of the colonial powers aimed at subverting the independence of and dismembering the Republic of the Congo. Can it be that they want us to pay for the murder of Patrice Lumumba and hundreds of other patriots, or for the tripartite aggression against Egypt, and for other similar crimes? Let no one entertain the belief that the Soviet Union will divert a single kopeck, or a single cent to aiding the colonists to sanctify their criminal deeds.

Every time the conversation turns to the most urgent tasks of consolidating peace, you invariably return to the problem of concluding a German peace treaty and normalizing the situation in West Berlin on its basis. As far as its acuteness goes, this problem can even challenge the problem of disarmament.

✦ ✦ ✦ **9**

EXCERPT FROM STATEMENT BY AMBASSADOR
ADLAI E. STEVENSON IN REPLY TO FOREIGN
MINISTER GROMYKO, *September 21, 1962*

I had hoped that it would not be necessary to interrupt the general
debate, but the utterance of the representative of Communist Cuba
and of Mr. Gromyko today leave me no choice but to also exercise my
right of reply, not on all that has been said here, which unhappily
follows the pattern of persistent prosecution of the cold war, but with
respect to what has been said about Cuba.

The sober 17th session has ended on the fourth day. And I remind
the members of the United Nations that since the attack on Cuba by
refugees from Cuba in April, 1961, repeated complaints have been
brought to the United Nations by Cuba, accompanied by hysterical
charges that the United States was plotting, planning, preparing, immediate invasion. One of these complaints, as I recall, was filed in
August, 1961, but not pressed until six months later. The attack was
called imminent in August, but evidently even the Cubans did not
believe it.

As you know, all of these complaints were dismissed one by one,
by overwhelming votes. But only after the expenditure of much time
of the delegates and expense to the organization.

From what has been said here, it is apparent that we are going to
suffer another sustained assault on our patience and our credulity. I
would have thought that there was plenty of useful work to do here
without renewing these tired charges.

Mr. Gromyko says that the United States has asserted the right to
attack Cuba because it has another system. He says no nation should
interfere in the affairs of another. I marvel at the bland hypocrisy of
the nation that subverted the wholesome Cuban social revolution to
Communism, that crushed with tanks the independence of Hungary,
that holds in thrall all of Eastern Europe from the Baltic to the Black
Sea. Yet he presumes to lecture us on interference in the affairs of
others.

But as we know only too well, such righteous rhetoric is the standard Communist cloak for the very interference it charges to others.

Now, in direct answer, let me say to the representatives of the
Soviet Union and of Cuba, that we are not taking and will not take
offensive action in this Hemisphere, neither will we permit aggression
in this Hemisphere. For, as the President of the United States made
clear last week, we and other countries of the Americas will not be

deterred from taking whatever action is needed by threat from any quarters.

While we will not commit aggression, we will take whatever steps are necessary to prevent the Government of Cuba from seeking to subvert any part of this Hemisphere. We shall work closely with our inter-American partners and this intention does not, of course, derogate from our right, a right anchored in the United Nations Charter, to protect our vital national security.

The threat to peace in Cuba comes not from the United States but from the Soviet Union. The threat arises from the extraordinary and unnecessary flood of Soviet arms and military personnel pouring into Cuba.

It is this foreign intervention in the Western Hemisphere which is creating grave concern not only in this country, but throughout the hemisphere. For what purpose is this great military build-up in Cuba intended? No one can be sure, but all of Cuba's neighbors are justified in feeling themselves threatened and anxious.

If the Soviet Union genuinely desires to keep the peace in the Caribbean, let it stop this warlike posturing. This stuffing of Cuba with rockets, military aircraft, advanced electronic equipment and other armament [is] all out of proportion to any legitimate needs.

This military intervention from outside of this hemisphere is the threat to which the states of the Western Hemisphere cannot remain indifferent, any more than states could anywhere else.

But I think, Mr. President, the time is long past to graduate — if I can use that word — from this sort of strident talk to address ourselves to the real and urgent business of this General Assembly, which is not propaganda and abuse, but peace. The United States will exercise its opportunity to respond to other aspects of the utterances we have heard this afternoon at an appropriate time and place.

Thank you, Mr. President, and my apologies for detaining you.

The New York Times, September 22, 1962, p. 2. Copyright by The New York Times. Reprinted by permission.

✧ ✧ ✧ **10**

INTERVIEW OF SECRETARY OF STATE DEAN RUSK
BY JOHN SCALI OF ABC NEWS, *September 29, 1962*

Mr. Scali: Mr. Secretary, in the past we have said that the arms
build-up in Cuba is defensive even though Castro has been supplied
with missiles. Is it possible, now that Russia plans to build a so-called
fishing port, the balance tips from a defensive to an offensive build-up?
Secretary Rusk: Well, those announcements have to do with action to
be taken in the future. We will be watching that very carefully and
closely indeed, and we will make a judgment when we see what in
fact actually happens Now I don't think that we ought to play with
words on this question of defensive and offensive weapons. Any
weapon is offensive if you are on the wrong end of it. But the configuration of the military forces in Cuba is a configuration of defensive
capability. What we are concerned about is the development of any
significant offensive capability against Cuba's neighbors in the Caribbean, or against this country, and we are keeping a very close watch
indeed on just that point. We have very great power in that area,
and the President has made it very clear that whatever arms are in
Cuba will stay in Cuba and that there will be no effort by Castro to
move these arms into other countries.
Mr. Scali: Mr. Secretary, how will the Government be able to make a
judgment of when the arms buildup shifts from a defensive to an offensive status?
Secretary Rusk: Well, that would be a matter of detail, affirmation,
and judgment based upon all the military views available and that
would be done with our own military advisers taking a full part in an
assessment of capabilities.
Mr. Scali: How would you evaluate the Soviet arms build-up in Cuba
in terms of the total Soviet cold-war strategy?
Secretary Rusk: Oh, I think that the Soviets have had to face the fact
that this regime in Cuba has been getting into very serious trouble
indeed on the island. Foodstuffs are in very short supply, production
has dropped off severely, there has been undoubtedly a sense of un-
easiness and alarm on the part of the rulers there. They have called,
for example, for a considerable number of what seemed to have
[been] phony alerts. I think they may be trying to draw attention
away from some of the problems that they are having on the island. I
think that the Cuban situation is certainly becoming very expensive
indeed for the bloc to shore up the failures there; but it is also a very
serious problem for us and has to be treated as such.

Mr. Scali: Mr. Secretary, which is the greatest danger to the United States, the potential alienating of much of world opinion by taking firm action against Cuba, or the potential loss of prestige and respect for permitting Russia to outflank us and build a base for subversion next door to us?

Secretary Rusk: Well, I think neither one of those is a full basis for deciding what action is right and wise and necessary in a given situation. It is clear that the power of the United States is such that you could put armed forces ashore in Cuba, but that means a lot of casualties and it means a lot of Cuban casualties; it means bloodshed. And if we could find an answer without that, we should try to do so.

But the question of prestige is primarily a question of solidarity in this Hemisphere. I think that general world opinion is much less interested in Cuba than we are here, for quite understandable reasons. And we have seen here in this Hemisphere and are seeing a rapidly growing solidarity with respect to Cuba. The Communists' voices in the Hemisphere have become more vocal. But on the other hand, the Castro regime has been losing the sympathy of what might be called the democratic left. It is quite clear that the moderates and conservatives throughout the Hemisphere are losing their complacency about Castroism and are becoming more and more active and concerned about it. There has been a dramatic change since the Costa Rica conference of 1960, reflected in the Punta del Este conference in January of this year, and that movement of both peoples and governments in this Hemisphere continues. And I am now talking to foreign ministers here in New York, and we will be talking to them next week, to see what further steps we ought to take in the situation.

Mr. Scali: Mr. Secretary, in this coming week of course you will have the so-called informal meetings with the inter-American foreign ministers. Could you tell us why this meeting is an informal one and not a formal one?

Secretary Rusk: Well, the principal reason is to have a chance to meet as quickly as possible and without all of the problems that are concerned in convening a formal meeting under the organization of the OAS Charter and encounter many of the other questions that exist there among the different members of the Hemisphere. The foreign ministers were gathering here for the United Nations General Assembly. We thought that we ought to take advantage of that fact to meet just as informally as possible. It is not a meeting which can in fact take decisons under the treaties of the OAS because it is so very informal, but I already know from my own talks here in preparation for that meeting that it will be a very profitable and worthwhile meeting.

Mr. Scali: Mr. Secretary, in the past you have put a great premium on the desirability of unity within the inter-American family. Unhappily, several Latin American countries have dragged their feet on taking effective action against Castro. Is it possible that at this informal meeting you will come up with some sort of plan whereby the nations most immediately threatened by Castroism in the Central American and Caribbean area might join with the United States in some kind of tougher action?

Secretary Rusk: Well, that was already anticipated in the Punta del Este conference in January. One of the resolutions that was passed, I think by a seventeen-vote majority, did provide for joint actions by groups within the Hemisphere to deal with this specific question if necessary. We will of course continue not only our consultation with the other countries within the Caribbean area, but we will continue our close cooperative work with them on matters of common security interest — for example, on surveillance in the Caribbean, in being sure that there is no illicit arms traffic in the Caribbean area coming out of Cuba, and a variety of other actions which are being taken behind the scenes with the full cooperation of the governments in that area.

Mr. Scali: Mr. Secretary, on another point, we find that many of the Cuban exile organizations in the United States are complaining rather bitterly in some cases against the restrictions being put on them by the American Government. Many of them have all sorts of plans for returning to the homeland. Why aren't we supporting some of these exile organizations in the United States in allowing them more freedom?

Secretary Rusk: Well, we have, as you know, been giving considerable support to the refugees as such.

Mr. Scali: Right.

Secretary Rusk: Now, as happens so frequently with refugees or exile organizations, there is very little unity among them. There is a contest for influence. They find it difficult to work together. This is the principal problem insofar as any single organization is concerned. Also I think it has to be borne in mind that there are anti-Castro people on the island of Cuba who need to be recognized as having a real stake and part in this whole problem. So I realize that there are certain groups or certain committees that feel that they ought to be a chosen instrument of some sort. But the great problem and the great need is for all non-Castro Cubans to get together as closely as possible in a great unity of purpose to restore Cuba to the democratic life of the Western Hemisphere.

Mr. Scali: Mr. Secretary, you have mentioned the anti-Castro underground in Cuba, which we know exists. There are also many people who say that we should take a more active role in supporting this anti-Castro underground, perhaps by supplying them weapons and giving them encouragement through other means. What do you say to this?

Secretary Rusk: Well, I obviously can't get seriously into that question.

The anti-Castro elements in Cuba do know that they have the encouragement and support of everyone in this Hemisphere who is opposed to Castroism, but I think that this is the sort of thing or question I can't really get into.

Mr. Scali: Is it our information, sir, that considerable anti-Castro senti-
ment exists in Cuba?

Secretary Rusk: I think that that is very definitely our impression and
that this is growing, because of the ruthlessness of the regime and the
great severity of the regime on the people and their economy and their
traditional way of life. I think we know that the Castro regime has
great organized support. It has the accouterments of a police state,
but it also has underneath it what has happened in so many dictator-
ships of that sort — deep resentment on the part of the people themselves.

Mr. Scali: Mr. Secretary, the Republicans on Capitol Hill seem to be
making quite an issue of the administration policy on Cuba. Now,
granted that both Republicans and Democrats have united behind
this single resolution supporting the President, do you think that many
of the Republican demands which may come up during the election
are really political in nature?

Secretary Rusk: Well, I think that in the present campaign candidates
of both parties are going to be and should be talking about Cuba with
the people in their constituencies. I do not believe that, except for an
occasional instance, this debate can take on a straight partisan line.
Cuba has been a problem for two administrations. It is still an un-
solved problem. And in my discussions with the committees and the
leaders in our Congress, I find that the Democrats and the Republicans
are equally concerned about the problem and that they are equally
concerned about finding the right and wise course of action under all
the circumstances.

We have a national problem here in front of us, and I think vigorous
debate is to be desired and is in any event unavoidable, but I would
hope that what is necessarily a national problem does not break itself
up into alleged partisan points of view, because I feel and know that
the leadership of both parties are deeply concerned — concerned that
no satisfactory answer has yet been found and that the penetration of
this hemisphere by Castro communism is something which cannot be
accepted in the hemisphere and by the United States.

Mr. Scali: Mr. Secretary, in discussing Cuba with some of the foreign
ministers here, I know that you have heard the view expressed by some
that Cuba is a United States problem. Do you agree that this is a
strictly United States problem?

Secretary Rusk: Well, it is in the first instance a major problem for
this Hemisphere because of the commitments of the Hemisphere under
its treaties and charters, and in those commitments the United States
plays a very important role. It is a problem for us because it is a

problem in the Hemisphere as well. It would be a problem for us had we not had the Hemisphere organizations. But it is here. But it is also a part of a worldwide struggle for freedom. It is involved in a worldwide confrontation between the Communist bloc and the free world, and therefore it is one of those problems which is of concern to all the free world because this struggle is relentless and unending in every continent, and no one can be, I think, disregardful of it.

Mr. Scali: Mr. Secretary, since this is part of a worldwide Communist plot, could we not soon be approached with a deal to shut down some of our bases overseas in return for which Russia would close down her base in Cuba?

Secretary Rusk: This is not a negotiable point. This would not be a way to meet this struggle for freedom. You cannot support freedom in one place by surrendering freedom in another. In any event, we have special commitments here in this Hemisphere under our Hemisphere charters, and we cannot connect in negotiations or in trades the problem of Cuba with the defense of freedom in other places. No. This [deal] is not on.

Mr. Scali: This would also apply to any effort to link Cuba, say, with Berlin?

Secretary Rusk: Exactly.

Mr. Scali: Mr. Secretary, are you a baseball fan?

Secretary Rusk: Yes, I have been for many years.

Mr. Scali: Do you keep close tab on what the lowly Washington Senators are doing?

Secretary Rusk: Well, some of my friends think that I am a man of little conscience because I am automatically a hometown fan. I was a New York Yankee fan for many years, and now I am a Washington Senator fan. It hasn't given me too much to cheer about this season, but nevertheless it is a good ball club and I have enjoyed following them.

Mr. Scali: Do you have any hope that next year it will wind up any better?

Secretary Rusk: Well, when you wind up in the cellar, you always say, "Wait until next year!"

Mr. Scali: Thank you very much, Mr. Secretary.

U.S., Department of State, *Bulletin,* Volume XLVII, No. 1217 (October 22, 1962), pp. 595–598. (Department of State press release 590 dated September 29, 1962.)

✧ ✧ ✧ **11**

EXCERPT FROM STATEMENT BY CUBAN PRESIDENT OSVALDO DORTICOS TORRADO BEFORE U.N. GENERAL ASSEMBLY, *October 8, 1962*

Reiterated and insolent and insulting statements [about Cuba] have been made by Senators and Representatives of the United States.

Use is most wholeheartedly made in the most absurd fashion of all circumstances to feed this campaign of aggressive hysteria against our country, until it culminates, for example, in the ridiculous statement that the establishment in our territory of a fishing port, following friendly and amicable relations with the Soviet Union, also implies a threat of armed aggression, which jeopardizes the security of the United States itself, namely, that they are raising to the level of threat of war the use of codfish and herring.

We know that this atmosphere of hysteria, we know that this campaign, we know that this interminable series of slander and libel are part and parcel of pressures being exercised by the Government of the United States.

We know that that pressure exists, but we also believe that it is the Government of the United States itself that is responsible, when all is said and done, for this pressure. This pressure is the unavoidable result of the policy of constant and permanent aggression and harassment that has been followed since the new Administration took over in this country.

And everyone can see and watch the activities that are being carried out under the tutelage of this climate of anti-Cuban hysteria.

For example, not in the United Nations, but as obvious contempt for the United Nations, there is an invitation sent out to the foreign ministers of Latin America to meet at the State Department and they are invited to conspire to join the domestic subversion of my country.

Once again the so-called inter-American system is wielded, that system that the Government of the United States itself has been good enough to disdain.

Why was the system not invoked at the time of the aggression, why was the system sidestepped at the time of the invasion of the Bay of Pigs?

Doubtless it will also be this same system that will be overlooked in the case of a new armed aggression against my country.

We have seen that the Secretary of State of the United States of America was not even present at the United Nations. He has not shown his care for disarmament and peace and tranquility.

33

He has been outside our organization, taken up with his work of subversion, of conspiracy against my country. We also know full well that at that meeting of Latin American foreign ministers respectable representatives of countries of Latin America went and, despite their ideological differences with our revolution, they have defended the principles of non-intervention and self-determination of peoples.

From this rostrum I have to praise some of those foreign ministers and I challenge them to tell us what was discussed at that meeting and what was discussed outside the meeting, so that one and all will know that it is not Cuba that upsets peace in this continent, it is not Cuba that attacks sister republics, but Cuba that is the victim and doubtless will be pointed out as the next victim of interference and new aggression and new obstacles to its development.

Without consulting any of the international bodies, with contempt for one and all, the Government of the United States, by taking unilateral decisions still carries out activities that flagrantly flout and violate the principles of the Charter of the United Nations.

Coercions are used to force the naval blockade of our island. In open daylight pressures are exercised on the countries of NATO themselves to have them stop their ships from carrying cargo to our country.

And if this is unsuccessful there is still another tool — reprisals against ships that do carry cargoes to my country.

This pressure for blockades, the carrying out of unilateral acts to force this blockade, gentlemen, in a time of peace and I ask myself and I throw the question at you gentlemen whether a blockade is or is not an act of war.

And I ask you gentlemen whether the Government of the United States is entitled or empowered or allowed, outside this international organization, showing its contempt for the organization, to take such unilateral decisions having such repercussions.

And I ask you gentlemen whether this can be made to jibe with the purposes of improving and widening international relations, which led to the setting up and the establishment of the United Nations organization. I ask and I wonder whether the United Nations organization can impassively watch such events take place.

Cuba asks the condemnation of such aggressive acts, a condemnation from the United Nations.

Cuba has said in the past and repeats it here that we do not intend nor shall we ever carry out any activities extending the ideology of our revolutionary process to any other countries or parts of this hemisphere.

We shall not give as a free gift to the United States the pretext for aggression.

We hope that this will be a dispute and a controversy that one day will be settled by peaceful negotiations, but until that day dawns, and while we wait the moment to exercise that right in accordance with international law, we wish to denounce from this rostrum any effort to use, as a pretext for aggression, any self-provocation and aggression coming from the base at Guantanamo.

Gentlemen, from the beginning of the deterioration of Cuban-United States relations, Cuba has constantly been ready to negotiate.

And as Cuba is ready, so we have the moral right to challenge the delegation of the Government of the United States to tell us whether the Government of the United States of America is equally ready to take the necessary and useful steps to overcome the present international tensions around Cuba.

We are pessimistic; unfortunately, we can more or less anticipate the answer that will be given us.

Those steps, and you gentlemen can stand as witnesses, those steps will not be taken. We would like them to be taken. We are lovers of peace. We wish to work, we want to speed up the progress of our country. We don't want war. We don't want to fight. But we have to follow the lead of patriotism, we have to follow the lead of serenity, and that of the responsibility of the leaders.

Unfortunately, the road followed by the United States of America is not this. Their powers have led them down the road of arrogance, hunger for domination and panic in the light of the Cuban revolution.

Cuba is not an aggressive country. The problem of Cuba is the question of the sovereign decision of a people and a right of that people to self-determination. Cuba did not wish to add its name to the roster of those involved in the cold war.

Cuba only wishes to develop its economy, assist its culture and plan and carry out a good future in peace. Cuba is ready at any given moment to prove those aims.

If it be true that there is no intention of attacking our country, then in this°Assembly we urge the head of the United States delegation to be good enough to stand here and give us true guarantees that his Government does not intend to attack Cuba.

Let us not be told, gentlemen, that the problem of Cuba is not a bilateral difference between Cuba and the United States, that Cuba is really a hemispheric problem.

We have said and repeated and we repeat it now that we respect the principle of non-intervention. Our respect for sovereignty and independence of the rest of the countries of Latin America has also been stated.

We are not a hemispheric problem. Cuba is not the problem of this continent. Underdevelopment is a hemispheric problem. We are not a hemispheric problem. Hunger, famine and need are hemispheric problems, but Cuba is not. Lack of culture, illiteracy are hemispheric problems in this Hemisphere, not Cuba. American interference in the domestic affairs of the countries of this continent is a hemispheric problem, not Cuba.

The preparation and the training of armed forces, specifically on the part of the Government of the United States in different countries of this continent in order to unleash repression against popular movements in the continent until the danger of a new colonial warfare has been unleashed on this continent, this is a hemispheric problem, not Cuba.

Cuba is not a hemispheric problem, the United States is a hemispheric problem because of its lack of respect for the sovereignty of other states.

We can only point out the danger we have suffered and, for the benefit of the United Nations, the possible ramifications.

Our position is this one, very clear — ready to do what is necessary to achieve peace. But if once again arrogance, if once again the greed for domination is again the error of the hemispheric example to be drawn from the Cuban revolution, an error to the American Government, the people of Cuba, ready as always to live in peace, is ready daily to fight with weapons for its independence.

The New York Times, October 9, 1962, p. 14. Copyright by The New York Times. Reprinted by permission.

❖ ❖ ❖ **12**

REPLY OF AMBASSADOR STEVENSON TO PRESIDENT DORTICOS IN U.N. GENERAL ASSEMBLY, *October 8, 1962*

I have asked to speak to a point of order. For seventeen years we have come to expect that, when a chief of state asks for the privilege of this podium, he has an obligation not to abuse it and not to demean the United Nations and the dialog of diplomacy, but to speak here in a constructive and statesmanlike manner.

But the President of Cuba, Mr. President, speaking as chief of state on a ceremonial occasion, has seen fit to use this rostrum to attack my country with unparalleled calumnies, slanders, and misrepresentations for one hour and forty-five minutes.

Yet, Mr. President, I will not claim a right of reply from this platform this morning. Instead, I shall respond to his intemperate and false charges outside of this hall and at once. And, with your permission, Mr. President, I will have my response placed before the members of the General Assembly in printed form during the day.

Mr. President, the traditions of etiquette and of good taste which have been established here have built respect for this organization, and for my part I do not want to descend even by reply to the levels of the chief of state we have just heard on this ceremonial occasion.

He is right, however, on one point. The last word will be written by history.

U.S., Department of State, *Bulletin*, Volume XLVII, No. 1219 (November 5, 1962), p. 706.

✧ ✧ ✧ **13**

STATEMENT BY AMBASSADOR STEVENSON TO THE PRESS IN FURTHER REPLY TO PRESIDENT DORTICOS, *October 8, 1962*

Slander and invective are no substitute for facts, and the weaker a case is the longer it takes to present. I think I can be very brief indeed.

The charges just rehearsed by President Dorticos of Cuba against my Government are neither original nor true. Four times within the last eight months, once in the Political Committee of the Assembly, once in the plenary, and twice in the Security Council, the United Nations has decisively rejected accusations similar to those we have heard today.

I repeat the policy of the United States:

The Government of the United States, like the governments of the other independent American Republics, will honor its commitments to the United Nations Charter and to the inter-American system. As we have stated so often, the United States will not commit aggression against Cuba. But let it be equally clear that the United States will not tolerate aggression against any part of this Hemisphere. The United States will exercise the right of individual and collective self-defense — a right expressly recognized in the charter — against aggression in this hemisphere.

The charges made by Cuba against the United States are dictated by two factors. One is that the Castro regime has associated itself with the Communist bloc in its pursuit of world domination. A tactic always used in seeking this objective is to ridicule, malign, and vilify anyone with the courage to oppose them.

The second factor is Cuba's self-inflicted exclusion from the American family of nations. The Castro regime has turned its back on its history, tradition, religion, and culture. Cuba has turned away from its neighbors, and it is at the mercy of the political riptides that sweep through the Communist world with such frequence.

Thus the other nations of the Americas are understandably anxious and alert. But vigilance cannot and should not be equated with intervention, nor alarm with aggression.

The Hemisphere — and the world — were prepared to accept the original promises of the Castro government that economic and social justice would be brought to the Cuban people. But its original pledges have now been discarded by the Cuban regime, and we condemn with all the force at our command the violations of civil justice, the drumhead executions, and the suppression of political, intellectual, and religious freedom which have been inflicted on the Cuban people.

But even these excesses would not constitute a direct threat to the peace and independence of other states. However, Cuba has been opened to a flood of Soviet weapons and "techniques" and to the Soviet Union's so-called "fishing fleet," which is a long way from the fishing grounds off the north shore of Cuba. The cod and the herring, gentlemen, are a long way from the new fishing fleet's headquarters. Cuba has not only armed itself to a degree never before seen in any Latin American country, but it has also welcomed penetration by the foremost exponent of a doctrine condemned in this Hemisphere as "alien" and "incompatible." What we cannot accept — and will never accept — is that Cuba has become the springboard for aggressive and subversive efforts to destroy the inter-American system, to overthrow the governments of the Americas, and to obstruct the peaceful, democratic evolution of this Hemisphere toward social justice and economic development.

The statements of the President of the United States on this subject and the recent joint resolution of the Congress of the United States amply attest to this concern.

Nor can these developments be ignored by the American Republics as a whole Let there be no doubt as to the solidarity of the nations of this Hemisphere on the problem of Cuba.

The foreign ministers and special representatives of the American Republics have just concluded two days of informal discussion on Communist intervention in Cuba. Speaking unanimously, they declared that the most urgent problem facing the Hemisphere is this foreign intervention in Cuba and its threat to convert the island into an armed base for penetration and subversion of the democratic institutions of the Hemisphere.

The Hemisphere representatives unanimously affirmed their will to strengthen our common security against all aggression and all situations threatening peace and security in this Hemisphere. Noting the special characteristics of the inter-American regional system, they stated that a military intervention by Communist powers in Cuba cannot be justified as a situation analogous to the defensive measures adopted in other parts of the free world in order to resist Soviet imperialism.

The communiqué issued by the foreign ministers in Washington last week reflected the sense of increased gravity with which the American states have witnessed a succession of developments in Cuba since the Punta del Este meeting, where the Communist government of Cuba was found to be incompatible with the American system.

In the face of this threat the foreign ministers have again unanimously reaffirmed their will to strengthen the security of the Hemisphere against all aggression, from inside and outside the Hemisphere, and against all developments and situations capable of threatening its peace and security.

The historic support of the members of the Organization of American States for the principles of self-determination and nonintervention is well known. These principles have been enshrined in acts of inter-American conferences, antedating by decades even the conception of the United Nations.

The United States has already begun to take effective measures concerning shipping and trade with Cuba and the surveillance of traffic in arms and other strategic items in accordance with the discussions of the ministers of foreign affairs, the resolutions of the Eighth Meeting of Consultation, and other inter-American instruments.

The purpose of these measures is the collective defense of the Hemisphere. As I have said, these measures have no offensive purpose.

There was incessant talk this morning about economic strangulation and economic blockade. Neither of these terms has any application to this case. The current regime in Cuba has pronounced its intention to overthrow other governments in this Hemisphere. Could anyone, therefore, take part in any trade, or aid trade designed to boost the Cuban economy and to arm its military services?

To say that our self-protective actions are aggressive or a warlike gesture is absurd. It is the most normal and, indeed, the least violent way in which we can express our strong disapproval of the threats and sword rattling emanating from Cuba.

No threat to peace in this Hemisphere arises out of the unanimous determination of American Republics in this regard.

The President of Cuba professes that Cuba has always been willing to hold discussions with the United States to improve relations and to reduce tensions. But what he really wishes us to do is to place the seal of approval on the existence of a Communist regime in the Western Hemisphere. The maintenance of communism in the Americas is not negotiable. Furthermore, the problem of Cuba is not a simple problem of United States-Cuban relations. It is a collective problem for all the states of this Hemisphere.

If the Cuban regime is sincere in its request for negotiations and wishes to lay its grievances before the appropriate forum — the Organization of American States — I would suggest the Cuban government might start by some action calculated to awaken the confidence of the inter-American system. The obvious place to begin would be the severing of its multiple ties to the Soviet bloc.

Let no one mistake the impact of this Soviet intervention in Cuba on the hope we all share for world peace. If the Soviet Union persists in the course it has chosen, if it continues to try to prevent the peaceful social revolution of the Americas, it will increasingly excite the deep indignations of the people of my country and of other American states. The result will be to make the resolution of issues far more difficult in every other part of the world. A consequence of this gratuitous Soviet initiative is to postpone even further the hope for world stabilization. I cannot state this point with sufficient gravity.

The tragedy of Cuba is still unfolding. How short has been the time since the two continents of the Western Hemisphere acclaimed the downfall of the Batista dictatorship and hailed what promised to be a democratic and progressive revolution. How quickly that promise was replaced by a reign of terror, confiscation, and the suppression of political, intellectual, and religious freedom.

Just as fear is the first price of oppression, it would also have been the final price, if the Cuban oppressor had not been saved from the Cuban people by the Soviet Union. How many times in history has fear of the people's wrath driven tyrants to sell their nation to more powerful tyrants?

Can the Cuban electorate send the Russian forces home? Do the Cuban leaders dare face their people without these alien protectors? A country bristling with Soviet missiles and "protectors" is your answer.

We will constantly work to reassure the Cuban people that they have not been forgotten or abandoned and make clear to freedom-loving Cubans, both within and without that country, that they can count on the sympathy and support of the American people in their efforts to escape the grip of Soviet domination and recapture their own revolution. We did this for those who sought the overthrow of Batista. We can do no less today.

The foreign ministers meeting at Washington voiced the fraternal affection of all American peoples for the people of Cuba and fervently wish to see them embraced again in the American family of nations. The United States joins wholeheartedly in this desire.

If the Cuban regime wishes to establish normal friendly relations in this Hemisphere, let it return to the concepts and obligations of the inter-American system, let it cease its subservience to the Soviet Union, let it cease to be an avenue of intervention, which threatens the fundamental principles and the peace and security of all its neighbors with an alien doctrine.

The way is clear, and the choice is Cuba's.

U.S., Department of State, *Bulletin*, Volume XLVII, No. 1219 (November 5, 1962), pp. 706–708. (Read to press correspondents outside U.N. General Assembly hall.)

◇ ◇ ◇ **14**

ADDRESS BY PRESIDENT KENNEDY, *October 22, 1962*

Good evening, my fellow citizens. This Government, as promised, has maintained the closest surveillance of the Soviet military build-up on the island of Cuba. Within the past week unmistakable evidence has established the fact that a series of offensive missile sites is now in preparation on that imprisoned island. The purposes of these bases can be none other than to provide a nuclear strike capability against the Western Hemisphere.

Upon receiving the first preliminary hard information of this nature last Tuesday morning (October 16) at 9:00 A.M., I directed that our surveillance be stepped up. And having now confirmed and completed our evaluation of the evidence and our decision on a course of action, this Government feels obliged to report this new crisis to you in fullest detail.

The characteristics of these new missile sites indicate two distinct types of installations. Several of them include medium-range ballistic missiles capable of carrying a nuclear warhead for a distance of more than 1,000 nautical miles. Each of these missiles, in short, is capable of striking Washington, D.C., the Panama Canal, Cape Canaveral, Mexico City, or any other city in the southeastern part of the United States, in Central America, or in the Caribbean area.

Additional sites not yet completed appear to be designed for intermediate-range ballistic missiles capable of traveling more than twice as far — and thus capable of striking most of the major cities in the Western Hemisphere, ranging as far north as Hudson Bay, Canada, and as far south as Lima, Peru. In addition, jet bombers, capable of carrying nuclear weapons, are now being uncrated and assembled in Cuba, while the necessary air bases are being prepared.

This urgent transformation of Cuba into an important strategic base — by the presence of these large, long-range, and clearly offensive weapons of sudden mass destruction — constitutes an explicit threat to the peace and security of all the Americas, in flagrant and deliberate defiance of the Rio Pact of 1947, the traditions of this nation and Hemisphere, the Joint Resolution of the 87th Congress, the Charter of the United Nations, and my own public warnings to the Soviets on September 4 and 13.

,This action also contradicts the repeated assurances of Soviet spokesmen, both publicly and privately delivered, that the arms build-up in Cuba would retain its original defensive character and that the Soviet Union had no need or desire to station strategic missiles on the territory of any other nation.

The size of this undertaking makes clear that it has been planned for some months. Yet only last month, after I had made clear the distinction between any introduction of ground-to-ground missiles and the existence of defensive antiaircraft missiles, the Soviet Government publicly stated on September 11 that, and I quote, "The armaments and military equipment sent to Cuba are designed exclusively for defensive purposes," and, and I quote the Soviet Government, "There is no need for the Soviet Government to shift its weapons for a retaliatory blow to any other country, for instance Cuba," and that, and I quote the Government, "The Soviet Union has so powerful rockets to carry these nuclear warheads that there is no need to search for sites for them beyond the boundaries of the Soviet Union." That statement was false.

Only last Thursday, as evidence of this rapid offensive build-up was already in my hand, Soviet Foreign Minister Gromyko told me in my office that he was instructed to make it clear once again, as he said his Government had already done, that Soviet assistance to Cuba, and I quote, "pursued solely the purpose of contributing to the defense capabilities of Cuba," that, and I quote him, "training by Soviet specialists of Cuban nationals in handling defensive armaments was by no means offensive," and that "if it were otherwise," Mr. Gromyko went on, "the Soviet Government would never become involved in rendering such assistance." That statement also was false.

Neither the United States of America nor the world community of nations can tolerate deliberate deception and offensive threats on the part of any nation, large or small. We no longer live in a world where only the actual firing of weapons represents a sufficient challenge to a nation's security to constitute maximum peril. Nuclear weapons are so destructive and ballistic missiles are so swift that any substantially increased possibility of their use or any sudden change in their deployment may well be regarded as a definite threat to peace.

For many years both the Soviet Union and the United States, recognizing this fact, have deployed strategic nuclear weapons with great care, never upsetting the precarious status quo which insured that these weapons would not be used in the absence of some vital challenge. Our own strategic missiles have never been transferred to the territory of any other nation under a cloak of secrecy and deception; and our history, unlike that of the Soviets since the end of World War II, demonstrates that we have no desire to dominate or conquer any other nation or impose our system upon its people. Nevertheless, American citizens have become adjusted to living daily on the bull's eye of Soviet missiles located inside the U.S.S.R. or in submarines.

In that sense missiles in Cuba add to an already clear and present danger — although it should be noted the nations of Latin America have never previously been subjected to a potential nuclear threat.

But this secret, swift, and extraordinary build-up of Communist missiles — in an area well known to have a special and historical relationship to the United States and the nations of the Western Hemisphere, in violation of Soviet assurances, and in defiance of American and hemispheric policy — this sudden, clandestine decision to station strategic weapons for the first time outside of Soviet soil — is a deliberately provocative and unjustified change in the status quo which cannot be accepted by this country if our courage and our commitments are ever to be trusted again by either friend or foe.

The 1930's taught us a clear lesson: Aggressive conduct, if allowed to grow unchecked and unchallenged, ultimately leads to war. This nation is opposed to war. We are also true to our word. Our unswerving objective, therefore, must be to prevent the use of these missiles against this or any other country and to secure their withdrawal or elimination from the Western Hemisphere.

Our policy has been one of patience and restraint, as befits a peaceful and powerful nation, which leads a worldwide alliance We have been determined not to be diverted from our central concerns by mere irritants and fanatics. But now further action is required — and it is underway; and these actions may only be the beginning. We will not prematurely or unnecessarily risk the costs of worldwide nuclear war in which even the fruits of victory would be ashes in our mouth — but neither will we shrink from that risk at any time it must be faced.

Acting, therefore, in the defense of our own security and of the entire Western Hemisphere, and under the authority entrusted to me by the Constitution as endorsed by the resolution of the Congress, I have directed that the following initial steps be taken immediately:

First: To halt this offensive build-up, a strict quarantine on all offensive military equipment under shipment to Cuba is being initiated. All ships of any kind bound for Cuba from whatever nation or port will, if found to contain cargoes of offensive weapons, be turned back. This quarantine will be extended, if needed, to other types of cargo and carriers. We are not at this time, however, denying the necessities of life as the Soviets attempted to do in their Berlin blockade of 1948.

Second: I have directed the continued and increased close surveillance of Cuba and its military build-up. The Foreign Ministers of the Organization of American States in their communiqué of October 3 rejected secrecy on such matters in this Hemisphere. Should these offensive military preparations continue, thus increasing the threat to the Hemisphere, further action will be justified. I have directed the Armed Forces to prepare for any eventualities; and I trust that in the interests of both the Cuban people and the Soviet technicians at the sites, the hazards to all concerned of continuing this threat will be recognized.

Third: It shall be the policy of this nation to regard any nuclear missile launched from Cuba against any nation in the Western Hemisphere as an attack by the Soviet Union on the United States, requiring a full retaliatory response upon the Soviet Union.

Fourth: As a necessary military precaution I have reinforced our base at Guantanamo, evacuated today the dependents of our personnel there, and ordered additional military units to be on a standby alert basis.

Fifth: We are calling tonight for an immediate meeting of the Organ of Consultation, under the Organization of American States, to consider this threat to hemispheric security and to invoke articles six and eight of the Rio Treaty in support of all necessary action. The United Nations Charter allows for regional security arrangements — and the nations of this Hemisphere decided long ago against the military presence of outside powers. Our other allies around the world have also been alerted.

Sixth: Under the Charter of the United Nations, we are asking tonight that an emergency meeting of the Security Council be convoked without delay to take action against this latest Soviet threat to world peace. Our resolution will call for the prompt dismantling and withdrawal of all offensive weapons in Cuba, under the supervision of United Nations observers, before the quarantine can be lifted.

Seventh and finally: I call upon Chairman Khrushchev to halt and eliminate this clandestine, reckless, and provocative threat to world peace and to stable relations between our two nations. I call upon him further to abandon this course of world domination and to join in an historic effort to end the perilous arms race and transform the history of man. He has an opportunity now to move the world back from the abyss of destruction — by returning to his Government's own words that it had no need to station missiles outside its own territory, and withdrawing these weapons from Cuba — by refraining from any action which will widen or deepen the present crisis — and then by participating in a search for peaceful and permanent solutions.

This nation is prepared to present its case against the Soviet threat to peace, and our own proposals for a peaceful world, at any time and in any forum in the Organization of American States, in the United Nations, or in any other meeting that could be useful — without limiting our freedom of action.

We have in the past made strenuous efforts to limit the spread of nuclear weapons. We have proposed the elimination of all arms and military bases in a fair and effective disarmament treaty. We are prepared to discuss new proposals for the removal of tensions on both sides — including the possibilities of a genuinely independent Cuba, free to determine its own destiny. We have no wish to war with the Soviet Union, for we are a peaceful people who desire to live in peace with all other peoples.

But it is difficult to settle or even discuss these problems in an atmosphere of intimidation. That is why this latest Soviet threat — or any other threat which is made either independently or in response to our actions this week — must and will be met with determination. Any hostile move anywhere in the world against the safety and freedom of peoples to whom we are committed — including in particular the brave people of West Berlin — will be met by whatever action is needed.

Finally, I want to say a few words to the captive people of Cuba, to whom this speech is being directly carried by special radio facilities. I speak to you as a friend, as one who knows of your deep attachment to your fatherland, as one who shares your aspirations for liberty and justice for all. And I have watched and the American people have watched with deep sorrow how your nationalist revolution was betrayed and how your fatherland fell under foreign domination. Now your leaders are no longer Cuban leaders inspired by Cuban ideals. They are puppets and agents of an international conspiracy which has turned Cuba against your friends and neighbors in the Americas — and turned it into the first Latin American country to become a target for nuclear war, the first Latin American country to have these weapons on its soil.

These new weapons are not in your interest. They contribute nothing to your peace and well being. They can only undermine it. But this country has no wish to cause you to suffer or to impose any system upon you. We know that your lives and land are being used as pawns by those who deny you freedom.

Many times in the past Cuban people have risen to throw out tyrants who destroyed their liberty. And I have no doubt that most Cubans today look forward to the time when they will be truly free — free from foreign domination, free to choose their own leaders, free to select their own system, free to own their own land, free to speak and write and worship without fear or degradation. And then shall Cuba be welcomed back to the society of free nations and to the associations of this Hemisphere.

My fellow citizens, let no one doubt that this is a difficult and dangerous effort on which we have set out. No one can foresee precisely what course it will take or what costs or casualties will be incurred. Many months of sacrifice and self-discipline lie ahead — months in which both our patience and our will will be tested, months in which many threats and denunciations will keep us aware of our dangers. But the greatest danger of all would be to do nothing.

The path we have chosen for the present is full of hazards, as all paths are; but it is the one most consistent with our character and courage as a nation and our commitments around the world. The cost of freedom is always high — but Americans have always paid it. And one path we shall never choose, and that is the path of surrender or submission.

Our goal is not the victory of might but the vindication of right —

not peace at the expense of freedom, but both peace and freedom, here in this Hemisphere and, we hope, around the world. God willing, that goal will be achieved.

U.S., Department of State, *Bulletin*, Volume XLVII, No. 1220 (November 12, 1962), pp. 715–720. (Delivered from the White House by television and radio at 7:00 P.M. E.S.T. on October 22, 1962. A White House press release, as delivered text.)

✧ ✧ ✧ **15**

U.S. REQUEST FOR CONVENING U.N. SECURITY COUNCIL, *October 22, 1962*

EXCELLENCY: I have the honor to request an urgent meeting of the Security Council to deal with the dangerous threat to the peace and security of the world caused by the secret establishment in Cuba by the Union of Soviet Socialist Republics of launching bases and the installation of long-range ballistic missiles capable of carrying thermonuclear warheads to most of North and South America.

The United States now has incontrovertible evidence that the Union of Soviet Socialist Republics has been installing in Cuba a whole series of facilities for launching offensive nuclear missiles and other offensive weapons and installing the weapons themselves. These steps are far in excess of any conceivable defense requirements of Cuba. The Soviet action in establishing them signals an acceleration of the process by which the U.S.S.R. has moved to snuff out the integrity and independence of the Cuban nation. The establishment of bases for nuclear missiles capable of raining thermonuclear destruction throughout most of the Western Hemisphere constitutes a grave threat to the peace and security of this Hemisphere and of the whole world.

The size of the Soviet undertaking in establishing missiles and other offensive weapons in Cuba makes clear that it was planned some months ago. Yet, throughout these months, the U.S.S.R. has given repeated assurances, both in public and in private, that no offensive weapons were being delivered to Cuba.

On September 11, 1962, the Soviet Union said in an official statement that the "armaments and military equipment sent to Cuba are designed exclusively for defensive purposes. . . . There is no need for the Soviet Union to shift its weapons for the repulsion of aggression, for a retaliatory blow to any other country, for instance Cuba. . . . The Soviet Union has so powerful rockets to carry these nuclear warheads that there is no need to search for sites for them beyond the boundaries of the Soviet Union." Similarly, Foreign Minister Gromyko told the General Assembly on September 21 that any "sober minded man" knew that Cuba was not "building up her forces to such a degree that she can pose a threat to the United States, to the passage of the United States to the Panama Canal, or else a threat to any State of the Western Hemisphere. . . . The Aid rendered by the Soviet Union to Cuba to strengthen her independence does not pursue any of these goals. . . ."

Upon satisfying itself as to the deliberately provocative steps which have in fact been taken, the United States Government has commenced a series of measures designed to halt this offensive build-up.

The United States has called for a meeting of the Organ of Consultation to invoke Articles 6 and 8 of the Rio Treaty.

In order to give effect to the determination of the countries of the Western Hemisphere which they have recently reaffirmed to safeguard and defend the peace and security of the region against external interference and aggression, the United States is initiating a strict quarantine of Cuba to interdict the carriage of offensive weapons to that country.

In accordance with its obligations under the United Nations Charter, the United States now brings before the Security Council the fact of nuclear missiles and other offensive weapons in Cuba, and proposes the prompt and effective discharge of the Council's responsibilities for the maintenance of international peace and security.

What is at stake is the peace and security both of a single region and of the whole world. The developments of modern science and technology have created capacities for catastrophic destruction. The diffusion of these capacities through the Soviet actions in Cuba can only be regarded as the gravest kind of threat to the peace.

It should be the purpose of Security Council action to bring about the immediate dismantling and withdrawal of the Soviet missiles and other offensive weapons in Cuba, under the supervision of United Nations observers, to make it possible to lift the quarantine which is being put into effect. As part of this process, we are willing to confer with the Soviet Union on measures to remove the existing threat to the security of the Western Hemisphere and the peace of the world.

With these objectives in mind, the United States requests an urgent meeting of the Security Council. Attached is a draft resolution which the United States hereby presents to the Security Council.

Accept, Excellency, the renewed assurances of my highest consideration.

(s) ADLAI E. STEVENSON

U.S., Department of State, *Bulletin*, Volume XLVII, No. 1220 (November 12, 1962), p. 724. (U.N., *Security Council Document S/5181*, October 22, 1962, pp. 1–3. Letter addressed to the President of the Security Council.)

❖ ❖ ❖ **16**

U.S. DRAFT RESOLUTION PRESENTED TO U.N. SECURITY COUNCIL, *October 22, 1962*

HAVING CONSIDERED the serious threat to the security of the Western Hemisphere and the peace of the world caused by the continuance and acceleration of foreign intervention in the Caribbean,

NOTING WITH CONCERN that nuclear missiles and other offensive weapons have been secretly introduced into Cuba,

NOTING ALSO that as a consequence a quarantine is being imposed around the country,

GRAVELY CONCERNED that further continuance of the Cuban situation may lead to direct conflict,

1. CALLS as a provisional measure under Article 40 for the immediate dismantling and withdrawal from Cuba of all missiles and offensive weapons;

2. AUTHORIZES AND REQUESTS the Acting Secretary General to dispatch to Cuba a United Nations observer corps to assure and report on compliance with this resolution;

3. CALLS FOR termination of the measures of quarantine directed against military shipments to Cuba upon United Nations certification of compliance with Paragraph 1;

4. URGENTLY RECOMMENDS that the United States of America and the Union of Soviet Socialist Republics confer promptly on measures to remove the existing threat to the security of the Western Hemisphere and the peace of the world, and report thereon to the Security Council.

U.S., Department of State, *Bulletin*, Volume XLVII, No. 1220 (November 12, 1962), p. 724. (U.N., *Security Council Document S/5182*, October 22, 1962, p. 1.)

❖ ❖ ❖ **17**

CUBAN REQUEST FOR CONVENING THE U.N. SECURITY COUNCIL, *October 22, 1962*

In accordance with instructions from the Revolutionary Government of Cuba, I have the honour to request you to convene an urgent meeting of the Security Council whose distinguished President you are, to consider the act of war unilaterally committed by the Government of the United States in ordering the naval blockade of Cuba.

The United States Government is carrying out this act of war in disregard of the international organizations; in particular, in absolute contempt of the Security Council whose distinguished President you are, is creating an imminent danger of war.

This unilateral and direct aggression is merely the culmination of a series of aggressive acts committed against the Revolutionary Government of Cuba and the Cuban people by the Government of the United States of America, whose record of aggression we have reported to the United Nations and our President, Dr. Osvaldo Dorticos Torrado, denounced in the General Assembly on 8 October last.

The Revolutionary Government of Cuba bases this request on Article 34, Article 35 (1), and Article 39, and it also cites Article 1 (1), Article 2 (4) and Article 24 (1) of the United Nations Charter, and the relevant articles of the rules of procedure of the Security Council.

I take this opportunity of repeating to your Excellency my assurance of my distinguished consideration.

(s) Dr. Mario García-Inchaustegui
Ambassador
Permanent Representative of Cuba
to the United Nations

U.N., *Security Council Document S/5183*, October 22, 1962, p. 1. (Letter addressed to the President of the Security Council.)

❖ ❖ ❖ **18**

SOVIET REQUEST FOR CONVENING THE U.N. SECURITY COUNCIL AND STATEMENT BY THE SOVIET GOVERNMENT, *October 23, 1962*

On the instructions of the Soviet Government I would ask you to convene a meeting of the Security Council immediately in order to examine the question of "Violation of the Charter of the United Nations and threat to the peace on the part of the United States of America."

The grounds for the request to convene the Security Council are set forth in the Statement by the Soviet Government on Cuba which is annexed to this letter.

Please arrange for this letter and the said Statement by the Soviet Government to be issued as an official Security Council document.

Accept, Sir, the assurance of my highest consideration.

(s) P. Morozov
Deputy Permanent Representative
of the U.S.S.R. to the United Nations

U.N., *Security Council Document S/5186*, October 23, 1962, p. 1. (Letter addressed to the President of the Security Council.)

Last night Mr. Kennedy, the President of the United States of America, announced that he had given orders to the United States Navy to intercept all ships bound for Cuba, to subject them to inspection, and to turn back ships carrying weapons which, in the judgment of the United States authorities, were offensive in character. Orders had also been given for continued and close surveillance of Cuba. Thus the United States Government is in effect placing the Republic of Cuba under naval blockade. At the same time, the landing of additional United States troops at the United States Guantanamo base, situated in the territory of Cuba, has begun, and the United States armed forces are being placed in a state of combat readiness.

The President is endeavouring to justify these unprecedented aggressive acts by arguments to the effect that a threat to the national security of the United States is arising in Cuba.

The Soviet Government has repeatedly drawn the attention of the Governments of all countries and of world public opinion to the serious danger to world peace created by the policy pursued by the United States towards the Republic of Cuba. The statement by the President of the United States shows that the United States imperialist circles will stop at nothing in their attempts to stifle a sovereign State Member of the United Nations. To do this they are prepared to push the world towards the abyss of military catastrophe. The peoples of all countries must clearly realize that, in embarking on such a venture, the United States of America is taking a step towards the unleashing of a world thermonuclear war. Insolently flouting the international rules of conduct for States and the principles of the Charter of the United Nations, the United States has arrogated to itself — and has so announced — the right to attack the vessels of other States on the high seas: in other words, to engage in piracy.

Imperialist circles in the United States are trying to dictate to Cuba what policy it must pursue, what dispositions it is to make at home, and what weapons it must possess for its defence. But who has authorized the United States to assume the role of arbiter of the destinies of other countries and peoples? Why must the Cubans settle the

domestic affairs of their own State, not as they see fit, but according
to the wishes of the United States? Cuba belongs to the Cuban people, and only they can be masters of their fate.

Under the Charter of the United Nations, all countries, large or
small, have the right to organize their lives in their own way, to take
such measures as they consider necessary to protect their own security, and to rebuff aggressive forces encroaching on their freedom and
independence. To ignore this is to undermine the very basis of
existence of the United Nations, to bring jungle law into international
practice, and to engender conflicts and wars without end.

In this anxious hour, the Soviet Government considers it its duty to
address a serious warning to the United States Government, to advise
it that, in carrying out the measures announced by President Kennedy,
it is taking on itself a heavy responsibility for the fate of the world,
and recklessly playing with fire.

The United States leaders must at last understand that times have
changed completely. Only madmen can now take their stand on "positions of strength" and expect that policy to bring them any success,
to allow them to force their own dispositions on other States. While
in the past the United States could consider itself the greatest Power
on the world scene, there is no foundation for such a view today.
There is another force in the world which is no less powerful, and
which takes the position that peoples should arrange their life as they
please. Today, as never before, statesmen must show calm and prudence, and must not countenance the rattling of weapons.

The Soviet Government emphasizes once again that all weapons in
the Soviet Union's possession are serving and will serve the purposes
of defence against aggressors. Under existing international conditions,
the presence of powerful weapons, including nuclear rocket weapons,
in the Soviet Union is acknowledged by all the peoples in the world
to be the decisive factor in deterring the aggressive forces of imperialism from unleashing a world war of annihilation. This mission the
Soviet Union will continue to discharge with all firmness and con-
sistency.

The President of the United States said in his statement that, if
even one nuclear bomb fell on United States territory, the United
States would make a retaliatory response. Such an assertion is imbued
with hypocrisy, since the Soviet Union has already declared repeatedly that not a single Soviet nuclear bomb will fall either on the
United States or on any other country unless aggression has been committed. The nuclear weapons made by the Soviet people are in the
people's hands, they will never be used for purposes of aggression.

But if the aggressors unleash war, the Soviet Union will inflict the
most powerful blow in response.

The Soviet Union has always been true to the principles of the
Charter of the United Nations; it has consistently pursued, and still

pursues, a policy designed to preserve and strengthen peace. The whole world knows what great efforts the Soviet Union is making to lessen international tension, to eliminate the breeding-grounds of conflict and disputation between States, and to make the principles of peaceful coexistence between States with different social structures a living reality. It is the Soviet Union which has put forward and justified a programme of universal and complete disarmament, the application of which would open real prospects for the establishment of a peace without wars, without weapons. These proposals are gaining ever-increasing support throughout the world; they have fired the imagination of the people; they have become the order of the day. If the cause of disarmament has made no progress so far, the fault lies with the United States of America and its allies in NATO. They fear disarmament; they do not want to part with the big stick with whose help they are trying to dictate their will to other countries.

The United States Government accuses Cuba of creating a threat to the security of the United States. But who is going to believe that Cuba can be a threat to the United States? If we think of the respective size and resources of the two countries, of their armaments, no statesman in his right mind can imagine for one moment that Cuba can be a threat to the United States of America or to any other country. It is hypocritical, to say the least, to say that little Cuba may encroach on the security of the United States of America.

The Cubans wish to secure their homeland, their independence, against the threat emanating from the United States of America. The Government of Cuba is appealing to reason and conscience, and is calling upon the United States to refrain from making threatening passes at Cuba's independence and to establish normal relations with the Cuban State. Is there not a ring of conviction in the official declaration by the Cuban Government concerning its ambition to settle all questions at issue through negotiations with the United States Government?

Only recently, in speaking at the session of the United Nations General Assembly, Mr. Dorticos, the President of the Republic of Cuba, reiterated that Cuba has always expressed its readiness to negotiate through the normal diplomatic channel or by any other means with a view to discussing the differences existing between the United States and Cuba. The President of the United States now implies that such statements by the Cuban Government are not enough. But it would be possible to justify any aggressive action, any adventure in this way.

With regard to the Soviet Union's assistance to Cuba, this assistance is exclusively designed to improve Cuba's defensive capacity. As was stated on 3 September 1962 in the joint Soviet-Cuban communiqué on the visit to the Soviet Union of a Cuban delegation composed of Mr. E. Guevara and Mr. E. Aragones, the Soviet Government has responded to the Cubán 'Government's request to help Cuba with arms. The communiqué states that such arms and military equipment are intended solely for defensive purposes. The Governments of the two countries still firmly adhere to that position.

Soviet assistance in strengthening Cuba's defences is necessitated by the fact that, from the outset of its existence, the Republic of Cuba has been subjected to continuous threats and acts of provocation by the United States. The United States is stopping at nothing, even going so far as to organize armed intervention in Cuba in April 1961, in order to deprive the Cuban people of the freedom and independence they have won, to bring the country once more under the heel of the United States monopolies and to make Cuba a United States puppet.

The United States is demanding that the military equipment Cuba needs for its own defense should be withdrawn from its territory, a step to which no State prizing its independence can, of course, agree.

The Soviet Union considers that all foreign troops should be withdrawn from the territory of other States and should be brought back within their own national frontiers. If the United States was genuinely concerned to strengthen friendly relations with States and was striving to ensure lasting peace throughout the world, as President Kennedy asserts in his address of 22 October, it should have accepted the Soviet proposal and withdrawn its troops and military equipment and dismantled its military bases that are situated in the territory of other States in various parts of the world.

However, the United States, which has dispersed its armed forces and armaments throughout the world, stubbornly refuses to accept this proposal. It is using these armed forces and armaments for interference in the domestic affairs of other States and for the implementation of its own aggressive designs. It is United States imperialism which has assumed the role of international *gendarme*. The representatives of the United States constantly boast that United States aircraft can attack the Soviet Union at any time, can drop United States bombs on peaceful towns and villages and can deliver heavy blows. Not a day passes without the statesmen, military leaders and the Press of the United States uttering threats that United States submarines, which are ranging through many seas and oceans with Polaris missiles on board, can launch an atomic attack against the Soviet Union and other peace-loving States. President Kennedy's statement that the United States Government is acting solely in the interests of peace in making its exaggerated demands that Cuba should be deprived of the means of defence rings particularly false in the light of these facts.

The peace-loving States cannot but protest against the piratical operations which the President of the United States has announced against ships bound for Cuban shores, against the institution of control over the ships of sovereign States on the high seas. As we know, United States statesmen like to talk about their adherence to the principles of international law and to dilate upon the need for law and order in the world. (But in reality they evidently consider that the laws are written not for the United States, but for other States. The institution by the United States of a virtual blockade of Cuban shores is a provocative act, an unprecedented violation of international law, a challenge to all peace-loving peoples.

It is also obvious that, if the United States is today attempting to prohibit other countries from trading with Cuba and from using their ships to transport goods and cargoes there, United States ruling circles may tomorrow demand that similar action should be taken against any other State whose policy or social system does not suit them.

The United States Government is assuming the right to demand that States should account to it for the way in which they organize their defence, and should notify it of what their ships are carrying on the high seas.

The Soviet Government firmly repudiates such claims. The high-handed acts of United States imperialism may lead to catastrophic consequences for all mankind, which is not desired by any people, including the people of the United States.

In view of the full gravity of the situation which the United States Government has created over Cuba, the Soviet Government has instructed its representative in the United Nations to raise the question of the immediate convening of the Security Council to consider the following question: "The violation of the Charter of the United Nations and the threat to peace by the United States of America."

The Soviet Union appeals to all Governments and peoples to raise their voice in protest against the aggressive acts of the United States of America against Cuba and other States, strongly to condemn such acts and to take steps to prevent the unleashing of a thermonuclear war by the United States Government.

The Soviet Government will do everything in its power to frustrate the aggressive designs of United States imperialist circles and to defend and strengthen peace on earth.

The Soviet Government expresses its firm belief that the Soviet people will still further increase their labour efforts to strengthen the economic and defense capacity of their Soviet fatherland. The Soviet Government is taking all the necessary steps to insure that the country is not taken by surprise and is in a position to mete out an appropriate rebuff to an aggressor.

U.N., *Security Council Document S/5186*, October 23, 1962, pp. 2–7. (Statement by the Soviet Government on Cuba.)

❖ ❖ ❖ **19**

CUBAN REQUEST TO PARTICIPATE IN MEETING OF U.N. SECURITY COUNCIL, *October 23, 1962*

I have the honour to inform you that I have received instructions from my Government to participate in the meeting of the Security Council that has been called at the request of the Governments of the United States of America and Cuba.

I take the liberty of requesting through you the required authorization of the Security Council.

I have the honour to be, etc.

(s) DR. MARIO GARCÍA-INCHAUSTEGUI
Ambassador
Permanent Representative of Cuba

U.N., *Security Council Document S/5185*, October 23, 1962, p. 1. (Letter addressed to the President of the Security Council.)

❖ ❖ ❖ **20**

U.S. PROCLAMATION ON INTERDICTION OF OFFENSIVE WEAPONS, *October 23, 1962*

A PROCLAMATION

WHEREAS the peace of the world and the security of the United States and of all American States are endangered by reason of the establishment by the Sino-Soviet powers of an offensive military capability in Cuba, including bases for ballistic missiles with a potential range covering most of North and South America.

WHEREAS by a Joint Resolution passed by the Congress of the United States and approved on October 3, 1962, it was declared that the United States is determined to prevent by whatever means may be necessary, including the use of arms, the Marxist-Leninist regime in Cuba from extending, by force or the threat of force, its aggressive or subversive activities to any part of this hemisphere, and to prevent in Cuba the creation or use of an externally supported military capability endangering the security of the United States; and

WHEREAS the Organ of Consultation of the American Republics meeting in Washington on October 23, 1962, recommended that the Member States, in accordance with Articles six and eight of the Inter-American Treaty of Reciprocal Assistance, take all measures, individually and collectively, including the use of armed force, which they may deem necessary to ensure that the Government of Cuba cannot continue to receive from the Sino-Soviet powers military material and related supplies which may threaten the peace and security of the Continent and to prevent the missiles in Cuba with offensive capability from ever becoming an active threat to the peace and security of the Continent:

NOW, THEREFORE, I, JOHN F. KENNEDY, President of the United States of America, acting under and by virtue of the authority conferred upon me by the Constitution and statutes of the United States, in accordance with the aforementioned resolutions of the United States Congress and of the Organ of Consultation of the American Republics, and to defend the security of the United States, do hereby proclaim that the forces under my command are ordered, beginning at 2:00 P.M. Greenwich time October 24, 1962, to interdict, subject to the instructions herein contained, the delivery of offensive weapons and associated material to Cuba.

For the purposes of this Proclamation the following are declared to be prohibited material:

Surface-to-surface missiles; bomber aircraft; bombs, air-to-surface rockets and guided missiles; warheads for any of the above weapons; mechanical or electronic equipment to support or operate the above items, and any other classes of material hereafter designated by the Secretary of Defense for the purpose of effectuating this Proclamation.

To enforce this order, the Secretary of Defense shall take appropriate measures to prevent the delivery of prohibited materiel to Cuba, employing the land, sea and air forces of the United States in cooperation with any forces that may be made available by other American States.

The Secretary of Defense may make such regulations and issue such directives as he deems necessary to ensure the effectiveness of this order, including the designation, within a reasonable distance of Cuba, of prohibited or restricted zones and of prescribed routes.

Any vessel or craft which may be proceeding toward Cuba may be intercepted and may be directed to identify itself, its cargo, equipment and stores and its ports of call, to stop, to lie to, to submit to visit and search, or to proceed as directed. Any vessel or craft which fails or refuses to respond to or comply with directions shall be subject to being taken into custody. Any vessel or craft which it is believed is en route to Cuba and may be carrying prohibited materiel or may itself constitute such materiel shall, wherever possible, be directed to proceed to another destination of its own choice and shall be taken into custody if it fails or refuses to obey such directions. All vessels or craft taken into custody shall be sent into a port of the United State for appropriate disposition.

In carrying out this order, force shall not be used except in case of failure or refusal to comply with directions, or with regulations or directives of the Secretary of Defense issued hereunder, after reasonable efforts have been made to communicate them to the vessel or craft, or in case of self-defense. In any case, force shall be used only to the extent necessary.

IN WITNESS WHEREOF, I have hereunto set my hand and caused the seal of the United States of America to be affixed.

(SEAL) DONE in the City of Washington this twenty-third day of October in the year of our Lord, nineteen hundred and sixty-two, and of the Independence of the United States of America the one hundred and eighty-seventh.

(s) JOHN FITZGERALD KENNEDY
7:06 P.M.
October 23, 1962

By the President:
DEAN RUSK,
Secretary of State

U.S., Department of State, *Bulletin*, Volume XLVII, No. 1220 (November 12, 1962), p. 717. (No. 3504; 27 *Federal Register*, 10401.)

❖ ❖ ❖ **21**

U.S. EXECUTIVE ORDER MOBILIZING RESERVES, *October 23, 1962*

AN EXECUTIVE ORDER

ASSIGNING AUTHORITY WITH RESPECT TO ORDERING PERSONS AND UNITS IN THE READY RESERVE TO ACTIVE DUTY AND WITH RESPECT TO EXTENSION OF ENLISTMENTS AND OTHER PERIODS OF SERVICE IN THE ARMED FORCES.

By virtue of the authority vested in me by the Joint Resolution of

October 3, 1962 (Public Law 87–736), and by section 301 of title 3
of the United States Code, and as President of the United States, it
is hereby ordered as follows:

Section 1. The Secretary of Defense, and, when designated by
him for this purpose, any of the Secretaries of the military departments of the Department of Defense, and the Secretary of the Treasury with respect to the Coast Guard are hereby authorized and empowered to exercise the authority vested in the President until
February 28, 1963, by section 1 of the Act of October 3, 1962
(Public Law 87–736) to order, without consent of the persons concerned, any unit, or any member, of the Ready Reserve of an armed
force to active duty for not more than twelve consecutive months,
provided there are not more than 150,000 members of the Ready
Reserve thereby on active duty (other than for training) without
their consent at any one time.

Section 2. In pursuance of the provisions of section 2 of the said
Joint Resolution of October 3, 1962, the Secretary of Defense and the
Secretary of the Treasury with respect to the Coast Guard are hereby
authorized to extend enlistments, appointments, periods of active
duty, periods of active duty for training, periods of obligated service
or other military status in any component of an armed force or in
the National Guard that expire before February 28, 1963, for not
more than twelve months. However, if the enlistment of a member
of the Ready Reserve who is ordered to active duty under section 1
of this Executive Order would expire after February 28, 1963, but
before he has served the entire period for which he was so ordered to
active duty, his enlistment may be extended until the last day of that
period.

Section 3. In pursuance of the provisions of section 3 of the said
Joint Resolution of October 3, 1962, no member of the armed forces
who was involuntarily ordered to active duty or whose period of
active duty, his enlistment may be extended until the last day of that
Law 87–117 (75 Stat. 242), may be involuntarily ordered to active
duty under this Executive Order.

(s) John F. Kennedy

The White House,
October 23, 1962

U.S., Department of State, *Bulletin,* Volume XLVII, No. 1220 (November
12, 1962), p. 719. (No. 11058; 27 *Federal Register,* 10403.)

❖ ❖ ❖ **22**

SOVIET DRAFT RESOLUTION TO U.N.
SECURITY COUNCIL, *October 23, 1962*

*Violation of the United Nations Charter and threat to the
peace by the United States of America*

The Security Council,
Guided by the need to maintain peace and safeguard security
throughout the world,
Recognizing the right of every State to strengthen its defenses,
Considering inadmissible interference by some States in the internal affairs of other sovereign and independent countries,
Noting the inadmissibility of violations of the rules governing freedom of navigation on the high seas,
1. *Condemns* the actions of the Government of the United States
of America aimed at violating the United Nations Charter and at increasing the threat of war;
2. *Insists* that the Government of the United States shall revoke
its decision to inspect ships of other States bound for the Republic
of Cuba;
3. *Proposes* to the Government of the United States of America that
it shall cease any kind of interference in the internal affairs of the
Republic of Cuba and of other States which creates a threat to peace;
4. *Calls upon* the United States of America, the Republic of Cuba
and the Union of Soviet Socialist Republics to establish contact and
enter into negotiations for the purpose of restoring the situation to
normal and thus of removing the threat of an outbreak.

U.N., *Security Council Document S/5187*, October 23, 1962, p. 1. (Union
of Soviet Socialist Republics: draft resolution.)

❖ ❖ ❖ **23**

STATEMENT BY SECRETARY RUSK TO OAS,
October 23, 1962

Three weeks ago today, I met with your foreign ministers to consider the serious new situation created by the Soviet Military build-up

59

in Cuba. Most of you participated in that meeting,. You will recall
the discussion which took place culminating in a consensus on many
important aspects of the problem expressed in the final communiqué.
In that document the foreign ministers unanimously stated that the
efforts of the Sino-Soviet bloc to convert the island of Cuba. into an
armed base for Communist penetration of the Americas was the most
urgent problem confronting the Hemisphere. They also found that
the organs of our regional system which have responsibilities to deal
with the situation created by the Communist regime in Cuba should
intensify their efforts and should stand in readiness to consider what
measures, beyond those already authorized, might be required. And
the. foreign ministers also observed that it was desirable to intensify
surveillance of arms deliveries to Cuba in order to prevent the secret
accumulation in the island of arms that can be used for offensive
purposes against the Hemisphere.

When the foreign ministers prepared the communiqué, there was
no indication that the arms build-up was. taking on an offensive
character. Today we have incontrovertible evidence that despite repeated warnings. the Castro regime is permitting the establishment of
medium- and intermediate-range missile bases. on Cuban territory by
the Soviet Union. The facts are clear and incontrovertible and were
set forth by the President of the United States in his statement last
evening.. And these facts have been, of course,, also conveyed to you
by other means directly and to your governments. These facts demonstrate that the U.S.S.R. is making a major military investment in
Cuba with advanced weapons systems with substantial offensive
capability.

What do these facts mean to the independent nations of this Hemisphere? Their significance is immediate, direct, and perhaps fateful
to the maintenance of that independence. The principal implications
are:

First: The Communist regime in Cuba with the complicity of its
Soviet mentors has deceived the Hemisphere, under the cloak of
secrecy and with loud protestations of arming for self-defense, in
allowing an extracontinental power, bent on destruction of the national
independence and democratic aspirations of all our peoples, to establish an offensive military foothold in the heart of the Hemisphere. I
will not go into a detailed history of this partnership in deceit. Sufficient to recall that President Dorticos (Osvaldo Dorticos Torrado of
Cuba) in a speech before the United Nations General Assembly on
October 8 said: "We shall continue to strengthen our military defense,
to defend ourselves, not to attack anyone." The Soviet Government on
its part said in an official statement on September 11: "The armaments and military equipment sent to Cuba are designed exclusively
for defensive purposes." The statement added that Soviet rockets are
so powerful that "there is. no need to search for sites for them beyond
the boundaries of the Soviet Union." And last week the Soviet For-

eign Minister (Andrei A. Gromyko) in his talks with President Kennedy in the White House said that Soviet assistance to Cuba "pursued solely the purpose of contributing to the defense capabilities of Cuba," that "training by Soviet specialists of Cuban nationals in handling defensive armaments was by no means offensive," and that "if it were otherwise, the Soviet Government would never become involved in rendering such assistance."

Second: This offensive capability is of such a nature that it can reach into the far corners of our Hemisphere with its destructive force. These new weapons arriving in Cuba are not only directed against the United States. Let there be no misunderstanding. There are other strategic targets in this Hemisphere — in your countries — which they can devastate with their lethal loads. The missile sites in being for medium-range ballistic missiles are capable of carrying nuclear warheads as far west as Mexico City, as far south as the Panama Canal or Caracas, and as far north as Washington, D.C. The new sites for intermediate-range ballistic missiles in Cuba will be able to carry mass destruction to most of the major cities in the Western Hemisphere. In the face of this rapid build-up, no country of this Hemisphere can feel secure, either from direct attack or from persistent blackmail.

Third: This new Soviet intervention means a further tightening of the enslavement of the Cuban people by the Soviet power to which the Castro regime has surrendered the Cuban national heritage. It signifies for the rest of the Hemisphere a vast strengthening of the offensive capability of the Communist system, which talks of peaceful coexistence by which it appears to mean softening for subjugation, which uses the slogan of national liberation to crush every legitimate national aspiration.

Fourth: The Soviet intervention in this Hemisphere with major offensive weapons challenges as never before the determination of the American governments to carry out hemispheric commitments solemnly assumed in inter-American treaties and resolutions for the defense of the peace and security of the nations of this Hemisphere against extracontinental aggression or intervention. Here again I hardly need to review them because they are familiar to us all. Beginning with the Rio Treaty in 1947, and culminating in the decisions of the foreign ministers in Punta del Este and in their communiqué issued here this month, there has been a mounting conviction on the part of the American peoples and their governments that the growing intervention of the international Communist movement in this Hemisphere must stop and that the individual and collective means available within the regional system should be brought to bear as necessary to accomplish this objective.

The task before us is to meet this new phase of Soviet aggressive intervention in this Hemisphere. As free nations we must act in defense of our national independence and democratic heritage. We must confront and overcome the challenge now presented in Cuba. In doing so we must tailor our response, individually and collectively, to the degree and direction of the threat, be firm in our convictions and resolute and united in our actions.

In these circumstances the United States Government has sought a policy which would accomplish our purposes with the appropriate and necessary use of force and with necessary opportunity to remove this grave threat by means other than general war.

The President has therefore stated that it is necessary immediately to prevent the arrival of additional offensive military weapons in Cuba, to seek promptly to arrest further work on the offensive capacity being developed in Cuba, and to require that all these offensive weapons be withdrawn or eliminated before we can consider that this new threat to the peace of the Hemisphere will have been adequately dealt with.

The United States Government, therefore, strongly urges that the governments of this Hemisphere take the actions necessary under the Inter-American Treaty of Reciprocal Assistance to achieve these objectives.

As an initial measure, which is primarily the responsibility of this Hemisphere and of special concern to it, the United States believes that we should establish a strict quarantine to prevent further offensive military equipment from reaching Cuba. The immediate character of the nuclear military threat to our peoples from these bases in Cuba is such that we cannot tolerate any further opportunity to add to their capacity. To this end the United States has requested this urgent meeting of the Council to convoke the Organ of Consultation under article 6 of the Rio Treaty to deal with this new situation. We are convinced that the evidence presented can leave no doubt that the danger is present and real. Furthermore, because of the urgency of the situation, we believe that the Council, acting provisionally as Organ of Consultation, should immediately take the steps which are necessary at this time.

For these purposes my Government has prepared two draft resolutions, the texts of which have been circulated. The first is a procedural resolution by which the Council would decide to convoke the Organ of Consultation under the Inter-American Treaty of Reciprocal Assistance and would also decide to act provisionally as that Organ in accordance with Article 12 of that treaty. The second, more substantive resolution is one which would be formally considered by the Council, once it has approved the first and has constituted itself as the Organ of Consultation. Under this second resolution the Organ of Consultation would call for the immediate dismantling and withdrawal from Cuba of all missiles and other weapons of offensive capability and would recommend, though not seek to compel, the member states of the OAS to take the measures necessary to insure that this build-up does not continue to receive additional offensive weapons, to prevent the offensive capacity already acquired by the Castro regime from being used to destroy the peace and security of the Hemisphere.

Finally, Mr. Chairman, I want to say a word about the action being taken simultaneously in the Security Council of the United Nations. The threat is to our Hemisphere, and we have the primary responsibility and duty to act as we are now doing as a Hemisphere. But the threat originates from outside the Hemisphere, and it is appropriate that the extracontinental power which challenges our inter-American commitments and our deliberations must also be dealt, in that forum in which he participates. It is therefore fitting in this case that the Security Council of the United Nations be requested to call upon this member to refrain from his aggressive actions against us and to seek to enforce upon him its decisions.

Meanwhile, without awaiting the outcome of the United Nations approach we must insure that our Hemisphere is effectively quarantined against any further additions to Soviet offensive nuclear military power in our midst.

All the world will be watching how wisely, how resolutely, how unitedly this Council acts to meet a challenge within our Hemisphere and to our own interest. May I add that crucial in this present situation will be the judgment of others, some of them far away, about the unity and determination of the nations of this Hemisphere. The President made it clear last evening that we should prefer to resolve this problem through peace. But if others make a grave mistake the danger will be greatly increased. And therefore, gentlemen, I am deeply convinced that the unanimity of this Hemisphere is directly related to the opportunity to remove this threat within the limits of force which are now being employed. For the future of peace and freedom of the world has never before been so dependent upon the inter-American system as it is today.

U.S., Department of State, *Bulletin,* Volume XLVII, No. 1220 (November 12, 1962), pp. 720–722.

❖ ❖ ❖ **24**

EXCERPT FROM STATEMENT BY CUBAN AMBASSADOR GARCÍA-INCHAUSTEGUI TO OAS, *October 23, 1962*

We are deeply sorry that at a moment of serious tension and danger of nuclear war that a permanent member of the Security Council should see fit to use inadequate language when referring to representatives and agents of governments and in judging facts that belong to history and to the sovereign political position of states and jurisdiction of states.

The North American representative is very happy with his social system. We have a very different opinion from his. We reject his affirmations and statements regarding our history and our social system.

Who are these who accuse Cuba of being a threatening base against American territory? Those who possess the only foreign base in Cuba against the will of our people. Those who now reinforce it so that from that base they can attack us too.

According to the statement by the delegate of the United States, there are two types of military bases, and two types of rockets — the good military bases and the bad ones, the good rockets and the bad rockets.

Obviously the Government of the United States reserves the right to decide and determine when a rocket is good and when a rocket is bad or naughty, when a base is good and when a base is naughty.

What right have they to ask for dismantling and disarmament when they in Cuba occupy a base against the will of our own people. And in their continental territory and all over the world they possess bases that are aggressive bases against member states of this organization.

What rights support the United States when it asks for observers in Cuba? The United Nations observers should logically be sent to the American bases from which invasions and pirates emerge to punish and harass a small state, one whose only crime is that of struggling for the development of its own people.

We will accept no type of observers, observers of matters that fall within our domestic jurisdiction. The imperialistic maneuvers in the Congo will not be repeated in Cuba.

The New York Times, October 24, 1962, p. 22. Copyright by The New York Times. Reprinted by permission.

✧ ✧ ✧ **25**

RESOLUTION ADOPTED BY OAS, *October 23, 1962*

WHEREAS,

The Inter-American Treaty of Reciprocal Assistance of 1947 (Rio Treaty) recognizes the obligation of the American Republics to "provide for effective reciprocal assistance to meet armed attacks against any American State and in order to deal with threats of aggression against any of them."

Article 6 of the said Treaty states:

"If the inviolability or the integrity of the territory or the sovereignty or political independence of any American State should be affected by an aggression which is not an armed attack or by an extracontinental or intra-continental conflict, or by any other fact or situation that might endanger the peace of America, the Organ of Consultation shall meet immediately in order to agree on the measures which must be taken in case of aggression to assist the victim of the aggression or, in any case, the measures which should be taken for the common defense and for the maintenance of the peace and security of the Continent."

The Eighth Meeting of Consultation of the Ministers of Foreign Affairs of the American Republics in Punta del Este in January, 1962, agreed in Resolution II "To urge the member states to take those steps that they may consider appropriate for their individual and collective self-defense, and to cooperate, as may be necessary or desirable to strength their capacity to counteract threats or acts of aggression, subversion, or other dangers to peace and security resulting from the continued intervention in this hemisphere of Sino-Soviet powers, in accordance with the obligations established in treaties and agreements such as the Charter of the Organization of American States and the Inter-American Treaty of Reciprocal Assistance";

The Ministers of Foreign Affairs of the American Republics meeting informally in Washington, October 2 and 3, 1962, reasserted "the firm intention of the Governments represented and of the peoples of the American Republics to conduct themselves in accordance with the principles of the regional system, staunchly sustaining and consolidating the principles of the Charter of the Organization of American States, and affirmed the will to strengthen the security of the Hemisphere against all aggression from within or outside the Hemisphere and against all developments or situations capable of threatening the peace and security of the Hemisphere through the application of the Inter-American Treaty of Reciprocal Assistance of Rio de Janeiro. It was the view of the Ministers that the existing organizations and bodies of the inter-American system should intensify the carrying out of their respective duties with special and urgent attention to the situation created by the communist regime in Cuba and that they should stand in readiness to consider the matter promptly if the situation requires measures beyond those already authorized."

The same meeting "recalled that the Soviet Union's intervention in Cuba threatens the unity of the Americas and its democratic institutions, and that this intervention has special characteristics which, pursuant to paragraph 3 of Resolution II of the Eighth Meeting of Consultation of Ministers of Foreign Affairs, call for the adoption of special measures, both individual and collective";

Incontrovertible evidence has appeared that the Government of Cuba, despite repeated warnings, has secretly endangered the peace of the Continent by permitting the Sino-Soviet powers to have intermediate and middle-range missiles on its territory capable of carrying nuclear warheads;

THE COUNCIL OF THE ORGANIZATION OF AMERICAN STATES, MEETING AS THE PROVISIONAL ORGAN OF CONSULTATION, RESOLVES:

1. To call for the immediate dismantling and withdrawal from Cuba of all missiles and other weapons with any offensive capability;

2. To recommend that the member states, in accordance with Articles 6 and 8 of the Inter-American Treaty of Reciprocal Assistance, take all measures, individually and collectively, including the use of armed force, which they may deem necessary to ensure that the Government of Cuba cannot continue to receive from the Sino-Soviet powers military material and related supplies which may threaten the peace and security of the Continent and to prevent the missiles in Cuba with offensive capability from ever becoming an active threat to the peace and security of the Continent;

3. To inform the Security Council of the United Nations of this resolution in accordance with Article 54 of the Charter of the United Nations and to express the hope that the Security Council will, in accordance with the draft resolution introduced by the United States, dispatch United Nations observers to Cuba at the earliest moment;

4. To continue to serve provisionally as Organ of Consultation and to request the Member States to keep the Organ of Consultation duly informed of measures taken by them in accordance with paragraph two of this resolution.

U.S., Department of State, *Bulletin*, Volume XLVII, No. 1220 (November 12, 1962), pp. 722–723. (U.N. *Security Council Document S/5193*, October 25, 1962, pp. 1–4.) Adopted by OAS Council by a vote of 19 to 0, with one abstention. (Uruguay abstained on October 23 because its delegate had not received instructions, but on October 24 Uruguay cast an affirmative vote making the resolution unanimous.)

❖ ❖ ❖ **26**

STATEMENT BY AMBASSADOR STEVENSON TO U.N. SECURITY COUNCIL, *October 23, 1962*

I have asked for an emergency meeting of the Security Council to bring to your attention a grave threat to the Western Hemisphere and to the peace of the world.

Last night the President of the United States reported the recent alarming military developments in Cuba. Permit me to remind you of the President's sobering words:

"Within the past week unmistakable evidence has established the fact that a series of offensive missile sites is now in preparation on that imprisoned island. The purpose of these bases can be none other than to provide a nuclear strike capability against the Western Hemisphere.

"Upon receiving the first preliminary hard information of this nature last Tuesday morning (October 16) at 9:00 A.M., I directed that our surveillance be stepped up. And having now confirmed and completed our evaluation of the evidence and our decision on a course of action, this Government feels obliged to report this new crisis to you in fullest detail.

"The characteristics of these new missile sites indicate two distinct types of installations. Several of them include medium-range ballistic missiles capable of carrying a nuclear warhead for a distance of more than 1,000 nautical miles. Each of these missiles, in short, is capable of striking Washington, D.C., the Panama Canal, Cape Canaveral, Mexico City, or any other city in the southeastern part of the United States, in Central America, or in the Caribbean area.

"Additional sites not yet completed appear to be designed for intermediate-range ballistic missiles — capable of traveling more than twice as far — and thus capable of striking most of the major cities in the Western Hemisphere, ranging as far north as Hudson Bay, Canada, and as far south as Lima, Peru. In addition, jet bombers, capable of carrying nuclear weapons are now being uncrated and assembled in Cuba, while the necessary air bases are being prepared."

In view of this transformation of Cuba, into a base for offensive weapons of sudden mass destruction, the President announced the initiation of a strict quarantine on all offensive military weapons under shipment to Cuba. He did so because, in the view of my Government, the recent developments in Cuba — the importation of the cold war into the heart of the Americas — constitute a threat to the peace of this Hemisphere and, indeed, to the peace of the world.

Mr. President, seventeen years ago the representatives of fifty-one nations gathered in San Francisco to adopt the Charter of the United Nations. These nations stated with clarity and eloquence the high purpose which brought them together.

They announced their common determination "to save succeeding generations from the scourge of war . . . to establish conditions under which justice and respect for the obligations arising from treaties and other sources of international law can be maintained, and to promote social progress and better standards of life in larger freedom." And in one sentence, paragraph 4, article 2, they defined the necessary condition of a community of independent peoples:

"All Members shall refrain in their international relations from the threat or use of force against the territorial integrity or political independence of any state, or in any other manner inconsistent with the Purposes of the United Nations."

In this spirit these fifty-one nations solemnly resolved to band together in a great cooperative quest for world peace and world progress. The adventure of the United Nations held out to humanity the bright hope of a new world, a world securely founded in international peace, in national independence, in personal freedom, in respect for law, for social justice and betterment, and, in the words of the charter, for "equal rights and self-determination of peoples."

The vision of San Francisco was the vision of a world community of independent nations, each freely developing according to its own traditions and its own genius, bound together by a common respect for the rights of other nations and by a common loyalty to the larger international order. This vision assumes that this earth is quite large enough to shelter a great variety of economic systems, political creeds, philosophical beliefs, and religious convictions. The faith of the charter is in a pluralistic world, a world of free choice, respecting the infinite diversity of mankind and dedicated to nations living together as good neighbors in peace.

Like many peoples, we welcomed the world of the charter, for our society is based on principles of choice and consent.

We believe the principles of an open society in the world order survive and flourish in the competitions of peace. We believe that freedom and diversity are the best climate for human creativity and social progress. We reject all fatalistic philosophies of history and all theories of political and social predestination. We doubt whether any nation has so absolute a grip on absolute truth that it is entitled to impose its idea of what is right on others. And we know that a world community of independent nations accepting a common frame of international order offers the best safeguard for the safety of our shores and the security of our people. Our commitment to the world of the charter expresses both our deepest philosophical traditions and the most realistic interpretation of our national interest.

Had we any other vision of the world, had we sought the path of empire, our opportunities for self-aggrandizement immediately after the war were almost unparalleled. In 1945, we were incomparably the greatest military power in the world. Our troops and planes were dispersed at strategic points around the globe. We had exclusive possession of the terror and promise of atomic energy. Our economic strength was unmatched. If the American purpose had been world dominion there could have been no more propitious moment to set out on such a course.

Instead, our commitment, then as now, was to the world of the Charter — the creation of a community of freely cooperating independent states bound together by the United Nations. In the service of this commitment and without waiting for the peace treaties, we dismantled the mightiest military force we had ever assembled. Armies were disbanded wholesale. Vast supplies of war equipment were liquidated or junked. Within two years after the end of the war, our defense spending had fallen by nearly $70 billion. Our Armed Forces were slashed from more than twelve millions to one and one-half million men. We did not retain a single division in a state of combat readiness. We did not have a single military alliance anywhere in the world. History has not seen, I believe, a more complete and comprehensive demonstration of a great nation's hope for peace and amity.

Instead of using our monopoly of atomic energy to extend our national power, we contributed more than $2.6 billion to the United Nations Relief and Rehabilitation Administration, much of which went to the relief of suffering in the Communist countries. And after 1948 we contributed many more billions to the economic restoration of Europe — and invited the Communist countries to participate as recipients of our assistance.

Instead of using substance and strength to extend our national power, we supported the movement for independence which began to sweep through Asia and Africa, the movement which has added fifty-nine new members to the United Nations in the years since 1945. Since the war we have contributed $97 billion of economic and military assistance to other nations, and, of this sum, $53 billion has gone to the nations of Asia, Africa, and Latin America.

I have often wondered what the world would be like today if the situation at the end of the war had been reversed — if the United States had been ravaged and shattered by war and if the Soviet Union had emerged intact in exclusive possession of the atomic bomb and overwhelming military and economic might. Would it have followed the same path and devoted itself to realizing the world of the Charter?

To ask this question suggests the central paradox of the United Nations. For among the states which pledged their fidelity to the idea of a pluralistic world in San Francisco were some who had an incompatible vision of the future world order.

Has the Soviet Union ever really joined the United Nations? Or does its philosophy of history and its conception of the future run counter to the pluralistic concept of the charter?

Against the idea of diversity, communism asserts the idea of uniformity; against freedom, inevitability; against choice, compulsion; against democracy, dogma; against independence, ideology; against tolerance, conformity. Its faith is that the iron laws of history will require every nation to traverse the same predestined path to the same predestined conclusion. Given this faith in a monolithic world, the very existence of diversity is a threat to the Communist future.

I do not assert that communism must always remain a messianic faith. Like other fanaticisms of the past, it may in time lose its sense.

of infallibility and accept the diversity of human destiny. Already in some countries we see communism subsiding into a local and limited ideology. There are those who have discerned the same evolution in the Soviet Union itself; and we may all earnestly hope that Chairman Khrushchev and his associates will renounce the dream of making the world over in the image of the Soviet Union. It must be the purpose of other nations to do what they can to hasten that day.

But that day has not yet arrived. The conflict between absolutist and pluralistic conceptions of the destiny of mankind remains the basic source of discord within the United Nations. It has given rise to what is known as the cold war. Were it not for this conflict, this organization would have made steady progress toward the world of choice and justice envisaged at San Francisco.

But because of the Soviet rejection of an open world, the hope for progress and for peace has been systematically frustrated. And in these halls we spend much of our time and energy either engaged in or avoiding this incessant conflict.

It began even before the nations gathered at San Francisco. As soon as the defeat of the Nazis appeared certain, the Soviet Union began to abandon the policy of wartime cooperation to which it had turned for self-protection. In early 1945 Moscow instructed the Communist parties of the West to purge themselves of the sin of cooperation and to return to their prewar view that democratic governments were by definition imperialistic and wicked. Within a few weeks after the meeting at Yalta the Soviet Union took swift action in Romania and Poland in brutal violation of the Yalta pledges of political freedom.

At the same time it began a political offensive against the United States, charging that the American Government — the government of Franklin Roosevelt — was engaged in secret peace negotiations with Hitler. Roosevelt replied to Stalin that he deeply resented these "vile misrepresentations." At the end of March 1945 Roosevelt cabled Winston Churchill that he was "watching with anxiety and concern the development of the Soviet attitude" and that he was "acutely aware of the dangers inherent in the present course of events, not only for the immediate issue but also the San Francisco Conference and future world cooperation."

It is important to recall these facts because the Soviet Union has tried in the years since to pretend that its policy of aggression was a defensive response to the change of administration in the United States, or to Churchill's 1946 speech at Fulton, Missouri, or to some other event after the death of Roosevelt. But the historical record is clear. As soon as the Soviet Government saw no further military need for the wartime coalition, it set out on its expansionist adventures

The ink was hardly dry on the Charter before Moscow began its war against the world of the United Nations. The very first meeting of the Security Council — and I .was there — was called to hear a complaint by Iran that Soviet troops had failed to withdraw from the northern part of that country on the date on which they had agreed to leave. Not only had they declined to go; they had installed a puppet regime on Iranian soil and had blocked Iranian troops from entering part of Iran's territory. The Soviet Union, in short, was violating the territorial integrity and denying the political independence of Iran — and doing so by armed force. Eventually the United Nations forced a reluctant agreement from the Soviet Union to live up to its pledge.

This was only the beginning. At the time of the German surrender, the Red Army was in occupation of Romania, Bulgaria, Hungary, Poland, Eastern Germany, and most of Czechoslovakia. And there the Red army stayed. It stayed in violation of the agreement reached at Yalta by the heads of the Allied Powers — the agreement which pledged the independence and promised free elections to these nations. By 1948 five nations and half of a sixth, with a combined population of more than ninety million people, had been absorbed into the Communist empire. To this day the peoples of Eastern Europe have never been permitted to exercise the charter right of self-determination.

Before the suppression of Eastern Europe was complete, the Soviet Union was fomenting guerrilla warfare and sabotaging economic recovery in Greece and Turkey, assailing neighboring regimes through all the instrumentalities of propaganda and subversion.

Nor were such activities confined to Europe. In Malaya, in the Philippines, in Burma, in Indo-china, the Communists encouraged and supported guerrilla uprisings against constituted governments.

In one event after another, on one stage after another — the rejection in the United Nations of the American plan for the internationalization of atomic energy, the rejection of the Marshall Plan, the blockade of Berlin, and, finally, the invasion of South Korea — the Soviet Union assailed political independence, resisted the world of the charter, and tried to impose its design of a Communist future.

Let me recall to this Council, Mr. President, the record with regard to international agreements.

The Soviet Government has signed treaties of nonaggression, as it did with the Baltic states and Finland — and then systematically invaded the countries whose integrity it had solemnly promised to respect.

At Yalta, and in a succession of peace treaties, it pledged to the liberated countries of Eastern Europe "the right of all peoples to choose the form of government under which they will live — the restoration of sovereign rights and self-government to those peoples who have been forcibly deprived of them" — and then it systematically denied those rights and consolidated that deprivation.

In 1945 it signed a thirty-year pact of mutual assistance and nonaggression with China, pledging that its military aid and economic support would be "given entirely to the National Government as the Central Government of China" — and violated that treaty almost before the Chinese negotiators had left Moscow.

At Potsdam it promised that "all democratic political parties with rights of assembly and of public discussion shall be allowed and encouraged throughout Germany" — and within its own zone promptly repudiated that promise. At Geneva in 1954 it agreed not to introduce arms into Viet-Nam — and sent guns and ammunition to the Viet Minh.

It denounced nuclear testing — and then violated the moratorium which for three years had spared the world the danger of nuclear tests.

Within this Council it has thwarted the majority will 100 times by the use of the veto.

The record is clear: Treaties, agreements, pledges, and the morals of international relations were never an obstacle to the Soviet Union under Stalin. No one has said so more eloquently than Chairman Khrushchev.

With the death of Stalin in 1953, the world had a resurgence of hope. No one can question that Chairman Khrushchev has altered many things in the Soviet Union. He has introduced welcome measures of normalization in many sectors of Soviet life. He has abandoned the classic Communist concept of the inevitability of war. He has recognized — intermittently, at least — the appalling dangers of nuclear weapons.

But there is one thing he has not altered, and that is the basic drive to abolish the world of the Charter, to destroy the hope of a pluralistic world order. He has not altered the basic drive to fulfill the prophecies of Marx and Lenin and make all the world Communist. And he has demonstrated his singleness of purpose in a succession of aggressive acts — in the suppression of the East German uprisings in 1953 and the Hungarian revolution in 1956, in the series of manufactured crises and truculent demands that the Allies get out of West Berlin, in the resumption of nuclear testing, in the explosion — defying a resolution of the General Assembly — of a fifty-megaton bomb, in the continued stimulation of guerrilla and subversive warfare all over the globe, in the compulsive intervention in the internal affairs of other nations, whether by diplomatic assault, by economic pressure, by mobs and riots, by propaganda, or by espionage.

The world welcomed the process known as de-Stalinization and the movement toward a more normal life within the Soviet Union. But the world has not yet seen comparable changes in Soviet foreign policy.

It is this which has shadowed the world since the end of the Second World War, which has dimmed our hopes of peace and progress, which has forced those nations determined to defend their freedom to take measures in their own self-defense. In this effort the leadership has inevitably fallen in large degree on the United States. I do not believe that every action we have taken in the effort to strengthen the independence of nations has necessarily been correct; we do not subscribe to the thesis of national infallibility for any nation. But we do take great pride in the role we have performed.

Our response to the remorseless Soviet expansionism has taken many forms. We have sought loyally to support the United Nations, to be faithful to the world of the charter, and to build an operating system that acts, and does not talk, for peace.

We have never refused to negotiate. We have sat at conference after conference seeking peaceful solutions to menacing conflicts.

We have worked for general and complete disarmament under international supervision. We have tried earnestly — and we won't stop trying — to reach an agreement to end all nuclear testing.

We have declined to be provoked into actions which might lead to war — in face of such challenges as the Berlin blockade, such affronts to humanity as the repression of the Hungarian revolt, such atrocities as the erection of that shameful wall to fence in the East Germans, who had fled to the West in such vast multitudes.

We have assisted nations, both allied and unaligned, who have shown a will to maintain their national independence. To shield them and ourselves, we have rebuilt our armed forces, established defensive alliances, and, year after year, reluctantly devoted a large share of our resources to national defense.

Together with our allies, we have installed certain bases overseas as a prudent precaution in response to the clear and persistent Soviet threats. In 1959, eighteen months after the boasts of Chairman Khrushchev had called the world's attention to the threat of Soviet long-range missiles, the North Atlantic Treaty Organization, without concealment or deceit, as a consequence of agreements freely negotiated and publicly declared, placed intermediate-range ballistic missiles in the NATO area. The warheads of these missiles remain in the custody of the United States, and the decision for their use rests in the hands of the President of the United States of America in association with the governments involved.

I regret that people here at the United Nations seem to believe that the cold war is a private struggle between two great superpowers. It isn't a private struggle; it is a world civil war, a contest between the pluralistic world and the monolithic world, a contest between the world of the Charter and the world of Communist conformity. Every nation that is now independent and wants to remain independent is involved, whether they know it or not. Every nation is involved in this grim, costly, distasteful division in the world, no matter how remote and how uninterested.

We all recognized this in 1950, when the Communists decided to test how far they could go by direct military action and unleashed the invasion of South Korea. The response of the United Nations taught them that overt aggression would produce not appeasement but resistance. This remains the essential lesson The United Nations stood firm in Korea because we knew the consequences of appeasement.

The policy of appeasement is always intended to strengthen the moderates in the country appeased, but its effect is always to strengthen the extremists. We are prepared to meet and reconcile every legitimate Soviet concern; but we have only contempt for blackmail. We know that every retreat before intimidation strengthens those who say that the threat of force can always achieve Communist objectives and undermines those in the Soviet Union who are urging caution and restraint, even cooperation.

Reluctantly and repeatedly, we have to face the sad fact that the only way to reinforce those on the other side who are for moderation and peaceful competition is to make it absolutely clear that aggression will be met with resistance and force with force.

The time has come for this Council to decide whether to make a serious attempt to bring peace to the world — or to let the United Nations stand idly by while the vast plan of piecemeal aggression unfolds, conducted in the hope that no single issue will seem consequential enough to mobilize the resistance of the free peoples. For my own Government, this question is not in doubt. We remain committed to the principles of the United Nations Charter, and we intend to defend them.

We are engaged today in a crucial test of those principles. Nearly four years ago a revolution took place on the island of Cuba. This revolution overthrew a hated dictatorship in the name of democratic freedom and social progress. Dr. Castro made explicit promises to the people of Cuba. He promised them the restoration of the 1940 constitution abandoned by the Batista dictatorship; a "provisional government of entirely civilian character that will return the country to normality and hold general elections within a period of no more than one year"; "truly honest" elections along with "full and untrammeled" freedom of information and political activity.

That is what Dr. Castro offered the people of Cuba. That is what the people of Cuba accepted. Many in my own country and throughout the Americas sympathized with Dr. Castro's stated objectives. The United States Government offered immediate diplomatic recognition and stood ready to provide the revolutionary regime with economic assistance.

But a grim struggle took place within the revolutionary regime, between its democratic and its predominant Communist wings, between those who overthrew Batista to bring freedom to Cuba and those who overthrew Batista to bring Cuba to communism. In a few months the struggle was over. Brave men who had fought with Castro in the

Sierra Maestra and who had organized the underground against Batista in the cities were assailed, arrested, and driven from office into prison or exile, all for the single offense of anti-communism, all for the single offense of believing in the principles of the revolution they fought for. By the end of 1959 the Communist Party was the only party in Cuba permitted freedom of political action. By early 1960 the Castro regime was entering into intimate economic and political relations with the Soviet Union.

It is well to remember that all these events took place months before the United States stopped buying Cuban sugar in the summer of 1960 — and many more months before exactions upon our Embassy in Habana forced the suspension of diplomatic relations in December 1960.

As the communization of Cuba proceeded, more and more democratic Cubans, men who had fought for freedom in the front ranks, were forced into exile. They were eager to return to their homeland and to save their revolution from betrayal. In the spring of 1961 they tried to liberate their country, under the political leadership of Dr. Castro's first Prime Minister and of a Revolutionary Council composed without exception of men who had opposed Batista and backed the revolution. The people and Government of the United States sympathized with these men — as throughout our history Americans have always sympathized with those who sought to liberate their native lands from despotism. I have no apologies to make for that sympathy or for the assistance which these brave Cuban refugees received from our hands. But I would point out, too, that my Government, still forbearing, refrained from direct intervention. It sent no American troops to Cuba.

In the year and a half since, Dr. Castro has continued the communization of his unfortunate country. The 1940 constitution was never restored. Elections were never held and their promise withdrawn — though Dr. Castro's twelve months have stretched to forty-two. The Castro regime fastened on Cuba an iron system of repression. It eradicated human and civil rights. It openly transformed Cuba into a Communist satellite and a police state. Whatever benefit this regime might have brought to Cuba has long since been canceled out by the firing squads, the drumhead executions, the hunger and misery, the suppression of civil and political and cultural freedom.

Yet even these violations of human rights, repellent as they are — even this dictatorship, cruel as it may be — would not, if kept within the confines of one country, constitute a direct threat to the peace and independence of other states. The threat lies in the submission of the Castro regime to the will of an aggressive foreign power. It lies in its readiness to break up the relations of confidence and cooperation among the good neighbors of this hemisphere — at a time when the Alliance for Progress, that vast effort to raise living standards for all peoples of the Americas, has given new vitality and hope to the inter-American system.

Let me make it absolutely clear what the issue of Cuba is. It is not an issue of revolution. This Hemisphere has seen many revolutions, including the one which gave my own nation its independence.

. It is not an issue of reform. My nation has lived happily with other countries which have had thoroughgoing and fundamental social transformations, like Mexico and Bolivia. The whole point of the Alliance for Progress is to bring about an economic and social revolution in the Americas.

It is not an issue of socialism. As Secretary of State Rusk said at Punta del Este in January: "Our Hemisphere has room for a diversity of economic systems."

It is not an issue of dictatorship. The American Republics have lived with dictators before. If this were his only fault, they could even live with Dr. Castro.

The foremost objection of the states of the Americas to the Castro regime is not because it is revolutionary, not because it is socialistic, not because it is dictatorial, not even because Dr. Castro perverted a noble revolution in the interests of a squalid totalitarianism. It is because he has aided and abetted an invasion of this Hemisphere — and an invasion at just the time when the Hemisphere is making a new and unprecedented effort for economic progress and social reform.

The crucial fact is that Cuba has given the Soviet Union a bridgehead and staging area in this Hemisphere, that it has invited an extracontinental, anti-democratic, and expansionist power into the bosom of the American family, that it has made itself an accomplice in the Communist enterprise of world dominion.

There are those who seek to equate the presence of Soviet bases in Cuba with the presence of NATO bases in parts of the world near the Soviet Union.

Let us subject this facile argument to critical consideration. It is not only that the Soviet action in Cuba has created a new and dangerous situation by sudden and drastic steps which imperil the security of all mankind. It is necessary further to examine the purposes for which missiles are introduced and bases established.

Missiles which help a country defend its independence, which leave the political institutions of the recipient countries intact, which are not designed to subvert the territorial integrity or political independence of other states, which are installed without concealment or deceit — assistance in this form and with these purposes is consistent with the principles of the United Nations. But missiles which introduce a nuclear threat into an area now free of it, which threaten the security and independence of defenseless neighboring states, which are installed by clandestine means, which result in the most formidable nuclear base in the world outside existing treaty systems — assistance in this form and with these purposes is radically different.

Let me state this point very clearly. The missile sites in NATO countries were established in response to missile sites in the Soviet Union directed at the NATO countries. The NATO states had every right and necessity to respond to the installation of these Soviet missiles by installing missiles of their own. These missiles were designed to deter a process of expansion already in progress. Fortunately, they have helped to do so.

The United States and its allies established their missile sites after free negotiation, without concealment and without false statements to other governments.

There is, in short, a vast difference between the long-range missile sites established years ago in Europe and the long-range missile sites established by the Soviet Union in Cuba during the last three months.

There is a final significant difference. For 150 years the nations of the Americas have painfully labored to construct a Hemisphere of independent and cooperating nations, free from foreign threats. An international system far older than this one — the inter-American system — has been erected on this principle. The principle of the territorial integrity of the Western Hemisphere has been woven into the history, the life, and the thought of all the people of the Americas. In striking at that principle the Soviet Union is striking at the strongest and most enduring strain in the policy of this hemisphere. It is disrupting the convictions and aspirations of a century and a half. It is intruding on the firm policies of twenty nations. To allow this challenge to go unanswered would be to undermine a basic and historic pillar of the security of the Hemisphere.

Twenty years ago the nations of the Americas were understandably disturbed by the threat of Nazism. Just as they would have reacted with vigor had any American Republic given itself over to the doctrines and agents of Nazism, so today they look with equal concern on the conquest of Cuba by a foreign power and an alien ideology. They do not intend to applaud and assist while Dr. Castro and his new friends try to halt the march of free and progressive democracy in Latin America.

Yet, despite the ominous movement of affairs in Cuba, the reaction of the Hemisphere and of my own Government continued to be marked by forbearance. Despite Dr. Castro's verbal assaults on other nations in the Hemisphere, despite his campaign of subversion against their governments, despite the insurrectionary expeditions launched from Cuba, the nations of the Americas retained their hope that the Cuban revolution would free itself. But Dr. Castro's persistence in his campaigns against the governments of this Hemisphere, his decision to become the junior partner of Moscow, finally destroyed that hope.

If Cuba has withdrawn from the American family of nations, it has been Dr. Castro's own act. If Cuba is today isolated from its brethren of the Americas, it is self-inflicted isolation. If the present Cuban government has turned its back on its own history, tradition, religion, and culture, if it has chosen to cast its lot with the Communist empire, it must accept the consequences of its decision. The Hemisphere has no alternative but to accept the tragic choice Dr. Castro has imposed on his people — that is, to accept Cuba's self-exclusion from the Hemisphere.

One after another, the other governments of this Hemisphere have withdrawn their diplomatic representatives from Cuba. Today only three still have their ambassadors in Habana. Last January the American states unanimously declared that the Castro regime was incompatible with the principles on which the Organization of American States had been founded and, by a two-thirds vote, excluded that regime from participation in the inter-American system.

All this took place before Soviet arms and technicians began to move into Cuba in a massive, continuous stream. But, even then, the governments of the Hemisphere were willing to withhold final judgment so long as the Soviet weapons were defensive. And my Government — and the United Nations — were solemnly assured by the representatives of both Soviet Russia and Cuba that the Soviet arms pouring into the island were, in fact, purely defensive weapons.

On September 11, the Soviet Government said in an official statement: "The armaments and military equipment sent to Cuba are designed exclusively for defensive purposes." The Soviet Government added that Soviet rockets were so powerful that "there is no need to search for sites for them beyond the boundaries of the Soviet Union." And last week, on October 18th, Mr. Gromyko, the Soviet Foreign Minister, told the President of the United States at the White House that Soviet assistance to Cuba "pursued solely the purpose of contributing to the defense capabilities of Cuba," that "training by Soviet specialists of Cuban nationals in handling defensive armaments was by no means offensive," and that "if it were otherwise, the Soviet Government would never become involved in rendering such assistance." This once peaceable island is being transformed into a formidable missile and strategic air base armed with the deadliest, far-reaching, modern nuclear weapons.

The statement issued by the Soviet Government this morning does not deny these facts — which is in refreshing contrast to the categoric assurances on this subject which they had previously given.

However, this same statement repeats the extraordinary claim that Soviet arms in Cuba are of a "defensive character." I should like to know what the Soviets consider "offensive" weapons. In the Soviet lexicon evidently all weapons are purely defensive, even weapons that can strike from 1,000 to 2,000 miles away. Words can be stretched only so far without losing their meaning altogether. But semantic disputes are fruitless, and the fact remains that the Soviet has upset the precarious balance and created a new and dangerous situation in a new area.

This is precisely the sort of action which the Soviet Government is so fond of denouncing as "a policy of positions of strength." Consequently, I invite the attention of the Council to another remark in the Soviet Government's statement of this morning: "Only madmen bank on a policy of positions of strength and believe that this policy will bring any success, will help make it possible to impose their orders on other States."

I need only mention one other curious remark in the Soviet Government's statement of today, and I quote once more: "Who gave the United States the right to assume the role of the master of destinies of other countries and peoples? . . . Cuba belongs to the Cuban peoples and only they can be masters of their destiny." This latter sentence is, of course, a succinct statement of United States policy toward Cuba. It is, however, very far from being Soviet policy toward Cuba.

When the Soviet Union sends thousands of military technicians to its satellite in the Western Hemisphere, when it sends jet bombers capable of delivering nuclear weapons, when it installs in Cuba missiles capable of carrying atomic warheads and of obliterating the Panama Canal, Mexico City, and Washington, when it prepares sites for additional missiles with a range of 2,200 miles and a capacity to strike at targets from Peru to Hudson Bay — when it does these things under the cloak of secrecy and to the accompaniment of premeditated deception, when its actions are in flagrant violation of the policies of the Organization of American States and of the Charter of the United Nations, this clearly is a threat to this Hemisphere. And when it thus upsets the precarious balance in the world, it is a threat to the whole world.

We now know that the Soviet Union, not content with Dr. Castro's oath of fealty, not content with the destruction of Cuban independence, not content with the extension of Soviet power into the Western Hemisphere, not content with a challenge to the inter-American system and the United Nations Charter, has decided to transform Cuba into a base for Communist aggression, into a base for putting all of the Americas under the nuclear gun and thereby intensify the Soviet diplomacy of blackmail in every part of the world.

In our passion for peace we have forborne greatly. But there must be limits to forbearance if forbearance is not to become the diagram for the destruction of this organization. Dr. Castro transformed Cuba into a totalitarian dictatorship with impunity, he extinguished the rights of political freedom with impunity, he aligned himself with the Soviet bloc with impunity, he accepted defensive weapons from the Soviet Union with impunity, he welcomed thousands of Communists into Cuba with impunity — but when, with cold deliberation, he turns his country over to the Soviet Union for a long-range missile-launching base, and thus carries the Soviet program for aggression into the heart of the Americas, the day of forbearance is past.

If the United States and the other nations of the Western Hemisphere should accept this new phase of aggression, we would be delinquent in our obligations to world peace. If the United States and the other nations of the Western Hemisphere should accept this basic disturbance of the world's structure of power, we would invite a new surge of Communist aggression at every point along the frontier which divides the Communist world from the democratic world. If we do not stand firm here, our adversaries may think that we will stand firm nowhere — and we guarantee a heightening of the world civil war to new levels of intensity and danger.

We hope that Chairman Khrushchev has not made a miscalculation, that he has not mistaken forbearance for weakness. We cannot believe that he has deluded himself into supposing that though we have power, we lack nerve; that though we have weapons, we are without the will to use them.

We still hope, we still pray, that the worst may be avoided — that the Soviet leadership will call an end to this ominous adventure. Accordingly, the President has initiated steps to quarantine Cuba against further imports of offensive military equipment. Because the entire inter-American system is challenged, the President last night called for an immediate meeting of the Organ of Consultation of the Organization of the American States, to consider this threat to hemispheric security and to invoke articles 6 and 8 of the Rio Treaty in support of all necessary action. They are meeting now. The results of their deliberations will soon be available to you.

Mr. President, I am submitting today a resolution to the Security Council designed to find a way out of this calamitous situation.

This resolution calls, as an interim measure under article 40 of the charter, for the immediate dismantling and withdrawal from Cuba of all missiles and other offensive weapons.

It further authorizes and requests the Acting Secretary General to dispatch to Cuba a United Nations observer corps to assure and report on compliance with this resolution.

Upon U.N. certification of compliance, it calls for the termination of the measures of quarantine against military shipments to Cuba.

And, in conclusion, it urgently recommends that the United States of America and the Soviet Union confer promptly on measures to remove the existing threat to the security of the Western Hemisphere and the peace of the world and to report thereon to the Security Council.

Mr. President, I have just been informed that the Organization of American States this afternoon adopted a resolution by nineteen affirmative votes containing the following operative paragraphs:

THE COUNCIL OF THE ORGANIZATION OF AMERICAN STATES, MEETING AS THE PROVISIONAL ORGAN OF CONSULTATION, RESOLVES:

1. To call for the immediate dismantling and withdrawal from

Cuba of all missiles and other weapons with any offensive capability:

2. To recommend that the member states, in accordance with Articles six and eight of the Inter-American Treaty of Reciprocal Assistance, take all measures, individually and collectively, including the use of armed force, which they may deem necessary to ensure that the Government of Cuba cannot continue to receive from the Sino-Soviet powers military material and related supplies which may threaten the peace and security of the Continent and to prevent the missiles in Cuba with offensive capability from ever becoming an active threat to the peace and security of the Continent:

3. To inform the Security Council of the United Nations of this resolution in accordance with Article 54 of the Charter of the United Nations and to express the hope that the Security Council will, in accordance with the draft resolution introduced by the United States, dispatch United Nations observers to Cuba at the earliest moment.

Mr. President, the issue which confronts the Security Council today is grave. Since the end of the Second World War there has been no threat to the vision of peace so profound, no challenge to the world of the charter so fateful. The hopes of mankind are concentrated in this room. The action we take may determine the future of civilization. I know that this Council will approach the issue with a full sense of responsibility and a solemn understanding of the import of our deliberations.

There is a road to peace. The beginning of that road is marked out in the resolution I have submitted for your consideration. If we act promptly, we will have another chance to take up again the dreadful question of nuclear arms and military bases and the means and causes of aggression and war — to take them up and do something about them.

This is a solemn and significant day for the life of the United Nations and the hope of world community. Let it be remembered not as the day when the world came to the edge of nuclear war but as the day when men resolved to let nothing thereafter stop them in their quest for peace.

U.S., Department of State, *Bulletin,* Volume XLVII, No. 1220 (November 12, 1962), pp. 723–734. (U.S./U.N., press release 4070, October 23, 1962.)

✧ ✧ ✧ **27**

STATEMENT BY AMBASSADOR GARCÍA-
INCHAUSTEGUI TO U.N. SECURITY COUNCIL,
October 23, 1962

We are deeply sorry that, at a moment of serious tension and
danger of nuclear war, a permanent member of the Security Council
should see fit to use inadequate language when referring to Heads of
Government and in judging facts that belong to history and to the
sovereign political jurisdiction of States.

The North American representative is very happy with his social
system. We, as far as the social system that he represents, have a very
different opinion from his. We reject, primarily because they are
false and also because they are interventionist, his affirmations and
statements regarding our history and our social system.

However, there is something that we would like to highlight from
the recent statement of the representative of the United States. When
referring to our country, he said: "This once peaceful island. . . ."
Well, he was referring to the island of American investments, to the
island of racial discrimination, to the island of exploitation and of illiteracy, to the island of the bloody dictatorship of Batista supported
and armed by the Government of the United States. That island, and
I address myself to the representative of the United States, has disappeared forever and it will never reappear, however many armadas
your aggressive Government may send to our coasts.

To speak on behalf of the Revolutionary Government of Cuba has
always been an exceptional honour for us. And today, to speak on
behalf of our people and our Revolutionary Government, at these
moments when direct war on the part of American imperialism hangs
over our homeland more heavily than ever, is a twofold honour. We
belong to a people that is ready to die for its independence and its
sovereignty. And those of us who are ready to die have the inalienable
right to have our words and voices heard by those who are pushing
mankind to the holocaust.

We reject as false and dishonest all the accusations levelled by the
President of the United States and repeated here by his representative
to the United Nations.

The people and Government of Cuba have been forced to arm to
defend themselves against the repeated aggressions of the United
States Government. As Mr. Dorticos, the President of our country,
stated when he addressed the General Assembly recently:

"We still hope that we shall be able to throw all these weapons overboard. We are a peace-loving nation; we want peace; we do not want war. The people of Cuba has only one desire — to achieve great conquests in the development of its nation's future, but to do so by peaceful work, by creative labour.

We were forced to arm — not to attack anyone, not to assault any nation, but only to defend ourselves. And to the joint resolution of the United States Congress we replied in due course with a declaration, agreed to by our own Council of Ministers, which says in its pertinent paragraphs:

"Were the United States able to give Cuba effective guarantees and satisfactory proof concerning the integrity of Cuban territory, and were it to cease its subversive and counterrevolutionary activities against our people, then Cuba would not have to strengthen its defenses. Cuba would not even need any army, and all the resources that were used for this could be gratefully and happily invested in the economic and cultural development of the country."

Were the United States able to give up proof, by word and deed, that it would not carry out aggression against our country, then, we declare solemnly before you here and now, our weapons would be unnecessary and our army redundant. We believe ourselves able to create peace."

Cuba is a country which has seen United States aircraft set fire to its plantations without ever a declaration of war. Cuba is a country that has seen its plants and factories sabotaged, its workers wounded or killed at the criminal hands of agents of the United States Government, without a declaration of war between the two countries. Cuba is a country that has seen its territory invaded by mercenaries trained, directed and subsidized by the United States Government, with the public sanction of Kennedy, without a declaration of war. Cuba is a country that has suffered the economic boycott of the United States Government and the use of North American pressure in order economically and diplomatically to isolate us, without the existence of a state of war. This boycott and these pressures have come from the same United States Government which is the international protector of colonialists, dictators and discriminators; the United States itself is a discriminator and a colonialist.

Once again pirate ships have crossed the Gulf of Mexico and the Caribbean, operating from North American bases and with the assent of North American authorities — and these acts have occurred without the existence of a state of war between Cuba and the United States. The monarchs of the modern age, in their imperialist rivalries, were more respectful of international law than is the United States Government in the age of the United Nations and international co-operation.

As representatives to the United Nations who read the Press in the

United States may see for themselves — a few days ago *The New York Times* published photographs, and other newspapers did so too — Cuba is a country that has suffered from the training on American soil of armed groups and sabotage agents whose aim is to destroy our revolutionary Government — and this, without a declaration of war.

I have just been handed a communiqué containing information on the most recent violations of our airspace by the United States: on 22 October, at 22:50, 23:50, and so forth. I could cite many other instances, because there is an interminable list of violations of our airspace and our seas by the imperialist and aggressive Government of the United States.

And all these activities have been carried out against Cuba despite the fact that Cuba and the United States, among other Governments, signed the Convention of 1928 on the rights and duties of States in case of civil war. The first article of that Convention very clearly sets forth as follows the obligations of the High Contracting Parties:

First, to use all the means at their disposal to prevent the inhabitants of their territory, nationals or foreigners, from crossing the frontier to foment or encourage civil war;

Second, to disarm and intern all rebel forces that cross their frontiers;

Third, to prohibit traffic in arms and war material;

Fourth, to ensure that in the territory under their jurisdiction no ship will be equipped, armed or used for warlike purposes in the interests of the rebellion.

It might be interesting if the jurists of the various nations who at this moment are studying in the Sixth Committee of the United Nations the codification of international law and the necessity of ensuring its application were to examine in an objective way these very events that have occurred in the relations between Cuba and the United States of America. We understand now why it has been so extremely difficult to agree in the United Nations on a definition of the word "aggression." At this moment, when nuclear war threatens the world because of North American aggression against Cuba, it might be useful for the representatives in this Council and all the representatives in the United Nations to examine, in the light of the United Nations Charter and of international law, all these events that have occurred in the relations between Cuba and the United States.

The North American President said, and the North American representative repeated here, that our defensive arms affect the security of their territory. I appeal to the conscience of this Council: Are not the military potential and the aggressions of the North Americans a threat to our people? We do not quite understand the idea that the Americans may have of the juridical equality of States, which is set forth in Article 2, paragraph 1, of the Charter of the United Nations. Their idea is that the United States, as a military Power, as a developed country, can promote, stimulate and carry out all types of aggressions, boycotts, sabotage, and all acts contrary to international law — and Cuba, a small but nevertheless courageous country, cannot arm in its own defence.

After the consecration of such a violation of law, what small country could be secure in its independence and sovereignty? It would suffice for a great neighbouring Power to decide that the system of any small stage is a subversive system, or that its defences are a threat to security, for intervention and acts of war immediately to take place, such as those from which my country is suffering today. If we proceed along that line, there will be no sovereignty left unscathed, and only the law of the strongest will prevail in relations between States.

And who are these who accuse Cuba of being a threatening base against United States territory? Those who possess the only foreign base in Cuba, against the will of our people, and those who now reinforce it so that from that base, too, they can attack us. It is those who have soldiers in every corner of the world, thousands of miles from their own territory. It is those who occupy Formosa, South Korea, who intervene in South Viet-nam, who help the colonialists of Angola, and who have backed and continue to back the interventionist maneuvers in the Congo.

According to the statement made by the representative of the United States, there are two types of military bases and two types of rockets: the good military bases and the bad ones, the good rockets and the bad rockets. And obviously the Government of the United States reserves the right to determine when a rocket is good and when a rocket is naughty, when a base is good and when a base is naughty. It is a very convincing piece of logic as far as the American representation of it is concerned.

Hardly a week ago, when war hysteria against Cuba began among the United States Congressmen, Mr. Kennedy recognized publicly that the Cuban weapons were defensive. Now, and because his intelligence service informs him of it, he pushes the world to the brink of war without presenting proof of his statements, without even consulting his military allies. The United States has done a very bizarre thing here. It has sent its ships to Cuba, it has sent its planes to Cuba and around Cuba — and then it consulted its allies and the international organizations. From now on, war or peace — the ghastly nuclear war — will depend on what the United States intelligence service may deem it fit to affirm. It is as though international organizations and the Security Council have no reason to exist, as though any State could unilaterally assume the right to decide when certain measures affect its security. Why are you here, then, gentlemen? Why are you meeting as representatives of members of the Security Council? If such an idea is to prevail, if such an outlook is to be accepted, why are you here?

I should like the representatives on the Security Council to tell us what right one Member of the Organization has to insult and attack another Member State because of its social system. As far as we know, the United Nations was born of the common effort of many States, with different social systems, in their struggle against Nazi and fascist intolerance. Well, what is the difference between the threats and aggressions of Hitler against his victims and the present aggressions of the United States against Cuba because of its social system?

What does it mean that our system is not negotiable in this hemisphere, and what type of morality is it that guides a government to negotiate with systems in accordance with their geographical locations? What contempt for the principles of the Charter — a Charter signed by States enjoying different social systems — is inherent in such practices. The Charter imposes peaceful negotiations on States in the settlement of their disputes. Cuba has always been ready to carry out peaceful negotiations, and the verbatim records of the United Nations in all bodies of this Organization will bear that out. Cuba has always been ready to seek a peaceful settlement of its conflict with the United States. But what has been the North American reply? It has been the haughty reply of one who tries to impose might over the law.

Even now, what the United States has done is to adopt a unilateral measure of war, based on its thirst for domination and neo-colonialist control — that is what the naval blockade of Cuba adds up to — and then, after doing that, to convoke the Security Council and other international bodies, with the idea of having them confirm its flagrant violation of law. That is the purpose of the United States. It takes a measure behind the back of this Organization, it takes a measure behind the back of the regional organization, it takes a measure behind the back of international law — and then, through its pressures of all kinds, it tries to force the international bodies to confirm what international morality and law must repudiate.

To what international organization did the United States turn before the event, to inform it of the aggressive intent of the United States? Why did it not accuse us before this Council and await the decision of the Council? The United States did not do so because it does not have one legal or moral reason upon which to base its measures of force taken against our country — measures of force which hurl the world to the brink of nuclear war and extermination.

What right has the United States to ask for dismantling and disarmament when it occupies a base in Cuba against the will of our own people and possesses all over the world aggressive bases against Member States of this Organization? What basis has the United States for asking that observers should go to Cuba? Logically, United Nations observers should be sent to the United States bases from which invaders and pirates emerge to punish and harass a small State, whose only crime is that of struggling for the development of its own people. We will not accept any kind of observers in matters which fall within our domestic jurisdiction. The imperialistic maneuvers in the Congo will not be repeated in Cuba.

The United Nations has no reason to implicate itself in the aggressive measure adopted by a great Power against a small Member State unilaterally and without a word from the United Nations. The United States, which did not denounce Cuba to this international Organization, did take measures without the consent of the Organization and has no right whatever to expect a blessing from the Organization on its violation of the law. Such a blessing or endorsement would be a shameful page in the annals of this Organization; it would be the very seed of its destruction and the destruction of all mankind.

The United Nations must halt the arrogant intimidation that is being exercised over it by the United States. Either the United Nations will stop the United States in its headlong use of force, or the United States will destroy the United Nations and begin the extermination of thousands of people, including thousands of North Americans.

The naval blockade unilaterally decreed by the United States is an act of war against the sovereignty and independence of our country and it is a measure that our people will resist by all means and in all ways. It is a desperate act on the part of the United States Government. It failed in all its efforts to destroy our revolution; now it is taking its last stand — war, although this may endanger the lives of thousands of people all over the world. The United States sent saboteurs to our country, and failed; it sent invasions to our country, and failed. The Cuban fiasco, as it is called here — and perhaps it is better understood that way — is indelibly written as a Yankee failure and defeat. The United States felt that, by means of the economic boycott and other pressures, other countries would not trade with Cuba and that thus we might be besieged and finished by famine. How does that sound, Mr. President — to destroy a country, a Member of our Organization, by hunger? What heroism to try to destroy a country by hunger because of its social regime, in the so-called Decade of Development.

But once again the United States failed. We would not be too [proud to die from] hunger.

What could the United States do then to reach an agreement with Cuba? For the peace of the world, we wish it had done so, but that did not suit its pride, its arrogance, its background as an aggressor Government of which *The New York Times* today [gave] us a summing up. It matters not a whit that the Charter imposes on the United States the duty of settling its controversies peacefully; it matters not that the Charter imposes on Member States the duty to refrain from the threat or use of force. In the mind of the United States, this applies to the powerful nations, to those possessing nuclear weapons, but not to Cuba, a small country a mere ninety miles from the empire.

Well, Cuba has shaken off forever the shackles of the "sphere of influence." Cuba has ceased forever to belong to that area referred to by Mr. Kennedy as "well-known because of its historic and special relations with the United States." Cuba is in Latin America, the Latin America of Rodo and Martí, the Latin America of Benito Juárez and of the heirs of Chapultepec. And the United States has the shamelessness — and I regret to have to use such a word — to refer here to the background and history of the relations of the United States with the Latin American community during the last 150 years, a history of pillage and depredation of violence and intervention, a history of confiscation of territory and of domination unequalled by any empire in the history of humanity.

This America of ours, the America of Martí, has as its northern limits the River Bravo — perhaps the representative of the United States might ask his specialists to translate that word. Cuba is a territory free of all Yankee interventionist influence and is a member of that Latin American Community.

Finally, the United States calls upon the Soviet Union to discuss with it the Cuban question. Does the United States not realize that the majority of the States of the world respect Cuba and that, among those States which respect Cuban sovereignty, is the Soviet Union? So accustomed is the United States to settle problems in the colonialist way that it forgets that the relations between Cuba and other States are based on equality and on respect for the sovereignty of all, and that Cuba, and Cuba alone, has the right to discuss and to decide upon its disputes with other states — the United States among them.

Article 2 (4) of the Charter states:

> All Members shall refrain in their international relations from the threat or use of force against the territorial integrity or political independence of any State, or in any other manner inconsistent with the Purposes of the United Nations.

The American blockade against our country is an act of war. It is use of force by a great Power against the independence of our home. It is a criminal act violating the Charter and the Principles of our Organization. We shall resist those illegal measures of North American imperialism. The reply of our people and our Government to the imminent armed attack of the United States has been general mobilization.

Our great leader — and I say "great leader" from a heart filled with love and respect because it was he who led us to victory over tyranny, and he who has directed and guided our people in all the battles which we have fought against imperialism — Fidel Castro, stated recently:

> A Yankee who dies invading this land will die as a pirate in the eyes of the world, he will die as a bandit.
> The Cuban who dies defending his homeland will die in the eyes of the world surrounded by glory, accompanied by law and by the warm feelings of all the peoples of the world.
> And if they come, if they come . . . many Yankees will die because they will not catch us unawares, with our guard down; they are not going to surprise us and find us disarmed; they will not catch us napping.

We request the Security Council, on behalf and for the sake of the Charter, and for international morality and for the sake of the principles of law, and appeal for the immediate withdrawal of the aggressive forces of the United States around the coast of Cuba and the cessation of the illegal, unilateral blockade adopted by the Government of the United States, which thus shows its contempt for the Charter. We ask for the immediate withdrawal of all ships, troops and planes sent to our shores. We ask for the cessation of the provocative acts in Guantanamo and of the piratical attacks organized by agents in the service of the United States Government. We ask for the cessation of all interventionist measures taken by the United States Government which interferes in the domestic affairs of Cuba, and we ask for the cessation of all violations of our air and sea space.

When the United States decided on war against our country, it ignored its own public opinion. Recent investigations and polls of that opinion have shown that the majority of the American people do not share the aggressive intent of the American monopolies. The President of the United States recently made a hypocritical appeal to our people. It is the appeal of one that offends our peoples, it is an appeal from one who attacks our country and tries to destroy it by hunger and famine, who has no ways left to break our country and force it to its knees, as they had our country on its knees earlier, in a period which the representative of the United States so wistfully recalled here. Now that Government wishes to commit the "heroism" of attacking us with its armies.

Well, our people, which does not hate the American people, our people that loves freedom even more than its own life, that loves its independence more than its own existence, our people that loves peace itself will give the answer. It is already giving the answer as it has given it in the past. It will be the same answer of our statement and our motto: "Country or death, we shall conquer." Never have we felt that the words of our national anthem were more appropriate or truthful. Mr. Kennedy, aggressors, all of you: to die in Cuba for our homeland is to live and Cubans will live to see imperialism bite the dust of defeat in Cuba, and Cubans will live to see the new and promising socialist society.

U.N., *Security Council Document S/PV .1022*, October 23, 1962, paras 41–61.

⋄ ⋄ ⋄ **28**

EXCERPT FROM STATEMENT BY
SOVIET AMBASSADOR VALERIAN A. ZORIN
TO U.N. SECURITY COUNCIL, *October 23, 1962*

I should now like to speak in my capacity as the representative of the Soviet Union.

Before proceeding with the statement of the position of the Soviet Government on the question which has been introduced by the Soviet Union for discussion in the Security Council, I should like to say a few words on the speech made by the representative of the United States who was defending the position of the United States on the question which that Government deemed it essential to place before the Security Council.

I must say that even a cursory examination of what was said by Mr. Stevenson betokens the total paucity of argument in the position of the United States Government in a question which it deems essential to place before the Security Council, the total helplessness of the Government of the United States to defend its position in the face of the Council and of world public opinion.

Mr. Stevenson has touched upon numerous subjects. He gave a falsified — let us be frank about this — account of the history of postwar relations and has represented the whole position of the United States as being beneficent. He has tried to denigrate in every means possible the position of the Soviet Union. He has spoken of the history of the Cuban Revolution, although one might .well wonder what relationship there was between the United States and the internal affairs of the sovereign Cuban State. He drew an idyllic picture of the history of the Western Hemisphere during the past 150 years, but he seemed to have overlooked the policy of the "big stick" of a President of the United States, President McKinley, the Monroe Doctrine, the action of Theodore Roosevelt in connection with the Panama Canal and the actions taken there; the boastful statements of the American General Butler to the effect that with his soldiers and marines he could hold elections in any Latin American country. This is something he was silent about. The policy of the "big stick" is now being sought to be carried out by the United States on this occasion too. But Mr. Stevenson has apparently forgotten that times have changed since then.

Mr. Stevenson touched upon the question of bases in various parts of the world. However, he failed to mention that the United States has these bases in thirty-five countries of the world, appropriating to itself the role of world policeman. What is surprising is that Mr. Stevenson has said practically nothing about the political, legal and moral grounds, based on the United Nations Charter for those aggressive acts that were undertaken by the United States Government during the past twenty-four hours against the small Cuban State.

This is not by accident, since in fact the Government of the United States has nothing to say in defense of its aggressive position. The Government of the United States has no positive ideas. If I may be excused the expression, it seemed to me that during the statement of the representative of the United States, Mr. Stevenson, we were looking at a completely naked man, bereft of any of the adornments of a civilized man, for in the eyes of the entire world and in the eyes of this Council, Mr. Stevenson stood here as the representative of an aggressive American brand of imperialism which rattles the sabre and demands that its own order be set up in the Western Hemisphere and throughout the whole world.

I do not wish to go off into polemics with Mr. Stevenson and with the Government of the United States generally on those subjects that have been touched upon in the long statement of the representative of the United States; I understand full well that all of these matters raised by Mr. Stevenson are but a smoke screen, an attempt to distract the attention of the Council from the substance of the matter under discussion, a matter involving the provisions of the Charter of the United Nations and the flagrant violations of those provisions that have been committed by the United States before the eyes of the whole world. Accordingly I shall not follow Mr. Stevenson in that course and I shall not answer all of his bold and false statements concerning the position of the Soviet Union. The position of the Soviet Union is clear and definite; it is known to the whole world. I shall not minimize or downgrade my statement by answering these minor and insignificant issues that Mr. Stevenson has attempted to raise before the Council.

The Security Council has convened today in circumstances which can but give rise to the gravest concern for the fate of peace in the Caribbean region and in the whole world. It is not a trivial matter that is involved; it is a matter of a unilateral and arbitrary action by a great Power which constitutes a direct infringement of the freedom and independence of a small country. This involves a new and extremely dangerous act of aggression in a chain of acts of aggression committed earlier by the United States against Cuba. It involves the violation of the most elementary rules and principles of international law. It involves the violation of the fundamental provisions of the Charter of the United Nations and of the spirit and letter of that Charter at the end of which stand the signature and seal of the United States.

Yesterday the United States in fact instituted a naval blockade of the Republic of Cuba, thus trampling underfoot the norms of international behaviour and the principles enshrined in the Charter of the United Nations. The United States has appropriated to itself the right — and has stated so — to attack ships of other countries on the open seas, and this constitutes nothing other than undisguised piracy. At the same time, at the Guantanamo Base, a base located on the territory of Cuba, landings of additional troops have been effected and the armed forces of the United States brought to combat readiness. Such venturesome enterprises, together with the statements of the President of the United States to explain them, statements made yesterday on the radio and on television, give evidence of the fact that American imperialist circles will balk at nothing in their attempts to throttle a sovereign state, a Member of the United Nations, as that little country is. They are prepared, for the sake of this, to push the world to the brink of a military catastrophe.

. . . .

As is known, a request for an urgent convening of the Security Council in view of the act of war committed unilaterally by the actions of the United States, which has declared a naval blockade of Cuba, was submitted to the Security Council by the representative of Cuba, Mr. García-Inchaustegui.

These are the clear-cut requests addressed to the Security Council by two States whose actions are permeated with a conviction of the extreme gravity of the highly dangerous situation created by the United States, and permeated with the desire to strengthen international peace and security, now so gravely threatened by the aggressive actions of the United States. These two letters differ as night differs from day, from the hypocritical letter addressed by the United States to the Security Council while, behind the backs of the Security Council, it tramples upon the principles of the Charter of the United Nations and of international law, having already begun military actions against a small nation, a Member of the United Nations, while at the same time cynically attempting to wrap itself in the raiments of the peacemaker.

The present actions of the United States against Cuba are the logical link in that aggressive policy — fraught with the direst consequences — carried out by the United States with respect to Cuba as early as the Eisenhower Administration, and which was continued and intensified by the present Government of the United States, a

Government which proclaimed at the very outset of its entry into office, the era of the "New Frontier." These actions constitute the most eloquent and tragic evidence for the world of the justification of the accusations that have been advanced on numerous occasions by the Revolutionary Government of Cuba in the organs of the United Nations, accusations that the Government of the United States has made preparations for the unleashing of aggression against Cuba and has made that the principal objective of all of its hostile actions against that small country.

The complaint of Cuba against the policy of constant threats and aggressive actions by the United States was first discussed by the Security Council, as is known, as early as July 1960. Cuba also applied to the Security Council, unmasking further aggressive actions of the United States and the preparation by them of direct military aggression in January 1961, and the Security Council once again was obliged to revert to the consideration of the important actions that were brought to it at that time. The representative of the United States in the Security Council then had baldly denied all of these accusations. The genuine value of the false statements of the United States at that time, that they never had any plan whatsoever for any kind of aggression or for intervention in Cuba — these are the actual statements of the representatives of the United States — became quite clear, as to how bald they were, when three months after these statements the United States, in April of 1961, organized, prepared and carried out an intervention by mercenaries in Cuba.

The United Nations again, this time at the fifteenth session of the General Assembly, was obliged to consider the question of the aggressive actions of the United States against Cuba, the responsibility for which was officially assumed by the President of the United States. The April fiasco nevertheless had taught no lesson to the United States. Not only did they make preparations for a new and greater intervention in Cuba, but they first tried to isolate Cuba and attract to their aggressive actions against Cuba the Organization of American States. Cuba at that time already was indicating the danger of the continuation and intensification of that course for the work of peace in the world.

The complaints of Cuba against the aggressive actions by the United States, through the illegitimate use of the Organization of American States, was discussed at the sixteenth session of the General Assembly and at meetings of the Security Council in February and March of the present year. If there was any need for further proof of the justification or the justness of those accusations, they are more than amply provided, as we have indicated, in those aggressive actions of the Government of the United States against Cuba which were proclaimed yesterday and the component part of which is the campaign for creating a smoke screen for the justification of those aggressive actions, which is here being unfolded, quite cynically, by the delegation of the United States.

As a matter of fact, the covering role that is being carried out in the halls of the United Nations by the representatives of the United States is not new to them, as is known. One can but refer to the fact that Mr. Stevenson personally has already spoken, in this rather ungainly role, in the halls of this building in April of 1961 when United States ships were landing trained, armed and prepared mercenaries on the shores of Cuba, all of them trained and equipped from America. And Mr. Stevenson at that very moment was hypocritically denying the existence of such an aggression.

Everybody will remember the statement of Mr. Stevenson of 15 April to the effect that the United States was planning no aggression against Cuba; and on the 17th the mercenaries of the United States were landing at Playa Girón. What worth is there then in the statements of a representative of a great Power who dared to deceive world public opinion and the official organs of the United Nations; trying to salvage the errors of the Intelligence Agency of the United States which had ordered Stevenson not to say anything about it?

The delegation of the United States today, of course, has somewhat changed its tune. Today it is not denying any more the fact that the United States has undertaken unilateral arbitrary action of a military character against Cuba, and the argument used by the United States against Cuba is found to be a new one. Having searched in the pile of junk, the so-called detectives of the State Department proposed to their Government a variant involving the setting up of so-called rocket bases in Cuba. In other words, there might have been an order to find some cause for the justification of aggression. That is all that would have mattered and the rest is a question of the resourcefulness of the officials concerned. Let them find a good enough excuse. There we have emerging as clear as the light of day, in the statement of President Kennedy and in the letter of the representative of the United States, Mr. Stevenson, the thesis of some incontrovertible evidence of the presence in Cuba of Soviet rockets, the falsity of which is all too obvious.

If the Government of the United States has after all decided in these circumstances to embark upon open falsehood, if it has not shirked before the advancing of the completely false and slanderous thesis of the presence of offensive Soviet rockets in Cuba, this simply illustrates and proves the extent to which it has absolutely no value with respect to what sort of excuse should serve as the justification for the new aggressive acts against Cuba which they are already committing. This simply illustrates the depth to which the United States has fallen and the depth of cynicism of the present new policy of the United States labelled the "New Frontier."

The falsity of the accusations advanced now by the United States against the Soviet Union — which consist of the fact that the Soviet Union has allegedly set up offensive armaments in Cuba — is clear from the outset. The Soviet delegation first of all officially confirms the statement already made by the Soviet Union in this connection that the Soviet Government has not directed and is not directing to Cuba any offensive armaments. The Soviet delegation recalls in particular the statement of *TASS* of 11 September of this year in which, on the instructions of the Soviet Government the following was stated:

> The armaments and military materiel sent to Cuba is designed exclusively for defensive purposes. The Soviet Union does not need to relocate in any other country, for instance, in Cuba, the means available to it for repelling aggression and for a retaliatory blow. The Soviet Union has so powerful a series of rockets and missile carriers that there is no need to seek a location for their launching anywhere outside the territory of the Soviet Union.

The observers of the United States in the Pacific recently were able to be convinced of the accuracy of the firing of Soviet rockets.

The Soviet delegation recalls also the statement of the Minister for Foreign Affairs, Mr. Gromyko, made by him on 21 September 1962 in the General Assembly, when he said:

> Any sober-minded man knows that Cuba is not . . . building up her forces to such a degree that she can pose a threat to the United States or to the passage of the United States to the Panama Canal, or else a threat to any State of the Western Hemisphere.

Mr. Gromyko went on to say:

> They know full well that the aid rendered by the Soviet Union to Cuba to strengthen her independence does not pursue any of these goals either, since they are alien to our foreign policy.

We should also recall the statement made on 8 October 1962 at the plenary meeting of the General Assembly by the President of the Republic of Cuba, Mr. Osvaldo Dorticós — to which the representative of Cuba here has partly referred:

> We were forced to arm — not to attack anyone, not to assault any nation, but only to defend ourselves. . . . Cuba constitutes a danger to the security of no nation whatsoever of our continent, nor has Cuba harboured, in the past or at the present time, any aggressive intentions against any of them.

And finally, the Soviet Government only today in its official statement which was circulated to the members of the Council once again declared the following:

With regard to the Soviet Union's assistance to Cuba, this assistance is exclusively designed to improve Cuba's defensive capacity. As was stated on 3 September 1962 in the joint Soviet-Cuban communiqué on the visit to the Soviet Union of a Cuban delegation composed of Mr. E. Guevara and Mr. E. Aragones, the Soviet Government has responded to the Cuban Government's request to help Cuba with arms. The communiqué states that such arms and military equipment are intended solely for defensive purposes. The Governments of the two countries still firmly adhere to that position.

Soviet assistance in strengthening Cuba's defences is necessitated by the fact that, from the outset of its existence, the Republic of Cuba has been subjected to continuous threats and acts of provocation by the United States.

In the light of these clear-cut statements it is obvious that the assertion — let us call things by their proper names — these completely false statements, which are being disseminated by the United States of some alleged intentions on the part of Cuba or on the part of the Soviet Union, are but a fabrication and a tissue of imaginary dreams. They are utilized and have been raised in the United States to the level of Government statements for the sole purpose of shielding, justifying and finding at least some sort of excuse for the committing of further and much more far-reaching acts of aggression by the United States, which is violating the Charter of the United Nations and which is creating a direct threat to peace.

Mr. Stevenson quoted Article 2, paragraph 4 of the Charter of the United Nations. This Article states:

All Members shall refrain in their international relations from the threat or use of force against the territorial integrity or political independence of any state, or in any other manner inconsistent with the Purposes of the United Nations.

But the declaring of a naval blockade of Cuba and all those military measures that have been put into effect on the instructions of the President of the United States since yesterday, all these measures, are they not threats or use of force against the territorial integrity or political independence of a State — of Cuba in this instance? Every sensible person will understand that this is the most flagrant violation of this principle of the Charter of the United Nations, a principle to which the representative of the United States dared refer.

The delegation of the United States is now trying to utilize fabrications in the Security Council for horrendous purposes and in order to try to compel the Security Council to approve retroactively those unlawful, aggressive actions of the United States which have already been adopted by the United States against Cuba, and which the United States is carrying out unilaterally, in clear violation of the

Charter of the United Nations and of the elementary norms and principles of international law. The peoples of the world, however, must have a clear idea of the fact that in embarking upon an open adventure of this kind, the United States of America is taking a step toward the unleashing of a world thermonuclear war. This is the great terrible price which the world may have to pay for the present reckless and irresponsible actions of the United States.

Why did the United States begin its new aggressive action against Cuba in such haste, and why is it trying to pretend that it is appealing to the Security Council? The answer to that question is dictated by logic. The very priority of the actions of the United States Government demonstrates this. Such a course can be taken only by someone who is sure in advance that the Security Council will never support — indeed, it will never be able to support — the aggressive actions in question. The purpose of the United States is in fact to place before the Security Council the *fait accompli* of United States aggression. The appeal to the Council is only a gesture to satisfy the public. To speak bluntly, this gesture is intended to disorient public opinion.

Of course, when one indulges in such a cynical gesture one does not really need any proof whatsoever. A mere declaration about some alleged incontrovertible evidence will do.

Thus, in the present position of the United States delegation in the Security Council there is a sorry logic of sorts. There is no proof, no evidence. But the United States does not need any evidence, because the United States — and this is openly mentioned in the Press of the United States — is not counting on the Security Council's being able to justify or approve its aggressive actions against Cuba. As is known, the United States is already carrying out these actions in practice — and the Security Council has been apprised of all this simply for the sake of appearances.

What is the *fait accompli* before which the United States is placing the Security Council? First, the United States unilaterally has declared the implementation of an actual blockade of Cuba by the United States. Secondly, the United States has directed large-scale military forces not only to the Cuban area but to the very territory of Cuba, to the United States base at Guantanamo, and has ordered them to be in a state of combat readiness. Thirdly, the United States has officially stated that it intends not to limit itself to this, but to take further action against Cuba — and this was stated in Mr. Stevenson's letter — if and when it finds that necessary. In other words, the United States is trying to reserve its right to continue open military aggression against Cuba. However great the danger is today that is hovering over Cuba as a result of these aggressive actions on the part of the United States, it does not fully cover the seriousness of the critical situation that has been produced.

The principal aspect of the present reckless actions of the United

States against Cuba lies in the fact that on the basis of official United States statements the Government of the United States is prepared to move to the direct unleashing of a world thermonuclear war for the purpose of achieving its aggressive designs against Cuba.

In the letter addressed by Mr. Stevenson to the President of the Security Council we find this direct statement: "What is at stake is the peace and security both of a single region and of the whole world." Thus the whole world is confronted with the readiness of the United States to go to the brink, where the stake is the fate of the world, where the stake is millions and millions of human lives.

The peace-loving countries and peoples have for a long time now had fears that the reckless and aggressive policies of the United States with respect to Cuba might bring the world to the brink of catastrophe. The apprehensions of the peace-loving forces and their attempts to call upon the United States Government to heed the voice of reason and to settle the dispute with Cuba peacefully are clearly shown in the records of the general debate which the seventeenth session of the General Assembly has only recently completed. I shall mention only a few of the statements made in the course of that debate by the heads of delegations, statements made at the highest level on behalf of the Governments of the various countries.

The Foreign Minister of the United Arab Republic, Mr. Fawzi, said: "The situation around Cuba is a source of worry to many lovers of peace and of the rule of law in international relations."

The Minister for Foreign Affairs of Algeria, Mr. Khemisti, said the following:

> . . . each State, great or small, rich or poor, must recognize this right to its own political system and have that right recognized by others.
>
> It is because of this necessity that we feel that the efforts made to attack and undermine a political regime chosen by the friendly people of Cuba are dangerous for international peace. The people of Cuba have no aggressive intentions, and they have the right to wish for their economic and social liberation.

But the United States is preventing the Cubans from thinking of that. The Foreign Minister of Iraq, Mr. Jawad, said:

> "We are all neighbours of countries with differing social and political systems and none has the right to impose its system upon others" — except the United States, which wishes to arrogate to itself such a right.

Mr. Jawad continued:

> This is the essence of the accepted policy of peaceful coexistence, and any other policy would inevitably lead to aggression.

The people of Cuba are free to choose their own system of government and no State, however big and powerful, has the right to interfere in the internal affairs of other States.

In order to achieve the observance, by the United States, of the sovereign rights of the Cuban people to choose a regime that it likes, the need to settle peacefully the dispute between the United States and Cuba, the need to cause the United States to waive the use of force in solving this dispute, was something that found the adherence of these countries and many others. Now, after the effecting, by the United States, of the recent and far-reaching aggressive actions against Cuba, it is clearly obvious how cynical was the attitude of the United States towards these and many other invocations and appeals to adhere, in its policy in the international arena and in relations with Cuba, to the lofty principles of the Charter of the United Nations.

In declaring the introduction of a blockade against Cuba, the United States has committed an unprecedented step in relations between States — between which there is no formal state of war.

By this arbitrary, piratical act, the United States has placed under threat the shipping of many countries of the world, including shipping of its allies who do not agree with this reckless and dangerous policy with respect to Cuba.

By this aggressive action of theirs, which creates a threat to peace in the whole world, they have launched a direct challenge at the United Nations, and to the Security Council as the principal organ of the United Nations responsible for the maintenance of international peace and security.

In stating its intention to draw into the implementation of its aggressive actions against Cuba the Organization of American States — to which it is already dictating the effecting of collective sanctions against Cuba — the United States is openly violating the prerogatives of the Security Council which alone can offer powers for the carrying out of any enforcement measures. In throwing their armed forces around Cuba and upon the territory of Cuba itself, and in having declared their intention to use force when they deem that appropriate, the United States is committing an act of uncovered aggression. They have openly violated the Charter of the United Nations, which prohibits to States — Members of the United Nations — the threat or use of force in international relations.

In showing total indifference to the serious international consequences that may stem from their unilateral action against Cuba, the United States has directly placed international peace and security under threat, and automatically, by their actions, has raised the question of urgent convening of the Security Council for the consideration of the critical stipulation that has been produced.

The fact that the United States itself has applied to the Security

Council is but trying to maintain composure while losing the game. The United States realizes full well that, after having committed such clearly aggressive actions against Cuba, it will in any event have to appear before the Security Council, to be accountable for these defiant, adventuresome actions. Indeed, could the Security Council ignore the fact that the United States is arbitrarily setting up a blockade around Cuba and is committing a definitely provocative step in its unprecedented and unheard-of violation of international law; are trampling underfoot the whole of the Charter of the United Nations; and are throwing a challenge to all of the peace-loving peoples? Could the Security Council overlook the fact that the United States of America is openly installing the law of the jungle in international relations by its actions — that it has reached such a state of cynicism that, not only does it commit aggressive actions against a small country such as Cuba, but it is even demanding that Cuba explain itself to the United States as to the fashion in which it has organized its defense and, at the same time, that it remove from its territory the technology that is needed by it for its defence against United States aggression?

Mr. Stevenson has, in his statement today, permitted himself to use a series of sentences to the effect that Castro, as you will see, has done with impunity this, that and the other thing, that he has established relations with the Soviet Union — and all this with impunity — as if the United States were called upon to punish someone, whoever he may be, who is establishing new relations with any country of the world, including the Soviet Union.

Mr. Stevenson, perhaps you yourself will punish yourself for having set up relations with the Soviet Union and holding negotiations with it.

The Security Council would fail in its direct duty as the principal organ responsible for the maintenance of international peace and security if it were to ignore or overlook the aggressive actions of the United States, which are nothing else than the fact that the United States has openly embarked upon the course of liquidation of the United Nations, a course of unleashing of world war.

Thus, what are the realistic facts facing the Security Council? These facts can be summarized in the following fashion:

First, the Government of the United States has declared that it will use such measures in regard to the shipping of other countries in the high seas — which action can be qualified in no fashion other than piracy. The decision of the United States to stop and inspect the ships of other countries which are headed for the shores of Cuba leads to a great intensification of the tension in the international situation, and constitutes a step towards the unleashing of world thermonuclear war, because no self-respecting State will permit its shipping to be tampered with.

Secondly, for the concealment of its actions, the United States is advancing a completely fabricated set of excuses. The United States is trying to represent as distorted the measures undertaken by the Cuban Government — measures designed to achieve or enhance the defense of its State. As any country and government concerned over its sovereignty and independence, Cuba in the face of aggression cannot but show serious apprehension and concern over its own safety.

Thirdly, from the very first days of its existence, the Revolutionary Government of Cuba is subjected to continual threats and provocations on the part of the United States, which is not balking at any actions — including the armed intervention in Cuba in April of 1961.

Fourth, the American imperialists have openly declared that they do not force their proposals upon other countries. Yet they are blatantly demanding that military facilities be removed from the territory of Cuba, when these facilities have been designed for the defense of that country.

Fifth, the Soviet Union Government has consistently spoken in favour, and now speaks in favour, of the withdrawal of all foreign forces and armaments from foreign territories back to their own country. This Soviet proposal is designed to normalize the international climate and to create an atmosphere of confidence in relations between States. Yet the Government of the United States, which has deployed its armaments and forces throughout the whole world, stubbornly refuses to adopt this Soviet proposal. The United States utilizes the presence of its armed forces on foreign territories for interference in the domestic affairs of other States and for carrying out its aggressive plans. The Soviet Union Government has stood and still stands by the position that it is necessary to liquidate all bases on foreign territories and to withdraw from them all foreign military forces and facilities. The Soviet Union Government will not object to this being done under the observance of observers appointed by the United Nations.

Sixth, the United States has no right whatsoever to make the demands that were contained in President Kennedy's speech, either from the point of view of the normal practices of international law in regard to the freedom of shipping or from the point of view of the principles and provisions of the Charter. No State, however powerful it may be, has any right at all to define or determine what form of armaments may be required by another State for its defense. Each State, according to the Charter of the United Nations, has the right of self-defense and the right to the necessary weapons to secure that defense. The Soviet Union, at the request of the Cuban Government, is supplying military material to Cuba designed for defensive purposes and defensive purposes only. In this connection the Soviet Union Government does not seek to obtain any advantage for itself in Cuba. The Soviet Union Government is not threatening anyone. It is not pursuing any military objectives in this region, or in any other region of the world.

The Soviet Union does not possess military bases in thirty-five of the world's countries. The Soviet Union is merely striving very sincerely towards giving assistance to the young Cuban Republic for the maintenance and strengthening of its sovereignty and independence.

Seventh, the position of the United States, as set out in President Kennedy's statement, is flagrantly at variance with the Charter of the United Nations and other universally recognized norms of international law. The Charter of the United Nations requires that all States, independently of their social structure, base their relations on a footing of equality and that they do not interfere in the domestic affairs of other States. The course which the United States has embarked upon with respect to Cuba and the Soviet Union is a course which would involve the liquidation of the United Nations. It is the course involving an unleashing of war.

Eighth, the Soviet Union Government appeals to all the peoples of the world to raise their voices in defense of the United Nations and not to permit the disintegration of this Organization. It appeals to them to vote against the United States policy of piracy, banditry, and the unleashing of a new war. Realizing the great responsibility resting upon the Security Council at this moment, the Soviet Union delegation considers that it is necessary first of all urgently to halt and repeal all the aggressive measures put into effect by the United States against Cuba and other countries. Understanding the urgent need for the adoption of such measures, the Soviet Union delegation, on the instructions of the Soviet Government, is introducing for the consideration of the Security Council the following draft resolution on the violation of the Charter of the United Nations and the threat to peace by the United States of America (see Document 22).

U.N., *Security Council Document S/PV .1022*, October 23, 1962, paras 62–93.

✧ ✧ ✧ **29**

STATEMENT BY AMBASSADOR STEVENSON TO PRESS, *October 23, 1962*

I want to say just five quick things.

First, the U.S.S.R. did not deny that Soviet MRBM and IRBM sites and missiles have been secretly installed in Cuba.

Second, in consequence the representative of the Soviet Union has in effect admitted that the Soviet statement of September 11 that there was "no need for the Soviet Government to shift its weapons . . . to any other country, for instance Cuba" and that there was "no need to search for sites for them beyond the boundaries of the Soviet Union" was deliberate deceit.

Third, the U.S.S.R. has thus itself fully confirmed to the Security Council the urgent necessity of the measures we were forced to take in our own defense, in defense of the hemisphere, and in defense of other allies of the United States and unaligned powers alike.

Fourth, this sequence of events should put the Council and the world on the alert about all protestations of innocence which we may expect to hear in the next few days.

And finally, it is now apparent that President Dorticos of Cuba was admitting the existence of long-range nuclear weapons in Cuba when he told the General Assembly on October 8, "We have sufficient means with which to defend ourselves; we have indeed our inevitable weapons, the weapons which we would have preferred not to acquire and which we do not wish to employ."

U.S., Department of State, *Bulletin*, Volume XLVII, No. 1220 (November 12, 1962), p. 734. (Mr. Stevenson's statement to the Press on October 23, 1962, made at 8:45 P.M. after the Security Council had adjourned. U.S./U.N. press release 4071, October 23, 1962.)

❖ ❖ ❖ **30**

STATEMENT BY THE PEOPLE'S REPUBLIC OF BULGARIA, *October 23, 1962*

I have the honour, on the instructions of my Government, to transmit enclosed herewith the text of the statement of the Government of the People's Republic of Bulgaria of 23 October 1962 on the aggressive actions of the Government of the United States of America against the Republic of Cuba with a request that it be distributed as an official document of the United Nations.

Please accept, etc.

(s) MILKO TARABANOV
First Deputy Minister for Foreign Affairs
of the People's Republic of Bulgaria
Chairman of the Delegation

STATEMENT

of the Government of the People's Republic of Bulgaria

On 22 October the President of the United States, Mr. Kennedy, in a speech over the radio and television made a statement without a precedent in peacetime, a statement directed against Cuba, a peace-loving country and Member of the United Nations. At the same time the President announced a number of military measures whose consequences are an open threat to peace not only in the Caribbean but in the whole world.

Violating in a gross manner the accepted norms of International Law and the principles of the United Nations Charter the Government of the United States of America in fact proclaimed a complete blockade of the Republic of Cuba and assumed the right to interfere in the domestic affairs of others countries and to dictate its will.   '

Dispatches from the United States show that the open threats of President Kennedy are accompanied by practical military preparations. The United States armed forces in the whole world and especially in the Caribbean have been put on the alert. The United States Guantanamo base in Cuba has been considerably strengthened.

The armed forces of the United States allies in various parts of the world are being put in battle readiness under United States pressure.

No reasonable man can believe that small Cuba poses any threat to the United States, a country armed to the teeth. Therefore, it is clear to everybody that the actions of the United States Government are dictated by their wish to change through force the regime which is not advantageous to them, a regime established by the Cuban people in their country.

Under the alarming circumstances that have arisen, the Soviet Government, with its statement of 23 October, once again appealed to the leaders of the United States to show prudence and make a sober assessment of the eventual consequences of their aggressive actions.

Unmasking the provocative actions of the United States the Soviet Government warns against the danger of a world thermonuclear war and appeals to all Governments to bar the way of war.

The Government of the People's Republic of Bulgaria, voicing the feelings and will of the Bulgarian people and true to its peace-loving policies, issues a most decisive protest against the arbitrary decisions of the United States Government, decisions that are not justified by anything, decisions to the effect that all ships and aircraft on their way to Cuba must be stopped and searched and even fired upon. Such actions of the United States — such brazen acts — differ in no way from the actions of pirates. Using piratical methods in its relations with the other sovereign countries the Government of the United

States is playing with fire and poses a serious danger to peace not only in the Caribbean but in the whole world.

No Government and no people who respect their own dignity will bow their head to the gross dictates of the Government of the United States.

The Bulgarian people have always taken and will take the side of the freedom-loving and heroic Cuban people and consider it an irrevocable right of every people, the Cuban people included, to choose for themselves their social and political system, to arrange themselves their internal affairs.

Cuba is not alone! With her are and will be all freedom-loving peoples, all Governments who are in favour of preserving the peace, the freedom and the sovereignty of every country.

The Government of the People's Republic of Bulgaria fully supports the Declaration of the Soviet Government of 23 October and appeals to all Governments who hold dear the cause of peace, to condemn the aggressive measures of the United States and to insist that they be called off without delay.

Taking into consideration the genuine threat to peace that has arisen as a result of the perfidious actions of the United States imperialism, the Bulgarian Government gave instructions to its delegation in the United Nations to insist that the question of the violation of the United Nations Charter and the threat to peace on the part of the United States be discussed immediately.

At the same time the Bulgarian Government cannot fail to take into account the fact that the United States and their allies have begun practical actions in preparation of war. In connexion with that the Bulgarian Government gave instructions for raising the defence capability of the country and for putting its armed forces in a state of battle readiness. In these hours full of alarm for mankind the Government of the People's Republic of Bulgaria completely shares the anxiety of the peoples for the preservation of peace and voices its hope that in spite of all sanity will prevail and the forces of peace will bar the way of the firebrands.

U.N., *Security Council Document S/5189*, October 24, 1962, pp. 1–3. (Letter addressed to the Acting Secretary General.)

❖ ❖ ❖ **31**

COMMUNIQUÉ FROM HAITIAN DEPARTMENT OF FOREIGN AFFAIRS, *October 23, 1962*

I have the honour to transmit to you herewith the text of the communiqué from the Department of Foreign Affairs of Haiti on the Cuban question; I should be grateful if you would have this text published as a United Nations document.

Accept, Your Excellency, the assurances of my highest consideration.

(s) CARLET R. AUGUSTE
Ambassador
Permanent Representative

COMMUNIQUÉ FROM THE DEPARTMENT OF FOREIGN AFFAIRS

At 5 P.M. on Monday, 22 October, Dr. François Duvalier, the President of the Republic, granted an audience at the National Palace to His Excellency Mr. Raymond L. Thurston, the Ambassador of the United States of America.

In the course of this interview, which took place in an atmosphere of mutual understanding, the Ambassador informed the President of the Republic: (1) of his Government's serious anxieties regarding the threats to peace in the hemisphere presented by the offensive armament built up in Cuba by the Soviet Union; (2) of the decisions taken by the United States Government in view of the Cuban situation.

Emphasis was laid on the importance attaching to the role of the Government of the Republic of Haiti, Cuba's neighbour, and to the services which the armed forces of Haiti, the National Security Volunteers (VSN) and the public are called upon to render in keeping watch on the Haitian coasts and in defending Western democracy.

The United States Ambassador handed to His Excellency, Dr. François Duvalier, the President of the Republic, whose devotion to spiritual values and whose anti-communist position are well known, a special message from His Excellency John F. Kennedy, the President of the United States of America, urgently requesting the Haitian Government's co-operation in the grave Cuban situation, in the face of which any political differences which may have arisen between the peoples of the Americas are insignificant.

The United States Ambassador explained that he had hope for the future and that, once the Cuban crisis had been overcome in close Haitian-American co-operation, it would strengthen more and more, between the Governments of President Duvalier and President Kennedy, the good-neighbour policy that is so much in keeping with both peoples' traditions.

His Excellency, Mr. René Chalmers, Minister for Foreign Affairs, Dr. Adrien Raymond, Under Secretary of State for Foreign Affairs, and Mr. W. Thomas, Political Counsellor of the American Embassy, attended the audience.

Port-au-Prince, 23 October 1962

U.N., *Security Council Document S/5198*, October 27, 1962, pp. 1–2. (Letter dated 25 October 1962 addressed to the Secretary General.)

◇ ◇ ◇ **32**

DECLARATION OF THE CZECHOSLOVAK SOCIALIST REPUBLIC, *October 23, 1962*

I have the honour to enclose the Declaration of the Government of the Czechoslovak Socialist Republic of 23 October 1962 concerning the blockade against Cuba and to request you that the Declaration be circulated as a United Nations document.

Accept, Excellency, etc.

(s) Prof. JIRI HAJEK
Permanent Representative of
the Czechoslovak Socialist Republic
to the United Nations

U.N., *Security Council Document S/5192*, October 25, 1962, p. 1. (Letter dated October 24, 1962 addressed to the Acting Secretary General.

On 22 October 1962, the President of United States of America made a statement in which he announced that he had given orders to the armed forces of the United States of America to halt all ships, bound for Cuba, to search them, to turn back those carrying cargo described by American authorities as "offensive" weapons and to extend this measure arbitrarily to affect also other types of cargo and carriers. By resorting to these measures, the United States have in fact imposed a blockade on Cuba.

At the same time, the President of the United States ordered continued and increased close surveillance of Cuba and also gave orders for the dispatch of considerable reinforcements of military units to the American military base of Guantanamo in Cuba. United States armed forces are being alerted also outside the territory of the United States.

These acts of the United States, accompanied by a torrent of irresponsible hysterical attacks, a deliberate stepping-up of warlike psychosis and carefully pre-meditated military provocations, have justly aroused the indignation of the widest sections of the world public opinion. They constitute an unprecedented interference in matters within the exclusive internal competence of this free Latin American country, a criminal attempt at a reversal of the social development in Cuba, and are directed against all peace-loving nations, against peace in the entire world.

The imperialism of the United States has since the very beginning adopted an extremely hostile attitude against Revolutionary Cuba whose people has got rid of the domination of American monopolies and their Batista-type puppets. By all means at its disposal, the American imperialism was trying to strangle Cuba economically in the hope that a threat of starvation will bring the people of Cuba down to its knees. Indeed, it was not for the first time that the United States of America hoped to achieve similar results through economic blockade and a policy of gross pressure. But just as the attempt to blockade economically the socialist countries proved completely ineffectual, so the attempts of the United States of America at an economic blockade of Cuba equally ended in bankruptcy.

At the same time, American imperialism endeavoured to achieve a political and diplomatic isolation of Cuba. The United States severed diplomatic relations with Cuba and devoted no small effort to bringing particularly the Latin American countries into the anti-Cuban front. However, neither the grossest extortion nor pressure have brought the expected result to the American imperialists.

The United States did not shrink from engineering in April 1961 a treacherous invasion of Cuba by mercenaries which the United States had armed, trained and shipped to Cuba.

One would have expected that the American imperialists learned a lesson from the inglorious end at Playa Girón. However, the present measures for the blockade of Cuba testify to the contrary. The American imperialism is again preparing to raise an armed fist against the people of Cuba and in pursuing its ends does not hesitate to throw the world on the brink of a war catastrophe.

. The blockade from the United States is an overt aggressive action, and is even admitted and characterized by the United States itself as a forcible measure. In such a way, the United States has committed a most flagrant violation of the very fundamental principle of contemporary international law — the prohibition of aggression.

International law and the United Nations Charter oblige Members to refrain in their international relations from the threat or use of force against the territorial integrity or political independence of any State, or in any other manner inconsistent with the purposes of the United Nations. The United States of America not only has used and is using its force against Cuba in order to induce it to change the course of its development, but is even using threat of force against the Soviet Union which is offering selfless assistance to Cuba in the effort of Cuba to build the country and safeguard its defence against enemy forces.

By declaring blockade against Cuba, the United States has grossly and willfully encroached upon the freedom of the high seas, which is safeguarded under international law. The high sea is open to all nations, and, by the concurrent will of all States, it has been exempted from the jurisdiction of any individual State. An attack against the freedom of the high sea constitutes an attack on the rights and legitimate interests of all States. On the high seas, all States enjoy absolute freedom and equality in navigation, commerce, communications and scientific research and no State or group of States may claim sovereignty over a part of the high sea or interfere with its free and full use by other States.

No sovereign State can allow ships sailing under its flag to be halted and searched by another State and impeded in the pursuit of their course. Usurpation of such a right by the United States can, therefore only lead to unpredictable international conflicts. The declaration of a naval blockade and the decision of the Government of the United States to search cargoes carried by ships of third States bound for Cuba constitutes open interference into the internal affairs of those third States.

The imposition of blockade on Cuba is the grossest cynical mockery of all principles of humanity to which the United States likes to pay Pharisaic lip-service: it is a measure devised to plunge the Cuban people back into the serfdom of American monopolies and to frighten all nations trying to complete the liquidation of colonialism and secure free and independent life. At the same time, this act of piracy is a dangerous blow to world peace and an overt preparation for the unleashing of a general conflict which the American imperialism expects to stop the course of history.

The militarist circles in the United States of America should at last face the actual facts of present-day world. Irrevocably past are the times when the American imperialists, depending on their military power, were free to dictate their arbitrary will to freedom-loving nations. As a result of a new situation and changed balance of power in the world, they have lost their military supremacy. Today the most powerful missiles and nuclear weapons which are an important safeguard of peace and security are fortunately in the hands of the Soviet Union. Any aggressor — and the American militarists should not forget this — has to reckon with the fact that if he really dares to start aggression he will suffer a deserved devastating retaliatory blow.

Cuba is fully entitled to acquire and possess according to its consideraton weapons to protect freedom and independence of the country. This is an inalienable right of any State wishing to defend its security and sovereignty. It is all the more true about the people of Cuba which since the victory of its revolution has had to counter day by day continuous threats and aggressive actions perpetrated by the United States.

No one can be convinced by the ridiculous allegations of the United States representatives that such a small country as Cuba and its peace-loving people could endanger the security of the United States. These allegations serve only as a hypocritical pretext for the imperialist circles of the United States of America to cover in front of the world public their aggressive actions against the Cuban people.

In its endeavour to settle all outstanding problems with the United States by peaceful means, the Revolutionary Government of Cuba has already several times urged the United States Government to normalize its relations with Cuba, to refrain from all attempts to reverse the present national and revolutionary development in the country and to stop intrigues directed against the independence of Cuba. However, all these proposals of the Government of Cuba have been rejected by the United States Government.

Faithful to the principles of its peaceful foreign policy, the Czechoslovak Government resolutely condemns in front of the whole world public this new aggressive action of the United States Government and expresses its full support to the just struggle of the heroic people and the Revolutionary Government of Cuba against the American imperialism.

The Czechoslovak people and its Government will meet fully and honestly their commitments towards the Republic of Cuba ensuing from the friendly relations with that country and from the obligations under the United Nations Charter.

The Government and the people of the Czechoslovak Socialist Republic rightfully expect that the United States Government will realize in time the danger of playing with fire which is kindling and will revoke without delay all aggressive and provocative measures taken against the Republic of Cuba.

Being aware of the extraordinary gravity of the situation created as a result of the aggressive steps taken by the United States Government against Cuba, the Czechoslovak Government renders its unqualified support to the Declaration of the Government of the U.S.S.R. of 23 October this year and to its request that the Security Council should discuss without delay "the violation of the United Nations Charter and the threat to peace by the United States of America." The Security Council which was entrusted the basic responsibility for the preservation of international peace and security must adopt resolute measures to stop the aggressor and to prevent arbitrary defiance of the United Nations Charter by American imperialism.

The Czechoslovak people, dedicated to its peaceful creative work in building its socialist fatherland, will answer the insolent provocations of the imperialists by a still greater endeavour and unity in the interest of a further strengthening of the political, economic and defensive forces of the Republic.

Side by side with the Soviet Union and the other socialist countries and all peace-loving nations, the Czechoslovak Socialist Republic will on its part do everything to thwart the new imperialist aggression of the United States Government and to maintain and strengthen world peace.

23 October 1962

U.N., *Security Council Document* S/5192, October 25, 1962, pp. 2–7.

✧ ✧ ✧ **33**

STATEMENT BY ACTING SECRETARY GENERAL
U THANT TO U.N. SECURITY COUNCIL,
INCLUDING TEXT OF LETTER TO PRESIDENT
KENNEDY AND CHAIRMAN KHRUSHCHEV,
October 24, 1962

MR. PRESIDENT:

Today the United Nations faces a moment of grave responsibility. What is at stake is not just the interests of the parties directly involved, nor just the interests of all Member States, but the very fate of mankind. If today the United Nations should prove itself ineffective, it may have proved itself so for all time.

In the circumstances, not only as Acting Secretary General of the United Nations but as a human being, I would be failing in my duty if I did not express my profound hope and conviction that moderation, self-restraint and good sense will prevail over all other considerations. In this situation, where the very existence of mankind is in the balance, I derive some consolation from the fact that there is some common ground in the resolutions introduced in the Council. Irrespective of the fate of those resolutions, that common ground remains. It calls for urgent negotiations between the parties directly involved, though, as I said earlier, the rest of the world is also an interested party. In this context I cannot help expressing the view that some of the measures proposed or taken, which the Council is called upon to approve, are very unusual, and I might say even extraordinary, except in wartime.

At the request of the Permanent Representatives of a large number of Member Governments, who have discussed the matter amongst themselves and with me, I have sent, through the Permanent Representatives of the two Governments, the following identically worded message to the President of the United States of America and the Chairman of the Council of Ministers of the U.S.S.R.:

"I have been asked by the Permanent Representatives of a large number of Member Governments of the United Nations to address an urgent appeal to you in the present critical situation. These Representatives feel that in the interest of international peace and security all concerned should refrain from any action which may aggravate the situation and bring with it the risk of war. In their view it is important that time should be given to enable the parties concerned to get together with a view to resolving the present crisis peacefully and normalizing the situation in the Caribbean. This involves on the one hand the voluntary suspension of all arms shipments to Cuba, and also the voluntary suspension of the quarantine measures involving the searching of ships bound for Cuba. I believe that such voluntary suspension for a period of two to three weeks will greatly ease the situation and give time to the parties concerned to meet and discuss with a view to finding a peaceful solution of the problem. In this context I shall gladly make myself available to all parties for whatever services I may be able to perform. I urgently appeal to Your Excellency to give immediate consideration to this message."

I have sent an identical message to the President of the United States of America and the Chairman of the Council of Ministers of the U.S.S.R.

I should also like to take this occasion to address an urgent appeal to the President and the Prime Minister of the Revolutionary Government of Cuba. Yesterday Ambassador García-Inchaustegui of Cuba

recalled the words of his President, words which were uttered from
the rostrum of the General Assembly just over two weeks ago, and I
quote:

"Were the United States able to give us proof, by word and deed,
that it would not carry out aggression against our country, then, we
declare solemnly before you here and now, our weapons would be
unnecessary and our army redundant."

Here again I feel that on the basis of discussion, some common
ground may be found through which a way may be traced out of
the present impasse. I believe it would also contribute greatly to the
same end if the construction and development of major military facilities and installations in Cuba could be suspended during the period
of negotiations.

Mr. President, I now make a most solemn appeal to the parties concerned to enter into negotiations immediately, even this night, if
possible, irrespective of any other procedures which may be available
or which could be invoked.

I realize that if my appeal is heeded, the first subject to be discussed will be the modalities, and that all parties concerned will have
to agree to comply with those responsibilities which fall on them before any agreement as a whole could become effective. I hope, however, that the need for such discussion will not deter the parties concerned from undertaking these discussions. In my view it would be
short-sighted for the parties concerned to seek assurances on the
end result before the negotiations have even begun.

I have stated in my message to both the President of the United
States of America and the Chairman of the Council of Ministers of
the U.S S R that I shall gladly make myself available to all parties
for whatever services I may be able to perform. I repeat that pledge
now.

During the seventeen years that have passed since the end of World
War II, there has never been a more dangerous or closer confrontation
of the major powers. At a time when the danger to world peace was
less immediate, or so it appears by comparison, my distinguished
predecessor said.

"The principles of the Charter are, by far, greater than the Organization in which they are embodied, and the aims which they are
to safeguard are holier than the policies of any single nation or people."
He went on to say: "The discretion and impartiality . . . imposed on
the Secretary General by the character of his immediate task may not
degenerate into a policy of expediency. . . . A Secretary General cannot serve on any other assumption than that . . . within the necessary
limits of human frailty and honest differences of opinion — all Member
Nations honour their pledge to observe all articles of the Charter. . . ."

It is after considerable deliberation that I have decided to send the
two messages to which I have referred earlier, and likewise I have

decided to make this brief intervention tonight before the Security Council including the appeal to the President and Prime Minister of Cuba.

I hope that at this moment, not only in the Council Chamber but in the world outside, good sense and understanding will be placed above the anger of the moment or the pride of nations. The path of negotiation and compromise is the only course by which the peace of the world can be secured at this critical moment.

Mr. President, I thank you.

U.N., *Press Release SG/1353*, October 24, 1962, pp. 1–3.

❖ ❖ ❖ **34**

JOINT DRAFT RESOLUTION OF GHANA AND UNITED ARAB REPUBLIC TO U.N. SECURITY COUNCIL, *October 24, 1962*

The Security Council,

Having considered the recent serious developments in the Caribbean,

Noting with grave concern the threat to international peace and security,

Having listened to the parties directly concerned,

1. *Requests* the Acting Secretary General to promptly confer with the parties directly concerned on the immediate steps to be taken to remove the existing threat to world peace, and to normalize the situation in the Caribbean;

2. *Calls* upon the parties concerned to comply forthwith with this resolution and provide every assistance to the Acting Secretary General in performing his task;

3. *Requests* the Acting Secretary General to report to the Council on the implementation of Paragraph 1 of this resolution;

4. *Calls* upon the parties concerned to refrain, meanwhile, from any action which may directly or indirectly further aggravate the situation.

U.N., *Security Council Document S/5190*, October 24, 1962, p. 1.

✧ ✧ ✧ **35**

STATEMENT BY VENEZUELAN AMBASSADOR
DR. CARLOS SOSA-RODRÍGUEZ TO U.N. SECURITY
COUNCIL, *October 24, 1962*

The balance of terror — as this armed peace under which we live has been called — is about to be shattered on our American continent, and it is therefore our inescapable duty to avoid this shattering of peace if we want to avoid the great tragedy which terrifies us all.

When I say that we are seriously alarmed by the existence in Cuba of rocket sites and by the stockpiling in Cuba of nuclear weapons, and that we wish this state of affairs to cease, I am not speaking merely for Venezuela, I am speaking on behalf of the other countries — Brazil, Mexico, Colombia, Bolivia, Ecuador, Argentina. To sum up, I am speaking on behalf of the entire American Continent.

We trust that the Soviet Union, which has set up these bases in Cuba, will understand the enormous anxiety that these bases are causing all over the continent and that it will cooperate in trying to do away with this grave danger to peace in our continent.

It is enough that these weapons of mass destruction are in the hands of the nuclear powers themselves; we cannot indifferently allow these weapons to be handed over to the only Communist government existing in America, so that it may thereby increase its military potential to the point at which, without any discussions or arguments, it can dominate our American republics or cast the world into a nuclear holocaust.

The New York Times, October 25, 1962, p. 23. Copyright by The New York Times. Reprinted by permission.

✧ ✧ ✧ **36**

STATEMENT BY BRITISH AMBASSADOR
SIR PATRICK DEAN TO U.N. SECURITY COUNCIL,
October 24, 1962

In the view of my Government this is one of the most serious situations ever brought before the Security Council. The problem is

115

urgent, and the consequences of the events now before us are in-calculable. We must harshly and with clarity see the true facts of the situation.

What is happening is this: By a deliberate and deceitful act of provocation the Soviet Union is introducing into the Western Hemi-sphere nuclear missiles of mass destruction.

This affects the whole security of the Western Hemisphere and presents a situation which those responsible for its defense cannot tolerate. That is the real point at issue before us, and not, as has been pretended here, the right of a government to take such measures as it may think necessary for its own defense. Let there be no mistake about it.

The task facing us is easily described but difficult to accomplish. Somehow we must rebuild the worlds envisaged by the Charter, we must recreate the atmosphere of confidence and trust between the [G]reat [P]owers of the [W]orld.

My country has always held that a sovereign people have the right to choose their own ideology, government and political way of life.

We strongly believe too, that each country has the right and duty to look to its own defense. But not one, Mr. President, can fit the in-stallation of these missile sites in Cuba into this picture. Legitimate defenses are one thing; nuclear missiles with ranges from 1,000 to over 2,000 miles are quite another.

And then add to this the fact that these weapons of mass destruc-tion are being installed in secrecy and behind a mask of duplicity.

We are forced to believe that the Soviet Government sees for itself some significant advantage, and when it attempts to steal this ad-vantage in such an underhand way, the free world must alert itself to a potential threat to its security and to a grave danger to mankind.

The truth is, Mr. President, that the threat comes not from without against Cuba but from within Cuba against its neighbors. The representatives of the Latin American countries have, as we have heard, met to discuss the situation as provided for in the Rio Treaty of 1947. These countries represent a voluntary association of a freedom-loving peoples who have joined together for their mutual defense and mutual benefit in an organization whose existence is recognized under our Charter.

The consensus of our Latin American colleagues is that these latest moves in Cuba do indeed represent a real threat to their security. It is they who have the experience and the knowledge with which to judge these latest events. We agree with their assessment.

Furthermore, if they are threatened then we are threatened too. For in this nuclear age the whole free world stands or falls together.

My Government, Mr. President, fully supports the provisions of the resolution before this Council tabled by the representative of the United States and in so doing urges the Governments of the Soviet

Union and of Cuba to heed the appeal of all peace-loving peoples everywhere.

✧ ✧ ✧ **37**

STATEMENT BY ROMANIAN AMBASSADOR MIRCEA MALITZA TO U.N. SECURITY COUNCIL, *October 24, 1962*

Today, on the seventeenth anniversary of the coming into force of the United Nations Charter, a document expressing the hope of humanity, it is indeed painful to find ourselves meeting here to debate one of the most flagrant violations of that Charter, a violation by the United States of America, which threatens the very existence of our organization.

This is not the first time that the Government of the United States has undertaken actions against the heroic Cuban people. The efforts of the United States to strangle Cuba, to wrest by force the sacred and inalienable right of the Cuban people to peace and independence, began in the first months of the existence of the new revolutionary Government of that country.

The economic blockade, the numerous acts of sabotage, the break-ing off of diplomatic relations, the attempts to isolate Cuba from the rest of the Latin American countries, the brutal interference in its domestic affairs, the bombing of Cuban towns and villages — all these are examples.

But this time, an action has been taken which, because of its scope, its consequences and its character, surpasses everything that was done last year by the United States Government against Cuba.

The true reason for the action of the United States Government against Cuba is in [its] political regime chosen by the Cuban people, in full exercise of its sovereign prerogatives. The United States policy [of] overthrowing the legal Government of Cuba and of changing its social regime has been openly acclaimed.

In view of the fact that it cannot train troops to fight against ideas, the United States Government needs to seek pretexts for the purpose of justifying these warlike actions, and thus it was that the pretended danger to the United States by the small state of Cuba was created.

In reality, only one thing is at issue here:

It is the hate of the imperialist circles in the United States for the Cuban regime. These circles cannot resign themselves to the existence of sovereign and independent Cuban state which is freed from the colonial domination of the United States.

The naval blockade set up by the United States in time of peace is designed to limit the freedom of the high seas and to hand over such freedom to one state. The members of the United Nations that ratified the Geneva convention on the use of the high seas, which recognized the legal force of such an agreement, cannot allow such a violation to go uncondemned and unpunished.

It is surprising, to say the least, to hear the representatives of the United Kingdom, one of the greatest maritime powers of the world, state his agreement to the naval blockade, which has been applied abusively, insultingly and unilaterally by the United States.

Recently the leaders of the British Chamber of Shipping stated that the British ship-builders wanted their right of trade to be respected as well as their right to sail the high seas.

In setting up such a blockade against Cuba the United States has committed an act of war against that country.

The Romanian Government will give all support to measures tending to stop the aggression. At this grave moment we trust that responsible spokesmen and politicians will use all their resources of calm, wisdom and knowledge, that reason will prevail and that they will be able to stop this dangerous course of events.

The Romanian delegation considers that it is the duty of the Security Council to condemn firmly the action of the United States against Cuba — action which threatens international peace and security.

The Security Council must insist on the immediate annulment of the naval blockade and the cessation of all interference in the internal affairs of the republic of Cuba, as well as of any other state. In keeping with this, my delegation wholeheartedly supports the draft resolution submitted by the delegation of the Soviet Union.

◇ ◇ ◇ **38**

STATEMENT BY IRISH AMBASSADOR FRANK AIKEN
TO U.N. SECURITY COUNCIL, *October 24, 1962*

The leaders of the Cuban revolution choose to regard the part
played by United States interests in Cuba as the source of all their
country's ills and a brake upon its economic and social development.

In keeping with this view, they had recourse to confiscation and
other. measures directed against United States concerns, measures
which inevitably aroused widespread ill-feeling and resentment in the
United States.

I understand the concern which the revolutionary Government of
Cuba feels for their national security. It is all the more understandable in view of the attempt made by Cuban refugee elements to
invade their territory in April of last year. It is only natural that the
Cubans should seek to strengthen their defenses so as to be able to
cope with any similar attack in the future.

But it is a far cry from that to a military build-up of the kind which
the Cuban Government now appears to have embarked upon with
the massive assistance of the Soviet Union.

There is some force to the argument often used that whether a
weapon is to be regarded as offensive or defensive depends less on its
intrinsic character than on the intentions of those who possess it.

Whatever may be the intentions of the Soviet or the Cuban Government, however, it appears undeniable that the installations, missiles
and aircraft now in Cuba are capable, in the hands of ill-intentioned
persons, of constituting a deadly threat to the security of North and
South America. It is quite true, in principle, as the representative of
the Soviet Union has argued, that it is for Cuba in the exercise of its
national sovereignty to decide how best to organize its own national
defense. As he said: "Cuba belongs to Cuban people and only they
can be masters of their fate."

But all governments are bound to use the powers they derive from
their national sovereignty not only in the best interests of their own
peoples, but with due regard for the preservation of good relations
with their neighbors and for the peace of the world.

As the experience of this nuclear age has already shown, small
countries, by allowing new military, and particularly nuclear, bases on
their national territories may upset the world's strategic balance and
add greatly to existing tensions.

This is a political fact which we cannot ignore. The Soviet Union
may criticize the reactions of the United States in the case of Cuba,

119

but it cannot fail to understand them. On more than one occasion in
the past the Soviet Union has itself issued stern warnings to neighboring countries of the possible consequences of the stationing of nuclear
missiles on their territories.

We have reached the stage when the extension of nuclear bases
and the spread of nuclear weapons have become unacceptable to
reasonable men as methods of solving the problems of world security.
If the principals in the present crisis proceed on their present course,
a headlong collision is bound to occur which may well lead to world
war and all that it means.

I have searched carefully in the statements submitted to the Council
by the United States and the Soviet Union for some indication of a
willingness on both sides to seek a peaceful solution of the problem
now before us.

In his statement to the Security Council on 22 October, the representative of the United States stated that his Government was
willing to confer with the Soviet Union on measures to remove the
existing threat to the security of the Western Hemisphere and the
peace of the world.

In the draft resolution which he submitted to the Council yesterday, the representative of the Soviet Union proposed that the Council
should call upon the United States of America, the Republic of Cuba
and the Union of Socialist Republics to establish compacts and to
enter into negotiations with the purpose of normalizing the situation
and of thus removing the threat of war.

In both cases the compacts and negotiations were suggested as the
final step in a wider scheme of proposals upon which agreement may
take time to achieve.

But let us make no mistake about it, the danger to peace with
which we are faced will not brook delay. Moreover, it can only be
dispelled by agreement, and agreement cannot be achieved without
discussions and negotiations. Let us hope, therefore, that negotiations
will be entered into while there is still time.

The New York Times, October 25, 1962, p. 23. Copyright by The New
York Times. Reprinted by permission.

✧ ✧ ✧ **39**

STATEMENT BY FRENCH AMBASSADOR
ROGER SEYDOUX TO U.N. SECURITY COUNCIL,
October 24, 1962

The question placed on the agenda is one of the most serious that the Security Council has ever had before it. We cannot escape the fact that the situation which exists today in Cuba constitutes a threat to international peace and security.

In fact, according to the explanations given us by our colleague of the United States, launching sites have been set up in Cuba for missiles with a range of at least 1,100 miles. The construction of other launching sites for missiles with a range of 2,500 miles is in progress. These weapons cannot be considered as anything but offensive.

The appearance of foreign nuclear missiles on Cuban soil can thus appear only as a serious initiative aimed at creating a new war front in a region up to now sheltered.

My delegation finds in the reactions of the Latin American countries an additional reason for believing in the gravity of the situation created by the Soviet Union.

It would be paradoxical for the Security Council to refuse to take into account the aspirations of an entire continent and the determination of governments which, justifiably, consider themselves threatened.

For all these reasons, the French delegation considers, in conclusion, that the draft resolution presented by the United States meets with the exigencies of the situation.

Without minimizing its gravity, it demonstrates clearly that the American Government is seeking, in accordance with the principles of the Charter, a peaceful solution.

This solution France believes to be possible and she desires it, not only in the immediate interest of the countries most directly concerned to world peace by the recent developments in Cuba.

The New York Times, October 25, 1962, p. 23. Copyright by The New York Times. Reprinted by permission.

❖ ❖ ❖ **40**

DECLARATION OF THE DOMINICAN REPUBLIC,
October 24, 1962

I have the honour to request you to circulate the appended declaration of the Council of State of the Dominican Republic as an official
United Nations document.

The declaration reads as follows:

"In pursuance of a resolution adopted by the Council of State, it
is my duty to inform the Dominican people of the concern felt by
the Government at the offensive measures which the Government of
Cuba has been taking by permitting the installation of nuclear missile
bases in Cuban territory. This conduct, imposed by Russia, constitutes
a grave threat to the security of all the nations of America, and at the
same time offers proof of flagrant violations of the agreements per-
manently embodied in the inter-American juridical system.

"In consequence, the Council of State, conscious of the danger
which this represents to the security and peace of the continent and
faithful to the principles of democracy and continental solidarity
which it has maintained unswervingly since its establishment, has
resolved to participate unreservedly in any measure which may be
deemed desirable either by the Organization of American States or
by the United Nations with a view to removing the threat at present
hanging over the free peoples of the world. Similarly, the Dominican
Government appeals to the brother peoples of the continent to preserve, at this crucial moment, the spirit of solidarity which is essential
if our civilization is to surivive, forgetting any difference which may
in the slightest degree separate them. Lastly, the Dominican Government calls upon the people to give their firm support to this attitude,
and to place at the service of this cause the patriotism demanded by
the present highly serious and difficult circumstances." Accept, Sir,
etc.

(s) GUAROA VELASQUEZ
Ambassador,
Head of the Permanent Mission

U.N., *Security Council Document S/5191*, October 24, 1962, p. 1. (Letter
addressed to the Acting Secretary General.)

❖ ❖ ❖ **41**

STATEMENT BY PRIME MINISTER HAROLD MACMILLAN TO BRITISH HOUSE OF COMMONS, *October 25, 1962*

On Monday, October 22, President Kennedy in a personal message and through the United States Ambassador in London made clear to me his deep concern about the Soviet development of Cuba as a formidable base for offensive ballistic missiles.

It is of course true that the United States authorities had known for some time of the location of a number of surface-to-air missile sites in Cuba but these missiles, even though carrying nuclear warheads, may be regarded as of a defensive nature.

Very recently, however, a number of medium-range ballistic or ground-to-ground missile sites have been definitely identified in Cuba. Reports from all American intelligence sources confirm that at least thirty missiles are already present in Cuba.

Such missiles with their range of over 1,000 miles could reach a large area of the United States including Washington and nearly the whole of Central America and the Caribbean, including the Panama Canal.

In addition sites for intermediate-range ballistic missiles with an operational range of 2,200 nautical miles have been identified.

Further sites for both types of missiles are being constructed.

All these missiles are designed to carry and must be presumed to carry, nuclear bombs.

In addition Russia has supplied Cuba with IL–28 aircraft of which over twenty have been definitely identified.

These bombers are offensive and not defensive weapons.

Neither the Soviet Union nor the Cuban Government appears to have denied these facts. In addition, it is believed that there are at least 5,000 Soviet military technicians already on the island.

These facts, which are fully established on the basis of the evidence provided, serious though they are in themselves, take on a more sinister character because of the previous history of this affair.

The House may recall that on the 4th and 14th of September, President Kennedy issued a solemn warning about the build-up of offensive weapons in Cuba, and that on the 11th of September the official Soviet news agency *Tass*, said this: "The armaments and military equipment sent to Cuba are designed exclusively for defensive purposes," and added: "there is no need for the Soviet Union to shift its weapons for a retaliatory blow to any other country, for instance to Cuba."

That amounted to an official disclaimer by the Soviet Government. In addition, as recently as the 18th of October, Mr. Gromyko, the Soviet Foreign Minister, explicitly speaking on the instructions of his Government, assured President Kennedy in person that Soviet assistance to Cuba was of a purely defensive character.

At that very moment circumstantial evidence to the contrary was accumulating. In view of the President's pledge that the United States would take measures to oppose the creation of offensive military power in Cuba, the Russian action, contrary to their categorical assurances, to develop this power can be only regarded as deliberately adventure designed to test the ability and determination of the United States.

The President no doubt formed this view, and in my judgment rightly, that to have accepted this would have thrown doubt on American pledges in all parts of the world, and exposed the entire free world to a new series of perils.

The House is well aware of the action so far taken by the President of the United States in this situation, both in the area of Cuba itself and in the Security Council of the United Nations.

As regards the area of Cuba the measures announced in the President's proclamation are designed to meet a situation which is without precedent. Moreover it cannot be said that these measures are extreme.

Indeed, they are studiously moderate in that the President has only proclaimed certain limited types of war material, not even all armaments, to be prohibited.

The armaments specified are surface-to-surface missiles, bomber aircraft, bombs, air-to-surface rockets, and guided missiles together with warhead equipment.

None of the categories specified in the President's proclamation can honestly be described as defensive.

In the Security Council the United States representative has made a strong appeal for a resolution which calls for the dismantling and withdrawal from Cuba of all nuclear missiles and offensive weapons, and for international supervision of this process by United Nations observers corps.

The resolution also urgently recommends that the United Nations and the Soviet Union should confer promptly on measures to remove the existing threat to the security of the Western Hemisphere and the peace of the world and report thereon to the Security Council.

As the House knows, Sir Patrick Dean, speaking on behalf of the British Government gave his support to this resolution.

I understand that discussion in the Security Council has been adjourned until 4 P.M. New York time, today, 9 P.M. London time.

Meanwhile as the House will have heard, the Acting Secretary

General of the United Nations, U Thant, has addressed a message in identical terms to President Kennedy and Chairman Khrushchev. He has also sent, I am informed, a message to the Cuban Government.

U Thant's proposal is there should be a voluntary suspension on behalf of Russia to all arms shipments to Cuba and at the same time a suspension of the quarantine measures involving the search of ships.

His appeal to the Cuban Government adds the suggestion that the construction and development of military facilities and installations should be suspended, all these measures to last for two or three weeks to give time to the parties concerned to meet and discuss with a view to finding a peaceful solution to the problem.

I am not yet in a position to inform the House that any replies have been received from any of the three Governments to whom the Acting Secretary General has addressed his message.

The British Government is, of course, concerned that this new threat to security should be dealt with as rapidly as possible and will add their support to any measures which lead genuinely to that end.

They trust also that, based on some alleviation of the present state of tension, it might be possible to move to a wider field of negotiation.

Nevertheless I think what has happened in the last few weeks must confirm our view that in these grave matters we cannot rest upon mere words and promises. These need, if they are to restore confidence, to be independently verified and confirmed.

❖ ❖ ❖ **42**

LETTER FROM CHAIRMAN KHRUSHCHEV TO LORD BERTRAND RUSSELL, *October 25, 1962*

I received your telegram and express sincere gratitude for the concern you have displayed in connection with the aggressive actions of the United States in pushing the world to the brink of war.

I understand your worry and anxiety. I should like to assure you that the Soviet Government will not take any reckless decisions, will not permit itself to be provoked by the unwarranted actions of the United States of America and will do everything to eliminate the situation fraught with irreparable consequences which has arisen in connection with the aggressive actions of the United States Government. We shall do everything in our power to prevent war from breaking out. We are fully aware of the fact that if this war is un-leashed, from the very first hour it will become a thermonuclear and world war. This is perfectly obvious to us, but clearly is not to the Government of the United States which has caused this crisis.

The American Government is said to have embarked on such a reckless course not only because of hatred for the Cuban people and their Government, but also out of pre-election considerations, in the flurry of interparty pre-election excitement. But this is madness which may lead the world to the catastrophe of a thermonuclear war. The persons who are responsible for the United States policy should ponder the consequences to which their rash actions may lead if a thermonuclear war is unleashed. If the way to the aggressive policy of the American Government is not blocked, the people of the United States and other nations will have to pay with millions of lives for this policy.

I beg you, Mr. Russell, to meet with understanding our position, our actions. Realizing the entire complexity of the situation brought about by the piratic actions of the American Government, we cannot agree with them in any form. If we encourage piracy and banditry in international relations, this will not conduce to consolidation of the norms of international law and, consequently, of legal order on which normal relations are based between states, between nations, between people.

Therefore if the United States Government will crudely trample upon and violate international rights, if it does not follow in its actions the appeals of reason, the situation having tensed up to the limit may get out of hand and this may resolve into a world war with all the regretful consequences to the peoples of all countries.

This is why what is needed now is not only the efforts of the Soviet Union, the Socialist countries and Cuba, which has become, as it were, the main focus of the world crisis, but also the efforts of all states, all peoples and all segments of society to avert a military catastrophe. Clearly if this catastrophe breaks out, it will bring extremely grave consequences to mankind and will spare neither right nor left, neither those who champion the cause of peace nor those who want to stay aloof.

I want to say once more: we shall do everything possible to prevent this catastrophe. But it must be borne in mind that our efforts may prove insufficient. Indeed, our efforts and possibilities are efforts and possibilities of one side. If the American Government will be carrying the program of piratic actions outlined by it, we shall have to resort to means of defense against an aggressor to defend our rights and inter-national rights which are written down in international agreements and expressed in the United Nations Charter. We have no other way out. It is well known that if one tries to mollify a robber by giving him at first one's purse, then one's coat, etc., the robber will not become more merciful, will not stop robbing. On the contrary, he will become increasingly insolent. Therefore it is necessary to curb the highwayman in order to prevent the jungle law from becoming the law governing relations between civilized people and states.

The Soviet Government considers that the Government of the United States of America must display reserve and stay the execution of its piratical threats which are fraught with most serious consequences.

The question of war and peace is so vital that we should consider useful a top-level meeting in order to discuss all the problems which have arisen, to do everything to remove the danger of unleashing a thermonuclear war. As long as rocket nuclear weapons are not put into play it is still possible to avert war. When aggression is unleashed by the Americans such a meeting will already become impossible and useless.

I thank you once more for your appeal, prompted as it is by concern for the destinies of the world.

The New York Times, October 25, 1962, p. 22. Copyright by The New York Times. Reprinted by permission.

❖ ❖ ❖ **43**

STATEMENT BY THE HUNGARIAN PEOPLE'S REPUBLIC, *October 25, 1962*

I have the honour to forward to you the text of the Statement of the Government of the Hungarian People's Republic on the dangerous situation of Cuba.

In the view of my Government the unilateral aggressive actions of the Government of the United States against the Republic of Cuba are not only open and immediate threats to the sovereignty and independence of a Member State but at the same time are seriously endangering international peace and security.

I request Your Excellency to arrange for the circulation of the Statement of the Government of the Hungarian People's Republic to all delegations as an official document of the General Assembly of the United Nations.

Please accept, etc.

(s) KAROLY CSATORDAY
*Permanent Representative of
the Hungarian People's
Republic*

U.N., *Security Council Document S/5194,* October 25, 1962, p. 1. (Letter addressed to the President of the Security Council.)

President Kennedy of the United States of America has ordered a naval blockade of Cuba and taken other military measures of a provocative character. The Government of the Hungarian People's Republic states that by ordering the naval blockade the Government of the United States of America has committed aggression against Cuba. These aggressive measures constitute at the same time an attack upon all nations defending their freedom and national independence, upon the Charter of the United Nations, and are a serious threat to peace.

The Government of the Hungarian People's Republic emphatically condemns these steps of the Government of the United States of America and demands that it repeal its measures trampling international law underfoot, endangering the freedom of navigation and constituting direct war provocation.

The Government of the Hungarian People's Republic wholly agrees with the statements published on 23 October this year by the Governments of Cuba and the Soviet Union and accordingly, taking into consideration the interests of the Hungarian People's Republic, in concert with the Warsaw Treaty Organization and other peace-loving forces, has taken appropriate measures against the provocative steps of the Government of the United States of America.

The Government of the Hungarian People's Republic and the Hungarian people, together with all peace-loving peoples of the world, condemn with righteous anger the new war provocation committed by the United States. The Government of the United States, which has created throughout the world a chain of offensive military bases against the freedom and independence of the socialist countries and of all peoples, wants to deprive the people of Cuba of the right to self-defence. It asserts in a hypocritical manner that the people of Cuba threaten the United States. The peoples know, however, that Cuba does not threaten the United States, but representatives of American monopoly capital want to stifle the struggle for freedom of the Cuban people in order to restore in Cuba their colonial domination and the exploiting role of capitalists.

The Government of the Hungarian People's Republic expects the Security Council of the United Nations to take effective and quick measures against the warlike aggression of the United Nations.

The Government of the Hungarian People's Republic and the Hungarian people express their solidarity with and send their fraternal greetings to the Government and the heroic people of Cuba. They are convinced that the rapid mobilization of the forces of peace will again succeed in tying the hands of the aggressors, safeguarding the independence of Cuba and preserving international peace.

U.N., *Security Council Document* S/5194, October 25, 1962, pp. 2–3.

◇ ◇ ◇ **44**

PROPOSALS OF THE UNION OF AFRICAN AND MALAGASY STATES, *October 25, 1962*

The extreme seriousness of the international situation now being debated in the Security Council has not been overlooked by the members of the group of the Union of African and Malagasy States (UAM), which are deeply attached to the maintenance of peace and to the principle of peaceful negotiations as the only means of settling disputes between States.

It must be possible to arrive at a settlement of the dispute in question through negotiation before any irreparable act is carried out. We are persuaded that the anguish aroused throughout the whole world and the urgent appeals for a lessening of tension which are heard everywhere will find expression in positive action by the United Nations to which the opposing parties will be morally and legally obliged to submit.

We have followed with the greatest possible interest and keen satisfaction the efforts which you are making in this direction. We give our absolute support to your proposals, to which we should like to see added a guarantee of effective United Nations supervision of their implementation.

Our proposals are, more precisely:

(1) Suspension of all shipments of arms to Cuba.

(2) Suspension of quarantine measures against Cuba

(3) Supervision by the United Nations of the implementation of points 1 and 2

(4) Negotiations with a view to finding a lasting and just solution which will safeguard peace.

We ask you to be good enough to circulate this letter as an official document coming from the Governments of the following twelve States:

> Cameroon
> Central African Republic
> Chad
> Congo (Brazzaville)
> Dahomey
> Gabon
> Ivory Coast
> Madagascar
> Mauritania

Niger
Senegal
Upper Volta
to the President and members of the Security Council.
Accept, Sir, the assurances of our highest consideration.

(s) E. D. ZINSOU
Minister for Foreign Affairs of Dahomey
(s) J. AUBAME
Minister for Foreign Affairs of Gabon
(s) MAURICE DEJEAN
Minister for Foreign Affairs of the
Central African Republic

U.N., *Security Council Document S/5195*, October 25, 1962, pp. 1–2. (Letter addressed to the Acting Secretary General.)

❖ ❖ ❖ **45**

LETTER FROM PRESIDENT KENNEDY TO ACTING SECRETARY GENERAL U THANT, *October 25, 1962*

EXCELLENCY:

I deeply appreciate the spirit which prompted your message of yesterday.

As we made clear in the Security Council, the existing threat was created by the secret introduction of offensive weapons into Cuba, and the answer lies in the removal of such weapons.

In your message and your statement to the Security Council last night, you have made certain suggestions and have invited preliminary talks to determine whether satisfactory arrangements can be assured.

Ambassador Stevenson is ready to discuss these arrangements with you.

I can assure you of our desire to reach a satisfactory and peaceful solution of the matter.

(s) JOHN F. KENNEDY

His Excellency U Thant
Acting Secretary General of the United Nations

U.S., Department of State, *Bulletin,* Volume XLVII, No. 1220 (November 12, 1962), p. 740. (White House press release dated October 25, 1962.)

❖ ❖ ❖ 46

LETTER FROM CHAIRMAN KHRUSHCHEV TO
ACTING SECRETARY GENERAL U THANT,
October 25, 1962

I have received your appeal, and carefully studied the proposals it
contains. I welcome your initiative. I understand your concern about
the situation obtained in the Caribbean since the Soviet Government
also considers this situation as highly dangerous and requiring an immediate interference by the United Nations.

I am informing you that I agree with your proposal, which meets
the interest of peace.

The New York Times, October 26, 1962, p. 16. Copyright by The New
York Times. Reprinted by permission.

❖ ❖ ❖ 47

STATEMENT BY AMBASSADOR STEVENSON TO
U.N. SECURITY COUNCIL, *October 25, 1962*

Today we must address our attention to the realities of the situation
posed by the build-up of nuclear striking power in Cuba.

In this connection I want to say at the outset that the course
adopted by the Soviet Union yesterday to avoid direct confrontation
in the zone of quarantine is welcome to my Government. We also
welcome the assurance by Chairman Khrushchev in his letter to Earl
Russell that the Soviet Union will "take no reckless decisions" with
regard to this crisis. And we welcome most of all the report that Mr.
Khrushchev has agreed to the proposals advanced by the Secretary
General.

My Government is most anxious to effect a peaceful solution of
this affair. We continue to hope that the Soviet Union will work with
us to diminish not only the new danger which has suddenly shadowed
the peace but all of the conflicts that divide the world.

I shall not detain you with any detailed discussion of the Soviet

131

and the Cuban responses to our complaint. The speeches of the Communist delegates were entirely predictable. I shall make brief comment on some points suggested by these speeches and some other points which may have arisen in the minds of members of the United Nations.

Both Chairman Khrushchev in the letter to Earl Russell and Ambassador Zorin in his remarks to this Council argued that this threat to the peace had been caused not by the Soviet Union and Cuba but by the United States.

We are here today and have been this week for one single reason — because the Soviet Union secretly introduced this menacing offensive military build-up into the island of Cuba while assuring the world that nothing was further from their thoughts.

The argument, in its essence, of the Soviet Union is that it was not the Soviet Union which created this threat to peace by secretly installing these weapons in Cuba but that it was the United States which created this crisis by discovering and reporting these installations. This is the first time, I confess, that I have ever heard it said that the crime is not the burglar but the discovery of the burglar — and that the threat is not the clandestine missiles in Cuba but their discovery and the limited measures to quarantine further infection.

The peril arises not because the nations of the Western Hemisphere have joined together to take necessary action in their self-defense but because the Soviet Union has extended its nuclear threat into the Western Hemisphere.

I noted that there are still at least some delegates in the Council — possibly, I suspect, very few — who say that they do not know whether the Soviet Union has, in fact, built in Cuba installations capable of firing nuclear missiles over ranges from 1,000 to 2,000 miles. As I say, Chairman Khrushchev did not deny these facts in his letter to Earl Russell, nor did Ambassador Zorin on Tuesday evening. And if further doubt remains on this score, we shall gladly exhibit photographic evidence to the doubtful.

One other point I would like to make is to invite attention to the casual remark of the Soviet representative claiming that we have thirty-five bases in foreign countries. The facts are that there are missiles comparable to these being placed in Cuba with the forces of only three of our allies. They were only established there by a decision of the heads-of-government meeting in December 1957, which was compelled to authorize such arrangements by virtue of a prior Soviet decision to introduce its own missiles capable of destroying the countries of Western Europe.

In the next place there are some troublesome questions in the minds of members that are entitled to serious answers. There are those who say that conceding the fact that the Soviet Union has installed these offensive missiles in Cuba, conceding the fact that this constitutes a grave threat to the peace of the world, why was it necessary for the nations of the Western Hemisphere to act with such speed? Why could not the quarantine against the shipment of offensive weapons have been delayed until the Security Council and the General Assembly had a full opportunity to consider the situation and make recommendations?

Let me remind the members that the United States was not looking for some pretext to raise the issue of the transformation of Cuba into a military base. On the contrary, the United States made no objection whatever to the shipment of defensive arms by the Soviet Union to Cuba, even though such shipments offended the traditions of this hemisphere.

Even after the first hard intelligence reached Washington concerning the change in the character of Soviet military assistance to Cuba, the President of the United States responded by directing an intensification of surveillance. And only after the facts and the magnitude of the build-up had been established beyond all doubt did we begin to take this limited action of barring only these nuclear weapons equipment and aircraft.

To understand the reasons for this prompt action, it is necessary to understand the nature and the purpose of this operation. It has been marked, above all, by two characteristics — speed and stealth. As the photographic evidence makes clear, the installation of these missiles — the erection of these missile sites — has taken place with extraordinary speed. One entire complex was put up in twenty-four hours. This speed not only demonstrates the methodical organization and careful planning involved. But it also demonstrates a premeditated attempt to confront this hemisphere with a *fait accompli*. By quickly completing the whole process of nuclearization of Cuba, the Soviet Union would be in a position to demand that the *status quo* be maintained and left undisturbed.

If we were to have delayed our counteraction, the nuclearization of Cuba would have been quickly completed. This is not a risk which this hemisphere is prepared to take.

When we first detected the secret offensive installations, could we reasonably be expected to have notified the Soviet Union in advance, through the process of calling the Security Council, that we had discovered its perfidy and then to have done nothing but wait while we debated and then have waited further while the Soviet representative in the Security Council vetoed a resolution, as he has already announced that he will do? In different circumstances, we would have. But today we are dealing with dread realities and not with wishes.

One of the sites, as I have said, was constructed in twenty-four hours. One of these missiles can be armed with its nuclear warhead in the middle of the night, pointed at New York, and landed above this room five minutes after it is fired. No debate in this room could affect in the slightest the urgency of these terrible facts or the immediacy of the threat to peace.

There was only one way to deal with that urgency and with that immediacy; and that was to act and to act at once — but with the utmost restraint consistent with the urgency of the threat to the peace.

And we came to the Security Council, I remind you, immediately and concurrently with the Organization of American States. We did not even wait for the OAS to meet and to act. We came here at the same time. We immediately put into process the political machinery that, we pray, will achieve a solution of this grave crisis. And we did not act until the American Republics had acted to make the quarantine effective.

We did not shirk our duties to ourselves, to the Hemisphere, to the United Nations, or to the world. We are now in the Security Council on the initiative of the United States precisely because, having taken the hemispheric action which has been taken, we wish political machinery — the machinery of the United Nations — take over, to reduce these tensions, and to interpose itself to eliminate this aggressive threat to the peace and to assure the removal from this Hemisphere of offensive nuclear weapons and the corresponding lifting of the quarantine.

There are those who say that the quarantine is an inappropriate and extreme remedy — that the punishment does not fit the crime. But I ask those who take this position to put themselves in the position of the Organization of American States to consider what you would have done in the face of the nuclearization of Cuba. Were we to do nothing until the knife was sharpened? Were we to stand idly by until it was at our throats? What were the alternatives available?

On the one hand, the Organization of American States might have sponsored an invasion, or destroyed the bases by an air strike, or imposed a total blockade on all imports to Cuba, including medicine and food. On the other hand, the OAS and the United States might have done nothing. Such a course would have confirmed the greatest threat to the peace of the Americas known to history and would have encouraged the Soviet Union in similar adventures in other parts of the world. And it would have discredited our will, our determination, to live in freedom and to reduce — not increase — the perils of this nuclear age.

The course we have chosen seems to me perfectly graduated to meet the character of the threat. To have done less would have been to fail in our obligation to peace.

To those who say that a limited quarantine was too much, in spite of the provocation and the danger, let me tell you a story — attributed like so many of our American stories to Abraham Lincoln — about the passerby out in my part of the country who was charged by a farmer's ferocious boar. He picked up a pitchfork and met the boar head on. It died, and the irate farmer denounced him and asked him why he didn't use the blunt end of the pitchfork. And the man replied, "Why didn't the boar attack me with his blunt end?"

Some here have attempted to question the legal basis of the defensive measures taken by the American Republics to protect the Western Hemisphere against Soviet long-range nuclear missiles.

I would gladly expand on our position on this, but in view of the proposal now before us presented last night by the Secretary General, perhaps that is a matter and a discussion, in view of its complexity and length, which could be more fruitfully delayed to a later time.

Finally, let me say that no twisting of logic, no distortion of words, can disguise the plain, the obvious, the compelling commonsense conclusion that the installation of nuclear weapons by stealth — weapons of mass destruction in Cuba — poses a dangerous threat to the peace, a threat which contravenes Article 2, paragraph 4, and a threat which the American Republics are entitled to meet, as they have done, with appropriate regional defensive measures.

Nothing has been said by the representatives of the Communist states here which alters the basic situation. There is one fundamental question to which I solicit your attention. The question is this: What action serves to strengthen the world's hope of peace?

Can anyone claim that the introduction of long-range nuclear missiles into Cuba strengthens the peace?

Can anyone claim that the speed and stealth of this operation strengthens the peace?

Can anyone suppose that this whole undertaking is anything more than an audacious effort to increase the nuclear striking power of the Soviet Union against the United States and thereby magnify its frequently reiterated threats against Berlin? When we are about to debate how to stop the dissemination of nuclear weapons, does their introduction in a new hemisphere by an outside state advance sanity and peace?

Does anyone suppose that, if this Soviet adventure should go unchecked, the Soviet Union would refrain from similar adventures in other parts of the world?

The one action in the last few days which has strengthened the peace is the determination to stop this further spread of weapons in this Hemisphere.

In view of the situation that now confronts us and the proposals made here yesterday by the Acting Secretary General, I am not going to further extend my remarks this afternoon. I wish only to conclude by reading to the members of the Council a letter from the President of the United States which was delivered to the Acting Secretary General just a few minutes ago in reply to his appeal of last night. He said to Mr. U Thant:

I deeply appreciate the spirit which prompted your message of yesterday.

As we made clear in the Security Council, the existing threat was created by the secret introduction of offensive weapons into Cuba, and the answer lies in the removal of such weapons.

In your message and your statement to the Security Council last night, you have made certain suggestions and have invited preliminary talks to determine whether satisfactory arrangements can be assured.

Ambassador Stevenson is ready to discuss these arrangements with you.

I can assure you of our desire to reach a satisfactory and peaceful solution of the matter.

I have nothing further to say at this time, Mr. President.

U.S., Department of State, *Bulletin,* Volume XLVII, No. 1220 (November 12, 1962), pp. 734–737. (Ambassador Stevenson's first statement of October 25, 1962. U.S./U.N. press release 4073, October 25, 1962.)

❖ ❖ ❖ **48**

STATEMENT BY AMBASSADOR ZORIN,
October 25, 1962

When Mr. Stevenson today attempted to accuse the Soviet Union as the prime cause for these aggressive actions on the part of the United States, I should like to draw attention of the Council to a completely surprising fact.

In the statement of President Kennedy of the 22nd of October, Mr. Kennedy said that during the last week unmistakable evidence has established the fact that a series of offensive missile sites is now in preparation on that island.

On the 16th of October the President of the United States had in his hands incontrovertible information. What happened after that? On the 18th of October the President of the United States was receiving the representative of the Soviet Union, the Minister of Foreign Affairs, Mr. Gromyko, two days after he had already in his hands incontrovertible evidence.

One may well ask why did the President of the United States in receiving the minister of another power which the Government of the United States is now accusing of dispatching offensive arms to Cuba against the United States, why then did he not say a word to the Minister of Foreign Affairs of the Soviet Union with respect to these incontrovertible facts?

Why? Because no such facts exist. The Government of the United

States has no such fact in its hands except these [*sic*] falsified information of the United States Intelligence Agency, which are being displayed for review in halls and which are sent to the press.

Falsity is what the United States has in its hands, false evidence.

The Government of the United States has deliberately intensified the crisis, has deliberately prepared this provocation and had tried to cover up this provocation by means of a discussion in the Security Council.

. You cannot conduct world policies and politics on such an opportunistic matter. Such steps can lead you to catastrophic consequences for the whole world, and the Soviet Government has issued a warning to the United States and to the world on that score.

The Soviet Union considers that the Government of the United States of America must display reserve and stay the execution of its piratical threats, which are fraught with the most serious consequence.

The question of war and peace is so vital that we should consider useful a top level meeting in order to discuss all the problems which have arisen to do everything to remove the danger of unleashing a thermonuclear war.

The New York Times, October 26, 1962, p. 16. Copyright by The New York Times. Reprinted by permission.

✧ ✧ ✧ **49**

STATEMENT BY AMBASSADOR STEVENSON TO U.N. SECURITY COUNCIL, *October 25, 1962*

I want to say to you, Mr. Zorin, that I do not have your talent for obfuscation, for distortion, for confusing language, and for doubletalk. And I must confess to you that I am glad that I do not!

But if I understood what you said, you said that my position had changed, that today I was defensive because we did not have the evidence to prove our assertions, that your Government had installed long-range missiles in Cuba.

Well, let me say something to you, Mr. Ambassador — we do have the evidence. We have it, and it is clear and it is incontrovertible. And let me say something else — those weapons must be taken out of Cuba.

Next, let me say to you that, if I understood you, with a trespass on credibility that excels your best, you said that our position had changed since I spoke here the other day because of the pressures of world opinion and the majority of the United Nations. Well, let me say to you, sir, you are wrong again. We have had no pressure from anyone whatsoever. We came in here today to indicate our willingness to discuss Mr. U Thant's proposals, and that is the only change that has taken place.

But let me also say to you, sir, that there has been a change. You — the Soviet Union has sent these weapons to Cuba. You — the Soviet Union has upset the balance of power in the world. You — the Soviet Union has created this new danger, not the United States.

And you ask with a fine show of indignation why the President did not tell Mr. Gromyko on last Thursday about our evidence, at the very time that Mr. Gromyko was blandly denying to the President that the U.S.S.R. was placing such weapons on sites in the new world.

Well, I will tell you why — because we were assembling the evidence, and perhaps it would be instructive to the world to see how a Soviet official — how far he would go in perfidy. Perhaps we wanted to know if this country faced another example of nuclear deceit like that one a year ago, when in stealth, the Soviet Union broke the nuclear test moratorium.

And while we are asking questions, let me ask you why your Government — your Foreign Minister — deliberately, cynically deceived us about the nuclear build-up in Cuba.

And, finally, the other day, Mr. Zorin, I remind you that you did not deny the existence of these weapons. Instead, we heard that they had suddenly become defensive weapons. But today again if I heard you correctly, you now say that they do not exist, or that we haven't proved they exist, with another fine flood of rhetorical scorn.

All right, sir, let me ask you one simple question: Do you, Ambassador Zorin, deny that the U.S.S.R. has placed and is placing medium- and intermediate-range missiles and sites in Cuba? Yes or no — don't wait for the translation — yes or no?

(The Soviet representative refused to answer.)

You can answer yes or no. You have denied they exist. I want to know if I understood you correctly. I am prepared to wait for my answer until hell freezes over, if that's your decision. And I am also prepared to present the evidence in this room.

(The President called on the representative of Chile to speak, but Ambassador Stevenson continued as follows.)

I have not finished my statement. I asked you a question. I have had no reply to the question, and I will now proceed, if I may, to finish my statement.

I doubt if anyone in this room, except possibly the representative of the Soviet Union, has any doubt about the facts. But in view of his statements and the statements of the Soviet Government up until last Thursday, when Mr. Gromyko denied the existence or any inten-

tion of installing such weapons in Cuba, I am going to make a portion
of the evidence available right now. If you will indulge me for a
moment, we will set up an easel here in the back of the room where
I hope it will be visible to everyone.

The first of these exhibits shows an area north of the village of
Candelaria, near San Cristóbal, southwest of Habana. A map, to-
gether with a small photograph, shows precisely where the area is in
Cuba.

The first photograph shows the area in late August 1962, it was
then, if you can see from where you are sitting, only a peaceful
countryside.

The second photograph shows the same area one day last week.
A few tents and vehicles had come into the area, new spur roads had
appeared, and the main road had been improved.

The third photograph, taken only twenty-four hours later, shows
facilities for a medium-range missile battalion installed. There are
tents for 400 or 500 men. At the end of the new spur road there are
seven 1,000-mile missile trailers. There are four launcher-erector
mechanisms for placing these missiles in erect firing position. This
missile is a mobile weapon, which can be moved rapidly from one
place to another. It is identical with the 1,000-mile missiles which
have been displayed in Moscow parades. All of this, I remind you,
took place in twenty-four hours.

The second exhibit, which you can all examine at your leisure,
shows three successive photographic enlargements of another missile
base of the same type in the area of San Cristóbal. These enlarged
photographs clearly show six of these missiles on trailers and three
erectors.

And that is only one example of the first type of ballistic missile
installation in Cuba.

A second type of installation is designed for a missile of intermediate range — a range of about 2,200 miles. Each site of this
type has four launching pads.

The exhibit on this type of missile shows a lauching area being
constructed near Guanajay, southwest of the city of Habana As in
the first exhibit, a map and small photograph show this area as it
appeared in late August 1962, when no military activities were apparent.

A second large photograph shows the same area about six weeks
later. Here you will see a very heavy construction effort to push the
launching area to rapid completion. The pictures show two large
concrete bunkers or control centers in process of construction, one
between each pair of launching pads. They show heavy concrete
retaining walls being erected to shelter vehicles and equipment from
rocket blast-off. They show cable scars leading from the launch
pads to the bunkers. They show a large reinforced concrete build-

ing under construction. A building with a heavy arch may well be intended as the storage area for the nuclear warheads. The installation is not yet complete, and no warheads are yet visible.

The next photograph shows a closer view of the same intermediate-range launch site. You can clearly see one of the pairs of large concrete launch pads, with a concrete building from which launching operations for three pads are controlled. Other details are visible, such as fuel tanks.

And that is only one example, one illustration, of the work being furnished in Cuba on intermediate-range missile bases.

Now, in addition to missiles, the Soviet Union is installing other offensive weapons in Cuba. The next photograph is of an airfield at San Julián in western Cuba. On this field you will see twenty-two crates designed to transport the fuselages of Soviet Ilyushin-28 bombers. Four of the aircraft are uncrated, and one is partially assembled. These bombers, sometimes known as Beagles, have an operating radius of about 750 miles and are capable of carrying nuclear weapons. At the same field you can see one of the surface-to-air anti-aircraft guided missile bases, with six missiles per base, which now ring the entire coastline of Cuba.

Another set of two photographs covers still another area of deployment of medium-range missiles in Cuba. These photographs are on a larger scale than the others and reveal many details of an improved field-type launch site. One photograph provides an overall view of most of the site; you can see clearly three of the four launching pads. The second photograph displays details of two of these pads. Even an eye untrained in photographic interpretation can clearly see the buildings in which the missiles are checked out and maintained ready to fire, a missile trailer, trucks to move missiles out to the launching pad, erectors to raise the missiles to launching position, tank trucks to provide fuel, vans from which the missile firing is controlled, in short, all of the requirements to maintain, load, and fire these terrible weapons.

These weapons, gentlemen, these launching pads, these planes — of which we have illustrated only a fragment — are a part of a much larger weapons complex, what is called a weapons system.

To support this build-up, to operate these advanced weapons systems, the Soviet Union has sent a large number of military personnel to Cuba — a force now amounting to several thousand men.

These photographs, as I say, are available to members for detailed examination in the Trusteeship Council room following this meeting. There I will have one of my aides who will gladly explain them to you in such detail as you may require.

I have nothing further to say at this time.

(After another statement by the Soviet representative, Ambassador Stevenson replied as follows:)

Mr. President and gentlemen, I won't detain you but one minute.

I have not had a direct answer to my question. The representative of the Soviet Union says that the official answer of the U.S.S.R. was the Tass statement that they don't need to locate missiles in Cuba. Well, I agree — they don't need to. But the question is, have they missiles in Cuba — and that question remains unanswered. I knew it would be.

As to the authenticity of the photographs, which Mr. Zorin has spoken about with such scorn, I wonder if the Soviet Union would ask its Cuban colleague to permit a U.N. team to go to these sites. If so, I can assure you that we can direct them to the proper places very quickly.

And now I hope that we can get down to business, that we can stop this sparring. We know the facts, and so do you, sir, and we are ready to talk about them. Our job here is not to score debating points. Our job, Mr. Zorin, is to save the peace. And if you are ready to try, we are.[1]

---

[1] The Council adjourned at 7·25 P M., October 25, to give the Secretary General an opportunity to hold discussions with interested parties and report back.

U.S., Department of State, *Bulletin,* Volume XLVII, No. 1220 (November 12, 1962), pp 737–740 (Ambassador Stevenson's second statement of October 25, 1962. U.S./U.N. press release 4074, October 25, 1962.)

✧ ✧ ✧ **50**

STATEMENT BY DEPARTMENT OF DEFENSE ON QUARANTINE, *October 25, 1962*

It now appears that at least a dozen Soviet vessels have turned back, presumably because, according to the best of our information, they might have been carrying offensive materials.

However, the first Russian ship that proceeded through the area patrolled by our forces was a Soviet tanker. It was ascertained by the United States naval vessel which intercepted her that the tanker had only petroleum aboard. Since petroleum is not presently included as prohibited material under President Kennedy's proclamation setting up the quarantine, the tanker was allowed to proceed.

The Navy satisfied itself that no prohibited material was aboard this particular ship. This encounter took place shortly after 8 A.M. E.D.T. today.

✧ ✧ ✧ **51**

STATEMENT BY POPE JOHN XXIII, *October 25, 1962*

"I beseech thee, O Lord, let Thy ear be attentive to the prayer of Thy servant, and to the prayer of Thy servants who desire to fear Thy name." (Nehemiah i.5.)

This ancient Biblical prayer rises to our trembling lips today from the depths of the touched and afflicted heart.

While the Second Vatican Ecumenical Council has just been opened, amidst the joy and the hopes of all men of goodwill, threatening clouds now come to darken again the international horizon, and to show fear in millions of families.

The church — as we repeated when welcoming the eighty-six extraordinary missions present at the opening of the Council — the church has nothing nearer to her heart than peace and brotherhood among all men, and she strives, without ever tiring, to establish them. We recalled this in regard to the grave duties of those who bear the responsibility of power. And we added: "In all conscience let them give ear to the anguished cry of 'Peace! Peace!' which rises up to Heaven from every part of the world, from innocent children and those grown old, from individuals to communities."

We repeat today that solemn warning. We supplicate all rulers not to remain deaf to the cry of mankind. Let them do everything in their power to save peace. By so doing, they will spare the world the horrors of a war that would have disastrous consequences, such as nobody can foresee.

Let them continue to negotiate, because this loyal and open attitude is of great value as a witness for the conscience of each one and in the face of history. To promote, favor and accept negotiations, at all levels and at all times, is a rule of wisdom and prudence which calls down the blessings of heaven and earth.

Let all our children, let all those who have been marked with the seal of baptism and nourished by Christian hope, let all those finally who are united to us by faith in God, join their prayers to ours in order to obtain from Heaven the gift of peace: a peace which will be true and lasting only if it is based on justice and equity. And upon all those who contribute to this peace, upon all those who, with a sincere heart, work for the true welfare of men, may there descend the special blessing which we lovingly give them, in the name of him who wished to be called the Prince of Peace.

The New York Times, October 26, 1962, p. 20. Copyright by The New York Times. Reprinted by permission.

❖ ❖ ❖ **52**

COMMUNIQUÉ FROM HAITIAN DEPARTMENT OF FOREIGN AFFAIRS, *October 25, 1962*

I have the honour to enclose herewith a communiqué from the Haitian Department of Foreign Affairs on the Cuban question and should be grateful if you would arrange for it to be issued as a United Nations document.

Accept, Sir, etc.

(s) CARLET R. AUGUSTE
Permanent Representative

The Department of Foreign Affairs announced that on 22 October the Government of the Republic of Haiti, acting within the framework of pan-American solidarity and in order to defend the peace and the security of the continent, which have been endangered by the installation in Cuba of offensive nuclear missile bases, decided to respond to the appeal made by his Excellency President John F. Kennedy in his message of the same date for the organization on the Hemisphere level of measures to counter the threat from outside the continent, which imperils the survival of Western democracy. Accordingly, His Excellency the Honourable Dr François Duvalier issued an order, on 22 October, to the Haitian coast-guard units and air force to increase, because of the present crisis, the number of their patrols keeping watch over the coasts of the Republic at the disposal of the United States naval and air units responsible for the quarantine operation.

The Department of Foreign Affairs also announces that as soon as President Kennedy's message to President Duvalier was received, the Chief Executive of the Haitian nation, moved by a strong spirit of pan-American co-operation, instructed his representative to the OAS to vote for the United States proposal to convene the provisional Organ of Consultation of the OAS and for the various points in the United States delegation's draft resolution, namely: (1) the immediate dismantling of the nuclear missile bases set up in Cuba by the Sino-Soviet Powers; (2) the organization of a quarantine operation to prevent, by force if necessary, the arrival of offensive weapons in Cuba; (3) the transmittal of the text adopted to the United Nations Secretariat. The Permanent Representative of Haiti to the United Nations received instructions on the same date to give the United

States delegation the fullest possible moral support in order to preserve forever the great principles of democracy upon which all the
actions of the Government of the Republic are based.

Port-au-Prince, 25 October 1962

U.N., *Security Council Document S/5199*, October 29, 1962, pp. 1–2. (Letter dated October 29, 1962, addressed to the Acting Secretary General.)

❖ ❖ ❖ **53**

LETTER FROM ACTING SECRETARY GENERAL U THANT TO PRESIDENT KENNEDY, *October 25, 1962*

25 October 1962
I would be grateful if you would be so kind as to transmit the
enclosed message to the President of the United States, John F. Kennedy.

Sincerely yours,

(s) U THANT
Acting Secretary General

H.E. Hr. Adlai E. Stevenson
Permanent Representative to the United Nations
United States Mission to the United Nations
United Nations Plaza,
New York, N Y.

I have today sent a further message to Chairman Khrushchev expressing my grave concern that Soviet ships already on their way to
Cuba might challenge the quarantine imposed by your government
and produce a confrontation at sea between Soviet ships and United
States vessels, which could lead to an aggravation of the situation. I
have also stated that what concerns me most is the fact that such a
confrontation and consequent aggravation of the situation would
destroy any possibility of the discussions that I have suggested as a
prelude to negotiations on a peaceful settlement. I have accordingly
expressed to him my earnest hope that Soviet ships already on their
way to Cuba might be instructed to stay away from the interception
area for a limited time only, in order to permit discussions of the
modalities of a possible agreement which could settle the problem
peacefully in line with the Charter of the United Nations.

In continuation of my message of yesterday and my speech before the Security Council, I would now like to appeal to Your Excellency that instructions may be issued to United States vessels in the Caribbean to do everything possible to avoid direct confrontation with Soviet ships in the next few days in order to minimize the risk of any untoward incident. If I could be informed of the action taken by your government on the basis of this appeal, I could inform Chairman Khrushchev that I have assurances from your side of your cooperation in avoiding all risk of an untoward incident. I would express the further hope that such cooperation could be the prelude to a quick agreement in principle on the basis of which the quarantine measures themselves could be called off as soon as possible.

(s) U Thant
Acting Secretary General

U.N., *Press Release SG/1358*, October 26, 1962, pp. 1–2.

❖ ❖ ❖ **54**

LETTER FROM PRESIDENT KENNEDY TO ACTING SECRETARY GENERAL U THANT, *October 25, 1962*

25 October 1962

EXCELLENCY:

I have the honor to transmit a reply from the President of the United States to your message to him of 25 October:

"I have your further message of today and I continue to understand and welcome your efforts for a satisfactory solution. I appreciate and share your concern that great caution be exercised pending the inauguration of discussions.

"If the Soviet Government accepts and abides by your request 'that Soviet ships already on their way to Cuba . . . stay away from the interception area' for the limited time required for preliminary discussion, you may be assured that this government will accept and abide by your request that our vessels in the Caribbean 'do everything possible to avoid direct confrontation with Soviet ships in the next few days in order to minimize the risk of any untoward incident.' I must inform you, however, that this is a matter of great urgency in view of the fact that certain Soviet ships are still proceeding toward Cuba and the interception area.

"I share your hope that Chairman Khrushchev will also heed your appeal and that we can then proceed urgently to meet the requirements that these offensive military systems in Cuba be withdrawn, in order to end their threat to peace. I must point out to you that present work on these systems is still continuing."

Accept, Excellency, the renewed assurances of my highest consideration.

Sincerely yours,
(s) Adlai E. Stevenson

His Excellency U Thant
Acting Secretary General
of the United Nations

U.N., *Press Release SG/1358,* October 26, 1962, pp. 2–3.

❖ ❖ ❖ 55

LETTER FROM ACTING SECRETARY GENERAL
U THANT TO CHAIRMAN KHRUSHCHEV,
October 25, 1962

25 October 1962

I would be grateful if you would be so kind as to transmit the enclosed message to the Chairman of the Council of Ministers of the Soviet Union.

Sincerely yours,

(s) U Thant
Acting Secretary General

H.E. Mr. V. A. Zorin
Permanent Representative to the United Nations
Permanent Mission of the U.S.S.R. to the United Nations
136 East 67th Street
New York, N.Y.

25 October 1962

In continuation of my message of yesterday and my statement before the Security Council, I would like to bring to Your Excellency's attention my grave concern that Soviet ships already on their way to

Cuba might challenge the quarantine imposed by the United States and produce a confrontation at sea between Soviet ships and United States vessels, which could lead to an aggravation of the situation. What concerns me most is that such a confrontation and consequent aggravation of the situation would destroy any possibility of the discussions I have suggested as a prelude to negotiations on a peaceful settlement. In the circumstances I earnestly hope that Your Excellency may find it possible to instruct the Soviet ships already on their way to Cuba to stay away from the interception area for a limited time only, in order to permit discussions of the modalities of a possible agreement which could settle the problem peacefully in line with the Charter of the United Nations.

I am confident that, if such instructions could be issued by Your Excellency, the United States authorities will take action to ensure that a direct confrontation between their ships and Soviet ships is avoided during the same period in order to minimise the risk of any untoward incident taking place.

If I could be informed of the action taken by Your Government on the basis of this appeal, I could inform President Kennedy that I have assurances from your side of your cooperation in avoiding all risk of an untoward incident.

I am at the same time addressing the enclosed appeal to President Kennedy.

(s) U THANT
Acting Secretary General

U.N., *Press Release SG/1357,* October 26, 1962, pp. 1–2.

❖ ❖ ❖ **56**

LETTER FROM CHAIRMAN KHRUSHCHEV TO ACTING SECRETARY GENERAL U THANT, *October 25, 1962*

DEAR U THANT,

I have received and studied your telegram of 25 October. I understand your anxiety for the preservation of peace, and I appreciate highly your efforts to avert military conflict.

Indeed, if any conflict should arise on the approaches to Cuba — and this may become unavoidable as a result of the piratical measures taken by the United States — this would beyond question seriously complicate the endeavours to initiate contacts in order to put an end, on a basis of negotiation, to the critical situation that has now been thrust on the world by the aggressive actions of the United States.

We therefore accept your proposal, and have ordered the masters of Soviet vessels bound for Cuba but not yet within the area of the American warships' piratical activities to stay out of the interception area, as you recommend.

But we have given this order in the hope that the other side will understand that such a situation, in which we keep vessels immobilized on the high seas, must be a purely temporary one; the period cannot under any circumstances be of long duration.

I thank you for your efforts and wish you success in your noble task. Your efforts to ensure world peace will always meet with understanding and support on our part.

The Soviet Government has consistently striven, and is striving, to strengthen the United Nations — that international Organization which constitutes a forum for all countries of the world, regardless of their socio-political structure, in order that disputes arising may be settled not through war but through negotiations.

Accept, Sir, the assurances of my highest consideration.

(s) N. KHRUSHCHEV

26 October 1962
His Excellency U Thant
Acting Secretary General
United Nations
New York

U.N., *Press Release* SG/1357, October 26, 1962, pp. 2–3. (Unofficial translation from Russian.)

❖ ❖ ❖ **57**

WHITE HOUSE STATEMENT ON CONTINUATION OF MISSILE BUILD-UP IN CUBA, *October 26, 1962*

The development of ballistic missile sites in Cuba continues at a rapid pace. Through the process of continued surveillance directly by the President, additional evidence has been acquired which clearly reflects that as of Thursday, October 25, definite build-ups in these offensive missile sites continued to be made. The activity at these sites apparently is directed at achieving a full operational capability as soon as possible.

There is evidence that as of yesterday, October 25, considerable construction activity was being engaged in at the intermediate-range ballistic missile sites. Bulldozers and cranes were observed as late as Thursday actively clearing new areas within the sites and improving the approach roads to the launch pads.

Since Tuesday, October 23, missile-related activities have continued at the medium-range ballistic missiles sites resulting in progressive refinements at these facilities. For example, missiles were observed parked in the open on October 23. Surveillance on October 25 revealed that some of these same missiles have now been moved from their original parked positions. Cabling can be seen running from the missile-ready tents to power generators nearby.

In summary, there is no evidence to date indicating that there is any intention to dismantle or discontinue work on these missile sites. On the contrary the Soviets are rapidly continuing their construction of missile support and launch facilities, and serious attempts are under way to camouflage their efforts.

U S., Department of State, *Bulletin,* Volume XLVII, No. 1220 (November 12, 1962), pp. 740–741. (White House press release dated October 26, 1962.)

✧ ✧ ✧ **58**

STATEMENT BY DEPARTMENT OF DEFENSE
ON BOARDING "MARUCLA," *October 26, 1962*

The Navy has intercepted and boarded the *Marucla,* a freighter registered under the Lebanese flag and bound for Cuba. It is out of the Baltic port of Riga, under Soviet charter.

The boarding party, composed of personnel from the destroyer *John R. Pierce,* was still aboard *Marucla* at 10:20 A.M., E.D.T.

First reports from the scene indicate that cooperation on the part of the freighter personnel was good.

Until the boarding party returns, after having looked at the manifest, searched the ship, inspected the cargo and interrogated the personnel, we cannot be sure of the composition of the cargo.

The boarding took place at 7:50 A.M., E.D.T., 180 miles northeast of Nassau.

The boarding party was led by the executive officer whose name is Lieut. Comdr. Dwight G. Osborne of East Paterson, N.J., and the executive officer of the *Kennedy*, Lieut. Comdr. Kenneth C. Reynolds of Coronado, Calif. The commanding officers of the two vessels are Comdr. James W. Foust of Greenburg, Pa., of the *Pierce;* and Comdr. Nicholas Nikhalevsky of the *Kennedy.*

Chronology of the events follows: (All times E.D.T.)

7:24 A.M. — Forces receive instructions to board.

7:29 A.M. — *U.S.S. Kennedy* lowered whaleboats.

7:32 A.M. — *Marucla* lowered Jacob's ladder over the side.

7:36 A.M. — *U.S.S. Kennedy* whaleboat under way to freighter.

7:39 A.M. — Whaleboat approaching freighter.

7:46 A.M. — Whaleboat alongside and boarding.

7:50 A.M. — Boarding party aboard. The executive officers of the *U.S.S. Kennedy* and the *U.S.S. Pierce* leading party.

First message after boarding: "Party aboard *Marucla* at 0750 (7:50 A.M.) Cooperation good. No difficulties expected."

The New York Times, October 27, 1962, p. 6. Copyright by The New York Times. Reprinted by permission.

✧ ✧ ✧ **59**

STATEMENT BY THE MONGOLIAN PEOPLE'S REPUBLIC, *October 26, 1962*

I have the honour to enclose herewith the Statement of the Government of the Mongolian People's Republic on the situation aroused by the recent dangerous actions of the United States Government and request that the Statement be circulated as a United Nations document.

Accept, Excellency, etc.

(s) B. JARGALSAIKHAN
*Permanent Representative of the
Mongolian People's Republic to
the United Nations*

Statement by the Government of the Mongolian People's Republic

It was with profound indignation that the Mongolian people and their Government learned that on 22 October Mr. J. Kennedy, President of the United States, had ordered the United States Navy to intercept all ships of other sovereign States bound for the coast of

Cuba, thus establishing a naval blockade of the Republic of Cuba. At the same time, imperialist circles in the United States have greatly intensified military preparations for armed aggression against revolutionary Cuba.

In undertaking ventures of this kind the United States Government is trying to suppress the Cuban revolution, to nullify the revolutionary achievements of the heroic Cuban people and to turn them into obedient slaves of United States imperialists.

On behalf of the entire Mongolian people, the Government of the Mongolian People's Republic makes the strongest possible protest against the aggressive acts of the United States against the Republic of Cuba, and condemns them as an attack on a sovereign Member State of the United Nations.

The Government of Mongolia, expressing the wishes of the Mongolian public, demands that an end be put immediately to the piratical actions of the United States Navy, which must be considered a gross violation of the generally accepted rules of international law and as an infraction of the rights of sovereign States.

The workers of Mongolia and the Government of the Mongolian People's Republic warmly approve of and support the statement made by the Soviet Government on 23 October concerning this new act of provocation by the United States militarists.

True to its consistently peaceful policy, the Soviet Government again appealed to the United States Government to abandon its belligerent policy towards Cuba, and warned it that in taking the measures announced by President Kennedy the United States Government was assuming a heavy responsibility for the fate of the world, and that it was recklessly playing with fire in a manner fraught with the most serious consequences for the whole of mankind.

Our people considers that the aggression initiated by United States imperialist circles against Cuba is an open challenge to all peace-loving forces in the world. The groundlessness and absurdity of the charges levelled by United States imperialist circles against peace-loving Cuba are clear to every sane person.

The Government of the Republic of Cuba, in the face of this direct threat from reactionary circles in the United States, took in full accordance with the provisions of the Charter of the United Nations the necessary measures to strengthen the defences of its country. Our people and its Government are convinced that no one has any right to prevent the Cuban people from deciding its own fate and from defending its revolutionary achievements against the infractions of the imperialists.

The American aggressors, blinded by hatred of the Cuban revolution, wish to impose a regime of their choice on the Cuban people by force of arms, but the imperialists will not succeed in this. Cuba is not alone in its struggle. It has on its side the solidarity of all peoples, of all the peace-loving forces of our planet.

The workers of Mongolia express their feelings of warmest sympathy and brotherly solidarity with the heroic Cuban people, and sincerely wish them success in the defence of their revolutionary achievements against the infractions of internationalist imperialist reaction headed by the United States monopolists.

The Government of the Mongolian People's Republic considers that, at this time of anxiety for the fate of the world, the United Nations should take the most effective and drastic measures to suppress the aggressive actions of the United States.

The Mongolian people and its Government express their firm conviction that the peace-loving forces of the whole world will succeed in bringing the extremist aggressors to their senses and in protecting universal peace from the threat of a new world war.

24 October 1962

U.N., *Security Council Document S/5196*, October 26, 1962, pp. 1–3. (Letter addressed to the Acting Secretary General.)

❖ ❖ ❖ **60**

LETTER FROM CHAIRMAN KHRUSHCHEV TO PRESIDENT KENNEDY, *October 26, 1962*

(Not available)

❖ ❖ ❖ **61**

LETTER FROM ACTING SECRETARY GENERAL U THANT TO PRIME MINISTER FIDEL CASTRO, *October 26, 1692*

DEAR MR. AMBASSADOR,

I would be grateful if the enclosed message could urgently be transmitted to His Excellency Señor Fidel Castro.

Sincerely yours,

(s) U THANT

H.E. Sr. Mario García-Inchaustegui
Permanent Representative of Cuba to
the United Nations

Message to His Excellency Señor Fidel Castro,
Prime Minister of the Revolutionary Government of Cuba

I hope that Ambassador García-Inchaustegui has conveyed to Your Excellency the appeal that I addressed to you and to President Dorticos through him in the course of the statement I made before the Security Council on 24 October. I then recalled the following words of President Dorticos, uttered from the rostrum of the General Assembly on 8 October:

"Were the United States able to give us proof, by word and deed, that it would not carry out aggression against our country, then, we declare solemnly before you here and now, our weapons would be unnecessary and our army redundant."

I added that I believed it would also contribute greatly to finding a way out of the present impasse "if the construction and development of major military facilities and installations in Cuba could be suspended during the period of negotiations."

As Ambassador García may have reported to you I have received fairly encouraging responses to my appeal for negotiations and a peaceful solution of the problem from the President of the United States and from the Chairman of the Council of Ministers of the U.S.S.R. Your Excellency can make a significant contribution to the peace of the world at this present critical juncture by directing that the construction and development of major military facilities and installations in Cuba, and especially installations designed to launch medium-range and intermediate-range ballistic missiles, be suspended during the period of negotiations which are now under way,

It would encourage me greatly to have an affirmative reply to this appeal very urgently.

(s) U Thant
Acting Secretary General

U.N., *Press Release SG/1359*, October 27, 1962, pp. 1–2. (Letter dated October 26, 1962.)

✧ ✧ ✧ **62**

LETTER FROM PRIME MINISTER CASTRO
TO ACTING SECRETARY GENERAL U THANT,
October 27, 1962

YOUR EXCELLENCY,
On the instructions of the Revolutionary Government of Cuba I
have the honour to transmit to you the following message.

"Your Excellency,
I have received your message dated 26 October, and express my
appreciation of your noble concern.

Cuba is prepared to discuss as fully as may be necessary, its differences with the United States and to do everything in its powei, in
co-operation with the United Nations, to resolve the present crisis.
However, it flatly rejects the violation of the sovereignty of our
country involved in the naval blockade, an act of force and war committed by the United States against Cuba. In addition, it flatly
rejects the presumption of the United States to determine what actions
we are entitled to take within our country, what kind of arms we
consider appropriate for our defense, what relations we are to have
with the U.S.S.R., and what international policy steps we are entitled
to take, within the rules and laws governing relations between the
peoples of the world and the principles governing the United Nations,
in order to guarantee our own security and sovereignty.

Cuba is victimizing no one; it has violated no international law; on
the contrary, it is the victim of the aggressive acts of the United
States, such as the naval blockade, and its rights have been out-
raged.

The Revolutionary Government of Cuba would be prepared to
accept the compromises that you request as efforts in favour of peace,
provided that at the same time, while negotiations are in progress, the
United States Government desists from threats and aggressive actions
against Cuba, including the naval blockade of our country.

At the same time I express to you our willingness to consider
attentively any new suggestion you may put forward; furthermore,
should you consider it useful to the cause of peace, our Government
would be glad to receive you in our country, as Secretary General of
the United Nations, with a view to direct discussions on the present
crisis, prompted by our common purpose of freeing mankind from
the dangers of war.

Unreserved respect for the sovereignty of Cuba is the essential
prerequisite if Cuba is to contribute with the greatest sincerity and

goodwill, grudging no step towards the solution of the present problem, and joining forces with all those people who are struggling to save peace at this dramatic moment in the life of mankind; Cuba can do whatever is asked of it, except undertake to be a victim and to renounce the rights which belong to every sovereign State.

I reiterate the assurances of my highest consideration.

Major Fidel Castro Ruz
Prime Minister of the Revolutionary Government of Cuba."

Accept, Your Excellency, the assurance of my highest consideration.

(s) Dr. Mario García-Inchaustegui
Ambassador
Permanent Representative of Cuba
to the United Nations

U.N., *Press Release SG/1359*, October 27, 1962, pp. 2–3.

❖ ❖ ❖ **63**

LETTER FROM CHAIRMAN KHRUSHCHEV TO PRESIDENT KENNEDY, *October 27, 1962*

DEAR MR. PRESIDENT:

It is with great satisfaction that I studied your reply to Mr. U Thant on the adoption of measures in order to avoid contact by our ships and thus avoid irreparable fatal consequences. This reasonable step on your part persuades me that you are showing solicitude for the preservation of peace, and I note this with satisfaction.

I have already said that the only concern of our people and government and myself personally as chairman of the Council of Ministers is to develop our country and have it hold a worthy place among all people of the world in economic competition, advance of culture and arts, and the rise in people's living standards. This is the loftiest and most necessary field for competition which will only benefit both the winner and loser, because this benefit is peace and an increase in the facilities by means of which man lives and obtains pleasure.

In your statement, you said that the main aim lies not only in reaching agreement and adopting measures to avert contact of our ships, and, consequently, a deepening of the crisis, which because of this contact can spark off the fire of military conflict after which any talks would be superfluous because other forces and other laws would begin to operate — the laws of war. I agree with you that this is only a first step. The main thing is to normalize and stabilize the situation in the world between states and between people.

I understand your concern for the security of the United States, Mr. President, because this is the first duty of the president. However, these questions are also uppermost in our minds. The same duties rest with me as chairman of the U.S.S.R. Council of Ministers. You have been worried over our assisting Cuba with arms designed to strengthen its defensive potential — precisely defensive potential — because Cuba, no matter what weapons it had, could not compare with you since these are different dimensions, the more so given up-to-date means of extermination.

Our purpose has been and is to help Cuba, and no one can challenge the humanity of our motives aimed at allowing Cuba to live peacefully and develop as its people desire. You want to relieve your country from danger and this is understandable. However, Cuba also wants this. All countries want to relieve themselves from danger. But how can we, the Soviet Union and our government, assess your actions which, in effect, mean that you have surrounded the Soviet Union with military bases, surrounded our allies with military bases, set up military bases literally around our country, and stationed your rocket weapons at them? This is no secret. High-placed American officials demonstratively declare this. Your rockets are stationed in Britain and in Italy and pointed at us. Your rockets are stationed in Turkey.

You are worried over Cuba. You say that it worries you because it lies at a distance of ninety miles across the sea from the shores of the United States. However, Turkey lies next to us. Our sentinels are pacing up and down and watching each other. Do you believe that you have the right to demand security for your country and the removal of such weapons that you qualify as offensive, while not recognizing this right for us?

You have stationed devastating rocket weapons, which you call offensive, in Turkey literally right next to us. How then does recognition of our equal military possibilities tally with such unequal relations between our great states? This does not tally at all.

It is good, Mr. President, that you agreed for our representatives to meet and begin talks, apparently with the participation of U.N. Acting Secretary General U Thant. Consequently, to some extent, he assumes the role of intermediary, and we believe that he can cope with the responsible mission if, of course, every side that is drawn into this conflict shows good will.

I think that one could rapidly eliminate the conflict and normalize the situation. Then people would heave a sigh of relief, considering that the statesmen who bear the responsibility have sober minds, an awareness of their responsibility, and an ability to solve complicated problems and not allow matters to slide to the disaster of war.

This is why I make this proposal: We agree to remove those

weapons from Cuba which you regard as offensive weapons. We agree to do this and to state this commitment in the United Nations. Your representatives will make a statement to the effect that the United States, on its part, bearing in mind the anxiety and concern of the Soviet state, will evacuate its analogous weapons from Turkey. Let us reach an understanding on what time you and we need to put this into effect.

After this, representatives of the U.N. Security Council could control on-the-spot the fulfillment of these commitments. Of course, it is necessary that the Governments of Cuba and Turkey would allow these representatives to come to their countries and check fulfillment of this commitment, which each side undertakes. Apparently, it would be better if these representatives enjoyed the trust of the Security Council and ours — the United States and the Soviet Union — as well as of Turkey and Cuba. I think that it will not be difficult to find such people who enjoy the trust and respect of all interested sides.

We, having assumed this commitment in order to give satisfaction and hope to the peoples of Cuba and Turkey and to increase their confidence in their security, will make a statement in the Security Council to the effect that the Soviet Government gives a solemn pledge to respect the integrity of the frontiers and the sovereignty of Turkey, not to intervene in its domestic affairs, not to invade Turkey, not to make available its territory as a *place d'armes* for such invasion, and also will restrain those who would think of launching an aggression against Turkey either from Soviet territory or from the territory of other states bordering on Turkey.

The U.S. Government will make the same statement in the Security Council with regard to Cuba. It will declare that the United States will respect the integrity of the frontiers of Cuba, its sovereignty, undertakes not to intervene in its domestic affairs, not to invade and not to make its territory available as [a] *place d'armes* for the invasion of Cuba, and also will restrain those who would think of launching an aggression against Cuba either from U.S. territory or from the territory of other states bordering on Cuba.

Of course, for this we would have to reach agreement with you and to arrange for some deadline. Let us agree to give some time, but not to delay, two or three weeks, not more than a month.

The weapons on Cuba, that you have mentioned and which, as you say, alarm you, are in the hands of Soviet officers. Therefore any accidental use of them whatsoever to the detriment of the United States of America is excluded. These means are stationed in Cuba at the request of the Cuban Government and only in defensive aims. Therefore, if there is no invasion of Cuba, or an attack on the Soviet Union, or other of our allies then, of course, these means do not threaten anyone and will not threaten. For they do not pursue offensive aims.

If you accept my proposal, Mr. President, we would send our representatives to New York, to the United Nations, and would give them exhaustive instructions in order to come to terms sooner. If you would also appoint your men and give them appropriate instructions, this problem could be solved soon.

Why would I like to achieve this? Because the entire world is now agitated and expects reasonable actions from us. The greatest pleasure for all the peoples would be an announcement on our agreement, on nipping in the bud the conflict that has arisen. I attach a great importance to such understanding because it might be a good beginning and, specifically, facilitate a nuclear test ban agreement. The problem of tests could be solved simultaneously, not linking one with the other, because they are different problems. However, it is important to reach an understanding to both these problems in order to make a good gift to the people, to let them rejoice in the news that a nuclear test ban agreement has also been reached and thus there will be no further contamination of the atmosphere. Your and our positions on this issue are very close.

All this, possibly, would serve as a good impetus to searching for mutually acceptable agreements on other disputed issues, too, on which there is an exchange of opinion between us. These problems have not yet been solved, but they wait for an urgent solution which would clear the international atmosphere. We are ready for this.

These are my proposals, Mr. President.

Respectfully yours,

(s) NIKITA KHRUSHCHEV

U.S., Department of State, *Bulletin,* Volume XLVII, No. 1220 (November 12, 1962), pp. 741–743. (Unofficial translation.)

❖ ❖ ❖ **64**

WHITE HOUSE STATEMENT ON SOVIET PROPOSALS, *October 27, 1962*

Several inconsistent and conflicting proposals have been made by the U.S.S.R. within the last twenty-four hours, including the one just made public in Moscow. The proposal broadcast this morning involves the security of nations outside the Western Hemisphere. But it is the Western Hemisphere countries and they alone that are subject to the threat that has produced the current crisis — the action of the Soviet Government in secretly introducing offensive weapons into Cuba. Work on these offensive weapons is still proceeding at a rapid pace. The first imperative must be to deal with this immediate threat, under which no sensible negotiations can proceed.

It is therefore the position of the United States that as an urgent preliminary to consideration of any proposals work on the Cuban bases must stop; offensive weapons must be rendered inoperable, and further shipment of offensive weapons to Cuba must cease — all under effective international verification.

As to proposals concerning the security of nations outside this hemisphere, the United States and its allies have long taken the lead in seeking properly inspected arms limitation, on both sides. These efforts can continue as soon as the present Soviet-created threat is ended.

U.S., Department of State, *Bulletin,* Volume XLVII, No. 1220 (November 12, 1962), p. 741. (White House press release dated October 27, 1962.)

❖ ❖ ❖ **65** .

LETTER FROM PRESIDENT KENNEDY TO CHAIRMAN KHRUSHCHEV, *October 27, 1962*

I have read your letter of October 26th with great care and welcomed the statement of your desire to seek a prompt solution to the problem. The first thing that needs to be done, however, is for work to cease on offensive missile bases in Cuba and for all weapons systems in Cuba capable of offensive use to be rendered inoperable, under effective United Nations arrangements.

Assuming this is done promptly, I have given my representatives in New York instructions that will permit them to work out this weekend — in cooperation with the Acting Secretary General and your representative — an arrangement for a permanent solution to the Cuban problem along the lines suggested in your letter of October 26th. As I read your letter, the key elements of your proposals — which seem generally acceptable as I understand them — are as follows:

1) You would agree to remove these weapons systems from Cuba under appropriate United Nations observation and supervision; and undertake, with suitable safeguards, to halt the further introduction of such weapons systems into Cuba.

2) We, on our part, would agree — upon the establishment of

adequate arrangements through the United Nations to ensure the carrying out and continuation of these commitments — (a) to remove promptly the quarantine measures now in effect and (b) to give assurances against an invasion of Cuba. I am confident that other nations of the Western Hemisphere would be prepared to do likewise.

If you will give your representative similar instructions, there is no reason why we should not be able to complete these arrangements and announce them to the world within a couple of days. The effect of such a settlement on easing world tensions would enable us to work toward a more general arrangement regarding "other armaments," as proposed in your second letter which you made public. I would like to say again that the United States is very much interested in reducing tensions and halting the arms race; and if your letter signifies that you are prepared to discuss a detente affecting NATO and the Warsaw Pact, we are quite prepared to consider with our allies any useful proposals.

But the first ingredient, let me emphasize, is the cessation of work on missile sites in Cuba and measures to render such weapons inoperable, under effective international guarantees. The continuation of this threat, or a prolonging of this discussion concerning Cuba by linking these problems to the broader questions of European and world security, would surely lead to an intensified situation on the Cuban crisis and a grave risk to the peace of the world. For this reason I hope we can quickly agree along the lines outlined in this letter and in your letter of October 26th.

(s) JOHN F. KENNEDY

U.S., Department of State, *Bulletin,* Volume XLVII, No. 1220 (November 12, 1962), p. 743. (White House press release dated October 27, 1962.)

❖ ❖ ❖ **66**

U.S. ANNOUNCEMENT ON TRANSITING WATERS IN VICINITY OF CUBA, *October 27, 1962*

The Department of State announced on October 27 the institution of a system of clearances to assist vessels which transit waters in the vicinity of Cuba and vessels destined for Cuban ports with cargoes containing no offensive weapons or associated materials.

The system, developed by the State, Defense, and Treasury Departments, is designed to avoid unnecessary delays and other difficulties to vessels arising out of the stoppage, inspection, or possible diversion of ships.

The system is for the convenience of shipping, and clearances are obtainable upon application by ships' owners, agents, or officers.

A vessel departing a United States port may obtain a special clearance from customs authorities at the port of departure. A vessel departing a foreign port may obtain the clearance from an American consulate.

The system covers two types of clearances. With respect to vessels departing American ports, whether destined for a Cuban port or merely transiting waters in the vicinity of Cuba, a Clearance Certificate (CLEARCERT) is obtainable from United States customs authorities.

With respect to vessels departing foreign ports, those which only transit waters in the vicinity of Cuba may file a Notice of Transit with the American consulate at the last port of departure; those destined for a Cuban port with a cargo containing no offensive weapons or other prohibited materiel may obtain a Clearance Certificate (CLEARCERT) from the American consulate at the last port of departure. In unusual circumstances it may be necessary to stop, inspect, or divert a ship despite the fact that it has a clearance.

U.S., Department of State, *Bulletin,* Volume XLVII, No. 1220 (November 12, 1962), p. 747. (Press release 644 dated October 27, 1962.)

✧ ✧ ✧ **67**

LETTER FROM CHAIRMAN KHRUSHCHEV TO PRESIDENT KENNEDY, *October 28, 1962*

DEAR MR. PRESIDENT:

I have received your message of 27 October. I express my satisfaction and thank you for the sense of proportion you have displayed and for realization of the responsibility which now devolves on you for the preservation of the peace of the world.

I regard with great understanding your concern and the concern of the United States people in connection with the fact that the weapons you describe as offensive are formidable weapons indeed. Both you and we understand what kind of weapons these are.

In order to eliminate as rapidly as possible the conflict which endangers the cause of peace, to give an assurance to all people who crave peace, and to reassure the American people, all of whom, I am certain, also want peace, as do the people of the Soviet Union, the Soviet Government, in addition to earlier instructions on the discontinuation of further work on weapons constructions sites, has given a new order to dismantle the arms which you described as offensive, and to crate and return them to the Soviet Union.

Mr. President, I should like to repeat what I had already written to you in my earlier messages — that the Soviet Government has given economic assistance to the Republic of Cuba, as well as arms, because Cuba and the Cuban people were constantly under the continuous threat of an invasion of Cuba.

A piratic vessel had shelled Havana. They say that this shelling was done by irresponsible Cuban *émigrés*. Perhaps so. However, the question is from where did they shoot. It is a fact that these Cubans have no territory, they are fugitives from their country, and they have no means to conduct military operations.

This means that someone put into their hands these weapons for shelling Havana and for piracy in the Caribbean in Cuban territorial waters. It is impossible in our time not to notice a piratic ship, considering the concentration in the Caribbean of American ships from which everything can be seen and observed.

In these conditions, pirate ships freely roam around and shell Cuba and make piratic attacks on peaceful cargo ships. It is known that they even shelled a British cargo ship. In a word, Cuba was under the continuous threat of aggressive forces, which did not conceal their intention to invade its territory.

The Cuban people want to build their life in their own interests without external interference. This is their right, and they cannot be blamed for wanting to be masters of their own country and disposing of the fruits of their own labor. The threat of invasion of Cuba and all other schemes for creating tension over China are designed to strike the Cuban people with a sense of insecurity, intimidate them, and prevent them from peacefully building their new life.

Mr. President, I should like to say clearly once more that we could not remain indifferent to this. The Soviet Government decided to render assistance to Cuba with means of defense against aggression — only with means for defense purposes. We have supplied the defense means which you describe as offensive means. We have supplied them to prevent an attack on Cuba — to prevent rash acts.

I regard with respect and trust the statement you made in your message of 27 October 1962 that there would be no attack, no invasion of Cuba, and not only on the part of the United States, but also on the part of other nations of the Western Hemisphere, as you said in your same message. Then the motives which induced us to render assistance of such a kind to Cuba disappear.

It is for this reason that we instructed our officers — these means as I had already informed you earlier are in the hands of the Soviet officers — to take appropriate measures to discontinue construction of the aforementioned facilities, to dismantle them, and to return them to the Soviet Union. As I had informed you in the letter of 27 October, we are prepared to reach agreement to enable U.N. representatives to verify the dismantling of these means. Thus in view of the assurances you have given and our instructions on dismantling, there is every condition for eliminating the present conflict.

I note with satisfaction that you have responded to the desire I expressed with regard to elimination of the aforementioned dangerous situation as well as with regard to providing conditions for a more thoughtful appraisal of the international situation, fraught as it is with great dangers in our age of thermonuclear weapons, rocketry, spaceships, global rockets, and other deadly weapons. All people are interested in insuring peace.

Therefore, vested with trust and great responsibility, we must not allow the situation to become aggravated and must stamp out the centers where a dangerous situation fraught with grave consequences to the cause of peace has arisen. If we, together with you, and with the assistance of other people of good will, succeed in eliminating this tense atmosphere, we should also make certain that no other dangerous conflicts, which could lead to a world nuclear catastrophe, would arise.

In conclusion, I should like to say something about a detente between NATO and the Warsaw Treaty countries that you have mentioned. We have spoken about this long since and are prepared to continue to exchange views on this question with you and to find a reasonable solution.

We should like to continue the exchange of views on the prohibition of atomic and thermonuclear weapons, general disarmament, and other problems relating to the relaxation of international tension.

Although I trust your statement, Mr. President, there are irresponsible people who would like to invade Cuba now and thus touch off a war. If we do take practical steps and proclaim the dismantling and evacuation of the means in question from Cuba, in so doing we, at the same time, want the Cuban people to be certain that we are with them and are not absolving ourselves of responsibility for rendering assistance to the Cuban people.

We are confident that the people of all countries, like you, Mr. President, will understand me correctly. We are not threatening. We want nothing but peace. Our country is now on the upsurge. Our people are enjoying the fruits of their peaceful labor. They have achieved tremendous successes since the October Revolution, and created the greatest material, spiritual, and cultural values. Our people are enjoying these values; they want to continue developing their achievements and insure their further development on the way of peace and social progress by their persistent labor.

I should like to remind you, Mr. President, that military reconnaissance planes have violated the borders of the Soviet Union. In connection with this there have been conflicts between us and notes exchanged. In 1960 we shot down your U-2 plane, whose reconnaissance flight over the U.S.S.R. wrecked the summit meeting in Paris. At that time, you took a correct position and denounced that criminal act of the former U[nited] S[tates] administration.

But during your term of office as president another violation of our border has occurred, by an American U–2 plane in the Sakhalin area. We wrote you about that violation on 30 August. At that time you replied that that violation had occurred as a result of poor weather, and gave assurances that this would not be repeated. We trusted your assurance, because the weather was indeed poor in that area at that time.

But had not your plane been ordered to fly about our territory, even poor weather could not have brought an American plane into our airspace, hence, the conclusion that this is being done with the knowledge of the Pentagon, which tramples on international norms and violates the borders of other states.

A still more dangerous case occurred on 28 October, when one of your reconnaissance planes intruded over Soviet borders in the Chukotka Peninsula area in the north and flew over our territory. The question is, Mr. President: How should we regard this? What is this, a provocation? One of your planes violates our frontier during this anxious time we are both experiencing, when everything has been put into combat readiness. Is it not a fact than an intruding American plane could be easily taken for a nuclear bomber, which might push us to a fateful step; and all the more so since the U[nited] S[tates] Government and Pentagon long ago declared that you are maintaining a continuous nuclear bomber patrol?

Therefore, you can imagine the responsibility you are assuming; especially now, when we are living through such anxious times.

I should like also to express the following wish; it concerns the Cuban people. You do not have diplomatic relations. But through my officers in Cuba, I have reports that American planes are making flights over Cuba.

We are interested that there should be no war in the world, and that the Cuban people should live in peace. And besides, Mr. President, it is no secret that we have our people on Cuba. Under a treaty with the Cuban Government we have sent there officers, instructors, mostly plain people: specialists, agronomists, zootechnicians, irrigators, land reclamation specialists, plain workers, tractor drivers, and others. We are concerned about them.

I should like you to consider, Mr. President, that violation of Cuban airspace by American planes could also lead to dangerous consequences. And if you do not want this to happen, it would be better if no cause is given for a dangerous situation to arise. We must be careful now and refrain from any steps which would not be useful to the defense of the states involved in the conflict, which could only cause irritation and even serve as a provocation for a fateful step. Therefore, we must display sanity, reason, and refrain from such steps.

We value peace perhaps even more than other peoples because we went through a terrible war with Hitler. But our people will not falter in the face of any test. Our people trust their government, and we assure our people and world public opinion that the Soviet Government will not allow itself to be provoked. But if the provocateurs unleash a war, they will not evade responsibility and the grave consequences a war would bring upon them. But we are confident that reason will triumph, that war will not be unleashed, and peace and the security of the peoples will be insured.

In connection with the current negotiations between Acting Secretary General U Thant and representatives of the Soviet Union, the United States, and the Republic of Cuba, the Soviet Government has sent First Deputy Foreign Minister V. V. Kuznetsov to New York to help U Thant in his noble efforts aimed at eliminating the present dangerous situation.

Respectfully yours,

(s) N. KHRUSHCHEV

U.S., Department of State, *Bulletin*, Volume XLVII, No. 1220 (November 12, 1962), pp. 743–745. (Unofficial translation.)

✧ ✧ ✧ **68**

STATEMENT BY PRESIDENT KENNEDY ON RECEIPT OF CHAIRMAN KHRUSHCHEV'S LETTER, *October 28, 1962*

I welcome Chairman Khrushchev's statesmanlike decision to stop building bases in Cuba, dismantling offensive weapons and returning them to the Sovet Union under United Nations verification. This is an important and constructive contribution to peace.

We shall be in touch with the Secretary General of the United Nations with respect to reciprocal measures to assure peace in the Caribbean area.

It is my earnest hope that the governments of the world can, with a solution of the Cuban crisis, turn their urgent attention to the compelling necessity for ending the arms race and reducing world tensions. This applies to the military confrontation between the Warsaw Pact and NATO countries as well as to other situatons in other parts of the world where tensions lead to the wasteful diversion of resources to weapons of war.

U.S., Department of State, *Bulletin*, Volume XLVII, No. 1220 (November 12, 1962), p. 745. (White House press release dated October 20, 1962.)

✧ ✧ ✧ **69**

LETTER FROM PRESIDENT KENNEDY TO CHAIRMAN KHRUSHCHEV, *October 28, 1962*

DEAR MR. CHAIRMAN:

I am replying at once to your broadcast message of October twenty-eight, even though the official text has not yet reached me, because of the great importance I attach to moving forward promptly to the settlement of the Cuban crisis. I think that you and I, with our heavy responsibilities for the maintenance of peace, were aware that developments were approaching a point where events could have become unmanageable. So I welcome this message and consider it an important contribution to peace.

The distinguished efforts of Acting Secretary General U Thant have greatly facilitated both our tasks. I consider my letter to you of October twenty-seventh and your reply of today as firm undertakings on the part of both governments which should be promptly carried out. I hope that the necessary measures can at once be taken through the United Nations, as your message says, so that the United States in turn will be able to remove the quarantine measures now in effect. I have already made arrangements to report all these matters to the Organization of American States, whose members share a deep interest in a genuine peace in the Caribbean area.

You referred in your letter to a violation of your frontier by an American aircraft in the area of the Chukotsk Peninsula. I have learned that this plane, without arms or photographic equipment, was engaged in an air-sampling mission in connection with your nuclear tests. Its course was direct from Eielson Air Force Base in Alaska to the North Pole and return. In turning south, the pilot made a serious navigational error which carried him over Soviet territory. He immediately made an emergency call on open radio for navigational assistance and was guided back to his home base by the most direct route. I regret this incident and will see to it that every precaution is taken to prevent recurrence.

Mr. Chairman, both of our countries have great unfinished tasks and I know that your people as well as those of the United States can ask for nothing better than to pursue them free from the fear of war.

Modern science and technology have given us the possibility of making labor fruitful beyond anything that could have been dreamed of a few decades ago.

I agree with you that we must devote urgent attention to the problem of disarmament, as it relates to the whole world and also to critical areas. Perhaps now, as we step back from danger, we can together make real progress in this vital field. I think we should give priority to questions relating to the proliferation of nuclear weapons, on earth and in outer space, and to the great effort for a nuclear test ban. But we should also work hard to see if wider measures of disarmament can be agreed and put into operation at an early date. The United States government will be prepared to discuss these questions urgently, and in a constructive spirit, at Geneva or elsewhere.

(s) JOHN F. KENNEDY

U.S., Department of State, *Bulletin,* Volume XLVII, No. 1220 (November 12, 1962), pp. 745–746. (White House press release dated October 28, 1962.)

❖ ❖ ❖ **70**

LETTER FROM CHAIRMAN KHRUSHCHEV TO
ACTING SECRETARY GENERAL U THANT,
October 28, 1962

DEAR MR. U THANT:

I am forwarding to you a copy of the message I sent today to the President of the United States, Mr. J. Kennedy, in order to enable you to familiarize yourself with our position, which we regard as exhaustive and which will help you to discharge your noble functions.

In connection with the negotiations you are conducting now with representatives of the Soviet Union, the United States of America and the Cuban Republic, the Soviet Government has sent to New York the First Deputy Foreign Minister of the U.S.S.R., V. V. Kuznetsov, to help you in your efforts aimed at eliminating the present dangerous situation.

Respectfully yours,

(s) N. KHRUSHCHEV

The New York Times, October 29, 1962, p. 16. Copyright by The New York Times. Reprinted by permission.

❖ ❖ ❖ **71**

LETTER FROM ACTING SECRETARY GENERAL U THANT TO CHAIRMAN KHRUSHCHEV, *October 28, 1962*

DEAR MR. AMBASSADOR,

I shall be grateful if you would be so good as to transmit the following message to Chairman Khrushchev:

"I wish to express my deep gratitude to Your Excellency for sending me a copy of your message to President Kennedy dated 28 October, in reply to President Kennedy's letter to Your Excellency of 27 October.

I note the constructive proposals you have made in order to remove tension in the Caribbean area. I believe that when these proposals are implemented the situation in the Caribbean area will be normalized.

I would like to inform Your Excellency that I have accepted an invitation extended to me by Prime Minister Fidel Castro on behalf of the Revolutionary Government of Cuba to visit his country. I feel that at the present time such a visit could contribute to the peaceful solution of the problem. As I stated in my letter to Premier Castro, the result of my discussions with him could lead to a solution 'by which the principle of respect for the sovereignty of Cuba would be assured, and it may also be possible for action to be taken which would reassure those countries which have felt themselves threatened by recent developments in Cuba.'

I am particularly gratified to note that you have already instructed your officers to take the necessary measures to stop the building of missile bases, to dismantle them, and to return the missiles to the Soviet Union, and that you are ready to come to an agreement that representatives of the United Nations may verify the dismantling of these bases.

I am also happy to note that the Soviet Government has sent to New York the First Deputy-Minister for Foreign Affairs of the U.S.S.R., Mr. Kuznetzov, with a view to assisting me in my efforts. Mr. Kuznetzov is an old and valued friend, and I look forward very much to exchanging views with him as soon as he arrives. I shall discuss with Mr. Kuznetzov, as well as with Premier Castro, the modalities of verification by United Nations Observers to which you have so readily agreed, and I hope that I shall be able to reach a satisfactory understanding with them.

168

I am convinced that, with the spirit of co-operation and concern for peace that you have shown, the outcome of these discussions will be successful and satisfactory to all the parties concerned."

Yours sincerely,

(s) U Thant
Acting Secretary General

His Excellency Mr. V. A. Zorin
Ambassador Extraordinary and Plenipotentiary
Permanent Representative of the Union of Soviet
   Socialist Republics to the United Nations
136 East 67th Street
New York 21, N.Y.

U.N., *Press Release SG/1363*, October 29, 1962, pp. 1–2.

❖ ❖ ❖ **72**

LETTER FROM PRIME MINISTER CASTRO TO ACTING SECRETARY GENERAL U THANT, *October 28, 1962*

SIR,
   On the instructions of the Revolutionary Government of Cuba, I have the honour to convey to you the following message:

"U Thant,
Acting Secretary General of the United Nations
   With reference to the statement made by Mr. John F. Kennedy, President of the United States, in a letter addressed to Mr. Nikita Khrushchev, Chairman of the Council of Ministers of the U S S R., to the effect that the United States would agree, after suitable arrangements had been made through the United Nations, to remove the blockade now in effect and to give guarantees against an invasion of Cuba, and with reference to the decision, announced by Mr. Nikita Khrushchev, to withdraw strategic defence weapons facilities from Cuban territory, the Revolutionary Government of Cuba wishes to make the following statement:
   The guarantees mentioned by President Kennedy that there will be no aggression against Cuba will be ineffective unless, in addition to the removal of the naval blockade which he promises, the following measures, *inter alia,* are adopted:

1. Cessation of the economic blockade and of all the measures of commercial and economic pressure being carried out by the United States against our country throughout the world.

2. Cessation of all subversive activities, of the dropping and landing of weapons and explosives by air and sea, of the organization of invasions by mercenaries, and of the infiltration of spies and saboteurs — all of which activities are being carried on from the territory of the United States and certain accomplice countries.

3. Cessation of the piratical attacks being carried out from bases in the United States and Puerto Rico.

4. Cessation of all violations of our air space and territorial waters by United States aircraft and warships.

5. Withdrawal of the naval base of Guantanamo and return of the Cuban territory occupied by the United States.

Accept, Sir, the assurance of my highest consideration."

(s) MAJOR FIDEL CASTRO RUZ
*Prime Minister of the Revolutionary
Government of Cuba.*

I request you to have the text of this note circulated as an official document of the General Assembly.

Accept, Sir, etc.

(s) MARIO GARCÍA-INCHAUSTEGUI
*Ambassador
Permanent Representative of Cuba
to the United Nations*

U.N., *General Assembly Document A/5271*, October 29, 1962, pp. 1–2.

✧ ✧ ✧ **73**

LETTER FROM ACTING SECRETARY GENERAL U THANT TO PRIME MINISTER CASTRO, *October 28, 1962*

DEAR MR. AMBASSADOR,

I shall be grateful if you would convey the following message to Prime Minister Fidel Castro:

"Your Excellency,

I have received with much gratitude and deep appreciation your kind letter of 27 October. I am particularly pleased to note that the Revolutionary Government of Cuba is prepared to accept the suggestion that I made as an effort in favour of peace, provided that, at the same time, while negotiations are in progress, the United States Government 'desists from threats and aggressive acts against Cuba including the naval blockade of your country.'

I am also glad to note your willingness to consider any new suggestion that may be put forward. I am deeply sensible to the honour that your Government has done me in inviting me, as Secretary General of the United Nations, to visit Cuba with a view to having direct discussions on the present crisis, prompted by our common concern to free mankind from the dangers of war.

I have much pleasure in accepting your invitation. I hope to be able to leave early next week. I hope to bring a few Aides with me and to leave some of them behind to continue our common effort towards the peaceful solution of the problem.

I also note and appreciate your feeling that the unreserved respect for the sovereignty of Cuba is an essential pre-requisite to any solution of the problem.

I would very much hope that it might be possible for me to discuss with you all important aspects of the problem. It would be my hope that as a result of these discussions, a solution would be reached by which the principle of respect for the sovereignty of Cuba would be assured, and it may also be possible for action to be taken which would reassure other countries which have felt themselves threatened by recent developments in Cuba."

Yours sincerely,

(s) U THANT

His Excellency Sr. Mario García-Inchaustegui
Ambassador Extraordinary and Plenipotentiary
Permanent Representative of Cuba to the
    United Nations
155 East 44th Street, 31st Floor
New York 17, New York

U.N., *Press Release SG/1360,* October 28, 1962, p. 1. (Letter dated October 28, 1962.)

❖ ❖ ❖ **74**

LETTER FROM O.A.S. SECRETARY GENERAL
JOSÉ A. MORA TO U.N. ACTING SECRETARY
GENERAL U THANT, *October 29, 1962*

In accordance with Article 54 of the Charter of the United Nations, I have the honour to inform you that up to this date and in compliance with the resolution approved on 23 October 1962 by the Council of the Organization acting provisionally as Organ of Consultation the Governments of Argentina, Colombia, Costa Rica, the Dominican Republic, Guatemala, Haiti, Honduras, Panama, and the United States of America have sent notes which I take pleasure in attaching to this letter and in which those Governments offer the co-operation of air and naval forces, port facilities, and other installations needed to carry out the collective action contemplated in the Inter-American Treaty of Reciprocal Assistance.

I should like to add with regard to this matter that I have received information to the effect that the Governments of other Member States of the Organization are about to communicate similar offers.

Accept, etc.

(s) Jose A. Mora
Secretary General

U.N., *Security Council Document S/5202*, November 1, 1962, p. 1. (Letter dated October 29, 1962.)

❖ ❖ ❖ **75**

STATEMENT BY PRESIDENT JOSIP BROZ TITO OF
YUGOSLAVIA, *October 30, 1962*

I have the honour to transmit herewith a message addressed to you by the President of the Federal People's Republic of Yugoslavia, Josip Broz Tito.

I should appreciate it if you would kindly bring the message to the immediate notice of the Member States of the United Nations, in accordance with the usual procedure, as a United Nations document.

Please accept, etc.

(s) VLADIMIR POPOVIC
Chairman of the Yugoslav Delegation to
the Seventeenth Session of the United
Nations General Assembly

Belgrade, 30 October 1962

It gives me sincere pleasure to address myself to you at a time when you are carrying out with a success which encourages us the noble task you have been entrusted with by the United Nations. The decision of the Government of the Union of Soviet Socialist Republics to dismantle the missile sites in Cuba, and the declared readiness of the United States to offer, in these conditions, guarantees through the United Nations for the independence and sovereignty of Cuba, signify a substantial turn for the better in this acute crisis. Important preconditions have, at the same time, thus been created, owing to the fact that reason prevailed in the final phase, for the successful initiation of direct negotiations between the countries involved in the dispute, and these will, we believe and sincerely hope, lead, with your continued assistance, to the ending of this crisis, which threatened to entail the most serious consequences and caused grave misgivings in our country and throughout the world.

The main purpose which should, in our opinion, now be achieved is to ensure the rapid implementation of all that had been agreed to in principle. This is necessary because it is only thereby that the situation will move towards normalization. Your visit to Cuba will undoubtedly contribute much towards this end. It is obvious that the situation must be considered as still dangerous while the blockade lasts, and also until the dismantling of the sites I have mentioned has begun, and even after that. All the more so as the question of ensuring the independence of Cuba and of preventing interference in her independent development had arisen, as you are certainly aware, even prior to recent events. It is therefore obvious that an essential element of the understanding that has been reached and of its implementation is an effective international guarantee to the security, the independence, the sovereignty and the integrity of Cuba, in accordance with the principles of the United Nations Charter, and this should be accepted by all countries, including, naturally, the Government of the United States. Cuba, too, would thus be ensured the essential conditions for participating in international relations on a footing of equality. The negotiations for the termination of the crisis would thus lead to the results we all expect, i.e., they would constitute a direct introduction into a more lasting settlement of relations and a stabilization of conditions in the area around Cuba.

A further contribution to peace in the area would be settlements which would guarantee the legitimate interests and rights of all the countries situated therein. What I have in mind here are, above all, the significant ideas and proposals put forth by the Government of Brazil in this sense.

I think, however, that we would all be remiss in our duty if we did not, on this occasion, when the very maintenance of peace has been brought into jeopardy, seek to perceive the more profound causes which led to so serious a situation, and if we failed to do our utmost to render impossible the occurrence of new crises through a gradual elimination of these causes. It is a fact that the unsatisfactory state of international relations and, above all, the tension between the blocs and the nature of the relations between the great Powers, all of which are closely linked with the constant aggravation of the armaments race, and more particularly of the nuclear weapons tests, rank foremost among these causes. It seems to me, therefore, that one of the main tasks should now be an increased general effort towards their removal. All the more so as this is a course which has already been clearly indicated at the present session of the General Assembly of the United Nations, and the Cuban crisis has shown that things should not be allowed to run the way they have been doing, merely because no formal agreement has yet been achieved on ending this dangerous trend of affairs. What I have in mind here is the fact that, for instance, amidst the Cuban crisis, behind its screen, so to speak, the nuclear weapons tests continued, not to mention the other acute problems which are also awaiting, or rather demanding, particularly in the light of the Cuban crisis, their urgent solution.

It is in this spirit and from this viewpoint that we have been following, from the outset, with keen interest and understanding your noble action and give it our full support. I wish to assure you that we shall continue to do so in the same spirit so as to ensure the desired and so essential success of this action.

Yours very sincerely,

(s) Josip Broz Tito

U.N., *Security Council Document S/5200*, October 31, 1962, pp. 1–3. (Letter addressed to the Acting Secretary General.)

✧ ✧ ✧ 76

STATEMENT BY ACTING SECRETARY GENERAL
U THANT ON RETURN FROM CUBA, *October 31, 1962*

I return from Havana after fruitful discussions with the leaders of Cuba. These discussions were conducted strictly in the context of my correspondence with Premier Fidel Castro, resulting from the proceedings of the Security Council meetings. There was agreement that the United Nations should continue to participate in the peaceful settlement of the problem.

During my stay in Havana I was reliably informed that the dismantling of the missiles and their installations was already in progress, and that the process should be completed by Friday. Thereafter there would come their shipment and return to the Soviet Union, arrangements for which are understood to be in hand.

One brief word. At my request the Cuban Government has agreed to return, on humanitarian grounds, the body of Maj. [Rudolf] Anderson [Jr.] to the United States.

✧ ✧ ✧ 77

STATEMENT BY FIRST DEPUTY PREMIER
ANASTAS I. MIKOYAN ON LEAVING NEW YORK
FOR CUBA, *November 2, 1962*

Yesterday, after we had arrived in New York, we called on U.N. Acting Secretary General U Thant and had a long conversation with him, during which we touched upon matters concerning the normalization of the situation in the Caribbean in the interests of strengthening the countries of this region.

We have agreed with U Thant that the conversation was a useful one. At the dinner last night, we had Mr. [John J.] McCloy and Mr. [Adlai E.] Stevenson, with whom we were exchanging views as to

how we could sooner and better implement the provisions contained
in the messages of Chairman N. S. Khrushchev and President J. F.
Kennedy on the elimination of the dangerous situation and the normalization in the Caribbean, and in the proposals of Premier Fidel
Castro, which comprise five well-known points.

These proposals of the Revolutionary Government of Cuba, aimed
at insuring the security of Cuba, are supported by the Soviet Union,
which considers them just.

It is with great pleasure that I am looking forward to coming to
the friendly Cuba where I already was in February, 1960, and saw
tremendous enthusiasm and unity of all working people of the Republic of Cuba headed by the hero of the Cuban people, Fidel Castro.

I have heard that the American press and radio, and in particular,
today's newspapers, venture absolutely groundless guesses and fan-
tasies about the purpose of my visit to Cuba.

I am going there for a friendly exchange of views with our close
friend, Premier Fidel Castro, on questions of the international situation.

When in Havana, I have met with the world-known American
writer, the late Ernest Hemingway, whose books are widely read in
the Soviet Union. He was a great American, and he once said to me
great words about Cuba: "I can say one thing with firm belief — as a
result of the revolution, Cuba has for the first time an honest government."

The Revolutionary Government of Cuba is enjoying complete confidence of the people. It threatens no one. It leads the people to
progress and happiness, building socialism, the social system, which
was chosen by the people of Cuba, and which they consider best for
themselves.

We entertain feelings of genuine friendship and profound respect
toward the Cuban people, their government and Premier Fidel Castro,
and render comprehensive support and assistance to Cuba.

In the message of N. S. Khrushchev to President Kennedy of
October 28, it is said firmly and clearly that we want to create confidence with the Cuban people, that we are with them and do not
shirk the responsibility for rendering help to the people of Cuba.

✧ ✧ ✧ **78**

BRIEF ADDRESS BY PRESIDENT KENNEDY
ON CUBA, *November 2, 1962*

MY FELLOW CITIZENS: I want to take this opportunity to report on
the conclusions which this Government has reached on the basis of
yesterday's aerial photographs which will be made available tomorrow,
as well as other indications, namely, that the Soviet missile bases in
Cuba are being dismantled, their missiles and related equipment are
being crated, and the fixed installations at these sites are being destroyed.

The United States intends to follow closely the completion of this
work through a variety of means, including aerial surveillance, until
such time as an equally satisfactory international means of verification
is effected.

While the quarantine remains in effect, we are hopeful that adequate procedures can be developed for international inspection of
Cuba-bound cargoes. The International Committee of the Red Cross,
in our view, would be an appropriate agent in this matter.

The continuation of these measures in air and sea, until the threat
to peace posed by these offensive weapons is gone, is in keeping with
our pledge to secure their withdrawal or elimination from this hemisphere. It is in keeping with the resolution of the Organization of
American States, and it is in keeping with the exchange of letters with
Chairman Khrushchev of October 27th and 28th.

Progress is now being made toward the restoration of peace in the
Caribbean, and it is our firm hope and purpose that this progress shall
go forward. We will continue to keep the American people informed
on this vital matter.

U.S., Department of State, *Bulletin,* Volume XLVII, No. 1221 (November
19, 1962), p. 762. (Address from White House by radio and television on
November 2.)

✧ ✧ ✧ **79**

RESOLUTION OF OAS, *November 5, 1962*

In accordance with Article 54 of the Charter of the United Nations,
I have the honour to transmit to you herewith, for the information of

the Security Council, a copy of the resolution adopted by the Council of the Organization of American States on 5 November 1962, serving provisionally as Organ of Consultation in application of the Inter-American Treaty of Reciprocal Assistance.

I am also enclosing a copy of the Note No. UP-J-34, of 31 October 1962, received from the Nicaraguan Ambassador on the Council of the Organization of American States, with reference to the action taken by his Government in connexion with the resolution approved by the Council serving provisionally as Organ of Consultation, at the meeting held on 23 October 1962.

Accept, Sir, etc.

(s) José A. Mora
Secretary General

RESOLUTION ADOPTED BY THE COUNCIL OF THE ORGANIZATION OF AMERICAN STATES, ACTING PROVISIONALLY AS ORGAN OF CONSULTATION, AT THE MEETING HELD ON 5 NOVEMBER 1962

WHEREAS:

On 23 October 1962, the Council of the Organization of American States, acting provisionally as Organ of Consultation in application of the Inter-American Treaty of Reciprocal Assistance, adopted measures intended to preserve the peace and the security of the Continent, which were seriously threatened by the constant and growing intervention of extracontinental Powers in Cuba when they installed ballistic missiles and other arms of an offensive capability on territory of that country;

The Organ of Consultation has recommended to the member states the adoption of individual and collective measures, including the use of armed force, for meeting that situation; and

Many member states have made formal offers of co-operation in accordance with the recommendation made in the second paragraph of the aforementioned resolution,

THE COUNCIL OF THE ORGANIZATION OF AMERICAN STATES,
ACTING PROVISIONALLY AS ORGAN OF CONSULTATION

RESOLVES:

1. To take due note of the offers of a military or other nature that the member states have made and are making in accordance with the terms of the resolution adopted on 23 October 1962 by the Council acting provisionally as Organ of Consultation.

To recommend that the member states participating with military forces or with other facilities in the defence of the Hemisphere work out directly among themselves the technical measures that may be necessary to the co-ordinated and effective action of the combined forces, and that they keep the Organ of Consultation informed of this action, in compliance with paragraph 4 of the above-mentioned resolution.

U.N., *Security Council Document S/5206*, November 13, 1962, pp. 1–2. (Letter dated November 8, 1962.)

❖ ❖ ❖ **80**

DEPARTMENT OF DEFENSE STATEMENT
ON REMOVAL OF MISSILES, *November 8, 1962*

The U[nited] S[tates] Government has confirmed through aerial reconnaissance that medium-range ballistic missile and intermediate-range ballistic missile equipment is being removed from Cuba. Within the next twenty-four hours it expects to obtain additional confirmation through the close alongside observation of Soviet vessels by U[nited] S[tates] Naval vessels. It is understood Soviet vessels will cooperate in this procedure.

As a result of aerial reconnaissance, the U[nited] S[tates] has photographs which indicate that all known MRBM and IRBM missile bases in Cuba have been dismantled.

Later photographs indicate the movement of significant items of equipment from the missile sites to port areas. Still later photographs give evidence that a substantial number of missile transporters have been loaded on to the main decks of certain Soviet cargo vessels and that several of these vessels have already departed Cuban ports.

Photographs and visual inspection from U[nited] S[tates] Naval vessels should provide further confirmation that the actual missiles (normally carried in missile transporters that have been photographed on board these vessels) have left Cuba.

Intensive discussions are continuing with respect to the other provisions of the understanding between President Kennedy and Chairman Khrushchev.

The New York Times, November 9, 1962, p. 3. Copyright by The New York Times. Reprinted by permission. Text of a statement issued by Assistant Secretary of Defense Arthur Sylvester on removal of Soviet Missiles from Cuba.)

❖ ❖ ❖ 81

COMBINED LETTER OF THE UNITED STATES, ARGENTINA, AND DOMINICAN REPUBLIC ON ESTABLISHMENT OF JOINT QUARANTINE FORCE, *November 9, 1962*

November 9, 1962

MR. CHAIRMAN:

We have the honor to address Your Excellency in order to refer to the resolution adopted on October 23, 1962, and November 5, 1962, by the Council of the Organization of American States, acting provisionally as the Organ of Consultation. Among the measures of a technical nature which the various contributing governments may undertake in order to achieve a coordinated and effective action, in conformity with the Resolution of November 5, 1962, arrangements have been made among the Governments of Argentina, the Dominican Republic, and the United States of America under which naval units of these countries are participating in the quarantine operations around Cuba established pursuant to the resolution adopted by the Organ of Consultation on October 23, 1962. By agreement among the participating governments, a combined force has been established known as the "Combined Quarantine Force" under the operational command of Rear Admiral John A. Tyree, Jr., (USN), whose flag ship is currently the *USS Mullinex*. Under this arrangement, officers of the participating navies act as members of the Staff of the Combined Quarantine Force, and the respective naval units are integrated in that force in order to carry out the operations mentioned above.

Accept, Excellency, the renewed assurances of our highest and most distinguished consideration.

(s) DELESSEPS S. MORRISON, *Ambassador,*
Representative of the United States of America
on the Council of the Organization of American States
(s) RODOLFO A. WEIDMANN, *Ambassador,*
Representative of the Argentine Republic
on the Council of the Organization of American States
(s) ARTURO CALVENTI, *Ambassador,*
Interim Representative of the Dominican Republic
on the Council of the Organization of American States

His Excellency
Alberto Zuleta Angel
Chairman of the Council of the
Organization of American States

U.N., *Security Council Document S/5208,* November 21, 1962, p. 13.

✧ ✧ ✧ **82**

LETTER FROM PRIME MINISTER CASTRO TO
ACTING SECRETARY GENERAL U THANT,
November 15, 1962

15 November 1962

His Excellency U Thant,
Acting Secretary General,
The United Nations

Your Excellency,

The conciliatory action which you are conducting as Acting Secretary General of this world organization is very closely linked with the latest world events concerning the crisis in the Caribbean.

There is no need, therefore, to dwell upon each and every one of the events, circumstances and incidents which have occurred in these weeks of extreme tension.

I should like to refer solely to the following matter: we have given you — and we have also given it publicly and repeatedly — our refusal to allow unilateral inspection by any body, national or international, on Cuban territory. In doing so we have exercised the inalienable right of every sovereign nation to settle all problems within its own territory in accordance with the will of its Government and its people.

The Soviet Government, carrying out its promise to Mr. Kennedy, has withdrawn its strategic missiles, an action which was verified by United States officials on the high seas.

We should like to repeat once more that the installation of these weapons was nothing other than act of legitimate self-defense on the part of the Republic of Cuba against the aggressive policy which the United States has been pursuing against our country since the very triumph of the Revolution. This did not confer any right upon the Government of the United States with respect to Cuba, since all our actions have been effected within the framework of international law and in exercise of the sovereign prerogatives of our state. It was, however, the pretext used to perpetrate acts of force which brought the world to the edge of war. The pretext has now disappeared. Nevertheless officials of the United States Government declare that they do not consider themselves bound by any promise, among other reasons because Cuba has not permitted the inspection of its territory.

The United States, resorting to the law of force, is constantly violating our territory through the use of air forces based in various parts of the Caribbean and on aircraft carriers which it is employing against us.

We have given proof that we are ready for a worthy peace. We have put forward five points as guarantees, the minimum which any sovereign nation can ask for. We have handed over the body of Major Anderson who died while carrying out an illegal flight over Cuban soil. We have warned the Government of the United States that it must stop these acts of violation of our sovereignty and at the same time we have done everything possible to prevent the occurrence of any incidents in connection with these acts.

What have we obtained in exchange? The violations have increased in number; every day the incursions of war planes over our territory become more alarming; military aircraft harass our air bases, make low-level flights over our military defenses and photograph not only the dismantled strategic missile installations but in fact our entire territory, foot by foot and inch by inch.

The capture of the leader of a group of spies trained by the CIA and directed by it, here in Cuba, has shown us how the photographs taken by the spying planes serve for guidance in sabotage and in their operations and has also revealed, among other things, a design to cause chaos by provoking the deaths of 400 workers in one of our industries.

This impairs in its essence the security of our nation and outrages the dignity of our people. The object has been not only to secure advantages for military and subversive purposes through information and detailed knowledge of our industrial installations and defense arrangements, but also in addition to humiliate and demoralize the Cuban people.

These are typically Hitlerite methods for softening the resistance of peoples.

Mr. Acting Secretary General, no sovereign state can allow its air space to be violated in this manner without feeling an impairment of its dignity. If in addition this violation is perpetrated by the reconnaissance aircraft of an enemy which openly threatens our country, tolerating it means, more than a lack of dignity, a shameful submission to the enemy. We cannot be asked to accept this by virtue of the discussions which are taking place with regard to the crisis, for the integrity of our physical space and the sovereignty of Cuba will never be negotiable.

We for our part have not failed to give constant warnings to the aggressors.

On 27 October, in the midst of the crisis, the Cuban Government declared that it would never acknowledge the vandalic and piratical privilege of any war plane to violate our air space since this was essentially a threat to our security and facilitated the conditions for a surprise attack. Cuba's right to resist such violations can never be renounced.

Today again through this communication which we are sending you as Secretary General of the United Nations, we wish to give warning that to the extent of the fire power of our anti-aircraft weapons, any war plane which violates the sovereignty of Cuba, by invading our air space, can only do so at the risk of being destroyed.

If the United States sincerely desires — as we ourselves desire — to take steps toward the solution of the present problems, it should begin by respecting these elementary rights of our country.

In the history of our Republic, the United States has more than once intervened in our domestic affairs, with the use of force. It secured this right in the first constitution of our Republic, by virtue of a law adopted by the United States Congress, and supported by an army of occupation. The present action of the United States is designed to reinstate, in fact, these militaristic and imperialist privileges.

The long history of struggle of our country, culminating in full sovereignty and national dignity after a century-long fight written in blood and heroism, cannot be reversed. A powerful military force could annihilate us but it could never make us yield and we should first demand a very high price of the pirates who dared to invade the soil of the Cuban fatherland. And even if we should die our banner would fly victoriously because we are defending something even more sacred than our right as a sovereign nation in the concert of free nations of the earth.

We are sounding the necessary alarm for the defense of world peace, we are defending the right of the small countries to be considered on a footing of equality, we are telling all the peoples of the earth that before the imperialist enemy there can be no weakening. The path of calm and stern vigilance, strong in the security of a response commensurate with the magnitude of the aggression, is the only way to the salvation of peace.

Our right to live is something which cannot be discussed by anyone.

But if our right to live is made conditional upon an obligation to fall to our knees, our reply once again is that we will not accept it.

We believe in the right to defend the liberty, the sovereignty and the dignity of this country, and we shall continue to exercise that right to the last man, woman or child capable of holding a weapon in this territory.

May I reiterate to you the expression of my highest consideration.

(s) FIDEL CASTRO
Prime Minister of the
Revolutionary Government

U.N., *Press Release SG/1378,* November 16, 1962, pp. 1–4.

✧ ✧ ✧ **83**

STATEMENT BY PRESIDENT KENNEDY ON CUBA AT PRESS CONFERENCE, *November 20, 1962*

I have today been informed by Chairman Khrushchev that all of the IL–28 bombers now in Cuba will be withdrawn in thirty days. He also agrees that these planes can be observed and counted as they leave. Inasmuch as this goes a long way toward reducing the danger which faced this Hemisphere four weeks ago, I have this afternoon instructed the Secretary of Defense to lift our naval quarantine.

In view of this action I want to take this opportunity to bring the American people up to date on the Cuban crisis and to review the progress made thus far in fulfilling the understandings between Soviet Chairman Khrushchev and myself as set forth in our letters of October 27 and 28. Chairman Khrushchev, it will be recalled, agreed to remove from Cuba all weapons systems capable of offensive use, to halt the further introduction of such weapons into Cuba, and to permit appropriate United Nations observation and supervision to insure the carrying out and continuation of these commitments. We on our part agreed that, once these adequate arrangements for verification had been established, we would remove our naval quarantine and give assurances against invasion of Cuba.

The evidence to date indicates that all known offensive missile sites in Cuba have been dismantled. The missiles and their associated equipment have been loaded on Soviet ships. And our inspection at sea of these departing ships has confirmed that the number of missiles reported by the Soviet Union as having been brought into Cuba, which closely corresponded to our own information, has now been removed. In addition the Soviet Government has stated that all nuclear weapons have been withdrawn from Cuba and no offensive weapons will be reintroduced.

Nevertheless, important parts of the understanding of October 27th and 28th remain to be carried out. The Cuban Government has not yet permitted the United Nations to verify whether all offensive weapons have been removed, and no lasting safeguards have yet been established against the future introduction of offensive weapons back into Cuba.

Consequently, if the Western Hemisphere is to continue to be protected against offensive weapons, this Government has no choice but to pursue its own means of checking on military activities in Cuba. The importance of our continued vigilance is underlined by our identification in recent days of a number of Soviet ground combat units in Cuba, although we are informed that these and other Soviet units were associated with the protection of offensive weapons systems and will also be withdrawn in due course.

I repeat, we would like nothing better than adequate international arrangements for the task of inspection and verification in Cuba, and we are prepared to continue our efforts to achieve such arrangements. Until that is done, difficult problems remain. As for our part, if all offensive weapons are removed from Cuba and kept out of the Hemisphere in the future, under adequate verification and safeguards, and if Cuba is not used for the export of aggressive Communist purposes, there will be peace in the Caribbean. And as I said in September, we shall neither initiate nor permit aggression in this Hemisphere.

We will not, of course, abandon the political, economic, and other efforts of this Hemisphere to halt subversion from Cuba nor our purpose and hope that the Cuban people shall some day be truly free. But these policies are very different from any intent to launch a military invasion of the island.

In short, the record of recent weeks shows real progress, and we are hopeful that further progress can be made. The completion of the commitment on both sides and the achievement of a peaceful solution to the Cuban crisis might well open the door to the solution of other outstanding problems.

May I add this final thought. In this week of Thanksgiving there is much for which we can be grateful as we look back to where we stood only four weeks ago — the unity of this Hemisphere, the support of our allies, and the calm determination of the American people. These qualities may be tested many more times in this decade, but we have increased reason to be confident that those qualities will continue to serve the cause of freedom with distinction in the years to come.

U.S , Department of State, *Bulletin,* Volume XLVII, No. 1224 (December 10, 1962), pp. 874–875. (Statement read by President Kennedy at the opening of his press conference.)

❖ ❖ ❖ **84**

U.S. PROCLAMATION TERMINATING INTERDICTION OF OFFENSIVE WEAPONS, *November 21, 1962*

I, JOHN F. KENNEDY, President of the United States of America, acting under and by virtue of the authority vested in me by the Constitution and Statutes of the United States, do hereby proclaim that at 11 P.M., Greenwich Time, November 20, 1962, I terminated the authority conferred upon the Secretary of Defense by Proclamation No. 3504, dated October 23, 1962, and revoked the orders contained therein to forces under my command.

IN WITNESS WHEREOF, I have hereunto set my hand and caused the Seal of the United States of America to be affixed.

DONE at the City of Washington this 21st day of November, in the year of our Lord nineteen hundred and sixty-two (Seal) and of the Independence of the United States of America the one hundred and eighty-seventh.

(s) JOHN F. KENNEDY

By the President:
Dean Rusk,
Secretary of State

U.S., Department of State, *Bulletin*, Volume XLVII, No. 1225 (December 17, 1962), p. 918. (No. 3507; 27 *Federal Register*, 11525.)

✧ ✧ ✧ **85**

LETTER FROM PRESIDENT DORTICOS AND PRIME MINISTER CASTRO TO ACTING SECRETARY GENERAL U THANT, *November 25, 1962*

The Permanent Mission of Cuba to the United Nations presents its compliments to the Secretary General of the United Nations and has the honour to transmit below the text of a statement by the Revolutionary Government of Cuba and to ask for it to be issued and circulated as an official United Nations document:

"The National Directorate of the Integrated Revolutionary Organizations and the Council of Ministers, meeting in joint session to deal with questions relating to the so-called Caribbean crisis, hereby resolve to make known to the people of Cuba and to the world the position of our Party and the Cuban Government.

In his latest public statement, President Kennedy announced the lifting of the blockade of Cuba in return for the withdrawal by the Soviet Union of the intermediate-range ballistic missiles and IL–28 medium bombers stationed in Cuba. Nevertheless, the statements by the President of the United States contain the seeds of a provocative and aggressive policy against our country, which must be exposed.

In one part of his speech, President Kennedy said: 'As for our part, if all offensive weapons systems are removed from Cuba and kept out of the Hemisphere in the future, under adequate verification and safeguards, and if Cuba is not used for the export of aggressive communist purposes, there will be peace in the Caribbean. And as I said in September, "We shall neither initiate nor permit aggression in this Hemisphere." We will not, of course, abandon the political, economic and other efforts of this Hemisphere to halt subversion from Cuba, nor our purpose and hope that the Cuban people shall some day be truly free. But these policies are very different from any attempt to launch a military invasion of the island.'

The position of strength adopted by the United States Government is wholly contrary to the rules of international law. Over and above the outrages which it has committed against Cuba, and which brought the world to the brink of war — an outcome avoided by means of agreements predicated upon an undertaking by the United States to abandon its aggressive and criminal policy against Cuba — it refuses even to give an assurance that it will not again violate the Charter of the United Nations and international law by invading the Republic of Cuba, on the pretext that our country has not agreed to international inspection.

It is quite evident that Cuba has a sovereign right, based on the Charter of the United Nations, to agree or not to agree to inspection of its territory. At no time has Cuba suggested or agreed to such verification.

The Soviet Government, for its part, complied with the verification requirement of which it spoke in its letter of 28 October, by allowing the United States to verify the withdrawal of the missiles on the high seas, and the United States agreed to this form of verification.

President Kennedy's claim is without foundation. It is merely a pretext for not carrying out his part of the agreement and for persisting in his policy of aggression against Cuba. As if that were not enough, even if permission were given for inspection, carrying with it all the guarantees which the United States Government might see fit to demand, the peace of the Caribbean would still be subject to the condition that 'Cuba is not used for the export of aggressive communist purposes.'

This is the same as saying that any effort by the peoples of Latin America to free themselves from the imperialist yoke might serve as a pretext for the United States Government to accuse Cuba, break the peace and attack our country. Flimsier guarantees would be difficult to imagine.

To all this must be added one further fact indicative of the warmongering and domineering policy of the United States Government.

In his latest statement, President Kennedy tacitly reasserted the right
— already claimed on several other occasions — for spy planes to fly
over the territory of Cuba and photograph it from one end to the
other. This too is a gross violation of international law.

Respect for international law is an essential condition if the nations of the earth are to live together regardless of their social or
economic systems.

The only effective way to guarantee that the rule of law will be
maintained in international affairs and that the provisions of the law
will be complied with is for all nations to respect the established rules.
At this time of acute rivalry between two conceptions of society, the
United States has arrogated to itself the right to break the existing
international rules and to make new rules as it pleases.

It is our view that when such a dangerous situation is reached,
when one country decides, by and for itself, how the law is to be
applied in its relations with other countries, there is no choice but
firmly to resist its claims.

The United States is trying to dictate what kind of arms we should
or should not have. The United States rulers who oblige us to expend
vast resources in order to defend ourselves against the aggression to
which we have been subjected during the four years of our Revolution's progress also claim to be the judges of what limit should be
placed on the armaments with which we defend our freedom.

It was the United States Government which, by its repeated and
overt attacks on our country, made it necessary for the Cuban people
to arm themselves. It was President Kennedy himself who ordered
an army of mercenaries to land at Playa Girón. It was under his
Administration that thousands of United States weapons were
dropped by parachute or landed on our shores with the aim of encouraging and organizing bands of counter-revolutionaries, who committed the worst possible crimes against teachers, mass literacy [sic]
personnel, peasants and workers.

The Governments of the United States — the previous one and
the present one — not only adopted criminal economic measures
against Cuba, which confronted our people with severe problems; in
addition their acts of military aggression forced us to devote great
energy and great resources to the defense of our integrity. What
would have become of our country and its Revolution if our people
had not offered stubborn and heroic resistance to the actions of that
powerful and aggressive country? The United States is guilty of
a policy of economic strangulation and of violence against Cuba, a
policy which has led to the Caribbean crisis with all its consequences
and dangers.

Furthermore, the United States violated the principle of freedom
of the seas by establishing the blockade of Cuba; it violated the
Charter of the United Nations by announcing the adoption of uni-

lateral measures against our country; and it now takes refuge in the OAS, seeking official sanction for its acts of piracy in the air. The OAS has no jurisdiction whatsoever on our soil; its decisions have no validity for us; to cite them is arbitrary — pure sophistry on the part of the imperialist aggressor.

The United States Government has reiterated its interventionist intentions. It has stated that it will in no circumstances abandon its political, economic 'and other' acts of aggression. What is meant by 'other efforts' against Cuba? International subversion, sabotage, acts of terrorism, pirate raids, infiltration by CIA agents, the landing and dropping of weapons in our territory, invasions by mercenaries — in fact everything which, in Pentagon jargon, is termed 'paramilitary warfare.'

If that is how matters stand, Cuba will have to defend itself by every available means. It reserves the right to acquire weapons of all kinds for its defence and will take such steps as it deems appropriate to strengthen its security in the face of this open threat. After examining President Kennedy's statement, then, it is possible to affirm that armed conflict has been averted but not that peace has been achieved. For our people there has been no peace, but incessant attacks. Many of their sons have died as a result of armed attacks, sabotage, murder, subversive acts and raids by pirate aircraft and ships instigated by the United States Government. President Kennedy's statement offers, not peace, but the continuation of such acts.

We therefore reiterate the five points which are essential to a genuine and final settlement of the crisis. First: cessation of the economic blockade and of all measures of commercial and economic pressure exercised against our country by the United States in every part of the world.

Second: the cessation of all subversive activities, of the dropping of weapons and explosives from the air and their landing from the sea, of the mounting of invasions by mercenaries, by infiltration by spies and saboteurs, all of which are being carried out from the territory of the United States and a few countries which are its accomplices.

Third: cessation of the pirate raids which are carried out from bases in the United States and Puerto Rico.

Fourth: the cessation of all violations of our air space and territorial waters by United States aircraft and warships.

Fifth: withdrawal from Guantanamo naval base and the restoration of the Cuban territory occupied by the United States.

These are no irrational demands; they do not conflict with the rights of anyone; they are claims so legitimate, and so clearly limited to the rights of the Cuban people, that no one can object to them.

The United States Government demands that the United Nations should verify in our territory the withdrawal of strategic weapons.

Cuba demands that the United Nations should verify in the territory of the United States, in Puerto Rico and in other places where attacks on Cuba are in preparation, the dismantling of the training camps for mercenaries, spies, saboteurs and terrorists; of the centres where subversion is prepared; and of the bases from which pirate vessels set out for our coasts.

In addition Cuba demands, as one of the required guarantees, that effective measures of control should be established to prevent any repetition of such acts in the future.

If the United States and its accomplices in aggression against Cuba do not agree to such inspection in their territories by the United Nations, Cuba will in no circumstances agree to inspection in its own territory.

Reciprocal concessions and guarantees will afford the only means of reaching a broad and fitting agreement acceptable to all.

If such an agreement is reached, Cuba will need no strategic weapons for its defence; the staff of foreign military technicians engaged to instruct our armed forces would be reduced to the minimum and the necessary conditions would be created for the normal development of our relations with the countries of this hemisphere.

A just and satisfactory settlement of this crisis would without doubt help towards solving the other problems awaiting action throughout the world; it would be a firm step on the true road to peace. And the world needs peace.

It is a legitimate aspiration of mankind that the enormous sums now being invested in the manufacture of costly and deadly armaments should be spent on making goods of use to man, especially for the benefit of the underdeveloped peoples whom the colonizing and imperialist countries have left immersed in the direst poverty.

War industry and the arms traffic can interest only the monopolists whose business it is to stifle the most lawful aspirations of the peoples and to batten, like birds of prey, on destruction and death.

As Marxist-Leninists, we defend peace by conviction and on principle. Weapons are to us a heavy burden imposed by the imperialists, which divert energy and resources from the creative tasks of the Revolution.

Our mission is to defend peace as the supreme aspiration of mankind. We believe in the possibility of averting war and we do not believe that war is a fatal and inexorable necessity. But this does not mean that the imperialists are entitled to be pirates, to be aggressors, or to commit acts of genocide against any people.

The imperialists must not confuse a position on principle with weakness in the face of their acts of aggression. It must be made quite clear to them that they are in no position today to impose their law on the world and that they will not be permitted to do so.

Cuba stresses once again that there is no better way than that of peace and discussion between Governments, but at the same time we repeat that we shall never falter before the imperialists. To their positions of strength we shall oppose our firmness; to the intent to humiliate us, our dignity; to aggression, the resolve to fight to the last man.

We do not believe in mere promises of non-aggression; we need deeds. Those deeds are set forth in our five points.

We have as little faith in President Kennedy's words as we feel fear at his veiled threats.

FATHERLAND OR DEATH! WE SHALL CONQUER!

Havana, 25 November 1962.

(s) OSVALDO DORTICOS
President of the Republic

(s) FIDEL CASTRO
*Prime Minister and Secretary General
of the Integrated Revolutionary
Organizations*

The Permanent Mission of Cuba to the United Nations takes this opportunity to reiterate to the Secretary General of the United Nations the assurances of its highest consideration.

New York, 26 November 1962

U.N., *Security Council Document S/5210*, November 26, 1962, pp. 1–6.

❖ ❖ ❖ **86**

COMBINED LETTER OF THE UNITED STATES, ARGENTINA AND DOMINICAN REPUBLIC ON DISESTABLISHMENT OF JOINT QUARANTINE FORCE, *November 30, 1962*

Washington, D.C.
30 November 1962

SIR:

We have the honour to refer to our communication of November 9, 1962.

Inasmuch as the progress of events has made possible the termination of naval quarantine operations in the vicinity of Cuba, the arrangements referred to in the joint communication mentioned above have been cancelled by common agreement among the governments represented by the signatories.

Accept, Sir, the renewed assurances of our highest consideration.

(s) deLesseps S. Morrison
Ambassador, Representative of the United States on the Council of the Organization of American States
(s) Rodolfo A. Weidmann
Ambassador, Representative of Argentina on the Council of the Organization of American States
(s) Arturo Calventi
Ambassador, Interim Representative of the Dominican Republic on the Council of the Organization of American States

Dr. Gonzalo Facio
Chairman of the Council of the Organization of American States
Washington, D.C.

U.N., *Security Council Document S/5217*, December 17, 1962, p. 8.

❖ ❖ ❖ **87**

LETTER FROM CUBAN AMBASSADOR CARLOS M. LECHUGA TO SECRETARY GENERAL U THANT, *December 5, 1962*

I have been instructed by the Revolutionary Government of Cuba to inform you of a new act of international piracy.

On the night of 4 December, members of counter-revolutionary organizations which operate in United States territory, manning a large vessel that came from the north, fired a considerable number of cannon and machine-gun shots at San Francisco Beach, situated some thirty kilometres east of the town of Caíbarion, on the north coast of the province of Las Villas.

The account of this event corresponds exactly with the statements made in New York by spokesmen for such organizations to the Associated Press agency. The fact that the spokesmen for these counter-revolutionary organizations are in New York, that the vessel came from the north and that it was armed with weapons with which only regular armed forces are equipped entitles one to conclude, without being exaggeratedly suspicious, that this operation was planned in the United States and that the ship came from United States territory.

This illegal action, occurring at a time when you are trying to bring about a permanent and satisfactory solution of the so-called Caribbean crisis, provides further justification for the position taken by the Revolutionary Government of Cuba that only a solution which includes specific measures to provide minimum safeguards, such as those contained in the five points proposed by the Prime Minister, Fidel Castro, would offer an effective and lasting guarantee of peace in this region and in the world.

The Revolutionary Government of Cuba considers that an objective evaluation of this event and of the circumstances in which it took place would enable you to draw the appropriate conclusions as to the most effective way of achieving the noble aims which you are pursuing.

On behalf of my Government, I ask for this letter to be circulated as an official United Nations document.

(s) CARLOS M. LECHUGA HEVIA
Ambassador
Permanent Representative of Cuba

U.N., *Security Council Document S/5214,* December 6, 1962, pp. 1–2.

✧ ✧ ✧ **88**

LETTER FROM CHAIRMAN KHRUSHCHEV TO PRESIDENT KENNEDY, *December 19, 1962*

DEAR MR. PRESIDENT:

In our recent correspondence related to the events in the Caribbean area we have touched on the question of cessation of nuclear weapon tests. Today I would like to come back again to that problem and set forth my views concerning possible ways of its speediest solution which would be mutually acceptable to both our sides.

It seems to me, Mr. President, that time has come now to put an end once and for all to nuclear tests, to draw a line through such tests. The moment for this is very, very appropriate. Left behind is a period of utmost acuteness and tension in the Caribbean. Now we have untied our hands to engage closely in other urgent international matters and, in particular, in such a problem which has been ripe for so long as cessation of nuclear tests. A certain relaxation of international tension which has emerged now should, in my view, facilitate this.

The Soviet Union does not need war. I think that war does not promise bright prospects for the United States, either. If in the past after every war America used to increase its economic potential and to accumulate more and more wealth, now war with the use of modern rocket-nuclear weapons will stride across seas and oceans within minutes. Thermonuclear catastrophe will bring enormous losses and sufferings to the American people as well as to other peoples on earth. To prevent this we must, on the basis of complete equality and with just regard for each other's interests, develop between ourselves peaceful relations and solve all issues through negotiations and mutual concessions.

One of such questions with which the governments of our countries have been dealing for many years is the question of concluding a treaty banning all tests of nuclear weapons.

Both of us stand on the same position with regard to the fact that national means of detection are sufficient to control banning experimental nuclear explosions in outer space, in the atmosphere, and under water. So far, however, we have not succeeded in finding a mutually acceptable solution to the problem of cessation of underground tests. The main obstacle to an agreement is the demand by the American side of international control and inspection on the territories of nuclear powers over cessation of underground nuclear tests. I would like to believe that you yourself understand the rightness of our arguments that now national means are sufficient to control also this kind of tests and be sure that agreement is observed by any side. But so far you do not want to recognize openly this actual state of things and to accept it as a basis for concluding without delay an agreement on cessation of tests.

Striving to find a mutually acceptable basis for agreement the Soviet Union has made lately an important step toward the West and agreed to installing automatic seismic stations. This idea, as is known, was put forward not by us. It was introduced by British scientists during the recent meeting in London of the participants of Pugwash movement. Moreover, it is well known to us, that when this idea was proposed, it was not alien to your scientists who were in London at that time.

We proposed to install such stations both near the borders of nuclear powers and directly on their territories. We stated our agreement that three such stations be installed on the territory of the Soviet Union in the zones most frequently subjected to earthquakes. There are three such zones in the Soviet Union where these stations can be installed: Central Asian, Altaian, and Far Eastern.

In the opinion of Soviet scientists the most suitable places for locating automatic seismic stations in the Soviet Union are area of the city of Kokchetav for central Asian zone of the U.S.S.R, area of the city of Bodaibo for Altaian zone, and area of the city of Yukutsk for Far Eastern zone. However, should, as a result of exchange of opinion between our representatives, other places be suggested for locating automatic seismic zones, we will be ready to discuss this question and find mutually acceptable solution.

Besides the above said zones there are two more seismic zones in the Soviet Union — Caucasian and Carpathian. However, these zones are so densely populated that conducting nuclear tests there is practically excluded.

Of course, delivery to and from [an] international center of appropriate sealed equipment for its periodic replacement at automatic seismic stations in the U.S.S.R. could well be made by Soviet personnel and on Soviet planes. However, if for such delivery of equipment to and from automatic seismic stations participation of foreign personnel were needed we would agree to this also, having taken, if necessary, precautionary measures against use of such trips for reconnaissance. Thus our proposal on automatic seismic stations includes elements of international control. This is a major act of good will on the part of the Soviet Union.

I will tell you straightforwardly that before making this proposal I have consulted thoroughly the specialists and after such consultation my colleagues in the government and I came to a conclusion that so far as the Soviet Union is concerned the above said considerations on the measures on our part are well founded and it seems to us, they should not cause objections on the part of the American side.

You, Mr. President, and your representatives point out that without at least a minimum number of on-site inspections you will not manage to persuade the United States to ratify an agreement on the cessation of tests. This circumstance, as we understand, ties you and does not allow you to sign a treaty which would enable all of us to abandon for good the ground where nuclear weapons are tested. Well, if this is the only difficulty on the way to agreement, then for the noble and humane goal of ceasing nuclear weapon tests we are ready to meet you halfway in this question.

We noted that on this October 30, in conversation with First Deputy Foreign Minister of the U.S.S.R., V. V. Kuznetsov in New York, your representative, Ambassador [Arthur H.] Dean, stated that, in the opinion of the United States Government, it would be sufficient to carry on 2–4 on-site inspections each year on the territory of the Soviet Union. According to Ambassador Dean's statement, the United States would also be prepared to work out measures which would rule out any possibility of carrying on espionage under the cover of these inspection trips, including such measures as the use of Soviet planes piloted by Soviet crews for transportation of inspectors to the sites, screening of windows in the planes, prohibition to carry photo cameras, etc.

We took all this into account and, in order to overcome the dead-lock and to arrive at last at a mutually acceptable agreement, we would agree, in those cases when it would be considered necessary, to 2–3 inspections a year on the territory of each of the nuclear powers in the seismic areas where some suspicious earth's tremors might occur. It goes without saying that the basis of control over an agreement on underground nuclear test ban would be the national means of detection in combination with automatic seismic stations. On-site inspections could be carried on with the precautions mentioned by Ambassador Dean against any misuse of control for purposes of espionage.

We believe that now the road to agreement is straight and clear. Beginning from January 1 of the new year of 1963 the world can be relieved of the roar of nuclear explosions. The peoples are waiting for this — this is what the United Nations General Assembly has called for. With the elimination of the Cuban crisis we relieved mankind of the direct menace of combat use of lethal nuclear weapons that impended over the world. Can't we solve a far simpler question — that of cessation of experimental explosions of nuclear weapons in the peaceful conditions? I think that we can and must do it. Here lies now our duty before the peoples of not only our countries but of all other countries. Having solved promptly also this question — and there are all the preconditions for that — we shall be able to facilitate working out an agreement on disarmament and with even more confidence proceed with solving other urgent international problems, which we and you unfortunately are not short of.

Sincerely,

(s) N. KHRUSHCHEV

U.S., Department of State, *Bulletin*, Volume XLVIII, No. 1233 (February 11, 1963), pp. 198–200.

✧ ✧ ✧ **89**

LETTER FROM PRESIDENT KENNEDY TO CHAIRMAN KHRUSHCHEV, *December 28, 1962*

DEAR MR. CHAIRMAN:

I was very glad to receive your letter of December 19, 1962, setting forth your views on nuclear tests. There appear to be no differences between your views and mine regarding the need for eliminating war in this nuclear age. Perhaps only those who have the responsibility for controlling these weapons fully realize the awful devastation their use would bring.

Having these considerations in mind and with respect to the issue of a test ban, I therefore sincerely hope that the suggestions that you have made in your letter will prove to be helpful in starting us down the road to an agreement. I am encouraged that you are prepared to accept the principle of on-site inspections. These seem to me to be essential not just because they seem to us to go to the heart of a reliable agreement ending nuclear testing.

If we are to have peace between systems with far-reaching ideological differences, we must find ways for reducing or removing the recurring waves of fear and suspicion which feed on ignorance, misunderstanding, or what appear to one side or the other as broken agreements. To me, the element of assurance is vital to peaceful relationships.

With respect to the question of on-site inspections I would certainly agree that we could accept any reasonable provision which you had in mind to protect against our concern that the on-site inspectors might engage in "espionage" en route to the area of inspection. In a statement at the United Nations, Ambassador Stevenson suggested that the United States would accept any reasonable security provision while the inspectors were being taken to the site, so long as they had reasonable provision for satisfying themselves that they were actually at the intended location and had the freedom necessary to inspect the limited designated area.

With respect to the number of on-site inspections there appears to have been some misunderstanding. Your impression seems to be that Ambassador Dean told Deputy Minister Kuznetsov that the United States might be prepared to accept an annual number of on-site inspections between two and four. Ambassador Dean advises me that the only number which he mentioned in his discussions with Deputy Minister Kuznetsov was a number between eight and ten. This represented a substantial decrease in the request of the United States as we had previously been insisting upon a number between twelve and twenty. I had hoped that the Soviet Union would match this motion on the part of the United States by an equivalent motion in the figure of two or three on-site inspections which it had some time ago indicated it might allow.

I am aware that this matter of on-site inspections has given you considerable difficulty although I am not sure that I fully understand why this should be so. To me, an effective nuclear test ban treaty is of such importance that I would not permit such international arrangements to become mixed up with our or any other national desire to seek other types of information about the Soviet Union I believe quite sincerely that arrangements could be worked out which would convince you and your colleagues that this is the case.

But in this connection, your implication that on-site inspections should be limited to seismic areas also gives us some difficulty. It is true that in the ordinary course we would have concern about events taking place in the seismic areas. However, an unidentified seismic event coming from an area in which there are not usually earthquakes would be a highly suspicious event. The United States would feel that in such a circumstance the U.S.S.R. would be entitled to an on-site inspection of such an event occurring in our area and feels that the United States should have the same rights within its annual quota of inspection.

Perhaps your comment would be that a seismic event in another area designated for inspection might coincide with a highly sensitive defense installation. I recognize this as a real problem but believe that some arrangement can be worked out which would prevent this unlikely contingency from erecting an insuperable obstacle.

Your suggestion as to the three locations in the Soviet Union in which there might be unmanned seismic stations is helpful but it does not seem to me to go far enough. These stations are all outside the areas of highest seismicity and therefore do not record all of the phenomena within those areas. These stations would be helpful in increasing the detection capability of the system but I doubt that they would have the same value in reducing the number of suspicious seismic events by identifying some as earthquakes. For this purpose unmanned seismic stations should be in the areas of highest seismicity, not outside them. To achieve this result there would be need for a number in the Tashkent area. It might be possible, of course, to reduce somewhat the number actually in the Soviet Union by arranging stations in Hokkaido, Pakistan, and Afghanistan. If the stations on Soviet territory were sited in locations free from local disturbances and could be monitored periodically by competent United States or international observers who took in portable seismometers and placed them on the pedestals it would be very helpful in reducing the problem of identification.

You have referred to the discussion of the "black box" proposal at the 10th Pugwash conference in London in September of this year as a United Kingdom proposal to which the United States has agreed. I do not believe that this was the situation. This proposal was reported to me as a Soviet proposal which was discussed with some United States scientists. Of the United States scientists who signed the statement none represented the United States Government or had discussed the matter with responsible officials. All were speaking as individuals and none were seismologists. Their agreement does not signify anything other than that this was an area which justified further study. The United States Government has given it that study and the results have been the conclusions which I have indicated above.

Notwithstanding these problems I am encouraged by your letter. I do not believe that any of the problems which I have raised are insoluble but they ought to be solved. I wonder how you think we might best proceed with these discussions which may require some technical development. It occurs to me that you might wish to have your representative meet with Mr. William C. Foster, the director of our Arms Control and Disarmament Agency, at a mutually convenient place, such as New York or Geneva. I will be glad to have your suggestions. After talks have been held we will then be in a position to evaluate where we stand and continue our work together for an effective agreement ending all nuclear tests.

Sincerely,

(s) JOHN F. KENNEDY

U.S., Department of State, *Bulletin,* Volume XLVIII, No. 1233 (February 11, 1963), pp. 200–201.

❖ ❖ ❖ **90**

PRESIDENT KENNEDY ACCEPTS FLAG FROM RANSOMED CUBAN BRIGADE, *December 29, 1962*

I want to express my great appreciation to the brigade for making the United States the custodian of this flag. I can assure you that this flag will be returned to this brigade in a free Habana.

I wonder if Señor [Secundo] Miranda, who preserved this flag through the last twenty months, would come forward so we can meet him. I wanted to know whom I should give it back to.

I always had the impression — I hope the members of the brigade will sit down again — I always had the impression that the brigade was made up of mostly young men, but standing over there is a Cuban patriot 57, one 59, one 61. I wonder if those three could stand so that the people of the United States could realize that they represent the spirit of the Cuban revolution in its best sense.

All of you members of the brigade, and members of their families, are following an historic road, one which has been followed by other Cubans in other days and, indeed, by other patriots of our hemisphere in other years — Juárez, San Martín, Bolívar, O'Higgins — all of whom fought for liberty, many of whom were defeated, many of whom went in exile, and all of whom came home.

Seventy years ago José Martí, the guiding spirit of the first Cuban struggle for independence, lived on these shores. At that time in 1889 the first international American conference was held, and Cuba was not present. Then, as now, Cuba was the only state in the Hemisphere still controlled by a foreign monarch. Then, as now, Cuba was excluded from the society of free nations. And then, as now, brave men in Florida and New York dedicated their lives and their energies to the freedom of their homeland.

The brigade comes from behind prison walls, but you leave behind you more than six million of your fellow countrymen who are also in a very real sense in prison, for Cuba is today, as Martí described it many years ago, as beautiful as Greece and stretched out in chains — a prison moated by water.

On behalf of my Government and my country I welcome you to the United States. I bring you my nation's respect for your courage and for your cause. Our primary gratitude for your liberation must go to the heroic efforts of the Cuban Families Committees, Mr. [Alvaro] Sánchez and others, and their able and skilled negotiator, Mr. James Donovan, and those many private American citizens who gave so richly of their time and their energies in order to save free men of Cuba from Castro's dungeons and to reunite you with your families and friends.

Their efforts had a significance beyond the important desire to salvage individual human beings. For your small brigade is a tangible reaffirmation that the human desire for freedom and independence is essentially unconquerable. Your conduct and valor are proof that, although Castro and his fellow dictators may rule nations, they do not rule people, that they may imprison bodies, but they do not imprison spirits; that they may destroy the exercise of liberty, but they cannot eliminate the determination to be free. And by helping to free you the United States has been given the opportunity to demonstrate once again that all men who fight for freedom are our brothers and shall be until your country and others are free.

The Cuban people were promised by the revolution political liberty, social justice, intellectual freedom, land for the *campesinos*, and an end to economic exploitation. They have received a police state, the elimination of the dignity of land ownership, the destruction of free speech and of free press, and the complete subjugation of individual human welfare to the service of the state and of foreign states.

Under the *Alianza para el Progreso* we support for Cuba and for all countries of this hemisphere the right of free elections and the free exercise of basic human freedoms. We support land reform and the right of every *campesino* to own the land he tills. We support the effort of every free nation to pursue programs of economic progress.

We support the right of every free people to freely transform the economic and political institutions of society so that they may serve the welfare of all.

These are the principles of the *Alianza para el Progreso*. They are the principles we support for Cuba. These are the principles for which men have died and fought, and they are the principles for which you fought and for which some died in your brigade. And I believe these are the principles of the great majority of the Cuban people today, and I am confident that all over the island of Cuba, in the government itself, in the army, and in the militia, there are many who hold to this freedom faith, who have viewed with dismay the destruction of freedom on their island and who are determined to restore that freedom so that the Cuban people may once more govern themselves.

I know that exile is a difficult life for any free man. But I am confident that you recognize that you hold a position of responsibility to the day when Cuba is once again free. To this end it is important that you submerge momentary differences in a common united front; that the brigade — those who serve in the brigade — will work together to keep alive the spirit of the brigade so that some day the people of Cuba will have a free chance to make a free choice. So I think it incumbent upon all of you who are here today to work together, to submerge those differences which now may disturb you, to the united end that Cuba is free, and then make a free choice as to what kind of a government and what kind of a country you freely wish to build.

The brigade is the point of the spear, the arrow's head. I hope they and the members of their families will take every opportunity to educate your children, yourselves, in the many skills and disciplines which will be necessary when Cuba is once more free.

Finally, I can offer no better advice than that given by José Martí to his fellow exiles in 1895, when the hour of Cuban independence was then at hand. "Let the tenor of our words be," Martí said, "especially in public matters not the useless clamor of fear's vengeance which does not enter our hearts, but the honest weariness of an oppressed people who hope through their emancipation from a government convicted of uselessness and malevolence, for a government of their own which is capable and worthy. Let them see in us," Martí said, "constructive Americans and not empty bitterness."

Gentlemen of the brigade, I need not tell you how happy I am to welcome you here to the United States and what a profound impression your conduct during some of the most difficult days and months that any free people have experienced — what a profound impression your conduct made upon not only the people of this country but all the people of this hemisphere. Even in prison you served in the strongest possible way the cause of freedom, as you do today.

I can assure you that it is the strongest wish of the people of this country, as well as the people of this Hemisphere, that Cuba shall one day be free again, and when it is, this brigade will deserve to march at the head of the free column.

U.S., Department of State, *Bulletin*, Volume XLVII, No. 1230 (January 21, 1963), pp. 88–90.

✧ ✧ ✧ **91**

JOINT LETTER FROM AMBASSADOR STEVENSON AND FIRST DEPUTY MINISTER OF FOREIGN AFFAIRS VASILY KUZNETSOV TO SECRETARY GENERAL U THANT, *January 7, 1963*

On behalf of the Governments of the United States of America and the Soviet Union we desire to express to you our appreciation for your efforts in assisting our Governments to avert the serious threat to the peace which recently arose in the Caribbean area.

While it has not been possible for our Governments to resolve all the problems that have arisen in connexion with this affair, they believe that, in view of the degree of understanding reached between them on the settlement of the crisis and the extent of progress in the implementation of this understanding, it is not necessary for this item to occupy further the attention of the Security Council at this time.

The Governments of the United States of America and of the Soviet Union express the hope that the actions taken to avert the threat of war in connexion with this crisis will lead toward the adjustment of other differences between them and the general easing of tensions that would cause a further threat of war.

(s) ADLAI E. STEVENSON
*Permanent Representative
of the United States
to the United Nations*

(s) V. KUZNETSOV
*First Deputy Minister of
Foreign Affairs of the
U.S.S.R.*

U.N., *Security Council Document S/5227*, January 7, 1963, p. 1.

LETTER FROM AMBASSADOR LECHUGA TO SECRETARY GENERAL U THANT,
January 7, 1963

On the instructions of my Government I have the honour to send you, with the request that they be forwarded to the President of the Security Council, copies of the letter which Fidel Castro, Prime Minister of the Revolutionary Government of Cuba, sent to you on 28 October 1962 and of the statement issued on 25 November 1962 by the National Directorate of the Integrated Revolutionary Organizations and the Council of Ministers, so that they may be included in the Security Council's documentation on the Caribbean crisis.

At the same time I should be grateful if you would request the President of the Security Council to give instructions for these documents to be circulated to Member States and if you would also arrange for the text of this letter to be circulated to all States Members of the United Nations.

As you know, the negotiations initiated with your generous assistance have not led to an effective agreement capable of guaranteeing permanent peace in the Caribbean and eliminating the existing tensions.

The Revolutionary Government of Cuba considers that the basic reason why these negotiations have not led to agreements acceptable to Cuba is that the Government of the United States, far from having renounced its aggressive and interventionist policy towards the Republic of Cuba, has maintained the position based on force which it took up in flagrant violation of the rules of international law.

The Cuban Government has stated — and it wishes to reiterate this condition on this occasion — that it cannot regard any agreement as effective unless it takes into consideration the five points or measures put forward as minimum guarantees for peace in the Caribbean by our Prime Minister, Fidel Castro, in his statement of 28 October 1962, which is attached.

These Cuban requests are based on elementary principles of international law. They are not irrational demands, and Cuba considers that no one in the United Nations could validly object to them without disregarding the very foundations of the world Organization. The Cuban Government therefore considers that the United States Government's mere promise not to invade Cuba, which, moreover, has never been given formal shape, would not be any safeguard for our country and would not guarantee peace in the Caribbean.

We wish to draw attention to the fact that the United States Government, apart from the acts of aggression it has committed against Cuba and its preparations to carry out an armed invasion of our country, which brought the world to the brink of war, an outcome avoided by means of agreements which presupposed a commitment by the United States to abandon its aggressive and criminal policy towards Cuba, refuses even to give an assurance that it will not again violate the United Nations Charter by invading the Republic of Cuba, on the pretext that our country has not agreed to international inspection, as has been publicly stated repeatedly throughout this whole affair.

The Cuban Government considers that it is a sovereign right of the nation concerned to agree or not to agree to inspection of its territory and that it is an absurd piece of insolence to offer an undertaking not to invade, the equivalent of an undertaking not to commit an international crime, upon the condition that the country liable to invasion agrees to inspection of its territory.

The Government of Cuba considers, on the other hand, that the Soviet Government has fulfilled the conditions concerning verification proposed by Chairman Nikita Khrushchev in his letter of 28 October 1962 by allowing the withdrawal of intermediate-range ballistic missiles with nuclear warheads to be verified on the high seas and by agreeing to similar methods of verification with regard to IL-28 bombers. Thus the United States Government's claim has no foundation or practical purpose and is merely an excuse for it not to carry out its part of the agreement and to persist in its policy of aggression against Cuba.

The Government of Cuba, moreover, categorically rejects the statement by the United States Government in which it reserves the right to use other means of inspection and verification on its own account. For a Power to officially announce its decision to inspect the territory of another Member State is truly alarming and amounts to a challenge to the United Nations. It implies an intolerable violation of national sovereignty, which Cuba denounces.

The Revolutionary Government of Cuba has already said that it would be ready to agree to the establishment of a system of multiple verification in the countries of the Caribbean region, including the corresponding parts of the United States, under which the extent of countries' compliance with their undertakings could be verified, provided that the United States, for its part, would agree to the adoption of the five measures or points requested by the Cuban Government.

The Cuban Government regrets the fact that the negotiations carried out with the agreement of the Security Council, which you yourself nobly and impartially set in motion, have not led to a satisfactory conclusion capable of guaranteeing peace in this hemisphere and thus throughout the world.

The recent history of this crisis, we repeat, gives palpable proof that the responsibility for this failure and for the maintenance of the tensions which dramatically aroused the fears of all mankind not long ago lies exclusively with the United States Government.

The Revolutionary Government of Cuba wishes to state once more on this occasion that there is no better procedure for solving crises such as this one than peaceful negotiations and discussion between the Governments concerned regarding the sovereign rights of each nation and respect for the rules of international law which govern the coexistence of nations. This is not the criterion which has determined the behaviour of the United States Government, and its stubborn resistance to any durable, satisfactory and fitting settlement is the reason why we are today unable to hail a real solution of the crisis.

Cuba reaffirms its peaceful policy and its desire for peaceful solutions, but wishes to state once more, in the words of the attached statement by the National Directorate of the Integrated Revolutionary Organizations and the Council of Ministers, that "to their positions of strength we shall oppose our firmness; to the intent to humiliate us, our dignity; to aggression, the resolve to fight to the last man."

The Cuban people, as our Prime Minister said during the recent ceremonies commemorating the fourth anniversay of the revolution, "reserve in full the right when confronted by their imperialist enemies and imperialist aggressors always to take any measures and to possess any weapons they consider appropriate."

We have not renounced this right.

Accept, sir, the assurances of my highest consideration.

(s) CARLOS M. LECHUGA
Ambassador
Permanent Representative of Cuba
to the United Nations

New York, 7 January 1963

U.N., *Security Council Document S/5228*, January 7, 1963, pp. 1–4.

❖ ❖ ❖ **93**

LETTER FROM SECRETARY GENERAL U THANT
TO AMBASSADOR STEVENSON,
January 8, 1963

I have received the letter of 7 January signed by you and the First Deputy Foreign Minister of the Union of Soviet Socialist Republics in which you have informed me that "while it has not been possible for our Governments to resolve all the problems that have arisen in connexion with this affair, they believe that, in view of the degree of understanding reached between them on the settlement of the crisis and the extent of progress in the implementation of this understanding, it is not necessary for this item to occupy further the attention of the Security Council at this time."

The letter has been issued as a Security Council document. I am also drawing the attention of the President of the Security Council to this letter, in order that he may inform the other members of the Council.

I share the hope expressed by your Governments that "the actions taken to avert the threat of war in connexion with this crisis will lead toward the adjustment of other differences between them and the general easing of tensions that could cause a further threat of war." I am also confident that all Governments concerned will refrain from any action which might aggravate the situation in the Caribbean area in any way.

I also take this opportunity to thank you and your Government for the appreciation expressed in the letter in regard to such assistance as I may have been able to render.

(s) U THANT
Secretary General

U.N., *Security Council Document* S/5229, January 9, 1963, p. 1.

❖ ❖ ❖ **94**

LETTER FROM SECRETARY GENERAL U THANT TO FIRST DEPUTY MINISTER KUZNETSOV, *January 8, 1963*

I have received the letter of 7 January signed by you and the Permanent Representative of the United States of America in which you have informed me that "while it has not been possible for our Governments to resolve all the problems that have arisen in connexion with this affair, they believe that, in view of the degree of understanding reached between them on the settlement of the crisis and the extent of progress in the implementation of this understanding, it is not necessary for this item to occupy further the attention of the Security Council at this time."

The letter has been issued as a Security Council document. I am also drawing the attention of the President of the Security Council to this letter, in order that he may inform the other members of the Council.

I share the hope expressed by your Governments that "the actions taken to avert the threat of war in connexion with this crisis will lead toward the adjustment of other differences between them and the general easing of tensions that could cause a further threat of war." I am also confident that all Governments concerned will refrain from any action which might aggravate the situation in the Caribbean area in any way.

I also take this opportunity to thank you and your Government for the appreciation expressed in the letter in regard to such assistance as I may have been able to render.

(s) U THANT
Secretary General

U.N., *Security Council Document* S/5230, January 9, 1963, p. 1.

APPENDIX

❖ ❖ ❖

ANNUAL MESSAGE OF PRESIDENT JAMES MONROE TO CONGRESS (MONROE DOCTRINE), PARAGRAPHS 7, 48, 49; *December 2, 1823*

At the proposal of the Russian Imperial Government, made through the minister of the Emperor residing here, a full power and instructions have been transmitted to the Minister of the United States at S. Petersburg, to arrange, by amicable negotiation, the respective rights and interests of the two nations on the northwest coast of this continent. A similar proposal has been made by his Imperial Majesty to the Government of Great Britain, which has likewise been acceded to. The Government of the United States has been desirous, by this friendly proceeding, of manifesting the great value which they have invariably attached to the friendship of the Emperor, and their solicitude to cultivate the best understanding with his Government. In the discussions to which this interest has given rise, and in the arrangements by which they may terminate, the occasion has been judged proper for asserting as a principle in which the rights and interests of the United States are involved, that the American continents, by the free and independent condition which they have assumed and maintain, are henceforth not to be considered as subjects for future colonization by any European powers.

. . . .

It was stated at the commencement of the last session that a great effort was then making in Spain and Portugal to improve the condition of the people of those countries, and that it appeared to be conducted with extraordinary moderation. It need scarcely be remarked that the result has been, so far, very different from what was then anticipated. Of events in that quarter of the globe with which we have so much intercourse, and from which we derive our origin, we have always been anxious and interested spectators. The citizens of the United States cherish sentiments the most friendly in favor of the liberty and happiness of their fellow-men on that side of the Atlantic. In the wars of the European powers in matters relating to themselves we have never taken any part, nor does it comport with our policy so to do. It is only when our rights are invaded or seriously menaced that we

resent injuries or make preparation for our defense. With the movements in this hemisphere we are, of necessity, more immediately connected, and by causes which must be obvious to all enlightened and
impartial observers. The political system of the allied powers is
essentially different in this respect from that of America. This difference proceeds from that which exists in their respective Governments.
And to the defense of our own, which has been achieved by the loss
of so much blood and treasure, and matured by the wisdom of their
most enlightened citizens, and under which we have enjoyed un-
exampled felicity, this whole nation is devoted. We owe it, therefore,
to candor, and to the amicable relations existing between the United
States and those powers, to declare that we should consider any attempt on their part to extend their system to any portion of this
hemisphere as dangerous to our peace and safety. With the existing
colonies or dependencies of any European power we have not inter-
fered and shall not interfere. But with the governments who have
declared their independence and maintained it, and whose independence we have, on great consideration and on just principles,
acknowledged, we could not view any interposition for the purpose of
oppressing them, or controlling in any other manner their destiny, by
any European power, in any other light than as the manifestation of
an unfriendly disposition toward the United States. In the war between these new governments and Spain we declared our neutrality at
the time of their recognition, and to this we have adhered and shall
continue to adhere, provided no change shall occur which, in the
judgment of the competent authorities of this Government, shall make
a corresponding change on the part of the United States indispensable
to their security.

The late events in Spain and Portugal show that Europe is still un-
settled. Of this important fact no stronger proof can be adduced than
that the allied powers should have thought it proper, on any principle
satisfactory to themselves, to have interposed, by force, in the internal
concerns of Spain. To what extent such interposition may be carried,
on the same principle, is a question in which all independent powers
whose governments differ from theirs are interested, even those most
remote, and surely none more so than the United States. Our policy
in regard to Europe, which was adopted at an early stage of the wars
which have so long agitated that quarter of the globe, nevertheless
remains the same, which is, not to interfere in the internal concerns of
any of its powers; to consider the government de facto as the legitimate government for us; to cultivate friendly relations with it, and to
preserve those relations by a frank, firm, and manly policy, meeting, in
all instances, the just claims of every power, submitting to injuries
from none. But in regard to these continents, circumstances are
eminently and conspicuously different. It is impossible that the allied
powers should extend their political system to any portion of either
continent without endangering our peace and happiness; nor can

anyone believe that our southern brethren, if left to themselves, would adopt it of their own accord. It is equally impossible, therefore, that we should behold such interposition, in any form, with indifference. If we look to the comparative strength and resources of Spain and those new governments, and their distance from each other, it must be obvious that she can never subdue them. It is still the true policy of the United States to leave the parties to themselves, in the hope that other powers will pursue the same course."

U.S., Congress, *American State Papers: Documents, Legislative and Executive, of the Congress of the United States,* Selected and Edited under the Authority of Congress by Asbury Dickins, Secretary of the Senate, and James C. Allen, Clerk of the House of Representatives, Second Series, Volume V, Foreign Relations (Washington: Gales & Seaton, 1858), pp. 245– 250.

THE CLARK MEMORANDUM ON THE MONROE DOCTRINE, (EXCERPT FROM INTRODUCTION), *December 17, 1928*

Finally, it should not be overlooked that the United States declined the overtures of Great Britain in 1823 to make a joint declaration regarding the principles covered by the Monroe Doctrine, or to enter into a conventional arrangement regarding them. Instead this Government determined to make the declaration of high national policy on its own responsibility and in its own behalf. The Doctrine is thus purely unilateral. The United States determines when and if the principles of the Doctrine are violated, and when and if violation is threatened. We alone determine what measures if any, shall be taken to vindicate the principles of the Doctrine, and we of necessity determine when the principles have been vindicated. No other power of the world has any relationship to, or voice in, the implementing of the principles which the Doctrine contains. It is our Doctrine, to be by us invoked and sustained, held in abeyance, or abandoned as our high international policy or vital national interests shall seem to us, and to us alone, to demand.

It may, in conclusion, be repeated. The Doctrine does not concern itself with purely inter-American relations; it has nothing to do with the relationship between the United States and other American nations, except where other American nations shall become involved with European governments in arrangements which threaten the security of the United States, and even in such cases, the Doctrine runs against the European country, not the American nation, and the United States would primarily deal thereunder with the European country and not with the American nation concerned. The Doctrine states a case of the United States *vs.* Europe, and not of the United States *vs.* Latin America. Furthermore, the fact should never be lost to view that in applying this Doctrine during the period of one hundred years since it was announced, our Government has over and over again driven it in as a shield between Europe and the Americas to protect Latin America from the political and territorial thrusts of Europe; and this was done at times when the American nations were weak and struggling for the establishment of stable, permanent governments; when the political morality of Europe sanctioned, indeed encouraged, the acquisition of territory by force; and when many of the great powers of Europe looked with eager, covetous eyes to the rich, undeveloped areas of the American Hemisphere. Nor should another equally vital fact be lost sight of, that the United States has only been able to give this protection against designing European powers because of its known willingness and determination, if and whenever necessary, to expend its treasures and to sacrifice American life to maintain the principles of the Doctrine. So far as Latin America is concerned, the Doctrine is now, and always has been, not an instrument of violence and oppression, but an unbought, freely bestowed, and wholly effective guaranty of their freedom, independence, and territorial integrity against the imperialistic designs of Europe.

J. REUBEN CLARK

December 17, 1928

U.S., Department of State, *Memorandum on the Monroe Doctrine: December 17, 1928,* prepared by J. Reuben Clark, Under Secretary of State (Washington: U.S. Government Printing Office, 1930), pp. xxiv–xxv.

✧ ✧ ✧ **C**

INTER-AMERICAN TREATY OF RECIPROCAL ASSISTANCE (RIO PACT), ARTICLES 1, 2, 3, 6, 7, 8, *September 2/December 19, 1947*

Article 1. The High Contracting Parties formally condemn war and undertake in their international relations not to resort to the threat or the use of force in any manner inconsistent with the provisions of the Charter of the United Nations or of this Treaty.

Article 2. As a consequence of the principle set forth in the preceding Article, the High Contracting Parties undertake to submit every controversy which may arise between them to methods of peaceful settlement and to endeavor to settle any such controversy among themselves by means of the procedures in force in the Inter-American System before referring it to the General Assembly or the Security Council of the United Nations.

Article 3. The High Contracting Parties agree that an armed attack by any State against an American State shall be considered as an attack against all the American States and, consequently, each one of the said Contracting Parties undertakes to assist in meeting the attack in the exercise of the inherent right of individual or collective self-defense recognized by Article 51 of the Charter of the United Nations.

Article 6. If the inviolability or the integrity of the territory or the sovereignty or political independence of any American State should be affected by an aggression which is not an armed attack or by an extra-continental or intra-continental conflict, or by any other fact or situation that might endanger the peace of America, the Organ of Consultation shall meet immediately in order to agree on the measures which must be taken in case of aggression to assist the victim of the aggression or, in any case, the measures which should be taken for the common defense and for the maintenance of the peace and security of the Continent.

Article 7. In the case of a conflict between two or more American States, without prejudice to the right of self-defense in conformity with Article 51 of the Charter of the United Nations, the High Contracting Parties, meeting in consultation shall call upon the contending States to suspend hostilities and restore matters to the *status quo ante bellum,* and shall take in addition all other necessary measures to reestablish or maintain inter-American peace and security and for the solution of the conflict by peaceful means. The rejection of the pacifying action will be considered in the determination of the aggressor and in the application of the measures which the consultative meeting may agree upon.

Article 8. For the purposes of this Treaty, the measures on which the Organ of Consultation may agree will comprise one or more of the following: recall of chiefs of diplomatic missions; breaking of diplomatic relations; breaking of consular relations; partial or complete interruption of economic relations or of rail, sea, air, postal, telegraphic, telephonic, and radiotelephonic or radiotelegraphic communications; and use of armed force.

U.S., Department of State, *Bulletin,* Volume XVII, No. 429 (September 21, 1947), pp. 565–567.

CHARTER OF THE ORGANIZATION OF AMERICAN STATES (ACT OF BOGOTÁ) ARTICLES 1, 20, 24, 25, *April 30, 1948/December 13, 1951*

Article 1. The American States establish by this Charter the international organization that they have developed to achieve an order of peace and justice, to promote their solidarity, to strengthen their collaboration, and to defend their sovereignty, their territorial integrity and their independence. Within the United Nations, the Organization of American States is a regional agency.

Article 20. All international disputes that may arise between American States shall be submitted to the peaceful procedures set forth in this Charter, before being referred to the Security Council of the United Nations.

Article 24. Every act of aggression by a state against the integrity or inviolability of the territory or against the sovereignty or political independence of an American State shall be considered an act of aggression against the other American States.

Article 25. If the inviolability or the integrity of the territory or the sovereignty or political independence of any American State should be affected by an armed attack, or by an act of aggression that is not an armed attack, or by an extra-continental conflict, or by a conflict by two or more American States, or by any other fact or situation that might endanger the peace of America, the American States, in furtherance of the principles of continental solidarity or collective self-defense, shall apply the measures and procedures established in the special treaties on the subject.

U S., Department of State, *Bulletin,* Volume XVIII, No. 464 (May 23, 1948), pp. 666-673.

SECOND RESOLUTION OF THE PUNTA DEL ESTE CONFERENCE, *January 22/31, 1962*

WHEREAS:

International communism makes use of highly complex techniques of subversion in opposing which certain states may benefit from mutual advice and support;

The American states are firmly united for the common goal of fighting the subversive action of international communism and for the preservation of democracy in the Americas, as expressed in Resolution XXXII of the Ninth International Conference of American States held in Bogotá, in 1948, and that for such purpose they can and should assist each other, mainly through the use of the institutional resources of the Organization of American States; and

It is advisable, therefore, to make available to the Council of the Organization of American States a body of an advisory nature, made up of experts, the main purpose of which would be to advise the member governments which, as the case may be, require and request such assistance.

The Eighth Meeting of Consultation of Ministers of Foreign Affairs, Serving as Organ of Consultation in Application of the Inter-American Treaty of Reciprocal Assistance,

RESOLVES:

1. To request the Council of the Organization of American States to maintain all necessary vigilance, for the purpose of warning against any acts of aggression, subversion, or other dangers to peace and security, or the preparation of such acts, resulting from the continued intervention of Sino-Soviet powers in this Hemisphere, and to make recommendations to the governments of the member states with regard thereto.

2. To direct the Council of the Organization to establish a Special Consultative Committee of experts on security matters, for the purpose of advising the member states that may desire and request such assistance, the following procedure being observed:

a. The Council of the Organization shall select the membership of the Special Consultative Committee on Security from a list of candidates presented by the governments, and shall define immediately terms of reference for the Committee with a view to achieving the full purposes of this resolution.

b. The Committee shall submit reports to such member states as may request its assistance; however, it shall not publish these reports without obtaining express authorization from the state dealt with in the report.

c. The Special Consultative Committee on Security shall submit to the Council of the Organization, no later than May 1, 1962, an initial general report, with pertinent recommendations regarding measures which should be taken.

d. The Committee shall function at the Pan American Union, which shall extend to it the technical, administrative, and financial facilities required for the work of the Committee.

e. The Committee shall function for the period deemed advisable by the Council of the Organization.

3. To urge the member states to take those steps that they may consider appropriate for their individual or collective self-defense, and

to cooperate, as may be necessary or desirable, to strengthen their capacity to counteract threats or acts of aggression, subversion, or other dangers to peace and security resulting from the continued intervention in this Hemisphere of Sino-Soviet powers, in accordance with the obligations established in treaties and agreements such as the Charter of the Organization of American States and the Inter-American Treaty of Reciprocal Assistance.

U.S., Department of State, *Bulletin,* Volume XLVI, No. 1182 (February 19, 1962), p. 279. (Special Consultative Committee on Security Against the Subversive Action of International Communism. Second Resolution — Adopted by a vote of nineteen to one [Cuba], with one abstention [Bolivia].)

✧ ✧ ✧ **F**

SIXTH RESOLUTION OF THE PUNTA DEL ESTE CONFERENCE, *January 22/31/1962*

WHEREAS:

The inter-American system is based on consistent adherence by its constituent states to certain objectives and principles of solidarity, set forth in the instruments that govern it:

Among these objectives and principles are those of respect for the freedom of man and preservation of his rights, the full exercise of representative democracy, nonintervention of one state in the internal or external affairs of another, and rejection of alliances and agreements that may lead to intervention in America by extra-continental powers;

The Seventh Meeting of Consultation of Ministers of Foreign Affairs, held in San Jose, Costa Rica, condemned the intervention or the threat of intervention of extra-continental communist powers in the Hemisphere and reiterated the obligation of the American states to observe faithfully the principles of the regional organization;

The present Government of Cuba has identified itself with the principles of Marxist-Leninist ideology, has established a political, economic, and social system based on that doctrine, and accepts military assistance from extra-continental communist powers, including even the threat of military intervention in America on the part of the Soviet Union;

The Report of the Inter-American Peace Committee to the Eighth Meeting of Consultation of Ministers of Foreign Affairs establishes that:

The present connections of the Government of Cuba with the Sino-Soviet bloc of countries are evidently incompatible with the principles and standards that govern the regional system, and particularly with the collective security established by the Charter of the OAS and the Inter-American Treaty of Reciprocal Assistance;

The above-mentioned Report of the Inter-American Peace Committee also states that:

It is evident that the ties of the Cuban Government with the Sino-Soviet bloc will prevent the said government from fulfilling the obligations stipulated in the Charter of the Organization and the Treaty of Reciprocal Assistance;

Such a situation in an American state violates the obligations inherent in membership in the regional system and is incompatible with that system; The attitude adopted by the present Government of Cuba and its acceptance of military assistance offered by extra-continental communist powers breaks down the effective defense of the inter-American system; and

No member state of the inter-American system can claim the rights and privileges pertaining thereto if it denies or fails to recognize the corresponding obligations,

The Eighth meeting of Consultation of Ministers of Foreign Affairs, Serving as Organ of Consultation in Application of the Inter-American Treaty of Reciprocal Assistance

DECLARES:

1. That, as a consequence of repeated acts, the present government of Cuba has voluntarily placed itself outside the inter-American system.

2. That this situation demands unceasing vigilance on the part of the member states of the Organization of American States, which shall report to the Council any fact or situation that could endanger the peace and security of the Hemisphere.

3. That the American states have a collective interest in strengthening the inter-American system and reuniting it on the basis of respect for human rights and the principles and objectives relative to the exercise of democracy set forth in the Charter of the Organization; and, therefore,

RESOLVES;

1. That adherence by any member of the Organization of American States to Marxism-Leninism is incompatible with the inter-American system and the alignment of such a government with the communist bloc breaks the unity and solidarity of the hemisphere.

2. That the present Government of Cuba, which has officially identified itself as a Marxist-Leninist government, is incompatible with the principles and objectives of the inter-American system.

3. That this incompatibility excludes the present Government of Cuba from participation in the inter-American system.

4. That the Council of the Organization of American States and

the other organs and organizations of the inter-American system adopt without delay the measures necessary to carry out this resolution.

U.S, Department of State, *Bulletin*, Volume XLVI, No. 1182 (February 19, 1962), p. 281. (Sixth Resolution of the Punta del Este Conference adopted by a vote of fourteen to one [Cuba] with six abstentions [Argentina, Bolivia, Brazil, Chile, Ecuador, Mexico].)

✧ ✧ ✧ **G**

U.S. PROCLAMATION ON EMBARGO OF TRADE WITH CUBA, *February 3, 1962*

WHEREAS the Eighth Meeting of Consultation of Ministers of Foreign Affairs, Serving as Organ of Consultation in Application of the Inter-American Treaty of Reciprocal Assistance, in its Final Act resolved that the present Government of Cuba is incompatible with the principles and objectives of the Inter-American system; and, in light of the subversive offensive of Sino-Soviet communism with which the Government of Cuba is publicly alined, urged the member states to take those steps that they may consider appropriate for their individual and collective self-defense;

WHEREAS the Congress of the United States, in section 620(a) of the Foreign Assistance Act of 1961 (75 Stat. 445), as amended, has authorized the President to establish and maintain an embargo upon all trade between the United States and Cuba; and

WHEREAS the United States, in accordance with its international obligations, is prepared to take all necessary actions to promote national and hemispheric security by isolating the present Government of Cuba and thereby reducing the threat posed by its alinement with the Communist powers:

Now, Therefore, I, John F. Kennedy, President of the United States of America, acting under the authority of section 620(a) of the Foreign Assistance Act of 1961 (75 Stat. 445), as amended, do

1. Hereby proclaim an embargo upon trade between the United States and Cuba in accordance with paragraphs 2 and 3 of this proclamation;

2. Hereby prohibit, effective 12:01 A.M., Eastern Standard Time, February 7, 1962, the importation into the United States of all goods of Cuban origin and all goods imported from or through Cuba; and I hereby authorize and direct the Secretary of the Treasury to carry out such prohibition, to make such exceptions thereto, by license or otherwise, as he determines to be consistent with the effective opera-

tion of the embargo hereby proclaimed, and to promulgate such rules and regulations as may be necessary to perform such functions;

3. And Further, I do hereby direct the Secretary of Commerce, under the provisions of the Export Control Act of 1949, as amended (50 U.S.C.App.2021–2032), to continue to carry out the prohibition of all exports from the United States to Cuba, and I hereby authorize him, under that Act, to continue, make, modify or revoke exceptions from such prohibition.

In Witness Whereof, I have hereunto set my hand and caused the Seal of the United States of America to be affixed.

Done at the City of Washington this third day of February in the year of our Lord nineteen hundred and sixty-two, and of the Independence of the United States of America the one hundred and eighty-sixth.

(s) John F. Kennedy

By the President:

Dean Rusk,
Secretary of State

U.S., Department of State, *Bulletin*, Volume XLVI, No. 1182 (February 19, 1962), p. 283.

"A STEP BY STEP REVIEW" OF THE CUBAN CRISIS, *November 1, 1962*

WASHINGTON, Nov. 1 — The Cuban crisis began in the whirring cameras of a single Air Force U–2 reconnaissance plane high above San Cristóbal on Sunday afternoon, October 14.

By 5:30 P.M. the next day intelligence officers in Washington had completed their preliminary analysis of the developed film and had made up their minds:

Soviet medium-range missiles, the mobile type used by the Red Army, were in place near San Cristóbal, 100 miles west of Havana.

Before the night was over, the incontrovertible evidence had hit the Administration with terrific impact.

"Remember," said an official later, "we had had a posture we'd all signed on to — that this [Soviet build-up] was not an offensive build-up."

Those first reconnaissance pictures set off two weeks of diplomatic thrust and parry, of military build-up and alert, and of strident propaganda activity that were perhaps without precedent in the peacetime history of the United States.

The crisis, though diminished in intensity, has not yet been resolved. For this reason, among others, the full story cannot yet be told. The following is as much as can now be pieced together and revealed:

The Soviet military build-up in Cuba started in the second half of July. At that time American intelligence sources reported suspicious movements of Soviet ships apparently laden with war materiel destined for Cuba.

All through August, according to intelligence reports, the build-up continued. More than thirty ships unloaded 2,000 Soviet technicians and instructors and such war materiel as surface-to-air missiles, patrol boats with missiles and MIG–21 fighters.

But photographic reconnaissance, which had been going on secretly for some time, showed nothing of an offensive character. The President said publicly on September 4 that as far as was known the Soviet arms in Cuba were defensive.

"Were it to be otherwise," he added, "the gravest issues would arise."

Within the Administration the possibility that some of the build-up was offensive was not being overlooked. The intelligence community — the Central Intelligence Agency, military intelligence and others — specifically raised the question whether there might be surface-to-surface missiles in Cuba with nuclear warheads.

Reports of such missiles were coming from Cuban refugees in Florida, who are regularly screened by intelligence agents. And refugee organizations published claims that Cuba had offensive missiles.

As a result of the persistent reports and intelligence concern, President Kennedy approved an order — apparently at the beginning of September — that the entire island of Cuba be photographed.

The Soviet ships heading for Cuba in increasing numbers also gave concern, and they were photographed. A picture taken on September 28 showed crates on a freighter's deck that could hold fuselages of the Ilyushin–28, a twin-engine Soviet jet bomber.

In early October the pictures gave what a high official said was "clear evidence" of Ilyushin–28's in Cuba. This may have been the reason for the secret dispatch of a squadron of Phantoms, a Navy fighter-bomber, to Florida October 6 and a sizable build-up of anti-aircraft and other air defense equipment there.

Hard evidence of missiles was another matter.

As late as September 5, high-altitude photographs of the San Cristóbal area showed an unmarred landscape. For the rest of the month the planes concentrated on the rest of the island, to the east.

But by the beginning of October, agents' reports had convinced officials in Washington that something suspicious was going on around San Cristóbal. On October 3 orders were accordingly issued to go back for more photographs.

The weather intervened. Hurricane Ella delayed flights for a week, and then a cloud cover docked high-altitude surveillance.

It was during this interval, on October 10, that Senator Kenneth B. Keating, Republican, of New York, said he had confirmed reports of intermediate-range missile sites under construction in Cuba.

At last, on the sunny Sunday afternoon of October 14, the cameras of the U–2 provided confirmation.

Looking back with all the evidence available later, officials estimated that the first medium-range missiles — or parts of them — began arriving in Cuba about September 10. Sections started moving to the launching sites about the middle of September.

It takes about twenty-four hours from the time photographs are taken over Cuba until they are processed and analyzed in Washington.

At 3 P.M. Monday, John A. McCone, Director of the Central Intelligence Agency, left Washington to take the body of a stepson who had been killed in Los Angeles to Seattle. The reconnaissance findings, therefore, were first communicated to his deputy, Lieutenant General Marshall S. Carter.

To make sure no mistake had been made, specialists analyzed the photographs through the early evening hours. At about 8.30 P.M. a Central Intelligence official telephoned to [Mc]George Bundy, the President's Special Adviser on National Security Affairs, at home. In security parlance, he informed Mr. Bundy of the incontrovertible evidence of offensive missiles and of the arrangements made for limited distribution of the evidence.

After the past caution, why did that telephone call so swiftly and completely persuade Mr. Bundy that there were offensive missiles in Cuba? This explanation is given:

"The difference was conviction on the part of the experts. And the reason for their conviction was the difference between refugee reports and photographs."

Other telephone calls began to spread the word that evening. Lieutenant General Joseph F. Carroll, Director of the Defense Intelligence Agency, made the calls at the Defense Department.

Even before the guarded call to Mr. Bundy, General Carroll had telephoned the news to Roswell L. Gilpatric, Deputy Secretary of Defense.

Then General Carroll took two civilian photo-analysts of his agency to dinner at the home of the Chairman of the Joint Chiefs of Staff, General Maxwell D. Taylor. At General Taylor's home — and joining in the briefing — were Mr. Gilpatric, General Carter of the Central Intelligence Agency and U. Alexis Johnson, Deputy Under Secretary of State for Political Affairs.

Defense Secretary Robert S. McNamara was not told that night.

He happened to have left the Pentagon unusually early, at 7 P.M., because he was host that night to "Hickory Hill University" — the intellectual gathering usually held at the home of Attorney General Robert F. Kennedy.

At the State Department it was Roger Hilsman, Director of Intelligence and Research. Mr. Hilsman got Secretary of State Rusk out of a dinner he was giving for Gerhard Schröder, the West German Foreign Minister. Mr. Rusk took the call in the pantry.

A team of intelligence experts had worked through the night on a report. At 8 A.M. an intelligence officer accompanied by two photo-analysts took the report and the pictures to Mr. Bundy at the White House.

At about 8:45 Mr. Bundy went to the President's bedroom. Mr. Kennedy was still in pajamas and robe, reading the papers.

Straightaway the President began indicating who should be called in. After less than 10 minutes with the President, Mr. Bundy left to start the machinery.

At the State Department, at 9 A.M., Secretary Rusk was briefed by the Under Secretary, George W. Ball, and Messrs. Hilsman, Johnson and Edward M. Martin, Assistant Secretary for Inter-American Affairs. At 10 Mr. Rusk had to leave to meet the Crown Prince of Libya at the Airport.

The President kept a 9:30 date at the White House with Commander Walter M. Schirra, the astronaut, his wife and two children. The President took them all out to see his daughter Caroline's ponies.

While this was going on General Carter arrived at the White House with other analysts and photographic enlargements. At 11:45 the group later known as the Executive Committee of the National Security Council assembled in the Cabinet room.

The President presided. Also present were Vice President Johnson, Secretary Rusk, Secretary of Defense McNamara, Secretary of the Treasury Douglas Dillon, Attorney General Kennedy, Under Secretary Ball, Deputy Secretary of Defense Gilpatric, General Carter, Assistant Secretary of State Martin, General Taylor, Mr. Bundy and Theodore C. Sorenson, Counsel and principal speech writer.

To those in the Cabinet room, it now seems in retrospect that the issues that dominated the week's deliberations were already visible, "in a sketchy way," at this meeting.

An air of challenge hung over the room. There was an awareness that any United States response might worsen the world situation. But not challenging the Soviet move would surely be the worst course of all.

In first analysis of what Premier Khrushchev was up to, Berlin bulked very large.

The first reading, as one official put it was, "This is a left hook designed to make him tougher when he comes at us in November, presumably on Berlin." Premier Khrushchev, they were convinced, planned to present the United States with a nasty set of alternatives.

If the United States did nothing, the credibility of its pledges would be destroyed. The Soviet Union would have made a military gain vis-à-vis this country, and a big political score in Latin America. One official said: "Latin American affairs would never have been the same. To the Latins Mr. Khrushchev might look like a winner."

If the United States bombed the bases or invaded Cuba, its moral position in the world would be tarnished. A great cry would go up from the neutral nations and the North Atlantic Treaty Organization alliance would be thrown into disarray. The Russians would have an excuse for counteraction in Berlin or some other spot.

The third possibility began to be considered at that first meeting was some sort of blockade. It, too, might provide grounds for a Soviet response in Berlin. It might irritate our North Atlantic Treaty allies because many of them are maritime powers sensitive to freedom of the seas. And it might not get at the missiles already in Cuba.

At this first meeting the President and his advisers were not yet clear on what was to be their objective — to get the offensive weapons out of Cuba. Some talked, rather, about getting Premier Castro out.

The meeting produced two immediate decisions. One was to intensify air surveillance of Cuba. The second was that action should await further knowledge, but should come as close as possible to disclosure of the Russian bases — which could not be long delayed. The President should disclose the news about the bases at the time he put in motion the United States' response.

The decision to time the announcement with the response necessarily put a tight time framework on the enterprise. To gain as much time as possible in traditionally loose-lipped Washington, the President ordered everyone at the meeting to keep the tightest security. Intelligence data would go only to those with a "need to know." Secretaries and friends would not be told.

By the end of the first meeting some of the enormous problems of staff work were evident.

The Pentagon had to produce estimates of the time factor, the kinds of units and the number of men involved in the various military alternatives.

The State Department would begin exploring the chances of support from Latin America and from our European allies, who had often said Cuba was our problem and who had themselves lived for years under the shadow of Soviet bases.

That afternoon at the State Department the "demonologists" — Federal language for Russian experts — were brought into the picture.

Ambassador-at-Large, Llewellyn E. Thompson Jr. and Charles E. Bohlen, who was about to leave for Paris to take up the duties of

Ambassador there, conferred with Mr. Rusk. Both were former Ambassadors to Moscow.

Adlai E. Stevenson, United States representative at the United Nations, was also brought into the discussions. He was in Washington to talk to a private session of newspaper editors at the State Department. In a similar session the day before, high officials had told the editors that the Government knew of no offensive missiles in Cuba.

Weeks before, the President had promised Connecticut Democrats to campaign for them Wednesday, October 17. After a meeting with Mr. McCone and Mr. Bundy he took off for speaking dates in Stratford, New Haven and Waterbury. He was gone until about midnight.

In his absence the top-level planning group met at the State Department, in Mr. Ball's conference room, most of the day and night. The meetings were neither formal nor orderly. Men would wander in and out doing jobs. Sandwiches were brought in when needed.

There was much discussion that day of a "surgical operation" — an air strike to take the missiles out of Cuba by force.

Invasion was not considered as a possible first action. It would take too long to mount. Surprise would be impossible. The effect on world opinion was certain to be unfavorable. The Soviet response might rapidly "escalate" the affair.

But the air strike did win significant support. So did a blockade.

New photographs coming in from the U–2's added to the urgency of the situation. They provided more evidence of the medium-range missiles at San Cristóbal and also showed intermediate (longer) range sites under construction in the Guanajay area between San Cristóbal and Havana. It was estimated that intermediate-range sites would be ready for missiles by December 1. Later other intermediate sites were found at Remedios in eastern Cuba.

Dean Acheson, the former Secretary of State, joined in the meetings most of that day. He had been called in that morning by Mr. Rusk.

On Thursday morning the newspapers carried a report that the Defense Department had begun a build-up of air power in the southeastern United States. A Pentagon spokesman called this "an ordinary thing to do" in the light of Cuban possession of jet fighters.

Actually, a considerable military deployment was under way — ostensibly under previous orders not connected with the Cuban crisis.

The Navy had long scheduled a Navy-Marine amphibious exercise called Philbriglex-62. By the middle of the week there were 5,000 marines at sea and forty ships converging on the Caribbean.

The purpose of the exercise was to liberate the mythical "Republican of Vieques" from the rule of a tyrant named Ortsac — Castro spelled backwards.

Eventually, of course, the exercise was canceled, and the ships and planes were used for blockade duty. But it was important to maintain the myth of the exercise as long as possible. Newsmen scheduled to board the ships in Puerto Rico were told that they could not because bad weather had dispersed the fleet.

President Kennedy's official schedule Thursday was an ordinary mixture of the serious and the ceremonial.

At 9:30 he presented some aviation trophies. At 10 he met with the Cabinet on domestic affairs. At noon he met with a former Japanese Finance Minister, Eifaku Sato. At 5 P.M. he was to meet Soviet Foreign Minister Andrei A. Gromyko. This meeting had been set before the crisis.

Unannounced sessions with the planners in the Cuba crisis were sandwiched into the President's schedule at 11 A.M. and 3 P.M. During the rest of the daylight hours they met without him, again at the State Department.

The absence of the President from these meetings was deliberate. During the whole week he, and sometimes Mr. Rusk and Mr. McNamara, stayed away at times so that their subordinates could speak their minds more freely on the ideas of both "the boss" and their own colleagues.

But at the decision-time meetings, in the White House, it was the President who gave the orders. "He held everyone under tight control," one official said. "He issued orders like a military officer expecting to be obeyed immediately and to be challenged only on grounds of overriding disagreement."

The meeting of the planners that afternoon was in Secretary Rusk's conference room. It moved the thinking of the group more clearly toward a blockade as opposed to a strike.

The tendency had been in that direction anyway. Those who had spoken for a strike were weighing the consequences of the most-certain casualties among Soviet military personnel.

At 5 P.M. Secretary Rusk and Mr. Thompson left for the White House to join the President's session with Foreign Secretary Gromyko. The meeting lasted two hours and fifteen minutes — and was a strange affair.

Mr. Gromyko repeated the public assurance of Soviet officials that assistance to Cuba was only for defensive purposes. He said he would speak frankly because he knew the President appreciated frankness.

The President, in response, called attention to his earlier statements that the Soviet effort in Cuba was defensive — and to his warning that any change in that estimate would have grave consequences.

There is still some question in the minds of officials whether Mr. Gromyko knew that day the full extent of the Soviet commitment in Cuba Officials are virtually certain that Soviet Ambassador Anatoly F. Dobrynin, who accompanied him to the White House, did not know.

Why did the President not confront Mr. Gromyko with what he

knew? A number of critics of United States policy have suggested that this should have been done, that the Russians should have been given a last chance to draw back.

One reason for not telling Mr. Gromyko, according to the President's advisers, was that the Administration had not yet decided what action to take. Another was the fear that, in the face of a warning, the Russians would not really back off, but would take some evasive action to blunt the effect of the eventual decision.

Mr. Gromyko was jovial with reporters as he came out of the meeting. He said the talk had been "useful, very useful."

The President had asked to see Robert A. Lovett, former Secretary of Defense, the only outsider brought in except for Mr. Acheson. He was briefed by Mr. Bundy during the Gromyko call, then brought upstairs to the President.

At eight o'clock Mr. Gromyko joined Secretary Rusk, Mr. Thompson and others for dinner on the eighth floor of the State Department Building. One floor below — unknown to Mr. Gromyko — the planning group continued its crisis discussions.

When Mr. McCone and Mr. McNamara arrived at the State Department reporters happened to see them and asked whether they were going to the Gromyko dinner. The two said they were.

There was one further security scare that evening, when someone remarked on the vast number of Government limousines parked outside the State Department. Mr. Ball sent all but one into the Department's underground garage.

At 9 P.M. nine members of the planning group (they called it "The Think Tank" among themselves at that time, or sometimes "The War Council") went over to the White House. They all piled into one limousine.

From there Attorney General Kennedy called his deputy, Nicholas deB. Katzenbach, at home and asked him to get to work on the legal basis for a blockade of Cuba.

Ambassador Thompson had emphasized in the meetings the need for a solid legal basis for any action taken. He said the Russians had a feeling for "legality," and there was general agreement that a good legal case would help with world reaction.

Mr. Katzenbach, a former professor of international law, met at the Justice Department with three department lawyers: Harold F. Reis, Leon Ulman and Richard K. Berg. He did not tell them precisely why they were there; he just said that the situation in Cuba was deteriorating, and that the possibility of a blockade had to be researched.

At the State Department, meanwhile, the Deputy Legal Adviser, Leonard C. Meeker, was doing his own research on blockade law. The Legal Adviser, Abram J. Chayes, was in Paris on a mission to halt Western shipping to Cuba.

The President had scheduled Friday for political campaigning. He and the "Think Tank" had decided he should stick to the plans, for one thing to avoid arousing suspicions.

The secret had been well kept despite the presence of some clues. It was announced this day, for example, that Secretary McNamara had asked the Joint Chiefs of Staff to stay in Washington for six weeks to consult on "budget planning."

Before leaving, the President indicated his approval of the trend of decision toward blockade. All along, the planners spoke of "blockade." The President himself came up later with the word "quarantine."

At 10 A.M. in Washington the planners met again at the State Department. Mr. Katzenbach and Mr. Meeker were included for the first time. Each gave a brief statement of his legal views.

They agreed that a resolution by the Organization of American States would provide strong legal support for a blockade. Mr. Katzenbach thought a unilateral order for a blockade could be justified legally if necessary; Mr. Meeker was less certain.

During that meeting there were some second thoughts about the blockade, some renewed interest in an air attack. The reason was the reading of what the group called a "scenario" — a paper indicating in detail the possible consequences of an action — for the blockade.

One decision was pretty well tied down that morning: the President would speak Monday night. That was the earliest time possible if all necessary steps were to be taken first.

The President left Cleveland just before 2. He stopped at Springfield, Ill., to lay flowers on Lincoln's tomb.

In Mr. Ball's conference room there was a critical session of the "War Council." The issue, again, was strike or blockade.

Attorney General Kennedy argued against a strike on moral grounds. He reminded the group of Pearl Harbor. For the United States to attack a small country like Cuba without warning, he said, would irreparably hurt our reputation in the world — and our own conscience.

The moral argument won general assent. As one official put it later: "A surprise attack would violate our deepest traditions and aspirations. What kind of a country would this be after such an action?"

The blockade proposal was recognized as the one raising the most serious dangers. As recently as October 6 Vice President Johnson had warned that "stopping a Russian ship is an act of war."

By the end of the afternoon meeting the blockade was clearly the indicated answer. But it was decided to do thorough staff work on alternatives, so the President could have everything before him when he decided. Mr. Bundy made it his special duty to keep the alternatives alive.

The President reached Chicago late in the afternoon and went to the Sheraton Blackstone, seemingly enjoying the crowds. One man held a sign about Cuba: "Less profile — More courage."

From Chicago Mr. Kennedy checked with the "War Council" by telephone. It was indicated that he probably should break off campaigning the next day and come home. But the final decision was put off until the next morning.

That evening Mr. Katzenbach called to his office the Defense Department's general counsel, John T. McNaughton, and Mr. McNamara's special assistant, Adam Yarmolinsky. He asked them to start drafting a blockade proclamation.

Mr. Ball kept a speaking date with the Board of the Chamber of Commerce.

At 9.35 A.M. (Central Daylight Time) on Saturday, in the Sheraton Blackstone, Pierre Salinger announced that the President was canceling the rest of his trip and flying back to Washington.

Mr. Salinger had gotten the word from Kenneth O'Donnell, the White House appointments secretary. He explained that Rear Admiral George Burkley, assistant White House physician, had found that the President had a slight infection of the upper respiratory tract, with one degree of fever. The story was false. The President had neither a cold nor a fever. He had instructed Mr. O'Donnell to pass the misleading report to Mr. Salinger so that he could get home without causing an upset.

Robert Kennedy had stepped out of a "Think Tank" meeting that morning to return a call from the President. Time was growing short. Besides, the secrecy that was the purpose of fulfilling the campaign plans was already crumbling.

There was tension in Washington. Reporters were beginning to ask questions. One called Mr. Salinger immediately after the President's return and asked point-blank whether there was an emergency. Mr. Salinger said he knew of none.

Mr. Kennedy reached the White House at 1:37 P.M., supposedly to go to bed. Mr. Bundy briefed him. He read a first draft of the proposed speech for Monday evening prepared overnight by Mr. Sorensen. Eventually the speech went through five drafts.

That afternoon, upstairs in the Oval Room, the President all but clinched the decision for blockade. He ordered operations to proceed, subject only to a final word from him the next day.

The smell of crisis hung over Washington that evening like the smell of burning leaves. Too many trips had been canceled, too many announcements made for what seemed "good" rather than real reasons.

All over town high officials failed to turn up for dinner parties or else left suddenly, murmuring apologies. Reporters used all their numbers and succeeded only in alerting half the diplomatic corps.

At the Pentagon Mr. Katzenbach, Mr. Chayes, Mr. McNaughton

and Mr. Yarmolinsky buttoned up the main points of the blockade proclamation.

At the State Department officials were preparing such things as the approach to the Organization of American States, Mr. Acheson was asked to take the news of the blockade to General de Gaulle and to the North Atlantic Treaty Organization Council.

Alexis Johnson turned out a "master scenario" for the whole Government, laying out everything that would have to be done before the President's speech — orders to embassies, ship movements and briefings. The scheduled hour of the speech 7 P.M. Monday was called P hour. The scenario began with 7 P.M. Saturday — "P minus 48."

Sunday was a golden fall day in Washington. It was also a day of tremendous activity.

At 11 A.M. there was a meeting of key officials with the President in the executive mansion. The President had wanted certain specific information from certain people. The information confirmed his view on the blockade, and the all-clear signal was given about noon.

At 2:30 P.M. in the White House the real, statutory National Security Council, with the Office of Emergency Planning represented for the first time, met formally.

In the State Department forty-three letters were drafted for the President's signature to the heads of government of all the alliances around the globe, as well as to Willy Brandt, Mayor of West Berlin. Also drafted was the letter from the President to Premier Khrushchev to be delivered with a copy of the speech.

In addition, instructions were drafted to sixty embassies concerning delivery of the letters or of the speech itself. All embassies or consulates were warned to take precautions against demonstrations and riots.

The Latin American nations were to be informed of the plan for a meeting of the Organization of American States Tuesday and given copies of the United States resolution to be introduced. This required work late into the night.

P Day had arrived.

At 9 A.M. the "Think Tank," including Messrs. Rusk, McNamara, Robert Kennedy, Ball, and Alexis Johnson, met in the White House. The National Security Council formally transformed the "tank" group into its own executive committee.

While the meeting was going on, Lawrence F. O'Brien, the President's Congressional liaison, began telephoning twenty leaders of both parties. The President wanted them back in Washington today, Mr. O'Brien told them.

Some could make it by commercial aircraft. Those who couldn't were fetched by Air Force planes. A few got the ride of their lives in jet fighters.

At noon Mr. Salinger announced that the President would make a speech of the greatest urgency by radio and television at 7 P.M.

At 1 P.M. the President took a quick swim in the White House pool, then lunched in the family dining room and returned to his office at about 2.

There were two moments of consternation:

First, Foreign Secretary Gromyko's departure for Moscow had been held up by bad weather in New York. Around noon, the Soviet United Nations mission announced it would soon have an important statement. There was fear the Russians had got wind of the United States plans. A plan was quickly formed to issue a short announcement of the blockade, which would be followed later by the speech. Mr. Salinger called in the microphones and cameras. But the Soviet statement turned out to be merely Mr. Gromyko's farewell. He took off early in the afternoon.

Second, at one point during the day a Soviet Ilyushin-18, a four-engine turboprop, was spotted heading for Cuba. There was a great to-do over whether it should be ordered away. Only at the last moment, Washington got word that it was heading for Brazil to pick up the remains of the Soviet Ambassador who had drowned the week before.

During the afternoon the State Department called Ambassador Dobrynin, who was in New York to see Mr. Gromyko off, and asked him to come to Mr. Rusk's office at 6 P.M.

There was frantic activity in the State Department to make sure all embassies had received Sunday's messages. It was discovered that a radio relay station in Nicosia, Cyprus, had blacked out, and that some of the embassies in Africa had not received the message. It was too late to do anything about it, and word was given to the African nations through their embassies here.

Last-minute changes in the speech were radioed, and then instructions for delivery of the speech and letters to all the foreign governments.

A message went to General Lauris E. Norstad, about to retire as NATO Commander in Chief, warning him to be on the alert for possible trouble in the NATO area.

In Brussels John J. McCloy was about to go into a big private business conference when he got a call from Mr. Rusk. He told the waiting businessmen, "Sorry, boys, I hate to drop names, but the Secretary needs me." He took the next plane home.

In Paris, Mr. Acheson called on President de Gaulle in the afternoon at the Elysée Palace and told him of the President's plans. President de Gaulle, Mr. Acheson reported later, was "splendid." If he resented the unilateral action being taken without prior consultation, he did not show it. He listened to Mr. Acheson courteously, asked some pertinent questions and expressed his support of the United States.

At 3 P.M., in Washington the National Security Council met at the White House. Then the Cabinet met. At 4 P.M., the President greeted the Prime Minister of Uganda, Milton Obote. Forty-five minutes later, when the President escorted Mr. Obote through the swarming news room to his waiting limousine, reporters crowded about him.

"It has been a very interesting day," the President said with the air of a man whose mind was elsewhere.

In front of the White House hundreds of pickets paraded with advice — "Don't chicken this time, Jack," "Cuba can be negotiated," "Peace, Mr. President."

It was P-minus two hours and time for the briefings. At 5 P.M. the President and Secretary Rusk laid the photos before the Congressional leaders.

"We have decided to take action," the President told them.

Senator Richard B. Russell, Democrat of Georgia and chairman of the Senate Armed Services Committee, spoke his mind. He thought invasion was the only solution. Blockade was too slow and therefore carried the greater risk. He found support in Senator J. W. Fulbright who, in April, 1961, had unavailingly urged the President not to support an invasion by Cuban refugees.

The President listened without anger, but was not to be dissuaded.

At 6 P.M. Ambassador Dobrynin was affable with newsmen as he entered Mr. Rusk's office.

With Mr. Rusk were Mr. Martin, John C. Guthrie, head of the Office of Soviet Affairs, and Helmut Sonnenfeld, a Russian-speaking expert on the Soviet Union.

When Mr. Dobrynin emerged twenty-five minutes later, the President's speech and letter clutched in his hand, he looked grim and shaken.

"Ask the Secretary," he said when a reporter asked whether there was a crisis. When he was asked to appraise the situation he snapped, "You can judge for yourself."

At 6:15 Under Secretary Ball and Mr. Hilsman, Director of the Department's Bureau of Intelligence and Research, briefed forty-six allied ambassadors in the State Department's International Conference Room.

In the President's study, as the minute hand moved toward the hour, Mr. Kennedy cast an eye over his speech. A sound of voices came through an open door at one side. The President looked around as if startled. The door was hastily closed. His secretary, Evelyn Lincoln, came in with a brush for a final swipe at his hair. The technicians gave the signal. He was on the air.

The President began with the evidence of the missile sites. He did not blame Cuba for the crisis, but the Soviet Union which, he said, had violated the most solemn assurances of its leaders that only defensive weapons were being sent to Cuba.

And he drew the line with the Soviet Union.

"This secret, swift and extraordinary build-up of Communist missiles — in an area well known to have a special and historical relationship to the United States and the nations of the Western Hemisphere is a deliberately provocative and unjustified change in the *status quo* which cannot be accepted by this country, if our courage and our commitments are ever to be trusted by either friend or foe."

The President said that he had ordered a quarantine on all such offensive weapons for Cuba and that ships carrying them would be turned back.

Furthermore, he said, the preparation of the missile sites must cease, and if it did not, "further action" would be taken. He was ordering the surveillance continued. Finally, he called upon Chairman Khrushchev to withdraw the weapons already there.

In the State Department the forty-six allied ambassadors who had been briefed watched the speech on a large screen.

At 7:30 Mr. Martin gave a further private briefing for the Latin American Ambassadors in Mr. Ball's office.

At 8 Secretary Rusk and Mr. Hilsman briefed the ambassadors of the so-called neutral nations, including Yugoslavia, in the International Conference room.

At the same hour Mr. Ball and Mr. Chayes, the State Department Legal Adviser, held a large briefing for diplomatic correspondents, and in the Pentagon Secretary McNamara briefed military correspondents. The Secretary of Defense made very clear that "whatever force is required" — even sinking — would be used to prevent ships from trying to run the blockade.

Meanwhile the United States had called for the Organization of American States to meet the next day in its highest capacity — as an organ of consultation.

And in New York, Mr. Stevenson delivered a letter to Valerian A. Zorin, head of the Soviet delegation to the United Nations, who was the October President of the Security Council, calling on him to summon an urgent meeting of the Council.

With the letter went a draft resolution calling on the Soviet Union to dismantle and withdraw the missiles under United Nations verification, after which the United States would end the quarantine and the two nations could confer "on measures to remove the existing threat to the security of the Western Hemisphere and the peace of the world."

During the evening Mr. Acheson in Paris had laid before the North Atlantic Treaty Organization Council the reasons for the United States action. He got a courteous, considered hearing. A few questions were asked and general support was expressed by the allies.

Thirteen hours after the President's speech came Moscow's first reaction. On Tuesday at 3 P.M. Moscow time — 8 A.M. Eastern daylight time — Tass, the Soviet press agency, began sending out a Government statement. At the same time Foy D. Kohler, the United States Ambassador, was handed the statement at the Foreign Office, together with a letter from Chairman Khrushchev to President Kennedy.

The statement was long and discursive. Accusations against the United States of "unheard of violation of international law," commission of "piracy," and "provocative" acts that might lead to thermonuclear war alternated with tributes to peace, professions of the most humanitarian motives toward Cuba and indignant denials that the missiles were intended for offensive purposes.

Altogether it was interpreted in Washington as betraying an uncertainty that convinced the experts that the Kremlin had been caught off guard and was playing for time to think out its next move. There was an almost immediate feeling that Soviet strategy, whatever its intended thrust, had been checked by the President's challenge.

This feeling grew as reaction came in from European capitals and the drama unfolded at the Organization of American States.

Prime Minister Macmillan, in the first of what were to become daily calls to the President, gave Mr. Kennedy full support. The Foreign Office straightaway issued a statement charging the Soviet Union with "deliberately" threatening the United States and Latin America.

In the morning Mr. Acheson left Paris for Bonn. He and Chancellor Adenauer are old and warm friends, and they had a long session. Later Mr. Acheson talked with Defense Minister Franz Josef Strauss. German support was wholehearted.

In New York, representatives of the other NATO nations said they had instructions to vote for the United States resolution.

The meeting of the Organization of American States began at 9 A.M. and ran into the early evening. Secretary Rusk represented the United States. He offered the resolution to authorize the use of force, individually or collectively, to enforce the blockade. He cited the Rio Pact of 1947.

Although the necessary two-thirds majority was assured, some delegates had not yet received detailed instructions from their governments.

To speed communications, Assistant Secretary Martin made arrangements with the telephone company to get top government priorities for the Latin American embassies.

As the meeting progressed, delegates darted back and forth between their seats and the telephones.

A few minutes before 5 P.M. the Council approved the resolution, 19 to 0. Emilio Oribe of Uruguay never got his instructions and abstained. Emilio Sarmiento Carruncho of Bolivia got through to La Paz, but could hear nothing over the bad connection. He took his political life in his hands and voted "Sí."

The unanimity of the council, together with the solid support of the NATO allies for the blockade decision, is believed by officials to have surprised the Soviet Union, and accounted for much of her diplomatic confusion during the week.

During the planning stage, no one expected such overwhelming support Why did the United States get it? In part, officials said, the sudden reality that missiles that could reach their own countries enabled some Latin American Presidents to defy the leftist opinion that had cowed them before.

In part, also, the outcome was credited to Assistant Secretary of State Martin who had organized, drafted, and argued all day and most of the night to round up the vote that would hit Moscow with staggering impact.

The President was prepared to act alone, but he wanted the support of the Organization of American States before issuing the proclamation of a blockade legally based on the Rio Pact. Therefore, the proclamation was held up until after the vote.

In it he declared and prohibited contraband — offensive missiles, their warheads and electronic equipment, and bomber aircraft. He authorized the Navy to stop and search any vessel believed to be carrying contraband to Cuba, to take it into custody if it refused to sail to another port and to use force if necessary.

The blockade would become effective at 10 the next morning.

At the Pentagon the same evening, Secretary McNamara said twenty-five Soviet merchant ships were heading toward Cuba, their course unchanged in the last twenty-four hours. He had sent orders to interdict these and all other ships headed for Cuba the next day.

Under authority granted the President by Congress October 3, Mr. McNamara ordered in the tours of duty of all Navy and Marine Corps personnel extended until further notice.

In New York the first round at the Security Council followed a familiar script. Ambassador Zorin countered the American resolution with one calling upon the United States to withdraw the blockade, stop interfering in Cuba's domestic affairs and enter talks with the Soviet Union to normalize the situation.

Mr. Stevenson said the Soviet Union had presented the "world of the Charter" with the most fateful challenge since World War II.

At the White House during the morning, the Executive Committee met with the President, and at the State Department the British, French and West German Ambassadors conferred with United States officials on a possible Soviet countermove against Berlin.

The blockade went into effect at 10 A.M. Wednesday.

From Moscow that morning came word that the Soviet Government had returned the President's proclamation of a blockade as unacceptable. Soon after the news agencies carried bulletins that Premier Khrushchev had proposed a summit meeting.

The proposal turned out to be a somewhat vague suggestion in a message to Bertrand Russell, the British philosopher and pacifist.

Mr. Khrushchev told Lord Russell — who once advocated dropping nuclear bombs on the Soviet Union if it refused international control of the atom — that he would take no "reckless decision."

The Premier's suggestion brought no response from the President, for officials here looked on it only as another delaying move that offered no real clue to Soviet intentions.

But a proposal that could not be ignored came from an unexpected quarter: U Thant, the Acting Secretary General of the United Nations. He acted largely on his own, but with the urging of the large group of non-aligned nations, whose thought was to draw the nuclear powers apart.

Mr. Thant sent letters to Mr. Kennedy and Mr. Khrushchev urging the suspension for two or three weeks of both the blockade and the arms shipments to Cuba while negotiations were held.

Mr. Khrushchev hastily accepted the proposal, but Washington was displeased and annoyed.

Washington thought the proposal would surely disarm its powerful diplomatic and military initiative and doubted that it could ever regain momentum if negotiations failed, as it was expected they would. The path of negotiation already had been rejected until the Russians agreed to undo their move, until they had dismantled Cuban bases.

Mr. Thant's proposal was not much sweetened in Washington's view by his subsequent expression that it would be helpful if work on "major military installations" in Cuba were also suspended during negotiations.

The President met with the executive committee during the day and with Congressional leaders who were leaving for home, subject to return on eight hours' notice from the White House. Mr. Kennedy ordered the Cabinet to follow his and the Vice President's example by canceling all campaigning.

At the State Department, Secretary Rusk met at 3 P.M. with the British, French and West German Ambassadors to keep them posted. In the afternoon, intelligence officials, at Britain's request, reviewed some passages in the speech that Prime Minister Macmillan was to deliver in the House of Commons the next day.

What about work on the missile bases?

To get that information accurately and speedily, the President this day authorized special low-level reconnaissance missions by Navy P-8U's flying in groups of four to eight planes, to supplement the high-level photography of the U-2's. The Navy planes found the work at the bases was continuing unabated.

And what about the blockade?

At about noon, Secretary McNamara said the Communist ship

nearest Cuba should make contact with the blockade by about 7:30 P.M. But later in the afternoon, Assistant Secretary Arthur Sylvester, the Pentagon press chief, announced that some of the Soviet ships had apparently altered course.

In the first day of the blockade, no contact was made. And that was the day's biggest news.

At 8 A.M. — twenty hours after the imposition of the blockade — a Navy ship made the first interception of a Soviet ship. It was the oil tanker *Bucharest,* and it was allowed to proceed to Cuba without search because the Navy was satisfied it carried only petroleum.

Although the day had begun rather auspiciously in low key, tension rapidly mounted as rumors began to circulate that the United States would invade Cuba, or at least bomb the missile sites, if the Soviet Union did not quickly stop construction.

In part this talk was set off by a statement of Representative Hale Boggs, Democrat of Louisiana, to his constituents.

"Believe me," he said, "if these missiles are not dismantled, the United States has the power to destroy them, and I assure you this will be done."

The rumors gained impetus with reports of the arrival of Marine contingents in the Florida keys and a continued military build-up there.

At the dinner hour and all through the evening millions of Americans viewed on television the melodramatic challenge of Ambassador Zorin by Mr. Stevenson in the Security Council that afternoon.

Leaning forward and looking directly at the Russian, Mr. Stevenson challenged him to say "yes or no" whether the Soviet Union was placing medium- and intermediate-range missiles and sites in Cuba.

"I am prepared to wait for my answer until hell freezes over if that is your decision," said Mr. Stevenson. Then: "And I am also prepared to present the evidence in this room."

With that he turned to the blow-up photographs of the missile sites waiting on easels behind him.

While this was great spectator sport, the significant developments of the day were the replies of Chairman Khrushchev and President Kennedy to the Thant appeal for a moratorium and the interpretation of the United States position which Washington officials supplied reporters for guidance.

Mr. Khrushchev wrote U Thant: "I agree with your proposal, which meets the interests of peace."

The President wrote: "The existing threat was created by secret introduction of offensive weapons into Cuba, and the answer lies in the removal of such weapons.

But the word from American intelligence sources was that work on the missile bases was continuing at full speed.

In Washington, officials made clear that Mr. Thant's proposal as it stood was unacceptable, even temporarily. The ultimate objective was the removal of the missiles. Nothing else would suffice. And there must be verification. There would be no reliance on the Soviet word and no relaxation of surveillance. The United States was always willing to talk, but without limitation on its freedom of action.

After the Executive Committee meeting at the White House, all the top State Department officials gathered in Mr. Rusk's office. The mood all around was grim and tough. The next move was up to Moscow.

In his speech to Commons, Prime Minister MacMillan made no concession to criticism of the United States by many Labor party members. He said the Soviet Union had launched "a deliberate adventure designed to test the ability and the determination of the United States." In any negotiations, the word of the Soviet Union must be verified, he said.

. This was the day, with the Kremlin still stalling, that the United States Government began to step up the psychological pressure.

Once again the prelude was deceptive, giving little hint of "the act coming on." Just before 8 A.M. two destroyers that had been tailing a Soviet-chartered freighter of Lebanese registry all night put search parties aboard her without incident. When the search disclosed no contraband the ship was cleared to proceed to Cuba.

At the usual morning Executive Committee meeting at the White House, Mr. Stevenson was understood to have been instructed to make it unmistakably clear to Mr. Thant that the United States was immovable in its determination to get the missiles out of Cuba. One high official said: "Adlai was down to pick up his Oscar."

In the regular noon briefing, the State Department press officer, Lincoln White, called attention to a sentence in the President's Monday night speech declaring that if the Soviet's offensive military preparations continued, "further action will be justified."

In the afternoon Mr. Salinger said at a White House news conference that the Russians "are rapidly continuing" work on the sites, and showed no intention "to dismantle or discontinue work" on them.

Early in the evening the White House issued a new intelligence report. In detail it reported the activities of bull-dozers and cranes at the intermediate-range missile bases and the refinements over the past few days at the medium-range sites. The Russians, the White House said, were obviously trying to achieve "full operational capability as soon as possible."

The Army moved antiaircraft missiles into Key West. The Commander of the Atlantic Fleet, Admiral Robert L. Dennison, said the strengthened Guantanamo Naval Base was now defensible against attack.

Amid reports of imminent military action newsmen asked: "Tomorrow or Monday?" The Pentagon spokesman declined to comment on a statement by Representative Clement Zablocki, Democrat of Wisconsin, that the United States might soon have to resort to "pinpoint bombing" of the missile bases.

At the Organization of American States headquarters, Latin diplomats were reported in agreement that the resolution authorized the United States to dismantle the bases by force if necessary.

That evening, after talks with Mr. Stevenson and Mr. Zorin, the United Nations chief made public the replies of the President and Mr. Khrushchev to a new appeal. Mr. Thant had asked the Premier to keep Soviet vessels away from the blockade zone for a few days and Mr. Kennedy to order the Navy to avoid direct confrontation with Soviet ships.

The two leaders agreed, but the President said that the withdrawal of the military systems was "a matter of great urgency," and he reminded Mr. Thant that the work still went on.

The late editions of many evening newspapers had headlines on possible invasion or bombing.

At the White House officials later had made plain to newsmen that any next step would almost certainly have been an expansion of the blockade rather than an attack.

"Invasion was hardly ever seriously considered," one official stated. Another said that the air-strike possibility did not disappear after the President's first decision, but that considerations of decency and caution had deferred it until a time when it might have been necessary and no longer a surprise.

That time, officials agree, had not arrived Friday night.

But the Kremlin might well have wondered if the time was fast approaching.

At about 9 P.M. — 4 A.M. Moscow time — a letter from Premier Khrushchev to the President began to come into the State Department message center from Moscow.

It came in bit by bit as it was translated by the embassy in Moscow. In the department officials read it eagerly. It was rambling, but the tone seemed conciliatory.

Secretary Rusk was called and he convened a meeting at about 9 P.M. Officials waited for a "catch," but it did not come. When the letter was all assembled, officials agreed that Mr. Khrushchev had "climbed down."

Never explicitly stated, but embedded in the letter was an offer to withdraw the offensive weapons under United Nations supervision in return for a guarantee that the United States would not invade Cuba.

The letter reached the President at 11 P.M. He read it with relief.

The next morning, after officials had given it further study, a reply would go off.

Saturday brought the climax of the crisis, but not the peaceful climax that the Executive Committee expected as it convened to draft a reply to the strange Khrushchev letter.

Suddenly there clattered over the wires a second Khrushchev letter, with the long-awaited catch: The Premier offered to trade his bases in Cuba for the North Atlantic Treaty missile base in Turkey.

It was to be hours before the diplomatic copy of the letter about the Turkey base was actually received at the White House. Which proposal was genuine and which merited a reply?

The second letter was markedly different in tone and style from the previous Khrushchev communications. Had the Premier been overruled? Was he raising the ante? Or was he applying pressure by demanding a higher price if his private proposal was rejected?

These were the questions before the committee as it received news of favorable reaction in many parts of the world to the Turkey-Cuba trade propsal. Such a proposal had already been rejected as unacceptable; though the Turkey missile base had no great military value, it was of great symbolic importance to a stout ally. To bargain Turkey's safety for the greater security of the United States would have meant shocking, and perhaps shaking, the Western alliance.

The conference drafted a terse White House statement revealing that there now were conflicting Soviet proposals and that there could be no sensible negotiation until work on the missile sites in Cuba had stopped.

Without formally rejecting the Turkey-Cuba deal, the statement made clear that Cuba was a special problem that had to be settled first.

Perhaps time would clear up some of the apparent confusion in Moscow, the conferees decided, but by the time they reconvened at 2:30 P.M. in Mr. Ball's office at the State Department the news was alarming.

Not only had Mr. Khrushchev's diplomacy changed, but his Cuban allies' action also had changed. A U-2 plane was missing over Cuba and presumed lost. Another reconnaissance plane had drawn antiaircraft fire. Premier Fidel Castro was shouting defiance on Cuban television, vowing to shoot down the intruders.

The committee went back to the White House at 4 P.M. so that the President could weigh the evidence of a widening of Cuban activity. United States surveillance had to continue, the meeting agreed, and if the shooting went on, fighter escorts would have to be provided.

Perhaps the antiaircraft batteries would have to be attacked directly; most were known to be in Cuban hands, but was the President prepared to run the risk of killing Russians?

The group decided to give the Russians a little more time — to gain control over Premier Castro if he had acted alone, to change their minds if they had ordered the shooting.

But there was to be no mistaking United States reaction: The Pentagon warned that it would resist interference with reconnaissance and it called up more than 14,000 air reservists to support the warning.

The Turkey note had been parried early in the day, but Washington realized that to much of the world its attitude seemed negative. Indirectly, at least, Mr. Khrushchev had admitted now that there were missiles in Cuba, allegedly for the same reason the West had missiles in Turkey. But with the secret Khrushchev letter still before it, the group now tried a diplomatic gamble.

It drafted a new letter to Moscow, all but ignoring the Turkey proposal. The letter tried to make sense of the secret Khrushchev offer and said that if the President had understood the Premier correctly — if he was offering to remove the offensive weapons from Cuba in return for an end of the blockade and a promise that the United States would not invade the island — then it was a deal.

The letter was published and delivered to the Russians at about the same time, 7 P.M. The conferees took an hour's break, from 8 to 9, then reconvened until 10.

One participant recalled that the group sat that evening with a "strong sense that we were coming right down to the wire of another decision — probably more than the public realized." It had no explanation for the conflicting letters from Moscow. Shooting had begun.

No decision was made on the next step, "but we were pretty close," one official reported. Probably, the decision would have been to expand the embargo, to keep Soviet petroleum from Cuba. But the possibility of having to knock out hostile antiaircraft batteries on the island deeply troubled the conferees and there was doubt about how much longer the crisis could be carefully controlled.

Even that night, none of the officials expected the Cuban showdown to "turn nuclear," as they put it. But they felt that large-scale fighting would probably force Moscow into counteraction elsewhere.

They sat with an over-all confidence in the nation's nuclear superiority over the Soviet Union, but this was of little comfort if the Russians chose to go to a war that neither side could win.

The President gravely remarked that evening that it seemed to him to be touch and go, that it could now go "either way."

The return to standard time that night brought the promise of an extra hour's sleep. But it was a troubled sleep.

Official Washington awoke to a glorious morning in a dismal mood. But the mood did not last.

A few minutes before 9 A.M. the Moscow radio announced that it would have an important announcement on this hour.

It was another letter from the Chairman, a response to the President's letter of the night before. All told, the two men had now exchanged ten letters — five each way — in seven days. In addition, there had been verbal contact between the sides, at least one meeting between Robert Kennedy and Ambassador Dobrynin, at least one telephone conversation between Mr. Thompson and Mr. Dobrynin. It was almost impossible to keep track of who was telling whom what and when.

The last letter from Mr. Khrushchev said the Premier had ordered work on the bases stopped, the missiles crated and returned to the Soviet Union. Representatives of the United Nations, he promised, would "verify the dismantling."

In return, Mr. Khrushchev trusted the President's assurance that there would be no attack, no invasion of Cuba. Going beyond the President's pledge, he added, "not only on the part of the United States, but also on the part of other nations of the Western hemisphere."

At 11 A.M. Secretary Rusk, and presumably some other officials, came to the White House. They stayed an hour. A quick statement was composed. It was to be released immediately while the letter was being transmitted by the Embassy in Moscow.

The statement was released at noon and directed at Moscow over Voice of America facilities.

The President welcomed Premier Khrushchev's "statesmanlike decision" to dismantle the bases in Cuba and return the offensive weapons to the Soviet Union under verification. This was a "welcome and constructive contribution to peace."

In the afternoon a fuller reply to the Khrushchev letter was drafted. When all of the Khrushchev letter had not arrived by 5 P.M., it was decided to broadcast the reply.

The President said he considered his letter of Saturday and Premier Khrushchev's reply as "firm undertakings" which should be "promptly" carried out. He hoped the necessary measures for United Nations inspection should be taken "at once" so that the United States could lift the quarantine.

There was immense relief in Washington, but no sense of jubilation. An armed clash had been avoided. The Premier had agreed to meet United States terms. The immediate crisis had been surmounted. But officials knew that a long road lay ahead, full of pitfalls and dangers and arduous negotiation. Time would tell whether the last fifteen days would prove to be the great, fortunate turning point in the cold war that the United States hoped for.

E. W. Kenworthy, Anthony Lewis and Max Frankel, with additional material from James Reston, Wallace Carroll, Marjorie Hunter, Jack Raymond, Tad Szulc and Kathleen Teltsch, "Cuban Crisis: A Step by Step Review," *The New York Times*, November 3, 1962, pp. 1, 6–7. Copyright by The New York Times. Reprinted by permission.

❖ ❖ ❖ **1**

AN INTERPRETATION BY DEPARTMENT OF STATE LEGAL ADVISER ABRAM CHAYES ON U.S. LEGAL POSITION, *November 3, 1962*

The Cuban crisis is not over yet. It may be a very long time before it is over. And such progress as we have made cannot, on the whole, be attributed to our legal position. The primary elements in the confrontation of the last weeks have been the ability and the will of the United States to deploy the necessary force in the area to establish and enforce the quarantine, and the mobilization of friends and allies — in the hemisphere, in Europe, and elsewhere in the world — in support of our action.

But if it would not have been enough merely to have the law on our side, that is not to say it is wholly irrelevant which side the law was on. The deployment of force, the appeal for world support, to say nothing of the ultimate judgment of history, all depend in some significant degree on the reality and coherence of the case in law for our action.

It is worthwhile I think to set out that legal case and to examine some of its implications.

The question was not, as most of my friends in and out of the press seemed to think, "Is it a legal blockade?" The effort to name and classify things has its place in the law as in other disciplines, but this audience needs no reminder that legal problems are something more than a search for pigeonholes within which to encase living phenomena.

In wartime the establishment of a blockade, of course, with all its classical elements, is justified according to the books. It represents minimal interference with neutral commerce consistent with the necessities of war. But even in the most hallowed of the texts, war is not the sole situation in which such interference is permissible.

It is instructive to examine the rules of blockade. They were developed in the nineteenth century. They reflect very accurately the problems of the international order — as well as the weapons technology — that then prevailed. The typical subjects of international law were European nation-states. Their relations with each other were episodic and largely bilateral.

The age of total war was only beginning; so the application of force as an instrument of national policy was recognized as legitimate, if not positively beneficial. When force was applied it was, at least in theory, a bilateral affair or, at most, something between small and temporary groupings of nations on each side. The operating legal rules — always nicer and more coherent in retrospect than at the time — had two principal objects: first, to help assure that these affrays were carried out with the smallest disturbance of the normal activities of all concerned; and second, to permit a state to make an unambiguous choice whether to join with one of the belligerents — and so have a chance to share in any political gains — or to remain uninvolved and make its profits commercially, which were in any event likely to be both larger and safer.

International law addresses different problems today and in a different context. Its overriding object is not to regulate the conduct of war but to keep and defend the peace. If nonalignment continues to be a goal for some countries, noninvolvement has become a luxury beyond price. We remember that war in this century has twice engulfed us all, willy-nilly. Paper commitments to right conduct did not stop it. Above all we are burdened with the knowledge and the power to destroy the world. The international landscape today, too, looks quite different than it did a century ago. It is peopled with permanent organizations of states — some more comprehensive, some less, some purely for defense, and some with broader purposes. It is through these organizations that we hope to give reality to our pledges to maintain the peace.

The Soviet Union's threat in Cuba was made in the context of this international system, and it was answered in the same context.

The United States saw its security threatened, but we were not alone Our quarantine was imposed in accordance with the recommendation of the Organization of American States acting under the Rio Treaty of 1947. This treaty, together with related agreements, constitutes the inter-American system. Twenty-one countries, including Cuba, are parties to that treaty. None has ever disaffirmed it.

The Rio Treaty provides for collective action not only in the case of armed attack but also "if the inviolability or the integrity of the territory or the sovereignty or political independence of any American State should be affected . . . by any . . . fact or situation that might endanger the peace of America. . . ." In such cases, a special body, the Organ of Consultation, is to "meet immediately in order to agree on the measures . . . which should be taken for the common defense and for the maintenance of the peace and security of the Continent." The Organ of Consultation acts only by a two-thirds vote.

The treaty is explicit as to the measures which may be taken "for the maintenance of the peace and security of the Continent." The "use of armed force" is specifically authorized, though "no State shall be required to use armed force without its consent."

On October 23rd, the Organ of Consultation met, in accordance with the treaty procedures, and considered the evidence of the secret introduction of Soviet strategic nuclear missiles into Cuba. It recommended that member states "take all measures, individually and collectively, including the use of armed force, which they may deem necessary to ensure that the Government of Cuba cannot continue to receive from the Sino-Soviet powers military material and related supplies. . . ." The quarantine was imposed to carry out this recommendation.

Action by regional organizations to keep the peace is not inconsistent with the United Nations Charter. On the contrary, the Charter assigns an important role to regional organizations in carrying out the purposes of the United Nations. Article 52 (1) prescribes the use of "regional arrangements or agencies for dealing with such matters relating to the maintenance of international peace and security as are appropriate for regional action. . . ." And it is certainly not irrelevant in the present context that provisions dealing with regional organizations were written into the Charter at San Francisco at the insistence of the Latin American countries and with the inter-American system specifically in mind.

The activities of regional organizations, of course, must be "consistent with the Purposes and Principles of the United Nations." It may seem self-evident that action to deal with a threat to the peace meets this requirement. But the principles of the United Nations are stated in Article 2 of the Charter and include the undertaking of all members to

> refrain in their international relations from the threat or use of force against the territorial integrity or political independence of any state, or in any other manner inconsistent with the Purposes of the United Nations.

The quarantine action involves a use of force and must be squared with this principle.

The promise not to use force is not absolute. One qualification comes readily to mind. Article 51 affirms that nothing in the Charter, including Article 2 (4), impairs "the inherent right of individual or collective self-defense if an armed attack occurs." The quarantine action was designed to deal with an imminent threat to our security. But the President in his speech did not invoke Article 51 or the right of self-defense. And the OAS acted not under Article 3, covering cases of armed attack, but under Article 6, covering threats to the peace other than armed attack.

Self-defense, however, is not the only justifiable use of force under the Charter. Obviously, the United Nations itself could sanction the use of force to deal with a threat to the peace. So it did in Korea and in the Congo. We accept use of force in these instances as legitimate for two reasons. First, all the members have constituted the United Nations for these purposes. In signing the Charter they have assented to its powers and procedures, second, the political processes by which the U.N. makes a decision to use force give some assurance that the decision will not be rashly taken.

I submit that the same two factors legitimize use of force in accordance with the OAS resolution dealing with a threat to the peace in the hemisphere. The significance of assent is attested by the fact that, though Cuba is now and has been for some time the object of sanctions and hostility from the OAS and has been suspended from participation in its agencies, she has remained a party to the treaties and a member of the inter-American system, as, in a like case, did the Dominican Republic. The significance of the political processes in the Organization is attested by the fact that, despite the disproportion of power between the United States and its neighbors to the south, it was not until the danger was clear and present that the necessary majority could be mustered to sanction use of armed force. But when that time came, the vote was unanimous.

Some have asked whether we should not first have gone to the Security Council before taking other action to meet the Soviet threat in Cuba. And I suppose that in the original conception of the United Nations, it was thought that the Security Council would be the agency for dealing with situations of this kind. However, the drafters of the charter demonstrated their wisdom by making Security Council responsibility for dealing with threats to the peace "primary" and not "exclusive." For events since 1945 have demonstrated that the Security Council, like our own electoral college, was not a viable institution. The veto has made it substantially useless in keeping the peace.

The withering away of the Security Council has led to a search for alternative peacekeeping institutions. In the United Nations itself the General Assembly and the Secretary General have filled the void. Regional organizations are another obvious candidate.

Regional organizations, even when they employ agreed processes and procedures, remain subject to check. They are subordinate to the U.N. by the terms of the Charter, and in the case of the OAS, by the terms of the relevant inter-American treaties themselves. Like an individual state, it can be called to account for its action in the appropriate agency of the parent organization. In recognition of this relation, the President ordered that the case be put immediately before the Security Council. The U.N., through the Council and the Secretary General, is, as a result, actively engaged in the effort to develop a permanent solution to the threat to the peace represented by the Soviet nuclear capability in Cuba.

You will not have failed to see that the legal defense of the quarantine I have outlined reflects what I would call an American constitutional lawyer's approach to international law.

There is normative content in the system: "Congress shall make no law . . . abridging the freedom of speech, or of the press . . ."; "Member States shall refrain in their international relations from the threat or use of force." But it recognizes that norms, to be durable, must be subject to growth and development as circumstances change.

For assurance of healthy decision within this range, there must be reliance upon institutional arrangements, checks and balances. And therefore, we must worry about the reality of the assent reflected in those arrangements.

There is recognition that in public international law, as in our domestic constitutional system, the membrane that separates law from politics is thin and permeable. And there must therefore be professional vigilance so that law is not corrupted by *raison d'état*.

The consequence of having a system with this kind of "play in the joints" is that we must live without the certainty, provided by more formal systems, that we have done well. Vindication or failure of the work of the lawyer, like that of the politician and other artists, must await the riper judgment of history. I am content to submit our efforts these past weeks to that judgment. I have some confidence, perhaps reflecting my parochial bias, that in the final decision the rigor of the logician will be tempered by the working precepts of the American constitutional lawyer.

U.S., Department of State, *Bulletin,* Volume XLVII, No. 1221 (November 19, 1962), pp. 753–765. (Address to the Tenth Reunion of the Harvard Law School Class of 1952 on November 3.)

✧ ✧ ✧ **J**

UNDER SECRETARY GEORGE W. BALL ADDRESSES THE NATO PARLIAMENTARIANS CONFERENCE ON "NATO AND THE CUBAN CRISIS" *November 16, 1962*

This conference meets at a time when the value and strength of the North Atlantic alliance have been severely tested. In recent weeks the alliance has witnessed a major confrontation between the power and aggressive intentions of the East and the strength and determination of the West. The immediate focus, as you all know, was a Caribbean island ninety miles off the American coast. The cause was the effort of the Soviet Union to extend its offensive striking force against the Western Hemisphere by secretly introducing missiles and bombers into Cuba.

This event, its implications, and the events that may follow — for the Cuban affair is not yet ended — all directly concern the Atlantic alliance. I propose this afternoon, therefore, to speak of certain of the lessons for NATO that may properly be derived from this experience.

For the past month I have been a member of a small group in Washington created to advise President Kennedy on the developing problems of the Cuban crisis. That crisis has served to set out in clear relief the central significance of the Atlantic alliance and the inter-relationship of the problems it faces. Already it seems to me possible to draw from it three lessons — three precepts that we have all dimly perceived in the past but which emerge with striking clarity from the events of the past month.

First, it is clear more than it ever was in the past that the Atlantic nations are in the Cuban crisis together — as they must necessarily be in every major East-West confrontation.

In one sense, to be sure, Cuba is peculiarly a problem of the Western Hemisphere. But there can be no doubt whatever that the intrusion of nuclear weapons into that unfortunate small country posed as much of a threat to Europe as to America. These missiles were to have been targeted on the strategic deterrent forces of the United States. In the last analysis the security of Europe and America alike — indeed of the whole free world — rests on the strength of that deterrent.

It seems clear enough from this that in removing the offensive threat from Cuba we were unquestionably acting as much in Europe's interest as in our own. We are still acting in that common interest, and it would be wholly wrong to turn attention away from Cuba simply because the immediate danger of nuclear conflict seems to have been averted.

The Cuban crisis, in other words, is still with us — with all of us. And we would be involved together in any similar confrontation elsewhere in the free world. This was the point President Kennedy was making when, in his report to the American people on the Cuban situation, he said: "Any hostile move anywhere in the world against the safety and freedom of peoples to whom we are committed — including in particular the brave people of West Berlin — will be met by whatever action is needed."

The *second* lesson of Cuba is the wisdom — indeed the necessity — of the measured response. There were, of course, several ways in which the United States and other nations in our Hemisphere could have reacted to the sudden disclosure of a new and growing menace to the deterrent strength of the free world. The most direct and obvious way would have been to eliminate the offensive weapons by force — through a sudden air strike or an invasion. Such a response might have seemed clean, surgical, and definitive. We had ample power to achieve a decisive stroke with a minimum of cost.

But President Kennedy chose not to take such action. He made his decision with full awareness of the importance of what he was deciding — with full knowledge that it involved the interests not merely of the United States but of the whole free world. He chose instead a more limited response — a quarantine, interdicting the build-up of offensive weapons in Cuba. Through that choice we could avoid resort to an immediate use of force that might have led the United States and the Soviet Union, and with them their allies, up an ascending scale of violence.

That choice also enabled the President to gain time — time to consult with our allies about the future steps we should take, time also to seek a political solution. Lastly, it enabled him to keep — and he still keeps — an option for further pressure if the situation should require it.

In short, the President applied a doctrine of measured choice and thereby minimized the risk of nuclear incineration. By establishing the quarantine he developed an effective weapon, a weapon with economic as well as military implications, that may usefully be included in the growing arsenal that provides for the free world the widest spectrum of response to military and political threats.

The *third* lesson of Cuba is the need for quick reaction to sudden danger. We know very well that the effect of the quarantine would have been diminished if there had not been wholehearted and immediate cooperation from our European allies.

There are those who suppose that the requirements of speed and secrecy necessarily preclude all possibility of consultation. They are wrong. Time factors may render it difficult to consult on every step in a swiftly developing situation; they may telescope the exchange of views at moments of crisis, but they should not impair the continuum of the consultative process.

The Cuban crisis, in our view, makes manifest the need for a deeper, franker, and more continuous exchange of views. For by such exchanges we can block out in advance large areas of agreement so that when the moment of crisis comes we will all instinctively move along similar lines.

The fact is that, if the nations of the alliance are to be able to respond with the necessary decisiveness to the challenges ahead, we must be able to act on the basis of solid planning directed at a great variety of contingencies. We are engaged in this planning in the case of Berlin — working through the North Atlantic Council and the quadripartite ambassadorial group in Washington. But I believe we can make more progress. I think we can and should develop further the technique of contingency planning, applying it across the board to situations of danger confronting the alliance.

For the peril we face is a common peril that springs from a common source. It is literally true, as Article 5 of the North Atlantic Treaty stipulates, that an attack at any point in the NATO area is an attack upon all of us. Not only is the peril common, but the response must be common, it must, in a word, be an Atlantic response. And it is along that guideline — the meeting of common peril by a common, Atlantic response — that we must shape the NATO alliance.

It is no accident that the first major progress toward Atlantic unity came in the organization of military power. The danger to which the free states of the West were — and are — exposed is the massive threat of disciplined and aggressive communism, which commands one-third of the world's population. Any effective response to such a threat must be designed on a commensurate scale. Thus it has all along been clear that even a united Western Europe could not, by itself, mobilize sufficient resources to provide adequate security. Safety lay in combining the military power of Western Europe with the military power of the United States.

This was the situation that underlay the creation, four years after the war, of the Atlantic alliance. In the beginning what was provided under the North Atlantic Treaty had many of the characteristics of a classical defensive alliance; in essence it was an arrangement between the United States and Western European countries to join together for their common defense. Had the alliance remained static in this posture, it might well have followed the course of similar alliances in the past. Its lifespan would have been brief, its vigor would have diminished with time; and its internal coherence might have been critically weakened whenever East-West tension was temporarily relaxed.

The North Atlantic Treaty structure, which is of special concern to you as parliamentarians, is growing in a very different way. It has developed an inner life and an organic force of its own. And like all living organisms it has shown a capacity of adjustment to change. NATO has responded not only to changes in military technology but equally to changes in the economic and political shape of world relationships.

In the thirteen years since the founding of NATO not a single inch of European territory has come under Communist domination. The alliance has been increased in membership and in geographic scope. It has kept pace with the rapid development of sophisticated weaponry. It has steadily augmented the strength at its command. Its institutions and staff have developed in capability and in confidence. The North Atlantic Council has come to function as a broad consultative organ, treating, besides military questions, political issues of the keenest importance and greatest variety.

In short, NATO has undergone a profound transformation into a major element in the Atlantic partnership. It has never been more significant than it is today. For NATO is, in the military field, what the Organization for Economic Cooperation and Development is becoming in the economic field. It is nothing less than the structure within which the military aims of the partnership will take on form and substance.

Paralleling the growth of the Atlantic defensive structure, we have seen the brilliant progress of Western Europe, now a strong and prosperous community moving toward greater economic and political unity. This development has had a striking effect not only within the alliance but indeed on the Soviet bloc and in the uncommitted world. It has revived Europe spiritually as well as economically. It promises still further institutional growth that can provide new lessons in statecraft for the rest of the world.

It is, I am certain, apparent to us all that the new Europe has succeeded only because it could evolve in an atmosphere of security. General [Lauris] Norstad made that point eloquently in an American television broadcast on Veterans Day, when he emphasized that the great growth in the European economy reflected the spirit of confidence made possible by the North Atlantic alliance. The economic miracle of Europe during the past ten years, in other words, could have developed only behind the shield of NATO.

We in the United States have been deeply impressed by the achievements of the European Economic Community. The lonely position of preponderance in the free world that we occupied at the end of the war was never congenial to our tastes. From the beginning we consistently encouraged measures for the integration of Europe, and we look forward today to a Europe more and more united, more and more prosperous, and speaking with a single voice on a widening area of subject matter. We welcome a Europe that can serve as an equal partner with the United States in an Atlantic partnership.

Yet, at the same time, we recognize that the shift in the allocation of power respresented by the advent of a new and strong Europe will inevitably cause some problems of adjustment on both sides of the Atlantic. It will necessitate some change not only in the attitudes but in the habits of both Americans and Europeans.

For America, the development of a powerful European partner must mean an increasingly effective voice for Europe in the councils of the Atlantic partnership, including the councils of the NATO alliance. Consultation with a united Europe will be more natural, less cumbersome, and more effective than consultation can possibly be today. Accordingly the practice of consultation is bound to encompass an increasingly large range of political, economic, and military matters. And we on our side, in phase with the new development of the European community, will have to adjust our own thinking and our habits.

We are, of course, heartened by the disposition of the new and stronger Europe to play a larger part in the common defense. Since World War II we have at all times identified our own security with the security of Western Europe. Indeed, so deep is our commitment that we could not possibly distinguish an attack upon Western Europe from an attack upon ourselves.

We maintain over 400,000 men in Europe, including the Sixth Fleet in the Mediterranean. If dependents of these men are added, we have about 700,000 people constantly in Europe. We have made available over twenty tactical air squadrons. We maintain in place major stockpiles of nuclear and conventional weapons and a diversity of means of delivery. Given the size and character of the United States involvement in Europe, any notion that we might abandon our European commitment is destructive, chimerical, and false.

Yet, as much as anybody else, we understand that the present organization of the Atlantic alliance is not perfect. As much as anybody else, we understand that in the defense field, as in all others, we need the cross-fertilization of fruitful ideas.

For defense in the nuclear age is not simple. It is expensive; it is technically complex; it is something relatively new in the world; and it is constantly changing because of the rapid rate of technological development. The fact that my own country, within a very short period, has moved from reliance on massive retaliation to a search for the widest range of possible retaliatory measures is no accident of political fortune. It is an expression of the pace and the sweep of change that technology forces upon us.

For in the field of modern defense there is no received wisdom, no tablets of the law, no copybooks, not even any demonstrated military precepts. On the contrary, modern strategy is a continuous process of thought — a ceaseless framing, testing, refining, and modifying of different hypotheses. In the United States this process of inner dialog goes on all the time and in many places. It is conducted in the military staffs of the Defense Department, in exchanges between the Defense and State Departments, in the Congress and its committees, in the research institutions and the universities, and in some organs of the press.

A process of thought similar in scope and intensity is getting under way in Western Europe. And, in that connection, you, as members of parliaments, as links between peoples and governments, have a special role to play. You have the ability to study the operations of government. You have the power to ask hard questions and to elicit full and frank answers. You serve as a cross section of public opinion. You are, in other words, ideally placed to launch and to guide the strategic debate that seems to us the necessary background to wise choice in security matters.

For a wide range of strategic problems confronts us, and the answers are neither obvious nor easy. Statesmen, as well as soldiers, must deal with the problems of survival. You have a responsibility to participate with your governments in defining the nature of the threat to Western security and the steps that can best be taken to provide safety for us all without inviting destruction. None of us can neglect these matters. But it is not enough to consider solely the details of strategic planning; we must also ask ourselves constantly whether we are contributing our fair share to the common defense, in terms of expenditures in relation to gross national product, in terms of manpower, in terms of other national assets. There can be no more critical matters for parliamentary consideration.

In the military field Europe shares with the United States responsibility for Western defense as a whole. It is our common duty to define the priority of needs. The most urgent need today is for the development of more effective conventional forces for NATO to complement the superior nuclear power already available to the alliance.

Hopefully, the contingencies most apt to arise in the future are not those likely to call forth a massive nuclear exchange. We can certainly expect localized political and military pressures, perhaps not too much unlike the recent challenge in Cuba. Those pressures can best be met — as that challenge has been met — by whatever response is appropriate, involving as it may the deployment and selective use of conventional land, sea, and air forces.

Challenges may be presented at any one of a number of sensitive points. To meet them with steady nerve, without alarms, excursions, and wasteful deployment, we need stronger conventional forces than are now available. That is why it is essential that a Europe growing more powerful and more unified should make an increasing effort to further the build-up of conventional forces. The undertaking of such a build-up is not only necessary as a military matter if NATO is to have at its command the widest range of measured response; it would have a positive and transforming effect on the European spirit. It would provide a critical increment of security and self-confidence that should give an even greater sense of assurance and achievement to what we have come to call the "new Europe."

The strengthening of conventional forces is, of course, eminently feasible. In population and gross national product, the NATO countries are more than a match for the Soviet Union and its East European satellites. NATO forces already dominate the sea. Our air strength is at least equal to that of the Soviet bloc. We do need more strength on the ground, not only in terms of manpower but in qualitative terms. We need more and better equipment and reserves of better quality and higher mobility. The additional effort required to make up these deficiencies can pay big dividends. There is no reason why the NATO countries cannot maintain in the NATO area conventional forces that are at least equal to those in Eastern Europe.

Let me draw on the Cuban experience for an illustration. Why were we able to modulate and attune our responses so closely to the degree of our need? Surely it was because we had the ability to deploy as required a very large variety of land, sea, and air forces in the fashion necessary to accomplish the task at hand. Because we had clear superiority of conventional forces, we were never confronted with the awful dilemma of having to utilize major nuclear weapons or to retreat from our objective.

In the same way we must increase the spectrum of our military choices on the continent of Europe. If we do so — always preserving intact the ultimate nuclear deterrent — we increase our ability to achieve the purposes of the alliance at the smallest risk of nuclear annihilation.

At the same time I understand fully that, as Europe grows stronger and more unified, as it develops an increasing sense of its own mission, it may wish to play a larger role in nuclear defense. From a strictly military standpoint, we do not feel that the alliance has an urgent need for a European nuclear contribution. But, should other NATO nations so desire, we are ready to give serious consideration to the creation of a genuinely multilateral medium-range ballistic missile force fully coordinated with the other deterrent forces of the North Atlantic Treaty Organization.

It is not for us — indeed, it would be out of keeping with the spirit of the Atlantic partnership — to dictate how such a force should be manned, financed, or organized. But it is a proper responsibility of the United States, which has had so much experience in the nuclear field, to make available to others our information and ideas with respect to the characteristics and capabilities of a multilateral force. And we are now in the process of doing so.

In this connection one thing is clear. The faster Europe approaches unity, the more the nations of Europe hammer out common policies and common institutions, the easier it will be for us to work together as equal partners within the Atlantic partnership, employing NATO as the military expression of that partnership to achieve the indivisibility of response — the indivisibility of command and direction — that is the indispensable element of an effective defense in this nuclear age.

America, as you will see from what I have said, looks to the Atlantic partnership with a great sense of expectation. We envisage that partnership developing as a framework for useful address to all our common problems. If mutual self-interest is present — and it definitely is — we also believe that what Pericles said of the Athenians is true of ourselves: A noble principle underlies our work. It is the principle of shared responsibility. And we believe that the Atlantic nations act not only from self-interest but in the interest of all free men, that the Atlantic partnership is the expression of a noble principle and a model for free nations everywhere.

U.S., Department of State, *Bulletin,* Volume XLVII, No. 1223 (December 3, 1962), pp. 831–835. (Department of State press release 678, November 16, 1962.)

SECRETARY RUSK DISCUSSES THE CUBAN CRISIS, *November 20, 1962*

The foreign policy of a democracy must rest upon the support of informed citizens. On Armistice eve, 1918, men like Paul Kellogg and Learned Hand, Harry Emerson Fosdick and Charles Beard brought into being an organization to help interested citizens to become more fully and intelligently informed about our relations with the rest of the world.

Now this is important not just because when a great democracy moves in foreign policy it must have the understanding and support of its citizens; it is also because foreign policy in fact, regardless of the abstractions of international law, reaches into every home in the community and in the country. If every county courthouse, for example, could display a map of the world showing where the country's men and women have served since 1941 throughout the world in defense of freedom and in defense of the security of this country, we would have a dramatic illustration of the fact that foreign policy is in fact the people's business.

The Foreign Policy Association has for almost half a century made a major contribution to public understanding of significant international problems facing this country.

For about half our history this great country of ours was under an illusion of irresponsibility. We were born; we grew, we were developed; we became prosperous through more than a century of the most intimate relations with nations beyond the oceans, beyond our own frontiers. Somehow, after World War I, we tried to put that aside. We tried to assume that we had no great burdens to bear, and we did not bring into the international field the full strength and resources and capacity to influence the course of events which rested here in the United States.

History has no chance to write about what might have been. But I think that we, as Americans, need to consider in quiet moments what the story might have been to prevent the tragedy of World War II and to stabilize international institutions, had we, during the first half of your own history as an organization, realized the responsibilities that go with the capacity to act.

During the second half of your history, we have had thrust upon us by the course of events a responsibility which we have never really known before as a people, imposing upon us great burdens, imposing upon us incredibly difficult and complex decisions, but also imposing

256

upon us an awareness that this country cannot be safe if others are insecure, that this country cannot be prosperous if others are ridden by poverty.

We meet today in an atmosphere of crisis, and I wish that I could report to you that that crisis has been resolved. I cannot, because much remains to be done. I suppose that many of you would like for me to say something about the present crisis. In fact, our policy and our course of conduct are already a matter of full public record. You will have a full understanding of the situation if you remind yourselves of the President's statements of September 4 and 13 about Cuba, the President's forthright address to the Nation on October 22nd, Ambassador Stevenson's classic speech before the Security Council at the United Nations the following day, and the public exchange of letters between President Kennedy and Chairman Khrushchev on October 27 and October 28.

There have been private talks among governments and with the Secretary General of the United Nations, and details of these talks have not been made fully public; but they are aimed at the accomplishment of publicly declared policy, of purposes we all understand, of results consistent with the security and well-being of the Western Hemisphere and of the peace of the world.

In his press conference today at six o'clock the President will, of course, comment on the Cuban situation as we now see it. But no citizen need suppose himself uninformed about his country's attitude on the issues to be resolved before we can write an end to what is called the Cuban crisis.

As a matter of fact, consultations in progress as we meet here now may very much affect the situation at today's end. So there are moments when the Secretary of State must try to make sense instead of making news — unless indeed that be news. (Laughter.)

May I say to my friends of the press that a text of what I have to say will be made available later in the day when my colleagues have a chance to discover what I am going to say, because the situation is so fluid that I have made some considerable revisions in what I thought I might say a few days ago. And, as for the photographs, I asked some photographers once why they kept taking pictures when they must have thousands already. And one of them said, "Well, because, Mr. Secretary, if you get shot, we want the last one." But as far as the text is concerned, I think it is worthwhile once in a while to remind the publishers and editors that working reporters are more valuable and have more to do than simply to snip excerpts from previously produced texts.

Today I should like to speak briefly and simply about some basic issues which underline the present crisis. The events of the past two months in Cuba and elsewhere have caused many capitals to look long and hard at the prospects for peace and the dangers of war.

I suspect that we are on the front edge of significant and perhaps unpredictable events, a period in which some of the customary patterns of thought will have to be reviewed and perhaps revised, a process that will affect governments in all parts of the world. It seems to me, therefore, that it would be appropriate for me to remind you of certain fateful decisions which the governments of the world must face in this present period, decisions which critically affect the prospects for peace and the survival of freedom.

The first of these fateful decisions is one which is to be made by the leaders of the Communist world. And I might remind you of a portion of President Kennedy's address to the United Nations in September of 1961, in which he called for a truce of terror. He said:

> This will require new strength and new roles for the United Nations. For disarmament without checks is but a shadow, and a community without law is but a shell. Already the United Nations has become both the measure and the vehicle of man's most generous impulses. Already it has provided — in the Middle East, in Asia, in Africa this year in the Congo — a means of holding violence within bounds.
>
> But the great question which confronted this body in 1945 is still before us: whether man's cherished hopes for progress and peace are to be destroyed by terror and disruption, whether the "foul winds of war" can be tamed in time to free the cooling winds of reason, and whether the pledges of our charter are to be fulfilled or defied — pledges to secure peace, progress, human rights, and world law.
>
> In this hall there are not three forces, but two. One is composed of those who are trying to build the kind of world described in Articles 1 and 2 of the Charter. The other, seeking a far different world, would undermine this Organization in the process.

I'm reminded of the great concern expressed by President Franklin Roosevelt before his death, before the end of World War II, that the trends of Soviet policy were causing him deepest concern and augured ill for the prospects of the United Nations conference then attempting to hammer out a United Nations Charter.

I am reminded that in 1947 and 1948 Secretary of State Marshall and President Truman invited the Soviet Union and other members of the Communist bloc to take part in what came to be known as the Marshall Plan for the reconstruction of war-devastated Europe and that that invitation was rejected and that soon thereafter Secretary Marshall was insistently and urgently inviting the Soviet Union really and truly to join the United Nations. Because in 1945, '46, '47, the great tragedy of our day is that we had such a "near miss" in the organization of world affairs. This country came out of World War II with unparalleled power in conventional forces, a monopoly on the atomic weapon; yet we committed ourselves fully to the attempt to make the United Nations a living reality.

One can describe those days either in terms of the "great commitment" or, in retrospect, as "the great mistake." But we laid down our arms. We sought to place the atomic bomb under the United Nations. We committed ourselves fully and wholeheartedly to the purposes of that Charter.

In 1946 we had no ally looking toward the future — only those allies which had been formed for the purposes of defeating Nazi Germany and militarist Japan, alliances which were expected to wither away. Our military budget dropped below $10 billion in 1947 and 1948. This was a signal: the determination of the American people to commit themselves to the purposes outlined in the preamble and articles 1 and 2 of the charter, in demonstration of their hope that this kind of world could in fact be brought into being.

One nation at that time stood in the way. I myself am convinced that, had it not been for that great abstention, the United Nations could have succeeded in handling efficiently and effectively the great issues which are brought before it that do not specifically involve that particular country.

The great decision that has to be made on the other side is whether in fact, as I have said on other occasions, they will pick up the great revolutionary responsibility that is waiting for them — the revolution of peace which can be brought about by a simple decision to live at peace with the rest of the world. For no other decision in the hands of a relatively few men can so transform the face of the earth as a simple decision to work to make the world for their children a living reality and not a frustrated hope.

We believe that in this period there are those on the other side who have had some sober reflections, perhaps are making some reappraisal, although there are others who obviously are not.

The harsh attack on India is a major problem for the entire free world, as well as for India, and those who are pressing this attack must not be permitted to believe that such conduct is consistent with the possibilities of peace in the modern world. But surely, having looked at the dangers in our present situation, we can express the hope that leaders in countries who for ideological or other reasons are not a part of the so-called free world, who have differences about what the future is going to hold, who have differences of comitment or prediction — surely we can express the hope that these leaders recognize the utter necessity of finding a path toward peaceful existence within the framework of the United Nations. Their own national interests, the needs — indeed, demands — of their own peoples give them the same great unfinished tasks in their societies which the rest of us have. Commitment to those purposes could open up great opportunities in the days ahead.

A second fateful decision for peace, I think, has to do with disarmament. There are many things which can and will, in due course, be said about the Cuban crisis. One of them is that Cuba has provided a dramatic example of the deadly dangers of a spiraling arms race. It is not easy to see how far-reaching disarmament can occur except as major political issues be resolved and as nations accustom themselves to living at peace with one another.

Nevertheless, it is also obvious, as we have seen in recent weeks, that modern weapons systems are themselves a source of high tension and that we must make an urgent and earnest effort to bring the arms race under control and to try to turn it downward if we possibly can.

In their exchange of messages, both Chairman Khrushchev and President Kennedy expressed the hope that a settlement of the Cuban crisis would be followed by other agreed measures to lessen the danger of thermonuclear war. In his letter President Kennedy said:

Mr. Chairman, both of our countries have great unfinished tasks and I know that your people as well as those of the United States can ask for nothing better than to pursue them free from the fear of war. Modern science and technology have given us the possibility of making labor fruitful beyond anything that could have been dreamed of a few decades ago.

I agree with you that we must devote urgent attention to the problem of disarmament, as it related to the whole world and also to critical areas. Perhaps now, as we step back from danger, we can together make real progress in this vital field. I think we should give priority to questions relating to the proliferation of nuclear weapons, on earth and in outer space, and to the great effort for a nuclear test ban. But we should also work hard to see if wider measures of disarmament can be agreed and put into operation at an early date. The United States government will be prepared to discuss these questions urgently, and in a constructive spirit, at Geneva or elsewhere.

That is the spirit with which we shall return next week to the eighteen-nation disarmament conference at Geneva. We earnestly hope that the Soviet negotiators will reflect a similar attitude. We also earnestly hope that they and all the other delegations will have taken to heart some important lessons underlined by the Cuban crisis and that all delegations, all countries, in all regions, will look upon disarmament as a high priority and urgent necessity.

This is not a matter that affects just the Soviet Union and the United States. There are other differences, other arms races. I would hope that some day we could call a conference on disarmament in which it would be out of order for any delegate to say anything more than what his own country was willing to contribute to the solution of disarmament problems — that it would be out of order for him to say what somebody else should contribute to these problems.

Perhaps I shouldn't say this, but I think it is of some importance that, at a time when the United Nations is voting unanimously for disarmament, seventy members are asking the United States for military assistance. This is not a problem in which two great powers have a monopoly. There are tasks to be taken up in every part of the world, although the greater danger is of course among the great powers themselves.

One of the plainest of the lessons we have learned in these recent weeks all over again — if we ever needed to learn it again — is that verbal assurances, however formal, cannot be taken at face value. Let us remember that we have just experienced an elaborate deception to cover the secret effort to develop in Cuba a serious nuclear threat to the United States and the Western Hemisphere. With this experience freshly in mind, surely no reasonable person would expect that arms control or related agreements can be effective without appropriate and adequate verification that commitments are in fact being met.

For sixteen years Soviet objections to inspection have stood as a barrier to concrete progress toward disarmament. Soviet representatives like to call inspection "espionage." I would not try to say whether this is a deep-seated, traditional passion for secrecy on the Russian scene or a consequence of the belief that secrecy is an important military asset. It is probably a combination of these and many other factors.

But whatever the reasons behind this alleged preoccupation with espionage, three things seem to me to be clear.

One is that the major powers know all that they need to know about each other to inflict devastating damage in the event of war. Espionage in its classical sense is no longer relevant to this great overriding issue.

Second, arrangements can be made for international inspection, particularly in the field of nuclear testing, which does not involve the gathering of information on any matter not central to the purpose of the inspection itself. You know, we have such short memories, we need, for example — all of us — to study over again the review of the post-World War II period which Adlai Stevenson made before the Security Council on October 23d.

I suspect that many of you have already forgotten that in March of this year, after the Soviet Union had exploded almost fifty nuclear tests and *before* we had resumed nuclear testing ourselves, the British and we offered the Soviet Union a comprehensive nuclear test ban which would involve having a look at less than one part in two thousand of Soviet territory in any given year. (This inspection would of course be reinforced by instrumentation and other means of knowing what in fact was happening.) One part in two thousand!

A farthing's worth of inspection insofar as general military information is concerned! Could that possibly be espionage?

Third, we must face the elementary fact that secrecy and disarmament are basically incompatible, for we cannot lay down our arms in the face of ignorance about what is happening in those various areas of the Eurasian landmass. Until the Soviet Union recognizes and accepts the elementary necessity of reliable safeguards, it is, quite frankly, difficult to see how urgently needed progress on disarmament can go forward.

Such agreements, under present conditions, cannot rest on naked trust. But it should not be necessary for anyone to worry about whether one side trusts the other, for the assurances of faithful performance must be built into the system through arrangements for independent verification.

We need the elementary institutional structure providing safeguards on which confidence can, in due course, be built. Otherwise we shall not have the possibility, either on our side or the other side of the Iron Curtain, of handling responsibly, honestly, and effectively the human tendency to suspect and to fear in the presence of ignorance about the other side.

In the Cuban crisis Chairman Khrushchev said that he was prepared to agree that representatives of the United Nations should verify the dismantling of the Soviet Union's offensive weapons in Cuba. But in the course of the brass tacks of negotiation, it has become evident that at least Mr. Castro's interpretation of such verification falls far short thus far of what others could in prudence accept as an adequate verification of a disarmament agreement.

In the disarmament negotiations at Geneva the Soviets have paid a certain attention, perhaps lip-service, to the need for international controls. But they have insisted that effective inspection should be installed only after there has been general and complete disarmament. During the process of disarmament, the Soviet plan would permit inspection at places where troops are being disbanded and where armaments are being destroyed. But it would not permit inspection of forces and armaments retained.

It seems obvious, indeed elementary, to us that such a plan cannot be regarded as a practical approach to disarmament. We hope that the Soviets will return to Geneva next week with a more realistic attitude toward this problem of assurance and of safeguards.

The United States believes, nevertheless, that major steps can be taken within the three-year period referred to as phase one. We have proposed a 30-percent cut in all major armaments. We would limit the production of armaments retained to replacement on a one-for-one basis. We have proposed other significant measures, including a halt to production of fissionable material for use in weapons and a reduction of the armed forces of the United States and the Union of

Soviet Socialist Republics to some 2,100,000 men each. These seem to us to be feasible measures. They are measures which can be undertaken, pending the beginnings of the transformation of international political life which opens the way for further measures to be adopted.

It is important to get started, to do something tangible and specific in this field and not wait until it is possible for everything to be done at once. Otherwise, we shall never get to that point and the arms race will continue. But if some of these measures could be adopted and carried out, they might indeed start a momentous revolution in international arrangements.

A final stage of general and complete disarmament is not in sight for the near future, since it would require a major transformation of international relations as an accompanying necessity. The institutions of law must be consolidated. The conduct of nations must be regularized. The possibilities of peace must be assured.

Meanwhile, however, we shall earnestly strive for measures to halt the arms race and to make progress along the road to disarmament. We most earnestly seek measures to reduce the danger of a great war. These measures might be of two kinds: preventing the future diffusion and development of nuclear weapons, and reducing the danger of war by accident or miscalculation.

In the first category are measures to prohibit the transfer of nuclear weapons to individual states and to establish nuclear-free zones, for example, in Latin America or Africa, if the states in those areas so desire. Also in this category are measures to keep outer space free of nuclear weapons in orbit and to stop nuclear testing.

When the Geneva conference recessed on September 8, negotiations on a nuclear test ban had reached an apparent deadlock. Talks among the United States, the United Kingdom, and the Union of Soviet Socialist Republics have continued in the nuclear test ban subcommittee of the eighteen-nation conference. So far these have only confirmed that the Union of Soviet Socialist Republics continues to resist any type of obligatory international on-site inspection. We ourselves would like to see a comprehensive ban on nuclear tests, that is, a ban on tests in all environments; but we cannot accept this unless we are certain that all parties live up to the agreement. In the case of earth tremors, such assurance requires a few on-site inspections to identify their cause.

If the other side has instruments which can do this job through instrumentation, we would press them to come forward with them. We cannot say with complete assurance that no such instruments exist. But we don't have them. If the other side does, we would like to see them. We have urged them at least twenty times to come forward with a demonstration of the capacity to detect nuclear testing, because this is a question of fact, not necessarily of policy. It is a question of what can be done to be reasonably sure that agreements are being carried out. But thus far we have not had any response on that point

As an alternative to a comprehensive test ban, we are ready to agree today to a ban on tests in the atmosphere, under water, and in outer space, for such tests can be detected by existing means. The Soviet Union says that it will agree to this only if we accept an unpoliced moratorium on underground tests while an inspection system for such tests is worked out. We did accept an unpoliced moratorium once, and there were secret preparations for a long series of tests by the other side. We do not need elaborate inspection, intrusive inspection, but only inspection to give us assurance that the events we are concerned about are not in fact occurring. If the other side cannot accept that much inspection, the prospects for disarmament remain, I'm afraid, somewhat dim.

The second kind of measures are those to reduce the danger of war by accident or miscalculation. One such measure would be an advance notice of major military movements and maneuvers outside of national territories. The United States has presented such a proposal at Geneva. We have also proposed the establishment of observation posts at key points to report on concentrations and movements of military forces.

The importance of these measures has been underlined by the events of the last few weeks in Cuba. Had these proposals been in effect, the chances are that the deployment to Cuba of offensive weapons would not have taken place. This experience underlined also the importance in times of crisis of extremely rapid and reliable communications between governments. Rapid communication was instrumental in this case in averting a possible war. But even more rapid communication would in fact be desirable. The United States proposed this early in the disarmament talks in Geneva. There has been some expression of interest in it on the other side, and we would hope that this measure is now ripe for agreement.

Even small and limited measures of agreement can serve to make a great war a little less likely. At the resumed sessions of the disarmament conference the United States will press for agreement on every measure which holds the prospects of reducing danger while we work on the more ambitious task of developing a treaty for general and complete disarmament in a peaceful and law-abiding world

· A third fateful decision for peace is one which rests with us here in this country — rests upon the American people — that is, whether we ourselves can fully comprehend the stakes which are at issue in this particular period of our history and can accept the burdens that go with the defense of our security and the long-range survival of freedom

Since World War II we have indeed been called upon to bear large burdens. Speaking as an American among Americans, I think we can be proud of the fact that we have responded so well to these demands.

But it is easy to become bored, or tired, or a bit frustrated or resentful if these burdens continue. But they must continue. They are not burdens that we can afford to tear ourselves to pieces about each year as though we were deciding each year all over again whether we want our nation to survive.

I mentioned the fact that in 1947 and 1948 our defense budget came down to just below $10 billion. Today it is more than $50 billion. If we look upon that earlier defense budget as the normal annual cost of the postwar defense establishment of a nation trying to make the United Nations work, we find that the accumulated increment in our defense expenditures since 1947 over that level has amounted to more than $425 billion. The growth of American defense expenditures corresponds with the tragic story of one aggression after another, spelled out in the debates and in the agenda of the United Nations — billions of additional expenditure because of someone else's refusal to join the United Nations *in fact*.

It is true that the American people have spent between ninety and a hundred billion dollars in the same period for what is called foreign aid. This is not an effort on which we can relax, because the failure to spend this lesser amount will multiply the necessity for spending larger amounts on the defense side.

This nation is deeply committed to a world of independent states freely cooperating, within the framework of the United Nations Charter and in their common interests, to get on with the recognized common tasks of mankind.

In 1946, no allies, in 1962, more than forty. Why? Because we have a commitment to the independence of states. What is our interest in the so-called unaligned countries? Their independence. If the 110 members of the United Nations were genuinely secure and genuinely independent (and these newly independent countries have shown a tough zeal for their independence), there would be no great tension between Washington and Moscow. The strictly bilateral issues between us are of relative unimportance. The independence of these nations is the issue; the structure of our world society is the issue — whether it is to be that spelled out in the charter or that imposed by a doctrine of world revolution.

We are, perhaps, as I said earlier, on the leading edges of some very important events. I think the free world can look forward to these with confidence. There is a great vitality of recovery and progress in the Atlantic community. There is a solidarity of commitment in purpose in the great alliances, such as the Organization of American States and North Atlantic Treaty Organization. There is a keen interest in their national existence, survival, and prosperity among the newly independent countries. There is a commitment on the part of the overwhelming majority of nations to the kind of world which we find congenial.

If we want to find a succinct statement of the long-range foreign policy of the American people, we can do worse than to read the opening sections of the United Nations Charter. It is no accident that this should be so, because we helped draft the charter, in a very important sense, at a time when this country was chastened by the fires of a great war. We were thinking deeply about ourselves and our future in those days, as we must today.

But those commitments are not only congenial with American tradition; they are congenial with the great humane tradition of man. These things we share with other people, regardless of race, geographical location, or indeed — when we talk about ordinary men and women — regardless of political system. These great commitments that are so deeply rooted in the nature of man himself makes allies of us all as we move into the future.

But if we shirk our responsibilities at this point, if we fail to carry these burdens through the period ahead, this could make a difference — a disastrous difference — and could shift the nature of our burdens into ever more dangerous channels.

I will say to you quite frankly we are not looking for a blank check in such matters as foreign aid. We have an obligation in Government — and those in other countries receiving American assistance have an obligation — to see that these funds are in fact well used. There have been, and there will be, mistakes. But we should not let the mistakes disrupt the entire effort.

Our friends abroad must recognize that these funds come out of taxes, not out of some mountain of gold hidden away in a Western desert, and that in good conscience we cannot mobilize these funds from the ordinary people of the United States in order to match waste with waste. We must match performance with performance.

The external resources of the Alliance for Progress will amount to something in the order of 2 percent of the gross national product of the Latin American countries. If by what we do with the 2 percent we can stimulate and invigorate what is done with the 98 percent, much can be accomplished. To the extent that we can assist other governments in mobilizing the interests and the loyalties of their own people in this great effort, we need not be concerned about whether development will in fact occur, it will occur.

So we have some great tasks in front of us. As free people, we can look forward to them with confidence. They won't be easy to carry. But we lay them down in the most literal sense at our very peril.

U.S., Department of State, *Bulletin*, Volume XLVII, No. 1224 (December 10, 1962), pp. 867–873. (Address by Secretary Rusk before the Foreign Policy Association in New York City. Department of State press release 691 dated November 21, 1962.)

◇ ◇ ◇ **L**

INTERVIEW OF SECRETARY RUSK BY DAVID SCHOENBRUN OF CBS NEWS, November 28, 1962

Q. Mr. Secretary, at this point can we bring up the Cuban question? From Monday, October 22d, when President Kennedy revealed the menace of Soviet missiles in Cuba, to Sunday morning, October 28th, when Khrushchev said he would dismantle and withdraw, the whole world knew that we were walking on the brink. But for one week before that, only you and a very few high officials knew what was going on. Can you tell us about that dramatic week?

A. I think the first information that indicated that something more than defensive weapons was present in Cuba came on late Monday night, the 15th [of October], I think it was. I was giving a dinner party for the German Foreign Minister, Mr. Schroeder, that evening, and late in the evening I had a telephone call indicating that something seemed to be there very definitely that was outside our understanding of defensive weapons. So we met the next morning and laid on measures which would tell us, for certain, exactly what was there throughout the island.

Now, we had several meetings a day through that week, on the one side assessing the information, on the other looking at all the questions. We had to give some thought, for example, as to why it was the Soviet Union departed from its long-standing policy with respect to such weapons and tried to put them into Cuba. So far as we have known, they have never put them outside of the Soviet Union before — the medium-range missiles or the intermediate-range missiles. We had to consider what was in their minds in Moscow to lead them to take this unusual and necessarily highly provocative and challenging step. We had to consider the wide range of possibilities and our own response to it, the effect on our more than forty allies all over the world, either in doing something or doing nothing, because whatever we do in a situation of this sort directly affects our involvement with everyone else. And so we had to spend that week being very sure that we knew what the facts were and boxing the compass of possibilities, of reactions, of the impact of the Soviet action on the one side, our action on the other, in order to put together the entire picture, in consultation with the President, so that the President would be in the best possible position to make the final decisions that only he can make.

Well, by the Friday of that week we had — I think, Friday evening — we had pretty full information. Then when the President's decision was made, we had to work out consultations with a great many governments — our allies in the Organization of American States, our allies in NATO, in other parts of the world, and consultations with the so-called unaligned countries. From a purely operational point of view, this was a very large undertaking. You recall that the President made his speech on Monday, October 22nd. We had a meeting of the Organization of American States the next morning. We had a meeting in the Security Council of the United Nations the next day. These were a part of a very far-reaching and comprehensive political discussion with governments all over the world, looking toward a protection of our vital interests, by peaceful means if possible.

Q. Mr. Rusk, never had we seen a story better kept than those seven secret days. How many people in this huge State Department of maybe 50,000 employees, all told, really knew about it? How did you keep your security? How did you run this extraordinary operation?
A. Well, first I can't, because of our relations with Congress, let you get away with that word "50,000"! We have about 6,000 here in the Department of State in Washington.

There were about twelve or fifteen men in government who knew the entire picture. The Vice President, Secretaries of State, Defense, and Treasury, Chairman of the Joint Chiefs, the Director of Central Intelligence, and a few others — Mr. McGeorge Bundy, of course, of the White House staff. But it was a very small group indeed, a small group indeed. Now, that meant that we had to go on a twenty-four hour basis here in the Department of State. My own colleagues, Under Secretary George Ball and Deputy Under Secretary Alex Johnson, took time about staying in the Department at night, so that we had a senior officer on duty at all times. We met in a variety of places, so that we did not create too much traffic at any one place. Senior officers did their own typing; some of my own basic papers were done in my own handwriting, in order to limit the possibility of further spread of the utterly vital matters that we were dealing with.

But by the end of the week, when the President's decision had been made, then it became necessary to extend the information to a considerable number of other people, because we had to be in a position to consult seventy-five or eighty governments.

Q. Mr. Secretary, after the President addressed the Nation, it became public knowledge, but then another problem came about and that is the channel of communications between ourselves and the adversary. Could you tell us about how one keeps communications open with the adversary in such a moment?

A. Well, I called in Ambassador Dobrynin of the Soviet Union an hour before the President's television speech and gave him a copy of the speech itself, with a covering memorandum. Then during the next several days there was a variety of contacts at the United Nations. But I think the — as a matter of fact, the most crucial exchanges were the public exchanges. The President's letter of October 27 and the broadcast message from Mr. Khrushchev on October 28, in combination, unlocked the crisis and made it possible to work toward a peaceful solution.

Q. Mr. Secretary, on Sunday morning, October 28, Radio Moscow broadcast the text of Khrushchev's letter before President Kennedy or you had actually received the letter. Now, this suggests a certain urgency of communications.
A. I think that there was a question of speed of communications through normal channels. The sheer physical problem of transmitting messages to people who use another language, requiring decoding and translation, with differences in office hours in their respective capitals, did remind us all over again that immediate communication is important; and I think these public communications turned out to be the fastest communication, so that this was, I think, the importance of the broadcast message on October 28. It was a fast response to the President's message of the day before and perhaps could not have been handled through the elaborate channels of code and translation and normal diplomatic patterns.

Q. Sir, perhaps you could take a tour around the world with us and tell us the impact of the Cuban affair on world affairs, beginning here at home, on the Organization of American States?
A. Well, I think that the sudden appearance in Cuba of these medium-range ballistic missiles and these light jet bombers gave an enormous impetus to a development which had been going on for a year or two in the Hemisphere — that is, growing concern about what Cuba meant to the rest of the hemisphere. And we were really not surprised, but we were deeply gratified, to see the immediate unification of the Hemisphere with unanimity on the nature of this threat and the necessity that it be removed.

I think that the unanimity in the Organization of American States and in NATO had some bearing on what Moscow's decision turned out to be in this situation. Had there been disunity, and had we fallen to quarreling among ourselves, I think the results might have been quite different. I think it gives us all some confidence for the future.

Now I don't want to mislead you on that, because we have cautioned our friends from drawing too many conclusions from the Cuban experience. The Soviet Union remains a great power. There were special circumstances in Cuba which are not necessarily present in other parts of the world. It would be, I think, wrong to say that, because this situation in Cuba came out the way it did, therefore a lot of other questions are going suddenly to take a new shape and new form in fundamental respects. I do think that this experience has caused an element of caution on all sides, in Moscow as well as elsewhere — that men have to look practically at the fact that nuclear war is a real danger and not just a theoretical danger.

Q. Is it possible, sir, that the Russians might have made a miscalculation in Cuba, and if so how can we help them not make another miscalculation somewhere else?
A. Well, I think it is very important that they understand that, when we talk about vital interests — all of us in the free world — when we talk about these great issues of war and peace, this is serious talk. And I think they do understand that most of the time. Because it is so easy for democracies to be underestimated. We normally do a lot more than we are willing to say in advance that we will do. And also, when you have a great sprawling democracy that is debating within itself all the time, as we are — we quarrel a good deal with each other, and we have an alliance of democracies, and there are times when it appears that, you know, we are not getting along very well together. The one thing that the outsiders must understand is that, on the great underlying issues of war and peace, we are united and firm and determined, and this is the signal we must get across; and I think there is good prospect that after this Cuban affair — that these signals can go across.

U.S., Department of State, *Bulletin,* Volume XLVII, No. 1225 (December 17, 1962), pp. 909–911. (Department of State press release 700, November 28, 1962.)

✧ ✧ ✧ CHRONOLOGY

NOVEMBER 6/16, 1686 — France and Great Britain concluded the Treaty of Whitehall which attempted to remove and exempt their respective holdings in North and South America from mutual or European conflict.

FEBRUARY 10, 1763 — The Treaty of Paris was signed ending the so-called "French and Indian Wars" between France, Great Britain, Portugal and Spain. By Articles VII and XX of this treaty Great Britain restored Cuba to Spanish control in return for concessions in northern Florida.

1778–1781 — The Spanish governors of Louisiana and Cuba supplied some arms and small sums of money to the rebels during the American Revolutionary War, largely on the grounds that independent American colonies would be less formidable adversaries than the British in the Americas. In addition Spain provided a subsidy of one million livres to the rebels in 1776.

AUGUST 3, 1786 — John Jay, then Secretary of Foreign Affairs, addressed the Congress on Spanish-American relations and urged that they be placed upon the best possible terms of reciprocity, particularly in trade and commerce, and urged the formulation of a treaty.

AUGUST 16, 1786 — Charles Pinckney, then a member of Congress, spoke against the proposed Jay treaty with Spain largely on the grounds that Spain had already made the proposed concessions and that the Spanish Empire was in the throes of dissolution and that the British would open the way to freer trade with Central and South America.

As Secretary of State during this period, Thomas Jefferson had aspirations for the acquisition of Cuba, which later became part of his "Large Policy" as President.

MARCH 22, 1793 — Secretary of State Thomas Jefferson wrote to Messrs. Carmichael and Short, U.S. ministers at Madrid, and said: "It is intimated to us in such a way as to attract our attention, that France means to send a strong force early this spring to offer independence to the Spanish-American colonies, beginning with those on the Mississippi, and that she will not object to the receiving of those on the east side into our Confederation. Interesting considerations require that we should keep ourselves free to act in this case according to the circumstances, and consequently that you should not, in any clause of treaty, bind us to guarantee any of the Spanish colonies against their own independence, nor indeed against any other nation."

MAY 6, 1794 — President Washington's instructions to John Jay, as envoy extraordinary to London, listed reciprocity in trade, "particularly to the West Indies" as the first object of consideration in his negotiations with the British to settle outstanding differences.

OCTOBER 27, 1795 — Charles Pinckney, then United States Minister to London, was sent to Spain as a special envoy to negotiate a treaty of commerce and navigation with Spain, which opened the Spanish Empire, particularly the West Indies, to trade with the United States and also extended the temporary right of deposit in New Orleans to the young country.

SEPTEMBER 17, 1796 — George Washington, then outgoing President, delivered his famous "Farewell Address" whereby, in view of the recent complications of United States foreign policy, he urged that the United States extend commercial relations but reduce political connections insofar as possible and pursue an independent course of neutrality.

1797 — The United States stationed "agents for seamen and commerce" in Cuba, and thus broke the Spanish trading monopoly.

SEPTEMBER 30, 1800 — The United States and France negotiated a Convention of Peace, Commerce and Navigation to try and reconcile their differences.

OCTOBER 1, 1800 — France and Spain signed the Treaty of St. Ildefonso whereby Spain retroceded the Louisiana Territory to France.

APRIL 30, 1803 — France, under Napoleon Bonaparte, ceded the Louisiana Territory to the United States for sixty million francs plus the assumption by the United States of private claims upon France up to twenty million francs. The sale was effected under Thomas Jefferson as President and Robert R. Livingston, U.S. Minister in Paris, and somewhat under the impetus of James Monroe as special envoy.

JANUARY–OCTOBER, 1805 — Charles Pinckney, U.S. minister to Madrid, was assisted by James Monroe, envoy extraordinary from London, in an attempt to resolve the U.S.-Spanish boundary dispute over Western Florida as a result of the purchase of the Louisiana Territory from France.

1805 — President Thomas Jefferson informed the British minister at Washington that if war broke out between Great Britain and Spain over Florida, the United States would take Cuba.

1808 — A delegation of Cubans visited President Jefferson, and suggested annexation to avoid possible domination by the French. Jefferson refused to give outright encouragement to the Cubans but his desires seemed to be clear enough.

OCTOBER 22, 1808 — The Cabinet of the United States unanimously supported the position of President Jefferson in regard to Cuba, but made it clear that it would not view with indifference the transfer of Cuba from Spain to either France or England.

OCTOBER 29, 1808 — President Thomas Jefferson wrote to Governor Claiborne of Louisiana: "We shall be well satisfied to see Cuba and Mexico remain in their present dependence; but very unwilling to see them in that of either France or England, politically or commercially. We consider their interests and ours as the same, and that the object of both must be to exclude all European influence from this Hemisphere."

1810–1811 — The United States sent "agents for seamen and commerce" to Buenos Aires, Chile and Peru. The revolting countries in turn sent numerous agents to the United States seeking diplomatic support and supplies. The United States assumed a position of watchful waiting and enjoyed new commercial privileges in these regions along with Great Britain.

JANUARY 15, 1811 — Congress passed a resolution, at the request of President James Madison, which embodied the non-transfer principle of American territory from one foreign power to another, mentioned by President Jefferson's Cabinet in regard to the possible independence or acquisition of Cuba.

MARCH 9, 1814 — The Treaty of Chaumont was concluded between Austria, Great Britain, Prussia and Russia for a period of twenty years. Article VI was the key to the treaty and stated the purpose: "To assure and facilitate the execution of the present Treaty, and to consolidate the intimate relations which to-day unite the four sovereigns for the good of the world, the High Contracting Parties have agreed to renew, at fixed periods, whether under the immediate auspices of the Sovereigns, or by their respective Ministers, reunions devoted to the great common interests and to the examination of the measures which, at any of these periods, shall be judged most salutary for the repose and prosperity of the peoples, and for the maintenance of the peace of the State."

NOVEMBER 20, 1815 — The Quadruple Alliance was concluded between Austria, Great Britain, Prussia and Russia which renewed the Treaty of Chaumont and partially implemented the Holy Alliance, which was designed to maintain the *status quo* and dedicated the nations to some broad conceptions of international cooperation.

SEPTEMBER 26, 1815 — The Holy Alliance was developed by Czar Alexander of Russia and presented to Great Britain, Austria and Prussia for adherence. It was based on the principles of Christianity, with God as the sovereign of the world and essentially constituted a moral reaffirmation of the victorious powers.

FEBRUARY 22, 1819 — Following the invasion of northern Florida by General Andrew Jackson, Secretary of State John Quincy Adams and Don Luis de Onis, the Spanish minister to Washington, negotiated the so-called Transcontinental Treaty which ceded the Floridas to the United States and regulated the western boundary of the Louisiana Territory.

SEPTEMBER 4, 1821 — Czar Alexander I of Russia promulgated a ukase which extended Russian control and trade monopoly down the west coast of North America.

MARCH 8, 1822 — President James Monroe addressed Congress on the recognition of the Central and South American states which had achieved independence from Spanish control. The policy of President Monroe was to accord the new states recognition as soon as there was a responsible government, which was in accordance with the commercial interests of the United States.

DECEMBER 17, 1822 — Secretary of State John Quincy Adams wrote to the U.S. minister at Madrid: "The present condition of the island of Cuba has excited much attention, and has become of deep interest to this Union. . . . [C]ommunicate to the Spanish Government in a manner adapted to the delicacy of the case the sentiments of this Government in relation to this subject, which are favorable to the continuance of Cuba in its connection with Spain."

1823 — Spain opened trade with Cuba and Puerto Rico to the United States partially in the hope of regaining influence or control over her former colonies.

APRIL 28, 1823 — Secretary of State John Quincy Adams wrote to Hugh Nelson, U.S. minister at Madrid: "Such, indeed, are, between the interests of that island and of this country, the geographical, commercial, moral, and political relations, formed by nature, gathering, in the process of time, and even now verging to maturity, that, in looking forward to the probable course of events, for the short period of half a century, it is scarcely possible to resist the conviction that the annexation of Cuba to our Federal Republic will be indispensable to the continuance and integrity of the Union itself."

SUMMER 1823 — Secretary of State John Quincy Adams was suspicious of the motivations of the British Foreign Minister, George Canning, in proposing a mutual declaration on the Western Hemisphere partially on the grounds that such a disclaimer might preclude the future acquisition of Cuba.

JULY 22, 1823 — John Quincy Adams as Secretary of State wrote a letter of protest to Henry Middleton, U.S. minister at St. Petersburg, taking exception to the Russian claim of "exclusive territorial jurisdiction" on the west coast of North America and the exclusive right of navigation and fishing in an area one hundred Italian miles from the claimed coastal region.

AUGUST 20, 1823 — The British Foreign Minister George Canning wrote to Richard Rush, the U.S. minister in London, proposing a mutual declaration of self-denial in regard to the emerging Spanish-American states and a declaration proposing that they should be left to their own destinies without European intervention or interference.

AUGUST 28, 1823 — Richard Rush, the U.S. minister at London, wrote to Secretary of State John Quincy Adams advocating that the United States and Great Britain make a mutual declaration to forestall the possibility of members of the Holy Alliance, and in particular France, from reasserting European control over the former Spanish colonies in Central and South America.

OCTOBER 9/12, 1823 — Prince de Polignac of France and the British Foreign Minister George Canning agreed to the so-called "Polignac Memorandum" whereby both France and Great Britain disclaimed any intent of acquiring parts of the former Spanish Empire in the Americas, but would not view with indifference the attempt of some other country to exert control, and that they were willing to see their respective countries ranked after Spain on the basis of the most-favored nation, assuming that Spain could make an amicable arrangement with her former colonies.

DECEMBER 2, 1823 — President James Monroe incorporated in his annual "State of the Union" address the essential features of the so-called "Monroe Doctrine" which were approximately as follows:

1. That the American continents were not to be considered for future colonization by European powers.
2. That the United States has not taken part in European wars, and does not desire to do so.
3. That the United States will not interfere with the existing colonies or dependencies of European powers.
4. That the United States would not view with indifference the extension of the European political system to the American continents. (Refer to Appendix A for selected paragraphs.)

1825 — President John Quincy Adams and Secretary of State Henry Clay wanted to send delegates to the first Pan-American Congress to be held at Panama. Their purpose was not to join an American alliance but to get the other states to uphold the doctrine of non-intervention and the principles of "good neighborhood." However, the U.S. delegates failed to arrive and the Congress was also a failure.

APRIL 27, 1825 — Secretary of State Henry Clay wrote to Edward Everett, then U.S. minister at Madrid, that "Of all the European powers, this country prefers that Cuba and Porto Rico should remain dependent on Spain."

OCTOBER 17, 1825 — Secretary of State Henry Clay wrote to Rufus King, U.S. minister at London, and stated that the United States was unwilling to bind itself to the neutralization of Cuba, but that it would not object if the other powers, France and Great Britain, desired to do so.

DECEMBER 20, 1825 — Secretary Clay addressed a note to the ministers of Colombia and Mexico, requesting them to use their influence to prevent any expeditions to Cuba or Puerto Rico until the Congress of Panama had expressed an opinion.

DECEMBER 10, 1827 — Edward Everett, U.S. minister at Madrid, prepared a confidential memorandum for the Spanish Secretary of State in which he pointed out that there were revolutionary movements underway in Great Britain for Cuba and "that the United States would not consent to Cuba passing to any third power."

OCTOBER 2, 1829 — Secretary of State Martin Van Buren wrote to Mr Van Ness, the U.S. minister at Madrid, that "the Government of the United States has always looked with deepest interest upon the fate of those islands, but particularly of Cuba."

OCTOBER 13, 1830 — Secretary of State Martin Van Buren instructed Mr. Van Ness, U.S. minister at Madrid, about the aspirations of Colombia and Mexico for Cuba and Puerto Rico, ". . . They inform you that we are content that Cuba should remain as it now is, but could not consent to its transfer to any European power. Motives of reasonable state policy render it more desirable to us that it should remain subject to Spain rather than to either of the South American States. Those motives will readily present themselves to your mind."

JULY 15, 1840 — Secretary of State John Forsyth wrote to the U.S. minister at Madrid; "Should you have reason to suspect any design on the part of Spain to transfer voluntarily her title to the island [of Cuba], whether of ownership or possession, and whether permanent or temporary, to Great Britain, or any other power, you will distinctly state that the United States will prevent it, at all hazards, as they will any foreign military occupation for any pretext whatsoever; and you are authorized to assure the Spanish Government that in case of any attempt from whatever quarter, to wrest from her this portion of her territory, she may securely depend upon the military and naval resources of the United States to aid her in preserving or recovering it."

JANUARY 14, 1843 — Secretary of State Daniel Webster instructed the U.S. consul at Havana to investigate some rumors about British plans for Cuba and observed that: "It is quite obvious that any attempt on the part of England to employ force in Cuba, for any purpose, would bring on a war, involving, possibly, all Europe, as well as the United States. . . ."

DECEMBER 2, 1845 — President James K. Polk gave an additional interpretation of the Monroe Doctrine in his annual message to Congress. The essence of Polk's interpretation seemed to be that "The United States . . . can not in silence permit any European interference on the North American continent, and should any such interference be attempted will be ready to resist it at any and all hazards." Polk went on to say that, "Should any portion of them, constituting an independent state, propose to unite themselves with our Confederacy, this will be a question for them and us to determine without any foreign interposition. We can never consent that European powers shall interfere to prevent such a union because it might disturb the 'balance of power' which they may desire to maintain upon this continent."

DECEMBER 12, 1846 — The United States and New Granada (Colombia) concluded a treaty whereby the United States would receive equal treatment and consideration with New Granada in the area known as the "Isthmus of Panama." Also, that if any communication or transportation across the isthmus were constructed in the future, the United States would continue to receive full and equal treatment with New Granada. In return for these concessions, the United States guaranteed the neutrality of the isthmus and the sovereignty of New Granada (Colombia) over the same area.

c. 1848 — Unrest prevalent in Cuba, but no organized insurrection against Spanish rule.

MAY 4, 1848 — Senator John C. Calhoun, a former member of President Monroe's cabinet, rose in the Senate and said: "So long as Cuba remains in the hands of Spain — a friendly power — a power of which we have no dread — it should continue to be, as it has been the policy of all Administrations ever since I have been connected with the Government, to let Cuba remain there; but with the fixed determination, which I hope never will be relinquished, that, if Cuba pass from her, it shall not be into any other hands but ours: This, not from a feeling of ambition, not from a desire for the extension of dominion, but because that island is indispensable to the safety of the United States, or rather, because it is indispensable to the safety of the United States that this island should not be in certain hands."

JUNE 17, 1848 — Secretary of State James Buchanan gave instructions to Romulus M. Saunders, the new U.S. minister to Madrid, to offer to purchase Cuba from Spain for a sum up to $100 million, to try and forestall the possible acquisition by Great Britain and to add to the strategic position of the United States. The Spanish government rejected the offer out of hand.

AUGUST 2, 1849 — Secretary of State John M. Clayton wrote to the U.S. minister at Madrid: "Whilst this Government is resolutely determined that the island of Cuba shall never be ceded by Spain to any other power than the United States, it does not desire, in future, to utter any threats, or enter into any guaranties with Spain on that subject. . . . The news of the cession of Cuba to any foreign power would, in the United States, be the instant signal for war. No foreign power would attempt to take it, that did not expect a hostile collision with us as an inevitable consequence."

1849–1854 — Numerous filibustering expeditions set out from the United States for Cuba to attempt to overthrow the Spanish control. The most notorious leader of these expeditions was Narcisio López, who led two unsuccessful attempts and was finally caught and garroted.

1850 — A combination of Southern slavery expansionists, Northern annexationists, and pro-U.S. attachment of Cubans developed a general atmosphere for the acquisition of Cuba. However, the slavery question in the United States (the Compromise of 1850) and the adamant opposition of Spain mitigated against annexation.

APRIL 19, 1850 — The United States and Great Britain concluded the "Clayton-Bulwer Treaty" whereby they mutually disclaimed exclusive jurisdiction or control of any canal which might be dug across Central America, and that each would have qual privileges in any such canal and the obligation of equal protection of such canal.

SEPTEMBER 27/OCTOBER 18, 1851 — Disturbed by the filibustering expeditions from the United States to Cuba, Spain successfully appealed to France and Great Britain to intercede on her behalf. The French and British informed Secretary of State Daniel Webster that a naval force had been sent to the Caribbean to forestall any further filibustering expeditions, to which Webster replied that the United States would not tolerate the surveillance of U.S. citizens on the high seas.

OCTOBER 4, 1851 — Secretary of State Daniel Webster wrote to President Millard Fillmore about his apprehensions over British interest in Cuba and observed that ". . . Mr. J. Quincy Adams often said that, if necessary, we ought to make war with England sooner than to acquiesce in her acquisition of Cuba. It is indeed obvious enough what danger there would be to us, if a great naval power were to possess this key to the Gulf of Mexico and the Caribbean Sea."

APRIL 23, 1852 — At the second instance of Spain, France and Great Britain proposed to the United States a tripartite agreement disclaiming any intention of excessive domination or control over Cuba. Secretary of State Edward Everett replied in circuitous reasoning that the United States would not accept European restraints on an essentially American affair.

DECEMBER 1, 1852 — Secretary of State Edward Everett replied to the French minister at Washington, Comte de Sartiges, that the United States is unwilling to sign a tripartite declaration with France and Great Britain disclaiming any intentions to exert control or influence over Cuba, and that the United States "considers the condition of Cuba as mainly an American question."

DECEMBER 6, 1852 — President Millard Fillmore discussed Cuba in connection with the disbarment of the mail packet *Crescent*

City from Havana in his annual address to Congress and stated that active representations were being made at Madrid.

MARCH, 1853 — President Franklin Pierce proclaimed for territorial expansion in his inaugural address, and soon thereafter dispatched James Buchanan to London, John Mason to Paris and Pierre Soulé to Madrid. The prime intent of the Pierce administration was clearly the acquisition of Cuba.

APRIL 3, 1854 — Secretary of State William L. Marcy instructed the U.S. minister to Spain, Pierre Soulé, to renew the offer of the United States to buy Cuba for a price up to $130 million. This offer was summarily rejected by Spain.

1854 — The U.S. packet ship *Black Warrior* was seized by Spanish authorities in Havana harbor for failing to produce a cargo manifest. The ship was later released after a vigorous protest by the United States but not without the imposition of a $6,000 fine. Spain subsequently made proper adjustments to reduce the matter.

OCTOBER 18, 1854 — The three U.S. ministers to Madrid, London and Paris, respectively, Pierre Soulé, James Buchanan and John Y. Mason, met at Aix-la-Chapelle and issued a joint declaration in regard to Cuba known as the "Ostend Manifesto." The essential features of this statement were that:
1. The United States had a reasonable right to try and buy Cuba for the fair price offered.
2. That if the offer of purchase were refused, the United States had the right to acquire Cuba for the sake of "internal peace and the existence" of the Federal Union.
Following an outburst at home and abroad, Secretary Marcy was forced to repudiate the "Ostend Manifesto."

1856 — The platform of the Democratic Party contained a plank calling for the annexation of Cuba. The Democrats also nominated James Buchanan, the real author of the "Ostend Manifesto," who was subsequently elected President. The Democratic Party split badly over the slavery issue, but persisted up to the Civil War in advocating the annexation of Cuba.

DECEMBER 6, 1858 — President James Buchanan discussed Cuba in his annual message to Congress: "The truth is, that Cuba, in its existing colonial condition, is a constant source of injury and annoyance to the American people. . . . It has been made known to the world by my predecessors that the United States have on several occasions endeavored to acquire Cuba from Spain by honorable negotiation. . . .
The Island of Cuba, from its geographical position, commands the mouth of the Mississippi and the immense and

annually increasing trade. . . . Whilst the possession of the island would be of vast importance to the United States, its value to Spain is comparatively unimportant. Such was the relative situation of the parties when the great Napoleon transferred Louisiana to the United States."

APRIL 1, 1861 — Secretary of State William H. Seward suggested to President Abraham Lincoln that the Civil War might be transformed from a party question into a national question by demanding "explanations from Spain and France" about their intentions in Santo Domingo and Mexico and "if satisfactory explanations are not received from Spain and France, would convene Congress and declare war against them." This was another interesting development in the interpretation of the Monroe Doctrine.

JANUARY 1866 — Secretary of State William H. Seward was one of the more ambitious expansionists after the Civil War, and made a cruise through the West Indies in early 1866 stopping at several islands including Cuba. The maritime experiences of the Civil War and the prospect of a trans-isthmian canal had convinced Seward and other members of the U.S. government that it might be desirable to acquire some islands or privileges in the Caribbean. Seward and President Ulysses S. Grant were the most active in various Caribbean schemes to acquire additional territory.

MAY 7, 1867 — Secretary of State William H. Seward had a confidential interview with the Spanish minister at Washington at which he said that Cuba would eventually "fall into the United States, without the practice of any injustice or unfriendliness and with the consent of the people of the island and of the Government of Spain."

1868–1878 — The approximate span of the so-called "First Revolt" of the Cubans against Spanish rule. Excessive brutality practiced by both the Spanish rulers and the insurrectionists.

1869 — President Ulysses S. Grant offered his good offices to Spain to settle the insurrection in Cuba on the basis of abolition of slavery, independence for Cuba, and an indemnity to Spain which would be guaranteed by the United States. Spain refused to negotiate unless the rebels surrendered and ceased insurrection, which put an end to the project.

DECEMBER 6, 1869 — President Ulysses S. Grant refers to the efforts of the United States to stop the revolution in Cuba in his annual address to Congress: "The United States, in order to put a stop to bloodshed in Cuba, and in the interest of a neighboring people, proposed their good offices to bring the existing

contest to a termination. The offer, not being accepted by Spain
on a basis which we believed could be received by Cuba, was
withdrawn."

JANUARY 10, 1870 — Secretary of State Hamilton Fish heard
that Spain was trying to negotiate a loan and pledge the
revenues of Cuba as security. He wrote to J. Lothrop Motley,
the U.S. minister at London, that the United States would look
with disfavor upon any arrangement which might "pledge the
revenues of that island, or compromise any interests connected
therewith or give to any foreign government a right to interpose
in the affairs of Cuba."

JUNE 13, 1870 — President Grant resisted Congressional pressure
and refused to recognize the belligerency of the Cubans in a
classic statement of international law interpreting the recognition
of a state of belligerency.

DECEMBER 5, 1870 — President Ulysses S. Grant discussed the
violation of United States citizens and property in Cuba in his
annual message to Congress, and threatened that unless Spain
came to some understanding on the settlement of the claims, "it
will then become my duty to communicate that fact to Congress
and invite its action on the subject."

1871 — Spain agreed to adjudicate the claims of U.S. citizens in
Cuba as a result of the "First Revolt." These claims were arbi-
trated before a mixed tribunal and the United States received a
total of $2,793,450.55 from Spain under this agreement.

DECEMBER 4, 1871 — President Grant again referred to the
worsening affairs in Cuba in his annual message to Congress:
"It is to be regretted that the disturbed condition of the island
of Cuba continues to be a source of annoyance and of anxiety.
The existence of a protracted struggle in such close proximity
to our own territory, without apparent prospect of an early
termination, cannot be other than an object of concern to a
people who, while abstaining from interference in the affairs of
other powers, naturally desire to see every country in an undisturbed enjoyment of peace, liberty and the blessings of free
institutions."

1873 — The Spanish government seized the *Virginius* on the high
seas as it was proceeding toward Cuba on a filibustering expedi-
tion. Fifty-three members of the crew and passengers were
briefly court-martialed and executed. The United States delivered an ultimatum to Spain for satisfaction, and the ship was
returned and an indemnity of $80,000 paid to the families of
the deceased.

The *Virginius* incident combined with the other grievances of the United States against Spain for the mistreatment of U.S. citizens and the despoliation of property provided a pretext for war with Spain. However, in spite of some demonstrations in the cities, there was little general demand for war.

NOVEMBER 5, 1875 — Secretary of State Hamilton Fish dispatched a message to Caleb Cushing, U.S. minister at Madrid, urging Spain to bring peace to Cuba on the basis of abolition of slavery and self-government. Fish also let it be known that the United States would welcome the support of the European powers in resolving the "Cuban Question," a maneuver for which he was severely criticized as violating the Monroe Doctrine and the principles of U.S. hegemony in the Western Hemisphere and avoidance of European entanglements or guarantees.

DECEMBER 7, 1875 — President Ulysses S. Grant expressed his opinion on the recognition of the insurgents in Cuba in his annual message to Congress: "While conscious that the insurrection in Cuba has shown a strength and endurance which make it at least doubtful whether it be in the power of Spain to subdue it, it seems unquestionable that no such civil organization exists which may be recognized as an independent government capable of performing its "international obligations and entitled to be treated as one of the powers of the earth."

NOVEMBER 19, 1881 — Secretary of State James G. Blaine wrote to James R. Lowell, the U.S. minister at London, advising him to attempt to revise the Clayton-Bulwer Treaty in favor of the United States.

JANUARY 7, 1882 — The British Foreign Minister, Lord Granville, advised the British minister at Washington, Lionel West, that Great Britain would not consider a reinterpretation of the Clayton-Bulwer Treaty.

1884 — By means of an executive agreement with Spain the United States removed a 10 percent *ad valorem* tariff on products from Cuba and Puerto Rico which greatly encouraged U.S. investment and development of the sugar industry in these islands.

1886 — Slavery was abolished and the Cubans were given limited representation in the Spanish *Cortes* (parliament).

OCTOBER 2, 1889–APRIL 19, 1890 — The First International Conference of American States held at Washington, D.C. Eighteen American Republics attended and formed the International Union of American Republics and the "Bureau of American Republics."

1890 — The so-called "McKinley Tariff" reduced import restrictions to a bare minimum and further encouraged U.S. trade with Cuba and Puerto Rico.

1894 — The so-called "Wilson Tariff" raised tariffs up to new highs and restricted the importation of Cuban and Puerto Rican sugar which caused considerable economic hardships in the islands.

1895–(1898) — The "Second Revolt" began and was characterized by ruthless suppression under General Weyler and his reconcentration policy, combined with equally ruthless retaliation by the insurgents. However, many more people died of starvation and disease than from actual warfare.

JULY 20, 1895 — Secretary of State Richard Olney wrote to Thomas F. Bayard, the United States ambassador at London, in regard to the Venezuelan-British boundary dispute: "That America is in no part open to colonization though the proposition was not universally admitted at the time of its first enunciation, has long been universally conceded. We are now concerned, therefore, only with that other practical application of the Monroe Doctrine the disregard of which by an European power is to be deemed an act of unfriendliness towards the United States."

1896–1898 — An estimated seventy-one filibustering expeditions set out from the United States for Cuba. Most of these expeditions failed but about twenty-seven managed to get through.

APRIL 4, 1896 — Secretary of State, Richard Olney informed the Spanish minister at Washington, Dupuy de Lôme, that the United States would not view with "complacency" another ten years of insurrection on the island of Cuba.

APRIL 6, 1896 — Both houses of Congress passed a concurrent resolution in favor of recognizing the belligerency of the Cuban insurgents and recommended to President Grover Cleveland that he extend his good offices to Spain in order to establish peace on the basis of Cuban independence. However, President Cleveland refused to do this citing President Grant's earlier statements on the requirements for the recognition of belligerency.

1896 — The Republican Party included a plank in its platform calling for the independence of Cuba; largely under the stimulation of Henry Cabot Lodge.

DECEMBER 7, 1896 — President Grover Cleveland referred to the possible recognition of the Cuban insurgents in his annual message to Congress: "The insurrection in Cuba still continues with all its perplexities. . . . If Spain has not yet re-established her authority, neither have the insurgents made good their title to be regarded as an independent state." President Cleveland had earlier proposed to cooperate with Spain on the establishment of home rule in Cuba under Spanish sovereignty, which had been refused.

SEPTEMBER 23, 1897 — President William McKinley contemplated trying to buy Cuba, but renewed the Grant and Cleveland offer of good offices to help establish peace in Cuba.

OCTOBER 23, 1897 — The Spanish Foreign Minister, the Duke of Tetuan, informed the U.S. minister at Madrid, Stewart L. Woodford, of the proposed Spanish reforms and attempts at quelling the rebellion while urging the United States to use its influence to restrain filibustering expeditions and financing of the rebels from the United States.

JANUARY–APRIL, 1898 — A newspaper rivalry in New York between the *Journal* of Mr. Hearst and the *World* of Mr. Pulitzer caused a distortion and exaggeration of the situation in Cuba which aroused U.S. sympathy and public opinion. "Jingoism" or the "Jingo Press" encouraged the young Republican expansionists led by Senator Henry Cabot Lodge, Assistant Secretary of the Navy Theodore Roosevelt and Captain Alfred T. Mahan, who in 1890 wrote *The Influence of Sea Power Upon History.*

JANUARY 25, 1898 — The battleship *Maine* dropped anchor in Havana harbor on a courtesy call which no one seems to have ordered.

FEBRUARY 9, 1898 — The Spanish minister at Washington, Dupuy de Lôme, had a private letter written to a friend in Cuba published without his knowledge in the New York *Journal*. The letter contained a candid appraisal of President McKinley, and expressed the opinion that the Spanish reforms in Cuba were not sincere.

FEBRUARY 15, 1898 — The battleship *Maine* blew up and sank in Havana Harbor with a loss of 260 lives. The cause or agents of the explosion were unknown, but the Spanish government immediately expressed condolences and proposed a joint commission to investigate the incident. The Jingo Press soon stirred up public opinion and the *Maine* affair became merged with the general Cuban Question.

MARCH 9, 1898 — At the suggestion of President McKinley, Congress passed a $50 million appropriation for national defense.

MARCH 17, 1898 — Senator Proctor of Vermont delivered a devastating account to the U.S. Senate of conditions and Spanish rule in Cuba after a recent visit.

MARCH 26, 1898 — Assistant Secretary of State William R. Day advised Stewart L. Woodford, the U.S. minister at Madrid, that President William McKinley urged the Spanish government to establish peace as quickly as possible in Cuba. The President also suggested:
1. That Spain revoke the reconcentration order in Cuba.
2. That Spain offer the Cubans full self-government.
3. That the United States would offer to assist in the achievement of these objectives.
4. That the President would offer his good offices for the mediation of the dispute.

MARCH 27, 1898 — Secretary of State William R. Day further advised the U.S. minister at Madrid, Stewart L. Woodford, to try and achieve:
1. An armistice until October 1, 1898, with negotiations toward a settlement through the "friendly offices" of the President.
2. Revocation of the reconcentration order with relief supplied from the United States.
3. If peace terms are not agreed upon by October 1, the President would act as the "final arbiter" in the dispute.
4. The President would attempt to get the insurgents to agree to the plan, subject to Spanish approval.

MARCH 30, 1898 — Spain revoked the reconcentration order in Cuba.

APRIL 5, 1898 — Stewart L. Woodford, the U.S. minister at Madrid, wrote to President McKinley strongly recommending that he accept the proposals of the Spanish government for the "immediate and unconditioned suspension of hostilities" for a period up to six months subject to acceptance by the Cuban insurgents.

APRIL 7, 1898 — At the instance of Spain, six European powers presented a joint note to President McKinley expressing the hope that the Cuban Question could be solved peaceably. McKinley replied that if the United States were to intervene it would be for "humanity's sake."

APRIL 10, 1898 — Report of the Spanish move to accept virtually all the terms expressed in the U.S. note of March 27, reached Washington.

APRIL 11, 1898 — In his special message to Congress, President William McKinley had this to say on recognition: "Turning to the question of recognizing at this time the independence of the present insurgent government in Cuba, we find safe precedents in our history from an early day. . . . Nor from the standpoint of expediency do I think it would be wise or prudent for this Government to recognize at the present time the independence of the so-called Cuban Republic. Such recognition is not necessary in order to enable the United States to intervene and pacify the island." However, the substance of the message to Congress was to request authority to use the armed forces to help pacify Cuba if necessary. The grounds for possible U.S. intervention as set forth by President McKinley were:
1. Humanitarian.
2. Protection of life and property.
3. Injury to U.S. commercial interests and destruction of property.
4. Situation in Cuba is a menace to peace.
5. Situation in Cuba has caused considerable expense to U.S.

APRIL 19, 1898 — Congress passed a joint resolution in response to McKinley's message:
1. Cuba should be independent.
2. Spain would have to withdraw.
3. Authorized the President to use the armed forces to accomplish objectives.
4. Disclaimed any "disposition or intention to exercise sovereignty, jurisdiction or control" over Cuba. (Teller Amendment)

APRIL 20, 1898 — President McKinley signed the joint resolutions and gave Spain until noon of April 23rd to comply with the intent of the resolutions.

APRIL 22, 1898 — President McKinley declared a partial blockade of Cuba.

APRIL 25, 1898 — Congress declared a state of war to have been in existence with Spain since April 21st.

MAY 1, 1898 — Under the command of Commodore George Dewey, part of the American fleet destroyed the Spanish Pacific fleet in the battle of Manila Bay in the Philippines.

JULY 3, 1898 — The American Atlantic fleet destroyed the Spanish Atlantic fleet in the battle of Santiago harbor.

AUGUST 12, 1898 — An armistice was signed between the United States and Spain through the good offices of the French ambassador in Washington.

SEPTEMBER 16, 1898 — President McKinley gave instructions to the United States peace commission which was to meet at Paris not later than October 1, 1898. Some features of the instructions were:

1. Evacuation by Spain of Cuba, Puerto Rico and all other Spanish islands in West Indies.
2. Occupation of these areas by U.S. military forces.
3. Cession of Guam to the United States.
4. Temporary waiver of Spanish indemnity to the United States.
5. Temporary concessions to the United States in the Philippines subject to further clarification.

DECEMBER 10, 1898 — A treaty of peace was concluded between the United States and Spain. A few of the provisions were:

1. Spain relinquished all title and claim of sovereignty over Cuba.
2. Spain ceded Puerto Rico and other islands in the West Indies along with Guam to the United States.
3. Spain ceded the Philippines to the United States, and the United States agreed to pay Spain $20 million.

FEBRUARY 6, 1899 — The U.S. Senate gave its advice and consent to the Treaty of Paris ending the Spanish-American War. The main terms were:

1. U.S. annexation of the Philippines.
2. U.S. protectorate over Cuba.
3. U.S. annexation of Puerto Rico and Guam.
4. U.S. indemnity to Spain of $20 million.

MARCH 3, 1899 — The army appropriations act had attached the "Foraker Amendment": "That no property, franchises, or concessions of any kind whatever shall be granted by the United States, or by any military or other authority whatever in the island of Cuba during the occupation thereof by the United States."

1898–1902 — U.S. military occupation of Cuba.

MARCH 2, 1901 — The army appropriations act had attached the "Platt Amendment":

1. Cuba was not to enter into any treaty or other compact with a foreign power which would impair its independence, nor permit colonization for military or naval lodgment or control.

2. Cuba was not to contract any public debt beyond its resources.

3. The United States would have the right to intervene "for the preservation of Cuban independence, the maintenance of a government adequate for the protection of life, property and individual liberty," and for discharging its obligations assumed by the Treaty of Paris.

4. Ratification of all acts of the United States during its military occupancy.

5. Execution by Cuba of the sanitary arrangements already undertaken by the United States.

6. The title of the Isle of Pines to be left for future adjustment.

7. The United States, for its defense as well as that of Cuba, to have the right to purchase or lease two naval stations.

8. These provisions to be embodied in a permanent treaty with the United States.

OCTOBER 22, 1901 — The Second International Conference of American States held in Mexico City with nineteen American Republics represented. The Conference produced a protocol of adherence to the "Hague Convention for the Pacific Settlement of International Disputes" and a Treaty of Arbitration for Pecuniary Claims.

NOVEMBER 18, 1901 — The United States and Great Britain concluded the so-called "Hay-Pauncefote Treaty" which abrogated the Clayton-Bulwer Treaty and gave the United States virtually unrestricted privileges in regard to the construction and administration of any trans-isthmian canal subject to the provisions of the Convention of Constantinople pertaining to the "internationalization" of the Suez Canal.

MAY 22, 1903 — The terms of the Platt Amendment were included in the Cuban constitution and in a treaty with the United States, known as the "Treaty of Havana."

DECEMBER 6, 1904 — President Theodore Roosevelt included in his annual message to Congress on the "State of the Union" a further interpretation of the Monroe Doctrine which became known as the "Roosevelt Corollary." The essential feature of this corollary was to unilaterally ascribe to the United States the right of intervention within the Western Hemisphere and particularly within the Caribbean area for "progress in stable and just civilization."

JULY 21–AUGUST 26, 1906 — The Third International Conference of American States held at Rio de Janeiro with nineteen out of the twenty-one American Republics represented. The conference was largely concerned with the forcible collection of debts and the Drago and Calvo doctrines.

1906–1909–1911–1919 — The United States intervened in Cuba primarily to maintain internal political stability and financial responsibility.

JULY 12–AUGUST 30, 1910 — The Fourth International Conference of American States held at Buenos Aires with twenty American Republics represented. The conference discussed economic and cultural cooperation, and also changed the name of the "International Bureau of American Republics" to the "Pan American Union."

AUGUST 3, 1912 — When rumors reached Washington that the Japanese might establish a fishing port in Lower California, Senator Henry Cabot Lodge proposed a resolution which passed the Senate and further expanded the Monroe Doctrine: "Resolved, that when any harbor or other place in the American continents is so situated that the occupation thereof for naval or military purposes might threaten the communications or safety of the United States, the Government of the United States could not see without grave concern the possession of such harbor or other place by any corporation or association which has such a relation to another Government, not American, as to give that Government practical power of control for national purposes."

OCTOBER 27, 1913 — President Woodrow Wilson delivered a speech at Mobile, Alabama, where he advocated that U.S. relations with Latin America be put on the basis of equality and respect, and not economic domination.

AUGUST 5, 1914 — The United States and Nicaragua entered into a treaty whereby the United States received exclusive proprietary rights in perpetuity from Nicaragua for the construction, maintenance and operation of any canal which might be constructed across the isthmus.

JANUARY 6, 1916 — President Wilson addressed the Pan-American Scientific Congress and recommended that the states of the Western Hemisphere mutually guarantee political independence and territorial integrity; and also agree to arbitrate all disputes and prevent external subversion. In regard to the Monroe Doctrine President Wilson observed that it "was proclaimed by the United States on her own authority. It has always been maintained, and always will be maintained, upon her own responsibility."

JUNE 28, 1919 — The twenty-first article of the Covenant of the League of Nations and simultaneously of the Treaty of Versailles stated: "Nothing in this covenant shall be deemed to affect the validity of international engagements, such as treaties of arbitration, or regional understandings like the Monroe Doctrine, for securing the maintenance of peace."

MARCH 25 to MAY 3, 1923 — The Fifth International Conference of American States met in Santiago, Chile, with eighteen of the American Republics in attendance. The "Gondra Treaty" was signed to try and avoid or prevent conflicts between American states.

JANUARY 16–FEBRUARY 20, 1928 — The Sixth International Conference of American States convened in Havana, Cuba, with all states represented. There was an attempt to prevent further American intervention in the Caribbean, but the only substance produced was a convention designed to forestall the use of one American country as a base for revolutionary attack on another country.

DECEMBER 17, 1928 — J. Reuben Clark, Under Secretary of the Department of State, submitted a memorandum to Secretary of State Henry L. Stimson which revised the U.S. policy toward Latin America and gave a re-definition to the Monroe Doctrine. According to this "Clark Memorandum," the Monroe Doctrine was a unilateral declaration which only had as much force and effect as the United States determined to give it. Also, that the Monroe Doctrine was not directed against or for the use of Latin America, but against Europe for the protection of Latin America. (Refer to Appendix B for text.)

DECEMBER 10, 1928–JANUARY 5, 1929 — An International Conference of American States on Conciliation and Arbitration met in Washington, D.C., with all countries in attendance except Argentina. The conference produced two conventions on inter-American conciliation and arbitration.

MARCH 4, 1933 — President Franklin D. Roosevelt enunciated the "Good Neighbor Policy" in these words: "In the field of world policy I would dedicate this nation to the policy of the good neighbor — the neighbor who resolutely respects himself and because he does so, respects the rights of others — the neighbor who respects his obligations and respects the sanctity of his agreements in and with a world of neighbors."

DECEMBER 3–26, 1933 — The Seventh International Conference of American States was held at Montevideo, Uruguay, with twenty states present. This produced a "Convention on Rights and Duties of States," which was largely concerned with the principle of nonintervention.

MAY 29, 1934 — A treaty of general relations was signed between the United States and Cuba which abolished the provisions of the Platt Amendment but retained the privileges at the Guantanamo Naval Station under the executive agreements of February 16 and 23, 1903. The protectorate of the United States over Cuba was thereby abolished.

DECEMBER 1–23, 1936 — An Inter-American Conference for the Maintenance of Peace was held in Buenos Aires. The conference was primarily concerned with the security of the Western Hemisphere in the event of war in Europe or the Far East.

DECEMBER 23, 1936 — At the Special Inter-American Conference held at Buenos Aires, the United States and twenty other American states entered into three separate treaties variously known as. "The Consultative Pact," "The Protocol on Non-Intervention," and "The Declaration of Principles of Inter-American Solidarity and Cooperation." The significance of these three conventions and the conference was to "multilateralize" the Monroe Doctrine and to lay the basis for an Inter-American confederation in the face of rising international tension and European disturbances.

DECEMBER 9–27, 1938 — The Eighth International Conference of American States was held in Lima, Peru. The conference was concerned with reducing Nazi and Fascist penetration into the Western Hemisphere on the eve of hostilities in Europe. Established the meeting of the consultation of foreign ministers.

OCTOBER 3, 1939 — At the Meeting of the Foreign Ministers of the American Republics in Panama, two resolutions were passed, one on "Neutrality" and the other referred to as the "Declaration of Panama." The first resolution attempted to remove the Western Hemisphere from the European conflict, and the second resolution laid the basis for a maritime buffer zone around the hemisphere.

JULY 30, 1940 — At the Second Meeting of Foreign Ministers of the American Republics in Havana a resolution was passed providing for the provisional administration of European colonies in the Americas to forestall possible German occupation.

JANUARY 28, 1942 — At the Third Meeting of Foreign Ministers of the American Republics in Rio de Janiero a resolution was passed known as the "Act of Rio de Janeiro" which declared that any act of aggression by a non-American state against any American Republic would be considered as an act of aggression against all and sufficient grounds for the breaking of diplomatic relations with the aggressor.

MARCH 6, 1945 — At the Inter-American Conference on Problems of War and Peace in Mexico City, a resolution was passed known as the "Act of Chapultepec." The essential features of this resolution were:

    1. Juridical equality of sovereign states.

    2. An act of aggression against one American state shall be considered as an act of aggression against all.

    3. Possible establishment of procedures to take measures in the face of aggression.

    4. Establishment of an international organization to accomplish the purposes of the resolution.

AUGUST 15–SEPTEMBER 2, 1947 — The Inter-American Conference for the Maintenance of Continental Peace and Security met in Rio de Janeiro and produced the "Rio Pact." The pact solidified the hemispheric unity in the face of possible Communist aggression or subversion.

SEPTEMBER 2, 1947 — At the Inter-American Conference for the Maintenance of Continental Peace and Security held in Rio de Janeiro, the Inter-American Treaty of Reciprocal Assistance known as the "Rio Pact" was developed. The essential features of this treaty are:

    1. An armed attack against one American state shall be considered as an armed attack against all

    2. An unarmed attack against the integrity, sovereignty or political independence of any American state, shall result in the Organ of Consultation meeting to consider the measures which should be taken to maintain the peace and security of the hemisphere.

    3. The measures which the Organ of Consultation may recommend include the use of force. (Refer to Appendix C for text of selected articles.)

MARCH 30–MAY 2, 1948 — The Ninth International Conference of American States met in Bogotá, Colombia, and formulated the Charter of the Organization of American States (OAS). In addition several agreements on the pacific settlement of disputes, rights and duties of man, and economic cooperation were worked out.

APRIL 30, 1948 — At the Ninth International Conference of American States held in Bogotá the Charter of the Organization of

American States also known as the "Act of Bogotá" was drawn up. The essential features of this agreement are:

1. Establishment of the Organization of American States.
2. Codification of existing principles and practices of the inter-American system.
3. Collective security through united action against violation of territorial integrity, sovereignty or political independence of any member. (Refer to Appendix D for text of selected articles.)

JULY 26, 1953 — Fidel Castro began his revolutionary movement to overthrow the regime of Fulgencio Batista in Cuba.

MARCH 1–28, 1954 — The Tenth International Conference of American States met in Caracas, Venezuela, which was primarily concerned with the "declaration of solidarity for the preservation of the political integrity of the Americas against the intervention of international communism."

JULY 25, 1957 — Upon presenting his credentials, U.S. Ambassador Earl T. Smith expressed the concern of the American people over the internal strife in Cuba.

MARCH 14, 1958 — The United States suspended arms deliveries to Cuba.

JUNE 22, 1958 — Raúl Castro, rebel commander in Oriente Province, issued an order for the detention of U.S. male citizens for the purpose of "stopping U.S. military shipments to the Batista government." Forty-three U.S. citizens are subsequently held and released on July 18th.

SEPTEMBER–OCTOBER, 1958 — The Cuban rebels set up a system levying of taxes on U.S. and Cuban businesses operating in eastern Cuba, in order to collect funds and equipment for the revolutionary movement.

OCTOBER 20, 1958 — Two Americans employed by the Texas Oil Company were captured and later released by the Cuban rebels.

JANUARY 1, 1959 — President Fulgencio Batista resigned and Fidel Castro came to power. President Batista and some of his personal aides left Cuba.

JANUARY 2, 1959 — Fidel Castro proclaimed a provisional Cuban government with Manuel Urrutia as President.

JANUARY 5, 1959 — José Miró Cardona appointed Prime Minister by President Urrutia.

JANUARY 7, 1959 — The Government of the United States recognized the new Cuban Government and expressed its satisfaction that the new Cuban Government would honor its international obligations and agreements.

La Hoy, the Communist Party daily newspaper, appeared in Havana for the first time since 1953.

JANUARY 9, 1959 — Ernesto "Che" Guevara, a leader of the revolutionary movement, declared that the Communists had earned the right to have a formal party in Cuba since so many members of the Communist Party had fought the Batista forces.

JANUARY 13, 1959 — About two hundred people were tried, convicted and executed by revolutionary tribunals. By the end of 1959 over six hundred people lost their lives under these tribunals.

JANUARY 21, 1959 — Daniel M. Braddock, the U.S. Chargé d'Affaires, informed Fidel Castro that the Government of the United States wanted cordial, friendly relations with the new Cuban Government.

JANUARY 27, 1959 — Nine U.S. companies operating in Cuba made advance tax payments of $2,560,000 to the new Cuban Government.

FEBRUARY 16, 1959 — Fidel Castro succeeded Miró Cardona as Prime Minister.

MARCH 2, 1959 — Philip W. Bonsal, the new U.S. ambassador to Cuba, upon presenting his credentials to President Urrutia stated that, "We wish you every success in your announced objective of raising the standard of living of your country. I shall devote particular attention to all the opportunities of increased cooperation in the economic field which may present themselves."

MARCH 4, 1959 — The Cuban Government "intervened" the Cuban Telephone Company, a U.S.-owned firm.

MARCH 22, 1959 — Premier Castro opposed backing the United States in the "Cold War."

MAY 17, 1959 — The Cuban Government passed an agrarian reform law which provided for the expropriation of land with compensation in twenty-year bonds at 4½ percent interest.

JUNE 11, 1959 — The United States expressed sympathy for the agrarian reform law and recognized the right of a state to take property for public purposes so long as there is prompt, adequate and effective compensation.

JUNE 12, 1959 — Ambassador Bonsal stressed the importance of close, friendly relations between the U.S. and Cuba because of the interrelated economies and geographic proximity of the two countries.

JUNE 25, 1959 — The Cuban Government seized three U.S.-owned cattle ranches under the agrarian reform law.

JULY 1, 1959 — Major Pedro Luis Diaz Lanz resigned as head of the Cuban Air Force charging that there was Communist infiltration of the armed forces and the new Cuban Government.

JULY 12, 1959 — President Urrutia stated on television that communism is not really concerned with the welfare of the people and that it was a menace to the Cuban revolution.

JULY 14, 1959 — Major Diaz Lanz testified on the Communist penetration of Cuba before the Senate Internal Security Subcommittee.

JULY 17, 1959 — Prime Minister Fidel Castro accused President Urrutia of treason over television, and Urrutia subsequently resigned.

JULY 31, 1959 — Cuban officials seized six more U.S.-owned lands.

SEPTEMBER 10, 1959 — Assistant Secretary of State Roy Rubottom informed the Cuban Government that the United States was still favorably disposed toward the Cuban Government despite the provocation of the previous nine months.

OCTOBER 26, 1959 — The Cuban Government passed a law which imposed confiscatory taxes on the U.S. Government-owned Nicaro nickel facility in reputed violation of an international agreement.

Premier Castro denounced the United States before a rally of 300,000.

OCTOBER 27, 1959 — U.S. Ambassador Philip Bonsal informed the Cuban Government that the "United States awaits a resolution by the Cuban Government of the issues involved on a basis of friendship and observance of international law which have traditionally characterized negotiations between Cuba and the United States."

NOVEMBER 6, 1959 — The Cuban Ministry of State published a brochure entitled "Cuba Renounces Before the World," repeating the charges of U.S. interference and provision of political asylum.

NOVEMBER 9, 1959 — The U.S. Government protested the Cuban brochure as inaccurate, and stated that no request had yet been made by Cuba under the extradition treaty with the United States.

DECEMBER 31, 1959 — Cuba and Communist China signed a trade agreement whereby Cuba would sell China 50,000 tons of sugar.

JANUARY 11, 1960 — The United States protested the seizure of U.S. property under the agrarian reform law, on the grounds that the provisions for compensation were not met.

JANUARY 23, 1960 — U.S. Ambassador Philip Bonsal was recalled.

JANUARY 27, 1960 — President Osvaldo Dorticos Torrado of Cuba stated that his government was fully disposed to discuss differences between Cuba and the United States through diplomatic negotiation, and would hear claims of individual U.S. citizens under Cuban and international law.

FEBRUARY 4, 1960 — Soviet First Deputy Premier Aanastas I. Mikoyan arrived in Cuba to open a Soviet exhibition.

FEBRUARY 13, 1960 — Prime Minister Fidel Castro and First Deputy Premier Anastas Mikoyan issued a joint communiqué and signed trade and economic aid agreements. The Soviet Union agreed to buy one million tons of Cuban sugar in each of the next five years, and Cuba received a $100 million credit for the purchase of equipment in the Soviet Union.

FEBRUARY 20, 1960 — Cuba signed a trade and payments agreement with East Germany.

FEBRUARY 24, 1960 — Armed Forces Minister Raúl Castro blamed the United States for the exploitation of Cuba since the turn of the century.

MARCH 2, 1960 — National Bank President Ernesto "Che" Guevara stated that the sugar which Cuba sells to the United States under a preferential agreement has meant economic slavery for the people of Cuba.

MARCH 4, 1960 — The French munitions ship *La Coubre* exploded in Havana harbor.

MARCH 5, 1960 — Prime Minister Fidel Castro identified the United States as the party responsible for the explosion of *La Coubre*.

The United States repudiated any connection with the explosion of *La Coubre*, and offered medical equipment and services for the relief of the victims.

MARCH 7, 1960 — The United States "categorically and emphatically" denied the charge of involvement in the explosion of *La Coubre*.

MARCH 20, 1960 — Ernesto "Che" Guevara stated that "Our war . . . is against the great power of the North."

MARCH 31, 1960 — Cuba signed a trade and payments agreement with Poland.

APRIL 19, 1960 — The Soviet oil tanker *Vishinsky* arrived in Cuba with a cargo of Soviet crude oil.

MAY 6, 1960 — A Cuban Coast Guard boat fired upon the U.S. submarine *Sea Poacher* eleven miles out from the Cuban shoreline.

MAY 8, 1960 — Cuba and the Soviet Union established diplomatic relations.

MAY 16, 1960 — Cuba and Czechoslovakia established diplomatic relations.

JUNE 8, 1960 — While on a visit to Moscow, Antonio Nuñez Jiminez, the Director of the Agrarian Reform Institute, said that Cuba is "the Soviet Union's greatest and most loyal friend."

JUNE 10, 1960 — The Cuban Government seized four U.S.-owned hotels in Havana.

Cuba signed a five-year trade and payments agreement with Czechoslovakia.

Prime Minister Fidel Castro stated that U.S. officials participated in a plot to mount an invasion in Cuba against Nicaragua. The U S. Government replied that the charges were false and designed to create dissension.

Raúl Roa, the Cuban Minister of State, declared the intent of Cuba "to break the structure of its commercial relations with the United States."

JUNE 15, 1960 — Cuba and Poland established diplomatic relations.

JUNE 18, 1960 — A joint Cuban-Soviet communiqué in Moscow noted the fruitful development of economic and cultural ties between the Soviet Union and Cuba.

JUNE 22, 1960 — The United States submitted a memorandum to the Inter-American Peace Committee on provocative actions of the Cuban Government. The memorandum took note of the *La Coubre* incident, the *Sea Poacher* incident, air incursions and the Cuban allegations of U.S. complicity in a plot to invade Nicaragua.

JUNE 29, 1960 — The Cuban Government seized the Esso and Texaco oil refineries on the grounds that they had violated Cuban law in refusing to refine Soviet crude oil.

JULY 3, 1960 — The U.S. Congress gave the President authority to reduce the import quota on Cuban sugar.

José Miró Cardona, Cuban ambassador-designate to the United States, resigned on the grounds that "the ideological differences between the plans of the Government . . . and my conscience were impossible to resolve." He received asylum in the Argentine Embassy.

JULY 5, 1960 — The United States protested the seizure of the U.S.-owned oil refineries as arbitrary, inequitable, and contrary to Cuban law and expressed the hope that these actions would be rescinded.

JULY 6, 1960 — The Cuban Government passed the "nationalization law" which authorized the nationalization of U S. properties through expropriation. Compensation was provided for in a rather complicated formula involving the export of Cuban sugar to the U.S.

JULY 6, 1960 — President Dwight Eisenhower cut the Cuban sugar quota to the U.S. in 1960 by 700,000 tons, largely on the grounds of developing relations between Cuba and the Soviet bloc.

JULY 9, 1960 — Soviet Premier Nikita Khrushchev stated that "Speaking figuratively, in case of necessity, Soviet artillerymen can support the Cuban people with rocket fire. . . ." President Eisenhower declared that Premier Khrushchev's statement underscored the close ties that have developed between Cuba and the Soviet Union.

JULY 10, 1960 — Ernesto "Che" Guevara stated that Cuba is defended by the Soviet Union which is the "greatest military power in history."

JULY 12, 1960 — Soviet Premier Nikita Khrushchev pledged to help Castro to oust the United States from the Guantanamo Naval Station and also declared that the "Monroe Doctrine" was "dead."

JULY 16, 1960 — The United States protested the nationalization law of July 6th as "discriminatory, arbitrary and confiscatory."

JULY 21, 1960 — Armed Forces Minister Raúl Castro stated in Moscow that Cuba "is grateful for political and moral support from the Soviet Union."

JULY 23, 1960 — Cuba and Communist China signed a five-year trade and payments agreement which provided for the Chinese purchase of 500,000 tons of Cuban sugar in each of the next five years.

JULY 29, 1960 — Cuban Economics Minister "Che" Guevara announced that the Cuban revolution had found the pattern set by Karl Marx.

AUGUST 1, 1960 — The United States submitted a statement to the Inter-American Peace Committee entitled "Responsibility of the Cuban Government for Increased Tensions in the Hemisphere." Among other charges the document stated that the Cuban Government had taken discriminatory actions against U.S.-owned properties totaling $850 million.

AUGUST 6, 1960 — The Cuban Government nationalized the properties of twenty-six companies partially or wholly owned by U.S. citizens.

AUGUST 7, 1960 — Prime Minister Castro justified the nationalization and expropriation of U.S. properties on the grounds that the U.S. had practiced "economic aggression" by reducing the Cuban sugar quota.

AUGUST 10, 1960 — The U.S. Government issued a document on the aggressive intent of the Cuban Government in its discriminatory trade and financial policies. The United States estimated that over $1 billion in U.S. properties had been expropriated.

AUGUST 16, 1960 — Prime Minister Castro reportedly sent a message to Premier Khrushchev in which he expressed appreciation "for the support of the Soviet people, which is irrefutable proof that the peoples fighting for their independence are not alone in their struggle."

AUGUST 24, 1960 — Prime Minister Castro charged the United States with supporting counterrevolutionaries and stated that Cuba would be friends with the Soviet Union and the Chinese People's Republic.

AUGUST 29, 1960 — The Foreign Ministers of the American Republics met in San José, Costa Rica, and approved a declaration which stated that the acceptance of extracontinental intervention by an American state endangered inter-American solidarity and security.

Prime Minister Castro repeated charges of U.S. aggression against Cuba and said that he would not renounce Soviet support.

SEPTEMBER 2, 1960 — In reply to the Declaration of San José, Prime Minister Castro enunciated his "Declaration of Havana" which denounced the United States and the Organization of American States.

Premier Castro recognized Red China and broke with Nationalist China.

SEPTEMBER 15, 1960 — Cuba and Hungary signed a trade and payments agreement.

SEPTEMBER 17, 1960 — Cuba nationalized three U.S.-operated banks through expropriation. The United States protested.

SEPTEMBER 23, 1960 — Cuba and North Korea established diplomatic relations.

SEPTEMBER 26, 1960 — Premier Castro delivered a rambling four-and-one-half-hour talk to the United Nations General Assembly accusing the United States of discrimination and economic imperialism among other charges.

SEPTEMBER 30, 1960 — Prime Minister Chou En-lai of Communist China stated that "in the event of necessity the Chinese Government and people will give all possible support and aid to the Cuban people. . . ."

OCTOBER 7, 1960 — Cuba and Bulgaria signed a trade and payments agreement.

OCTOBER 12, 1960 — The United States submitted a document to the U.N. Secretary General entitled "Facts Concerning Relations Between Cuba and the United States," which replied to Prime Minister Castro's charges of September 26th.

OCTOBER 19, 1960 — The United States ceased all exports to Cuba except non-subsidized foodstuffs, medicines and medical supplies.

OCTOBER 24, 1960 — Cuba nationalized an additional 166 properties wholly or partially U.S.-owned. The United States protested.

OCTOBER 26, 1960 — Cuba and Romania established diplomatic relations and signed trade and technical assistance agreements.

NOVEMBER 18, 1960 — The U.S. Government stated that at least twelve Soviet ships have delivered arms and ammunition to Cuba since July and that total Soviet bloc military aid to Cuba amounted to about 28,000 tons.

NOVEMBER 24, 1960 — President Osvaldo Dorticos Torrado declared that Cuba will continue its Communist ties even though John F. Kennedy was elected President.

DECEMBER 2, 1960 — Cuba and North Vietnam established diplomatic relations.

DECEMBER 19, 1960 — Cuba and the Soviet Union issued a joint communiqué whereby Cuba openly aligned itself with the domestic and foreign policies of the Soviet Union and indicated its solidarity with the Sino-Soviet bloc.

JANUARY 2, 1961 — Cuba held a military parade on the second anniversary of the Castro regime and displayed many items of Soviet bloc military equipment.

Prime Minister Castro demanded that the U.S. Embassy in Havana reduce the number of its officials to eleven within forty-eight hours.

JANUARY 3, 1961 — The United States terminated diplomatic and consular relations with Cuba and turned the handling of its affairs over to the Swiss Embassy. Cuba terminated its relations with the United States and turned its affairs over to the Embassy of Czechoslovakia.

JANUARY 12, 1961 — Uruguay expelled Cuban Ambassador García-Inchaustegui from country. Later assigned to the United Nations.

FEBRUARY 23, 1961 — Armed Forces Minister Raúl Castro stated that the Chinese People's Republic had sent Cuba hundreds of machine guns.

MARCH 31, 1961 — President John F. Kennedy reduced the Cuban sugar quota for the U.S. to zero.

APRIL 3, 1961 — The Government of the U.S. issued the "Cuba" pamphlet, which expressed a determination to support future democratic governments in Cuba and to help the Cuban people achieve freedom, democracy and social justice, and called upon the Cuban Government to sever its ties with the international communist movement.

APRIL 12, 1961 — President John F. Kennedy pledged that United States armed forces would not intervene in Cuba under any condition to help overthrow Castro.

APRIL 16, 1961 — Prime Minister Castro described his regime as "socialist."

Premier Castro ordered general mobilization and charged that the United States planned an invasion.

APRIL 17, 1961 — Cuban exile leader Miró Cardona announced that a sea-borne invasion of Cuba was underway.

APRIL 17–19, 1961 — A group of Cuban exiles attempted the abortive "Bay of Pigs" invasion of Cuba with U.S. assistance and support.

APRIL 18, 1961 — Cuban Foreign Minister Raúl Roa charged that Cuba was being invaded by mercenaries trained by the Central Intelligence Agency of the United States from bases in Florida and Guatemala.

Secretary of State Dean Rusk expressed sympathy for the rebel invaders but barred any direct U.S. intervention.

APRIL 19, 1961 — The invasion of Cuba by the Cuban exiles at the "Bay of Pigs" was a complete failure. Some 1,113 Cuban rebels were captured by Castro's forces shortly after the landing.

APRIL 21, 1961 — The United States suffered a loss of prestige after the failure of the Cuban invasion through its direct and indirect complicity.

Cuba voted with the Soviet Union on almost every major issue before the Fifteenth Session of the United Nations General Assembly.

APRIL 30, 1961 — Minister of Industries Ernesto "Che" Guevara declared that the Castro movement was "the first socialist revolution in Latin America."

MAY 18, 1961 — Premier Castro offered to trade the Cuban rebel captives for five hundred tractors.

JUNE 12, 1961 — Congressman William E. Miller maintained that President Kennedy revoked the plan of former President Dwight D. Eisenhower to provide U.S. air cover for the Bay of Pigs landing and thereby caused the "fiasco."

JUNE 14, 1961 — Premier Castro raised the ransom price for the Cuban captives to $28 million or one thousand tractors.

JUNE 17, 1961 — The failure of the Bay of Pigs venture resulted in solidification of the Castro regime at home and increased prestige abroad, particularly in Latin America.

SEPTEMBER 7, 1961 — The United States Congress prohibited assistance to any country which aids Cuba, unless the President determines that such assistance is in the U.S. national interest.

SEPTEMBER 11, 1961 — Former President Eisenhower said that no plan was made by or for him to invade Cuba.

SEPTEMBER 20, 1961 — A joint Soviet-Cuban communiqué proclaimed the "identity of positions of the Soviet Union and Cuba on all the international questions that were discussed."

OCTOBER 2, 1961 — A joint Communist Chinese-Cuban communiqué proclaimed complete agreement on "the current international situation and the question of further developing friendship and cooperation."

DECEMBER 2, 1961 — Prime Minister Fidel Castro stated "I believe absolutely in Marxism. . . . I am a Marxist-Leninist and will be a Marxist-Leninist until the last day of my life."

DECEMBER 6, 1961 — The United States submitted a document to the Inter-American Peace Committee entitled "The Castro Regime in Cuba" with information relating to Cuba's ties to the Sino-Soviet bloc and her threat to hemispheric security.

DECEMBER 20, 1961 — Cuba voted with the Soviet bloc on thirty-three out of thirty-seven major issues before the Sixteenth Session of the United Nations General Assembly.

JANUARY 14, 1962 — The Inter-American Peace Committee reported that Cuba's connections with the Sino-Soviet bloc were incompatible with the inter-American treaties, principles and standards.

JANUARY 22/31, 1962 — The Punta del Este Conference of the Organization of American States was held in Uruguay. Cuba was excluded from participation in the OAS and several actions were taken to counteract Cuban activities in the Western Hemisphere. (Refer to Appendix E, F, for texts of second and sixth resolutions.)

FEBRUARY 3, 1962 — President Kennedy declared an embargo on all trade with Cuba except medical necessities. (Refer to Appendix G for text.)

FEBRUARY 20, 1962 — Walt W. Rostow, Counselor of the Department of State, expressed the hope to the North Atlantic Council that NATO members would take the Punta del Este decisions into account in formulating their policies toward Cuba.

MARCH 24, 1962 — The United States excluded the importation of merchandise made in whole or in part from Cuban products.

MARCH 27, 1962 — The United States estimated that the Sino-Soviet bloc had furnished Cuba with about $100 million worth of military equipment and technical services.

APRIL 8, 1962 — The Cuban exiles who took part in the Bay of Pigs invasion of April 1961 were sentenced to prison subject to ransom totalling $62 million.

MAY 1, 1962 — The OAS Special Consultative Committee on Security submitted its initial report on Communist activities in the Western Hemisphere.

AUGUST 19, 1962 — Premier Fidel Castro informed Cuban peasants that their farms would be taken over by the government and that the entire Cuban agricultural economy would be based on collectives and cooperatives known as "state farms." This was thought to be a major economic and ideological milestone.

AUGUST 24, 1962 — U.S. officials disclosed that the flow of Soviet military equipment and technical personnel was increasing. It was estimated that twenty cargo ships and an unspecified number of passenger ships had arrived in Cuba since large-scale deliveries were resumed late in July. The number of technicians was estimated at 3,000 to 5,000 and the material was thought to include construction equipment, communications vans, radar vans, trucks and mobile generator units which appeared to be going to coastal defenses.

AUGUST 28, 1962 — The Soviet Union disclosed that the volume of maritime shipments to Cuba in 1962 would be double the volume in 1961.

AUGUST 29, 1962 — Premier Fidel Castro placed tight controls on the wages of Cuban workers, imposed penalties for absenteeism and authorized a reduction in vacations in an effort to increase production.

AUGUST 31, 1962 — A United States Navy plane was fired upon by two naval vessels, which were believed to be Cuban, off Cuba.

SEPTEMBER 1, 1962 — Senator Kenneth Keating of New York reported that there are about 1,200 uniformed Soviet troops in Cuba; the U.S. Government denied having any such data, and said that the U.S.S.R. continued to ship defense materiel. It was also reported that the Kennedy administration would attempt to curb Western shipping to Cuba.

SEPTEMBER 2, 1962 — The Soviet Union announced that it has agreed to supply arms and technical specialists to Cuba to train forces to meet threats from "aggressive imperialist quarters."

The Kennedy administration denied that there was anything new in Soviet-Cuban relations.

Senator Keating attacked the "do nothing" policy of the Kennedy administration toward Cuba, and suggested that the OAS send a mission to Cuba to study conditions and determine if there are any Soviet missile bases being established there.

SEPTEMBER 3, 1962 — The Soviet-Cuban military and technical assistance agreement was widely acclaimed in the Cuban press. The Soviet technicians were reportedly training the Cuban troops in the use of old radar equipment. Diplomatic sources reported that there was no reliable evidence that rocket launching pads had been installed.

SEPTEMBER 4, 1962 — President Kennedy released a statement which discussed the Soviet military equipment in Cuba and denied that it had any offensive military capability. The President also pledged that the United States would use "whatever means may be necessary" to prevent aggression from Cuba in the Western Hemisphere. (Refer to Document 1 for text.)

Senator Keating demanded that the United States urge its allies to stop letting the U.S.S R. use their ships for the transport of military equipment to Cuba.

SEPTEMBER 5, 1962 — Secretary of State Dean Rusk informed nineteen Latin American ambassadors that the United States would work to prevent the spread of communism from Cuba into the Western Hemisphere. Senator Mike Mansfield expressed the hope that the Republicans would keep the Cuban issue out of the political campaign.

SEPTEMBER 6, 1962 — The Soviet military personnel stationed in Cuba were reported to be organized into their own units either operating separately or in conjunction with the Cuban forces. It was also reported that there were about 4,000 Soviet troops stationed in Cuba.

SEPTEMBER 7, 1962 — Senator .Everett McKinley Dirksen and Representative Charles A. Halleck, the Republican Minority Leaders of Congress, issued separate statements urging a stronger U.S. policy toward Cuba. (Refer to Documents 2 and 3 for texts) Both Congressional leaders also proposed a joint resolution giving the President authority to use troops, if necessary, to defeat communism in Cuba

President Kennedy requested authorization from Congress to call up 150,000 reserves for a limited period. (Refer to Document 4 for text.) The President maintained that this standby authority to call up the reserves was required more by the Berlin situation than the Cuban situation.

SEPTEMBER 8, 1962 — Cuban exile leaders in the United States urged the Kennedy administration to permit and give support to the resumption of large scale subversive activities to try and topple the regime of Premier Fidel Castro.

Upon returning from a visit with Soviet Premier Nikita Khrushchev, poet Robert Frost held a news conference in New York and reported that Khrushchev told him the U.S. was "too liberal to fight" in defense of its own interests.

SEPTEMBER 11, 1962 — The Soviet Union warned that any attack by the United States on Cuba or upon Soviet ships bound for Cuba would mean war, and implied that it would be a nuclear rocket war. (Refer to Document 5 for text.) The Kennedy administration and Congress seemed unimpressed by the Soviet warning that an attack on Cuba could mean nuclear war.

Premier Fidel Castro declared that Congressional demands for energetic United States action against Cuba were proof of the "chaos" in the United States which is "playing with fire and with war."

SEPTEMBER 13, 1962 — President Kennedy stated that the United States would move quickly against Cuba to defend its security if necessary, but that at the present time military action is neither needed nor justified. (Refer to Document 6 for text.)

SEPTEMBER 14, 1962 — The Soviet Government accepted, with reservations, President Kennedy's declaration that United States military intervention in Cuba was not required or justifiable at the present time.

Senator Barry Goldwater of Arizona charged that President Kennedy's policy statement of September 13th "virtually promised the Communist world that the United States will take no action to remove the threat of Soviet armed might in the Western Hemisphere."

SEPTEMBER 16, 1962 — Senator Barry Goldwater attacked the Kennedy administration "do nothing policy" in regard to Cuba and maintained that Kennedy virtually promised the communists a free hand in Cuba.

The United States failed to get its allies to curb shipments to Cuba.

Columnist James Reston assailed the blockade suggestions of Senators Goldwater, Thurmond and Tower as irresponsible and said that they fail to show that a blockade is an act of war under international law.

Chester Bowles, special adviser on African and Asian affairs, sharply criticized that "hot-blooded, hot-headed minority of Americans" who believe that "life is based on power and that in the use of power everything goes."

SEPTEMBER 17, 1962 — Senators Hugh Scott and Kenneth Keating urged some form of economic and military blockade to screen out the military build-up in Cuba. Senator Jacob Javits also urged President Kennedy to demand that the Soviet Union stop extending military assistance to Cuba, and if the Soviet Union refused, to take whatever action is necessary.

Secretary of State Dean Rusk conferred for more than four hours in a joint session of Senate Foreign Relations and Armed Forces Committees on the developing situation in Cuba and the pending Senate resolutions on Cuba.

The view of the Kennedy administration was that the Soviet arms deliveries to Cuba were essentially defensive in character; however, several Senators publicly disagreed with this position. Secretary Rusk later said that a resolution expressing the sense of Congress on Cuba would be helpful.

SEPTEMBER 18, 1962 — Former Vice President Richard M. Nixon called for a "quarantine" of Cuba to halt the flow of Soviet arms. He urged President Kennedy to take "stronger action" immediately and pledged his "unqualified support" to the Administration in such a course. Mr. Nixon suggested that such a program could involve a naval blockade of the island and a commitment from the United States allies that their ships would not be used by the Soviet Union for shipments to Cuba.

SEPTEMBER 19, 1962 — The Senate Foreign Relations and Armed Services Committees approved the text of a joint resolution on Cuba sanctioning the use of force, if necessary, to defend the Western Hemisphere against Cuban aggression or subversion. The proposed resolution was understood to have the support of the Kennedy administration and the House Foreign Affairs Committee.

SEPTEMBER 20, 1962 — The Senate resolution on Cuba sanctioning the use of force, if necessary, to curb Cuban aggression and communist subversion in the Western Hemisphere, passed the Senate by a vote of 86 to 1. The lone dissenter was Senator Winston L. Prouty of Vermont who did not feel that the resolution went far enough. Prouty felt that the resolution should have "authorized" the President to use armed forces, and to warn the Soviet Union that it would be held responsible for any aggression stemming from Cuba. (Refer to Document 7 for text.)

SEPTEMBER 21, 1962 — Soviet Foreign Minister Andrei A. Gromyko issued a new warning in the United Nations that an attack on Cuba by the United States would mean war. (Refer to Document 8 for text.)

Ambassador Adlai E. Stevenson, the United States Representative to the United Nations, replied that "the threat to the peace in Cuba comes not from the United States, but from the Soviet Union." (Refer to Document 9 for text.)

SEPTEMBER 22, 1962 — President Kennedy maintained that Premier Castro had sealed his own doom by inviting Soviet military assistance.

SEPTEMBER 23, 1962 — Dr. Gilberto Arias, Finance Minister of Panama, proposed the establishment of a "NATO-type military alliance for defensive as well as offensive purposes, if such need arises." This would consist of the ten Central American and Caribbean nations presently exposed to communist subversion and possible aggression from Cuba.

Secretary of State Dean Rusk and British Foreign Secretary Lord Home discussed the question of British reluctance to place a strategic goods embargo on trade with Cuba. No resolution of the differences of opinion on this point was reported.

SEPTEMBER 24, 1962 — Secretary of State Dean Rusk requested of Norwegian Foreign Minister Halvard M. Lange that Norway cease carrying strategic goods from the Soviet Union to Cuba. The Italian and West German governments were reported to be more cooperative in the United States effort to isolate Cuba.

Senator Hubert Humphrey denied that the Kennedy administration had "set limits" on the Monroe Doctrine.

SEPTEMBER 25, 1962 — Premier Fidel Castro of Cuba announced the signing of a fishing treaty with the Soviet Union and the proposed construction of a joint Cuban-Soviet fishing port to be built on the north shore of Cuba.

SEPTEMBER 26, 1962 — The House of Representatives passed the joint resolution on Cuba by a vote of 384 to 7. The only question in the debate on the bill was whether the resolution as adopted by the Senate was worded strongly enough. (Refer to Document 7 for text.)

Secretary of State Dean Rusk informally discussed the possible creation of a Caribbean military organization to guard against Cuban aggression with other foreign ministers from Latin America.

SEPTEMBER 27, 1962 — At the request of the Turkish government, Turkish shipowners terminated all cargo movements to Cuba in their vessels. The United States was reported to have made firm representations on this point with Turkey and other NATO countries with merchant fleets.

The Soviet newspaper *Izvestia* ridiculed suggestions in the United States that the proposed Cuban-Soviet fishing port would be used for military purposes.

SEPTEMBER 28, 1962 — Soviet President Leonid Brezhnev announced in Yugoslavia on a visit with President Tito that an attack on Cuba by the United States would mean war with the Soviet Union.

SEPTEMBER 29, 1962 — The Polish Foreign Minister Rapacki attacked the United States position in relation to Cuba in the General Assembly of the United Nations.

SEPTEMBER 30, 1962 — Secretary of State Dean Rusk discussed the problem of Cuba. (Refer to Document 10 for text.)

President Kennedy and Lord Home, the British Foreign Secretary, met in Washington and discussed ways of "containing further Communist expansion and subversion in the Caribbean."

Premier Khrushchev invited President Kennedy to the Soviet Union for a visit by a personal invitation extended through Secretary of the Interior Stewart L. Udall.

OCTOBER 1, 1962 — The several hints by Premier Nikita S. Khrushchev that President John F. Kennedy visit the Soviet Union were labeled as "casual conversation" by the Department of State.

OCTOBER 2, 1962 — Secretary of State Dean Rusk assured a conference of American Foreign Ministers that the United States was prepared to provide the necessary leadership to defeat Communist subversion and possibly aggression in the Western Hemisphere.

OCTOBER 3, 1962 — The delegates to the informal inter-American foreign ministers conference in Washington labeled the Soviet intervention in Cuba as a threat to the hemisphere which required individual and collective countermeasures. In a closing communiqué the foreign ministers declared: "The Soviet Union's intervention in Cuba threatens the unity of the Americas and of its democratic institutions . . . it is desirable to intensify individual and collective surveillance of the delivery of arms and implements of war and all other items of strategic importance to the Communist regime of Cuba, in order to prevent the secret accumulation in the island of arms . . . used for offensive purposes against the hemisphere."

The United States government decided on drastic unilateral action to prevent the use of American, allied and neutral shipping between the Soviet Union and Cuba by excluding any ships engaged in this trade from ports in the United States. The President was also scheduled to issue orders prohibiting United States-owned ships sailing under foreign flags from trading with Cuba.

New York attorney James B. Donovan left for Cuba to discuss the possible exchange of prisoners held by Premier Castro in return for some undetermined ransom.

OCTOBER 4, 1962 — The United States government revealed its plan to penalize all shipowners who transport Soviet bloc supplies to Cuba. The plan includes loss of cargo from the United States government, closure of U.S. ports, prohibition of U.S. ports to countries that trade with Cuba, and prohibition of U.S. flag ships or U.S.-owned ships to trade with Cuba.

OCTOBER 5, 1962 — Brazilian Premier Hermes Lima assured Brazilian sympathizers of Fidel Castro that Brazil would never support punitive measures again Cuba simply because it has a form of government different from that of other Latin American countries Dr. Lima, who is also Brazil's foreign minister, stated that "Brazil's foreign policy maintains the principles of self-determination and respect for the sovereignty of each people."

OCTOBER 6, 1962 — Radio Havana began a program called "Radio Free Dixie" which was apparently aimed at the American Negroes in the South.

OCTOBER 7, 1962 — Reports were circulating in Miami that attorney James B. Donovan was removing many obstacles in the way of the release of the 1,113 Cuban prisoners captured after the unsuccessful invasion of April, 1961. There were also reports that if the $62 million "indemnity" in food and medicine demanded by Castro is raised, that the prisoners might be released in the near future.

President Osvaldo Dorticos Torrado of Cuba conferred with Premier Ahmed Ben Bella of Algeria today prior to placing the Cuban issue on the agenda of the General Assembly of the United Nations.

OCTOBER 8, 1962 — President Osvaldo Dorticos Torrado of Cuba addressed the General Assembly of the United Nations, attacked the United States and called upon the United Nations to condemn the United States "naval blockade" of Cuba. (Refer to Document 11 for text.)

Ambassador Adlai E. Stevenson rose to protest the attack by President Dorticos and issued a separate statement in reply immediately after the meeting of the General Assembly of the United Nations adjourned. (Refer to Documents 12, 13 for texts.)

Congress withheld economic and military assistance from any country which "sells, furnishes or permits any ships under its registry" to trade with Cuba "so long as it is governed by the Castro regime" under the terms of the Foreign Assistance Act of 1961, as amended, Section 107(a) and (b). Congress also withheld any economic or military assistance from any country which "is based upon that theory of government known as Communism" under the same Act, Section 109 (a) and (b).

OCTOBER 9, 1962 — Secretary of State Dean Rusk announced that the United States would work for the economic and social development of "the oppressed people of Cuba" if they were freed from Communist rule.

James B. Donovan, the attorney negotiating the release of the Cuban prisoners, was optimistic about an early agreement.

OCTOBER 10, 1962 — It was reported that the United States Government was deeply involved in trying to raise the ransom requested by Premier Castro for the release of the prisoners captured in the abortive "Bay of Pigs" invasion.

A Cuban exile group known as "Alpha 66" acknowledged that they staged a successful raid on Cuba on October 7th. The group maintained that they did considerable damage to Cuban civil and military installations. Alpha 66 was the group which attacked one British and two Cuban cargo vessels anchored off the north coast of Cuba on September 10th.

OCTOBER 11, 1962 — British shipowners insisted that they would accept no restriction on their trade with Cuba The British made it quite clear that they intended to retain their right to trade anywhere in the world.

The Swedish government also expressed disapproval of the United States ban on trade with Cuba.

OCTOBER 12, 1962 — Great Britain made representations to the United States in a carefully worded note about the proposed plan of Alpha 66, a Cuban exile organization, to attack all merchant ships carrying supplies to Cuba. A spokesman for the British Foreign Office earlier said that Great Britain "would take a serious view of any attacks on British shipping going about its lawful business."

The Department of State indicated that it was not prepared to act against the Cuban exiles who made threatening raids on Cuba and also warned foreign shippers that they would run risks in continued trade with Cuba. The Department of State further said that it did not sanction such assaults, but said that there were difficulties in guaranteeing the peace in the Caribbean.

President Manuel Ydigoras Fuentes of Guatemala apparently cancelled a plan by Cuban exiles to launch a bombing attack on Cuba. President Ydigoras also repeated the charge that the United States had promised Guatemala assistance in its dispute over British Honduras in return for permitting the United States to use Guatemala as a training ground for an invasion of Cuba. Ydigoras further indicated that he might favorably regard an application by a Cuban government in exile for recognition, but that he would not allow Guatemala to become the base of another Cuban invasion.

OCTOBER 13, 1962 — The policy of the Kennedy administration toward Cuba seemed to be one of imposing economic sanctions against the Castro regime in the face of massive Soviet economic, military and technical assistance. It was estimated that total Soviet bloc imports to Cuba for 1962 will come to about

$600 million, which will be partially covered by $500 million in Cuban exports. In addition, there had been an estimated $200 million in military supplies sent by the Soviet bloc in 1962, and the Soviet Union had promised $475 million in credits for the industrialization of Cuba.

OCTOBER 14, 1962 — It was reported that some United Nations delegates had been informed that the Soviet Union was willing to pursue a "more moderate" policy toward Cuba if the United States would relax its position on West Berlin.

It was felt in Washington that the Cuban Government had been extremely careful in recent weeks to avoid any chance of conflict with the United States or the imposition of sanctions by the Organization of American States.

President Kennedy abruptly changed his campaign plans and flew to New York for a conference with Adlai E. Stevenson, the United States Ambassador (Representative) to the United Nations. The discussions reportedly concerned the recent developments in the Congo.

OCTOBER 15, 1962 — Former President Dwight D. Eisenhower attacked the critics of his foreign policy in a campaign speech in Boston: "In those eight years [of the Eisenhower administration], we lost no inch of ground to tyranny. We witnessed no abdication of responsibility. We accepted no compromise of pledged word or withdrawal from principle. No walls were built. No threatening foreign bases were established. One war was ended and incipient wars were blocked."

Republican National Committee Chairman William E. Miller declared that the "irresolution" of the Kennedy administration is the dominant election issue in 1962.

Officials of the Kennedy administration observed that the Castro regime was being careful to avoid conflict and was not actively resisting aerial surveillance.

OCTOBER 16, 1962 — Soviet Premier Nikita S. Khrushchev and U.S. Ambassador Foy D. Kohler held a three-hour discussion on a wide range of topics including Berlin, Cuba, Soviet shipping, nuclear testing and disarmament. No substantive results of the meeting were announced, but a communiqué stated, "The conversation proceeded in an atmosphere of frankness and mutual understanding."

Algerian Premier Ben Bella praised the Castro revolution upon arriving in Havana from the United States for a short visit; later gave support to Castro demand for United States withdrawal from the Guantanamo Naval Station.

The Castro regime charged that U.S. Navy planes had flown "provocatively and repeatedly" over merchant ships in Cuban territorial waters.

OCTOBER 17, 1962 — New York attorney James Donovan, also a Democratic candidate for Senator, continued his role as intermediator in the possible exchange of the Cuban prisoners. Three days later Donovan received a ransom list of goods demanded by Castro for freedom of prisoners.

OCTOBER 18, 1962 — The Department of Defense announced that twelve Navy jet fighters were transferred to the southern tip of Florida on October 6th in response to reports that Cuba had acquired two dozen Soviet MIG jet planes.

The White House also announced that plans for a United States quarantine of Cuban shipping were still being worked out and probably would not be ready this week. According to the plans already made known, an executive order would impose various sanctions on foreign ships and shipping companies involved in Cuban trade.

Soviet Foreign Minister Andrei A. Gromyko met with President Kennedy at the White House and reportedly covered a wide range of topics in an extensive discussion of East-West issues. No report was immediately available on the substance of the issues discussed.

OCTOBER 21, 1962 — An atmosphere of crisis hung over Washington as President Kennedy met with top administration officials. President Kennedy placed a tight secrecy control over the issue of concern, but there were hints that he would address the nation over television in the next day or so.

The U.S. Navy and Marine Corps were reportedly staging extensive maneuvers involving about 20,000 men off Puerto Rico, interpreted by some as a show of force.

Increasing sympathy was reported among the Latin American States for the United States in its difficulties with Premier Castro and his regime. However, the Latin American States apparently viewed the idea of collective armed intervention with disfavor.

The Department of Defense denied that the unusual concentration of military forces off Puerto Rico was linked with crisis.

Senator Jacob Javits advocated the development of a "Caribbean-type NATO" to help enforce a quarantine.

OCTOBER 22, 1962 — Congressional leaders were flown in to Washington for special advance briefing on the crisis.

Forty-six pro-Western and neutral ambassadors were given advance briefing by Under Secretary George W. Ball

Secretary Rusk gave Soviet Ambassador Anatoly Dobrynin a special briefing on Cuban Crisis and an advance copy of President Kennedy's forthcoming address with a covering memorandum.

President Kennedy addressed the nation over radio and TV on the new "Cuban Crisis" and the finding of MRBM and IRBM missiles and other "offensive" weapons in Cuba. (Refer to Document 14 for text.)

Ambassador Adlai E. Stevenson requested an immediate meeting of the UN Security Council to discuss the Cuban Crisis. (Refer to Documents 15, 16 for texts.)

Secretary of State Rusk called for a meeting of the Council of the OAS.

Cuba requested that the United Nations Security Council meet to consider the developing Caribbean situation. (Refer to Document 17 for text.)

The Defense Department put all U.S. military forces throughout the world on an alert basis.

OCTOBER 23, 1962 — The Department of Defense released photographs of Soviet missile sites in Cuba.

The Cuban Crisis gripped the United Nations and all other business was temporarily postponed as delegates followed developments.

The Soviet Union requested the convening of a special session of the U.N. Security Council to consider the Caribbean situation. (Refer to Document 18 for text.)

Cuba requested permission to participate in the U.N. Security Council deliberations on the Caribbean situation. (Refer to Document 19 for text.)

President Kennedy signed proclamation of interdiction of offensive weapons establishing "quarantine" around Cuba. (Refer to Document 20 for text.)

President Kennedy issued an Executive Order mobilizing some reserve units. (Refer to Document 21 for text.)

The U.N. Security Council was seized with the Cuban Crisis. (Refer to Documents 22, 26, 27, 28, 29 for texts of resolutions and statements.)

The OAS unanimously passed U.S. resolution on Cuban Crisis. (Refer to Documents 23, 24, 25 for texts of resolution and statements.)

Former Secretary of State Dean Acheson flew to Paris to brief NATO members on Cuban Crisis.

Radio Moscow charged that "hysteria" had again gripped Washington and that the U.S. was threatening Cuba.

All Soviet and Warsaw Pact forces were reportedly put on an alert basis.

Premier Castro addressed the Cuban nation over TV and declared the U.S. blockade an act of piracy and that it will be fought. Castro also denied that Soviet military equipment was "offensive."

Premier Castro ordered full mobilization of all Cuban military forces and the civilian population.

The Department of Defense announced that all military dependents at Guantanamo were being evacuated and that the garrison was being reinforced.

The Department of Defense announced the interception of the Soviet oil tanker *Bucharest* which was allowed to proceed, with only alongside visual observation. Twelve other Soviet ships were reported to have altered course.

President Kennedy agreed to preliminary talks with Acting Secretary General U Thant on whether "satisfactory arrangements" for negotiations to resolve the Cuban Crisis could be developed. Premier Khrushchev agreed to U Thant's appeal for a moratorium on any further actions; if the United States would drop the quarantine, the Soviet Union would suspend arms shipments to Cuba. However, it was reported that Washington would continue the arms blockade until all offensive weapons in Cuba were under international supervision.

The People's Republic of Bulgaria issued a statement on the Cuban Crisis. (Refer to Document 30 for text.)

The Haitian Department of Foreign Affairs issued a communiqué on the Cuban Crisis. (Refer to Document 31 for text.)

OCTOBER 24, 1962 — Six Latin American nations offered military support to assist in U.S. blockade of Cuba.

President Kennedy's proclamation on the interdiction of offensive weapons (quarantine) went into effect at 10 A.M., Eastern Standard Time.

Communist China labeled the U.S. blockade as "piracy" and urged unity within the Communist bloc.

Lord Bertrand Russell of Great Britain appealed to Khrushchev for caution and urged President Kennedy to end the "madness."

The Czechoslovak Socialist Republic issued a declaration on the Cuban Crisis. (Refer to Document 32 for text.)

Acting Secretary General U Thant made a statement to the U.N. Security Council on behalf of forty member nations, and called upon President Kennedy and Premier Khrushchev to suspend all action for two or three weeks. (Refer to Document 33 for text of statement and letters to Kennedy and Khrushchev.)

The United Arab Republic and Ghana proposed a joint resolution essentially supporting the position of Acting Secretary General U Thant. (Refer to Document 34 for text.)

Dr. Carlos Sosa-Rodríguez of Venezuela supported the U.S. position before the U.N. Security Council. (Refer to Document 35 for excerpt from statement.)

Sir Patrick Dean of Great Britain supported the U.S. position before the U.N. Security Council. (Refer to Document 36 for excerpt from statement.)

Ambassador Mircea Malitza of Romania attacked the U.S. position before the U.N. Security Council. (Refer to Document 37 for excerpt from statement.)

Ambassador Frank Aiken of Ireland supported the U.S. position before the U.N. Security Council. (Refer to Document 38 for excerpt from statement.)

Ambassador Roger Seydoux of France supported the U.S. position before the U.N Security Council. (Refer to Document 39 for excerpt from statement.)

The Government of the Dominican Republic issued a declaration on the Cuban Crisis. (Refer to Document 40 for text.)

OCTOBER 25, 1962 — Prime Minister Harold Macmillan delivered an address to the House of Commons supporting the U.S. position on Cuba. (Refer to Document 41 for text.)

Premier Khrushchev replied to a letter from Lord Bertrand Russell and urged the U.S. not to carry out blockade and promised to avoid reckless decisions while proposing a summit conference to avert nuclear war. (Refer to Document 42 for text.)

The Hungarian People's Republic issued a statement on the Cuban Crisis. (Refer to Document 43 for text.)

The Union of African and Malagasy States issued a set of proposals on the Cuban Crisis. (Refer to Document 44 for text.)

President Kennedy replied to the appeal from Acting Secretary General U Thant and agreed to talks with him on arranging negotiations with the Soviet Union but indicated that the blockade would continue. (Refer to Document 45 for text.)

Premier Khrushchev sent a letter to Acting Secretary General U Thant which supported U Thant's position. (Refer to Document 46 for text.)

Ambassador Stevenson made two statements before the U.N. Security Council and challenged Soviet Ambassador Valerian A. Zorin to deny that the Soviet Union had offensive weapons in Cuba. Zorin refused to answer and Stevenson displayed photographs of missile bases under construction. (Refer to Documents 47, 49 for texts of statements.)

Ambassador Valerian A. Zorin of the Soviet Union replied to charges of Ambassador Stevenson and said that U.S. photos were false and that the Soviet Union had no offensive weapons stationed outside of the U.S.S.R. (Refer to Document 48 for text.)

The Department of Defense issued a statement on the quarantine of Cuba and procedures that would be followed. (Refer to Document 50 for text.)

Pope John XXIII issued a statement on the Cuban Crisis urging both sides to be reasonable and rational in the settlement of the dispute for the sake of mankind. (Refer to Document 51 for text.)

Haiti formally announced its support of the actions and policies of the United States. (Refer to Document 52 for text.)

Second message from Acting Secretary General U Thant to President Kennedy. (Refer to Document 53 for text.)

President Kennedy sent another letter to Acting Secretary General U Thant indicating that the United States will attempt to avoid any direct confrontation with the Soviet Union. (Refer to Document 54 for text.)

Acting Secretary General U Thant sent another message to Premier Khrushchev. (Refer to Document 55 for text.)

Premier Khrushchev sent another letter to Acting Secretary General U Thant indicating that he will keep Soviet ships away from the blockade area temporarily. (Refer to Document 56 for text.)

The White House issued a press release with new intelligence data showing that the Soviet missile build-up in Cuba was continuing at a rapid pace. (Refer to Document 57 for text.)

The Department of Defense issued a statement on the boarding of the *Marucla*. (Refer to Document 58 for text.)

The Mongolian People's Republic issued a statement on the Cuban Crisis. (Refer to Document 59 for text.)

Premier Khrushchev included a set of proposals for the resolution of the Cuban Crisis in a letter to President Kennedy. (Text of letter not yet available.)

Acting Secretary General U Thant sent a letter to Premier Castro attempting to approach him for a settlement. (Refer to Document 61 for text.)

OCTOBER 27, 1962 — Premier Castro sent a letter to Acting Secretary General U Thant indicating that he was willing to cooperate with him in trying to work out some arrangements for United Nations verification   (Refer to Document 62 for text.)

A U S U-2 reconnaissance plane was reported missing and presumed lost over Cuba

Premier Khrushchev sent yet another letter to President Kennedy proposing to swap the Soviet Cuban bases for the NATO bases in Turkey. (Refer to Document 63 for text.)

The White House issued a statement on the current status in the development of the Cuban Crisis. (Refer to Document 64 for text.)

President Kennedy sent another letter to Premier Khrushchev indicating that the bases swap deal is not acceptable but that the proposals set forth in Khrushchev's letter of October 26th contained the bases of an understanding. (Refer to Document 65 for text.)

The Department of State issued a press release concerning the prior clearance of vessels before departure for Cuba. (Refer to Document 66 for text.)

OCTOBER 28, 1962 — Premier Khrushchev had his reply letter of October 28th broadcast over Radio Moscow to expedite matters because events in the Cuban Crisis seemed to be running ahead of diplomacy. (Refer to Document 67 for text.)

President Kennedy replied to Premier Khrushchev's broadcast letter almost immediately with a statement and subsequently followed this with a letter confirming the proposals and arrangements. (Refer to Documents 68, 69 for texts.)

Chairman Khrushchev sent a copy of his reply to President Kennedy to Acting Secretary General U Thant with a cover note. (Refer to Document 70 for text.)

Acting Secretary General U Thant replied to Premier Khrushchev's note. (Refer to Document 71 for text.)

Prime Minister Fidel Castro sent a letter to Acting Secretary General U Thant on the apparent resolution of the Cuban Crisis. (Refer to Document 72 for text.)

Acting Secretary General U Thant replied to Premier Castro's letter (Refer to Document 73 for text.)

United States officials were reportedly reviewing the developments in the Cuban Crisis from the standpoint of the Soviet Union to determine if there were any serious shifts in Kremlin policy or power struggles between the "Stalinist" (hard line) or "co-existence" (soft line) elements. It was also reported that the United States was trying to help Premier Khrushchev save face in order to retain his position and carry out the proposals.

OCTOBER 29, 1962 — Acting Secretary General U Thant conferred with Soviet First Deputy Premier Vasily V. Kuznetsov on the morning after his arrival in New York, and later in the day with United States Ambassador Adlai E. Stevenson. The discussions were described as "fruitful" and U Thant announced that he was flying to Cuba on October 30th to confer with the Cuban government about arrangements for verification by the United Nations of the dismantling of Soviet missiles and a halt in the building of bases.

It was generally conceded among delegates at the United Nations that U Thant's election as permanent Secretary General of the United Nations was a virtual certainty on the basis of his tactful intercession and use of good offices in the Cuban Crisis.

OAS Secretary General José A. Mora sent a letter to Acting Secretary General U Thant of the U.N. (Refer to Document 74 for text.)

OCTOBER 30, 1962 — Acting Secretary General U Thant talked with Premier Castro for two hours about United Nations supervision of the dismantling of the Soviet missile bases. The talks were reported as "useful," but would be continued the next day.

The United States temporarily suspended its naval blockade and aerial surveillance of Cuba for the duration of U Thant's talks with Castro, at the request of the Acting Secretary General.

United States officials thought that Premier Castro would equivocate on United Nations supervision by insisting on his various conditions.

President Tito of Yugoslavia issued a statement on the recent developments in the Cuban Crisis. (Refer to Document 75 for text.)

OCTOBER 31, 1962 — Acting Secretary General U Thant issued a noncommittal statement on return from discussions with Premier Castro remarking that the talks were "fruitful." (Refer to Document 76 for text.)

Acting Secretary General U Thant's mission to Cuba to establish the bases of a United Nations observer corps in Cuba to inspect the dismantling of Soviet missiles was reported to be a failure. U Thant was returning to the United Nations with all members of his staff.

Dr. García-Inchaustegui was replaced as head of the Cuban delegation to the United Nations by Carlos Lechuga.

Premier Nikita Khrushchev ordered First Deputy Premier Anastas I. Mikoyan to go to Cuba. Mikoyan was expected to discuss the possible terms of United Nations inspection and verification of the removal of Soviet missiles from Cuba, and the general United States-Soviet Union resolution of the problem.

Sources in London believed that Premier Khrushchev's retreat from Cuba will produce a serious and significant strain over his control of the Soviet Government and the Communist bloc nations, particularly Communist China.

Officials of the Kennedy administration felt that the international climate had changed considerably as a result of the Cuban Crisis, and that many difficult issues such as Berlin, Latin America and disarmament may have a chance for solution. In any event, the consensus in Washington seemed to be that the Cuban Crisis was a "turning point" in the Cold War and had bought some time for the free world.

An editorial on the front page of *Jenmin Jih Pao*, the Chinese Communist newspaper, indirectly attacked Premier Khrushchev because he had acquiesced in the "U.S. imperialist attempt to browbeat the people of the world into retreat at the expense of Cuba."

NOVEMBER 1, 1962 — The United States resumed its selective blockade and aerial surveillance of Cuba after the return of Acting Secretary General U Thant to the United Nations.

The Soviet Union suggested that the International Committee of the Red Cross or possibly some observers from the diplomatic corps in Cuba might be used to check on Premier Khrushchev's promise to dismantle the missiles and return them to the Soviet Union. These proposals were alternatives to a United Nations inspection team originally accepted by Premier Khrushchev.

The United States expressed a willingness to consider using the Red Cross group.

Soviet First Deputy Premier Anastas Mikoyan left for Havana on what some believed the last chance to achieve a Cuban solution under the formula worked out by President Kennedy and Premier Khrushchev.

Some observers believed that the Cuban Crisis was causing strong internal strains within the Communist bloc.

NOVEMBER 2, 1962 — Soviet First Deputy Premier Anastas Mikoyan issued a brief statement prior to leaving New York for discussions with Premier Castro in Cuba. (Refer to Document 77 for text.)

Premier Castro rejected any form of international inspection or verification in Cuba.

President Kennedy made a brief address to the nation on the present status of the Cuban Crisis. (Refer to Document 78 for text.)

NOVEMBER 3, 1962 — The United States and the Soviet Union reportedly agreed to have the International Red Cross inspect Cuba bound ships at sea. The United States withheld any definitive guarantee of no invasion subject to an agreement on the international inspection of missile sites in Cuba.

Mr. Abram Chayes, the Legal Adviser to the Department of State, delivered an address to a Harvard Law School reunion group interpreting the U.S. legal position in regard to the Cuban Crisis. (Refer to Appendix I for text.)

The New York Times printed a "Step by Step Review" of the Cuban Crisis from October 14 through October 31. (Refer to Appendix H for text.)

NOVEMBER 4, 1962 — Acting Secretary General U Thant described the prospects for a settlement of the Cuban Crisis as "good," and that he was consulting with members of the Security Council about a meeting to review the situation.

NOVEMBER 5, 1962 — The United States reportedly received assurances from the Soviet Union that it still supported international inspection of the dismantling and removal of missiles from Cuba. However, officials of the United States made it clear that the "no invasion" pledge of President Kennedy was not binding without international verification of the removal of the offensive weapons.

In another front page editorial, *Jenmin Jih Poa*, the Chinese Communist newspaper, rejected any "appeasement policy" toward the United States and pledged "full support" to Premier Castro. Pro-Cuban demonstrations continued for the third day in Peking.

The OAS passed a second resolution relating to the Cuban Crisis. (Refer to Document 79 for text.)

NOVEMBER 6, 1962 — The Soviet Union was reported to have proposed that Swiss Army technicians of the International Red Cross inspect the ships loaded with Soviet missiles as they depart Cuba. However, the United States was reportedly holding firm to on-site inspection.

Acting Secretary General U Thant met with two representatives of the Red Cross at the United Nations to discuss the "inspection at sea of Soviet missiles being removed from Cuba."

The United States reportedly protested the failure of the Soviet Union to remove the IL-28 medium-range jet bombers.

NOVEMBER 7, 1962 — The United States and the Soviet Union reached an agreement whereby United States naval vessels would make contact with the Soviet ships leaving Cuba and verify that the missiles were being transshipped.

Assistant Secretary of Defense Arthur Sylvester read the following announcement: "The Soviet Union has reported ships are leaving Cuba with missiles aboard. Arrangements are being made with Soviet representatives for contact with these ships by United States naval vessels and for counting the missiles being shipped out."

In Moscow, Premier Khrushchev announced that forty Soviet missiles were emplaced in Cuba and that they are now on their way back to the Soviet Union.

In a message to Premier Khrushchev on the forty-fifth anniversary of the Bolshevik Revolution, Premier Castro maintained his position on the five conditions which he laid down for a settlement of the Cuban Crisis.

NOVEMBER 8, 1962 — The Department of Defense announced that "all known" Soviet missile bases in Cuba had been dismantled, and that a "substantial" number of missiles had been loaded aboard Soviet ships or were moving to port areas. It was also announced that the Navy will determine the evacuation of the missiles through "close alongside observation." (Refer to Document 80 for text.)

Members of the Cuban delegation to the United Nations made it known that the IL-28 medium-range bombers sent to Cuba by the Soviet Union are Cuban property and will not be returned. United States aerial reconnaissance indicated that there were thirty to forty IL-28 bombers in Cuba.

Informed sources in Washington indicated that the IL-28 bombers were included in the definition of offensive weapons.

Wu Hsiu-chuan, Communist Chinese delegate to the Bulgarian Communist Party Congress, reportedly asserted that Communist China supported Fidel Castro's five conditions of settlement and that the Peking regime would extend all the material and moral support it could to Cuba.

There were indications emanating from Cuba that it was re-examining its relations with the Soviet Union following the Soviet withdrawal of the IRBM and MRBM missiles.

NOVEMBER 9, 1962 — The Department of Defense announced that five Soviet freighters were intercepted on the high seas and submitted to inspection. Assistant Secretary of Defense Arthur Sylvester announced: "The responsible people of this Government are satisfied that what is being reported [through the Navy inspection procedure] are the missiles, but final determination will await analysis of the photographs."

It was reported that a representative of the Soviet delegation to the United Nations had given an official of the United States a list of forty-two missiles and equipment, which would leave Cuba by November 11th.

The Department of State announced that President Kennedy had received another letter from Soviet Premier Khrushchev, but described the contents as "technical." It was believed that the letter discussed the details of the inspection procedure for the departing missiles. Qualified sources also indicated that there were one or two other letters from Premier Khrushchev to President Kennedy which were not made public.

Senior members of the United Nations staff continued discussions with delegates of the International Red Cross, Paul J. Ruegger and Melchior Borsinger, on the inspection of Soviet ships going to Cuba to ascertain that no offensive weapons were being sent in.

Discussions continued at the United Nations between the special United States negotiator, John J. McCloy, and special Soviet negotiator, First Deputy Premier Vasily A. Kuznetsov. It was reported that no further progress had been made after a four-hour meeting between the two men and other representatives of both nations.

The Communist Party of the Soviet Union announced that the Central Committee of the CPSU would meet on November

19th. The speculation was that the meeting was called to assess the position of the Soviet Union in world affairs following the Cuban Crisis.

The United States, Argentina and the Dominican Republic issued a statement on the establishment of a quarantine force. (Refer to Document 81 for text.)

NOVEMBER 10, 1962 — The Department of Defense reported that it had intercepted and inspected five Soviet ships loaded with missiles leaving Cuba: No boarding parties, but alongside inspection and photographs.

NOVEMBER 11, 1962 — The new head of the Cuban delegation to the United Nations, Dr. Carlos Lechuga, announced that Cuba will not permit outside inspectors on Cuban soil.

Deputy Secretary of Defense Roswell Gilpatric stated on a television program that United States authorities had "counted" forty-two Soviet missiles leaving Cuba in the last few days. Mr. Gilpatric also indicated that there had only been a "partial fulfillment" of the U.S.-Soviet agreement and that the thirty to forty IL-28 medium bombers were also "offensive weapons" and would have to be withdrawn from Cuba.

The head of the United States delegation to the United Nations, Ambassador Adlai E. Stevenson, stated on a television program that the United Nations played an important role in the resolution of the Cuban Crisis. He also predicted that Acting Secretary General U Thant would be elected to a full term as Secretary General, partially on the basis of his performance in the Cuban Crisis.

Premier Castro stated that "the Cuban people and their Revolutionary Directorate are firmly decided to defend their Socialist revolution until death." No mention was made of the visit of Soviet First Deputy Premier Anastas Mikoyan.

NOVEMBER 12, 1962 — President Kennedy conferred with his top Cuban negotiators from the United Nations and Washington. The only tangible results of the meeting were that the United States would still insist on the withdrawal of the IL-28 bombers and would not give a "no invasion" pledge until there had been on-site inspection verifying the departure of the offensive weapons.

NOVEMBER 13, 1962 — The Soviet Union and Cuba submitted a joint proposal on the Cuban Crisis to Acting Secretary General U Thant. However, the proposal was not subsequently submitted to a joint meeting of the Soviet and United States representatives reportedly on the grounds that it would not have been acceptable.

It was reported that United States officials believed the prolonged visit of Soviet First Deputy Premier Anastas Mikoyan to Cuba was to survey the entire economic and political situation within Cuba as the basis for subsequent Soviet policy. Very little news of Mr. Mikoyan's visit reached the outside world.

NOVEMBER 14, 1962 — The United States negotiators at the United Nations became slightly optimistic when it appeared that Cuba no longer claimed the IL-28 bombers as their own, and that the Soviet negotiators had never flatly refused the United States demand that the bombers be withdrawn. It was also hinted that the United States might lift the selective blockade of Cuba if the bombers were withdrawn.

Informed sources at the United Nations said that the joint Soviet-Cuban proposal called for the inspection and verification procedure to be carried out by neutralist diplomats. This approach had been raised by Acting Secretary General U Thant earlier with Premier Castro, but had apparently been rejected by the United States.

NOVEMBER 15, 1962 — Premier Fidel Castro made it known to Acting Secretary General U Thant that Cuba would shoot down United States aircraft if aerial reconnaissance continued. (Refer to Document 82 for text.)

It was reported that in one of the private letters Premier Khrushchev sent to President Kennedy, he had proposed "unacceptable conditions" for the removal of the IL-28 bombers. United States officials said that they were still optimistic over an early settlement. It was also reported that President Kennedy had urged Premier Khrushchev not to delay too long in the removal of the bombers.

An Eastern European delegate to the United Nations predicted that Premier Khrushchev would withdraw the IL-28 bombers despite Premier Castro's claim that they were Cuban property.

There was also speculation that First Deputy Premier Anastas Mikoyan might arrive at the United Nations from Havana on November 16th.

NOVEMBER 16, 1962 — Under Secretary of State George W. Ball delivered an address on "NATO and the Cuban Crisis" before the NATO Parliamentarians Conference in Paris. (Refer to Appendix J for text.)

NOVEMBER 18, 1962 — The Central Committee of the Communist Party of the Soviet Union defended the policy of Premier Khrushchev in regard to the recent Cuban Crisis.

A page long statement from the Central Committee appeared in *Pravda*, a Soviet Communist Party newspaper, defending Premier Khrushchev's policy against his critics. In another front page editorial, *Jenmin Jih Pao*, the Chinese Communist Party newspaper, declared that it was "pure nonsense" to claim that "peace had been saved" by the withdrawal of Soviet missiles from Cuba.

John J. McCloy, chairman of a United States coordinating committee on Cuba, met with Vasily V. Kuznetsov, a Soviet First Deputy Premier at the Soviet delegation's Glen Cove estate, with no tangible results. It was also reported that a joint Soviet-Cuban memorandum had been submitted to Acting Secretary General U Thant on November 15th in addition to the joint Soviet-Cuban proposal of November 13th.

The memorandum of November 15th was revealed to U.S. Ambassador Adlai E. Stevenson, but its contents were not disclosed.

NOVEMBER 19, 1962 — Washington sources disclosed that President Kennedy was considering warning the Soviet Union and Cuba at the press conference on Wednesday, November 20th if assurances were not received that the IL-28 bombers would be removed promptly.

Prime Minister Castro stated that he would not obstruct a decision by the Soviet Union to remove the IL-28 bombers from Cuba.

NOVEMBER 20, 1962 — President Kennedy announced at his press conference that he had received assurances that the IL-28 bombers would be withdrawn from Cuba in the near future, and that the United States quarantine would be lifted. (Refer to Document 83 for text.)

Secretary of State Dean Rusk discussed the "Basic Issues Underlying the Present Crisis" before the Foreign Policy Association. (Refer to Appendix K for text.)

NOVEMBER 21, 1962 — The United States apparently planned to continue a flexible policy toward Cuba based on international inspection and verification with a view toward undermining Castro's regime.

Also, the Department of Defense released 14,200 air reservists and removed the involuntary extensions for the Navy and Marine Corps. Almost simultaneously the Soviet Union and the Warsaw Pact nations terminated the alert status of their forces.

President Kennedy issued a proclamation terminating the interdiction of offensive weapons. (Refer to Document 84 for text.)

NOVEMBER 23, 1962 — President Kennedy conferred with members of his executive committee of the National Security Council on the Cuban situation in Hyannisport.

Soviet First Deputy Premier Vasily V. Kuznetsov conferred again with Acting Secretary General U Thant. The nature of the talks was not revealed.

NOVEMBER 25, 1962 — Soviet First Deputy Premier Anastas I. Mikoyan announced that he would return to the United Nations on November 26th.

Acting Secretary General U Thant stated that he expected a reply on the joint Soviet-Cuban memorandum for a final settlement of the Cuban situation from the United States before the return of Mr. Mikoyan.

Premier Khrushchev and some of his deputies informed Western correspondents that the prime lesson to be learned from the Cuban Crisis was "compromise and mutual concessions" It was believed that this was the general policy line pursued by Premier Khrushchev in his correspondence with President Kennedy.

Premier Castro said that Cuba would permit United Nations investigators to verify the removal of Soviet missiles if the United States would agree to United Nations supervision of what he described as anti-Castro training bases in the United States. The United States indicated that it would reject the Cuban proposal. (Refer to Document 85 for text.)

NOVEMBER 26, 1962 — Soviet First Deputy Premier Anastas Mikoyan arrived at the United Nations after an extended stay in Cuba. Mr. Mikoyan met with Adlai Stevenson, John J. McCloy and Charles W. Yost at a dinner given by Acting Secretary General U Thant.

Earlier in the day the United States had rejected the joint Soviet-Cuban memorandum calling for immediate guarantees by the United States not to invade Cuba. The United States position was apparently that it would give no such pledge until there had been on-site inspection and verification in Cuba as agreed to by Premier Khrushchev in his letter of October 28th.

NOVEMBER 27, 1962 — Ambassador Adlai E. Stevenson and Cuban coordinator John J. McCloy briefed President Kennedy on their talks with Soviet First Deputy Premier Anastas I Mikoyan at the United Nations prior to Mikoyan's visit with President Kennedy in Washington. It was reported that in addition to Cuba and other East-West issues the question of a nuclear test ban and disarmament would be discussed by Mr. Kennedy and Mr. Mikoyan.

The Department of Defense announced that "a phased redeployment of forces sent to the Southeastern United States during the Cuban crisis has begun." The Department also announced that a special airborne alert of the Strategic Air Command had also been suspended.

NOVEMBER 28, 1962 — The Soviet Union agreed in principle to the re-election of U Thant to a full term as Secretary General despite earlier Soviet insistence that the current Cuban Crisis be settled first. The agreement came after a three-hour meeting at the Soviet Mission to the United Nations between Anastas I. Mikoyan, Vasily V. Kuznetsov and Valerian A. Zorin for the Soviet Union with Adlai E. Stevenson, Charles W. Yost and John J. McCloy representing the United States.

David Schoenbrun of CBS News interviewed Secretary of State Dean Rusk and discussed the Cuban Crisis. (Refer to Appendix L for excerpt from interview.)

NOVEMBER 30, 1962 — Acting Secretary General U Thant upon the unanimous recommendation of the Security Council and the unanimous vote of the General Assembly was elected to complete the unexpired term of Dag Hammarskold which ends on November 3, 1966.

Soviet First Deputy Premier Anastas I. Mikoyan completed two days of high-level discussions in Washington with President Kennedy and Secretary of State Dean Rusk. It was reported that no substantive progress was made on the issues of disarmament, Berlin and the banning of nuclear tests, but that agreement was reached to continue discussions on the Cuban Crisis at the United Nations.

The United States, Argentina and the Dominican Republic issued a combined letter on the disestablishment of their quarantine force. (Refer to Document 86 for text.)

DECEMBER 1, 1962 — Soviet First Deputy Premier Anastas I. Mikoyan left Washington by plane for Moscow after spending over five weeks in the Western Hemisphere. He departed saying that he was convinced of the goodwill of the United States and that the same spirit would be demonstrated by the Soviet Union.

DECEMBER 3, 1962 — The Department of Defense announced that the Soviet-made IL-28 medium range bombers sent to Cuba were being returned to the U.S.S.R. Assistant Secretary of Defense Arthur Sylvester said, "The IL-28 aircraft that have been seen on the island of Cuba are in the process of being withdrawn." It was estimated that the Soviet Union had sent about forty IL-28 bombers to Cuba.

DECEMBER 5, 1962 — Carlos Lechuga, the new Cuban ambassador to the United Nations, transmitted a letter and statement to Secretary General U Thant. (Refer to Document 87 for text.)

DECEMBER 6, 1962 — The Department of Defense announced that forty-two IL-28 jet bombers were on the way back to the

Soviet Union and that this number agreed with the earlier estimates. It was also reported that the Soviet troops stationed in Cuba were engaged in developing defensive fortifications and additional airfields throughout Cuba.

DECEMBER 7, 1962 — United States analysts expressed doubts that Cuba would be able to obtain sufficient Soviet bloc credits to overcome the present economic difficulties.

The Soviet Union and Cuba had earlier negotiated a two-way trade agreement which totaled $750 million for 1962, however, there is apparently little evidence that the trade has approached this amount.

DECEMBER 10, 1962 — Secretary of State Dean Rusk said that the United States cannot accept "any Soviet military presence" in Cuba as a normal situation.

DECEMBER 12, 1962 — Premier Khrushchev warned the United States to keep to its promise not to invade Cuba. Khrushchev told the Supreme Soviet that if the promise is not kept the Soviet Union would take "appropriate action."

President Kennedy did not directly reply to Khrushchev's remarks in his press conference but did say that regulations were being prepared to curb shipping from other nations to Cuba.

President Kennedy also indicated that in his best judgment, the offensive missiles and planes had been removed from Cuba, and that in the absence of international inspection the United States would continue its own method of verification to assure against the reintroduction of offensive weapons into Cuba.

DECEMBER 13, 1962 — Yugoslav President Josip Broz Tito praised Premier Khrushchev for his "statesmanlike" action on Cuba and stated that those who interpreted the Kremlin policy as a sign of weakness were "shortsighted and dangerous."

DECEMBER 17, 1962 — President Kennedy in a TV-radio review of his first two years in office, said that the United States is "better off with the Khrushchev view" of world problems "than we are with the Chinese Communist view." President Kennedy went on to say that the arms blockade of Cuba was about the only course available to the U.S. at the time.

DECEMBER 18, 1962 — Attorney James B. Donovan returned to Havana to resume negotiations for the release of the prisoners captured in the abortive Cuban invasion of 1961. The U.S. government was reported to have worked out a plan whereby contributions in kind by private corporations would be treated as tax deductible charitable contributions.

DECEMBER 19, 1962 — Chairman Khrushchev sent a letter to President Kennedy on the Cuban Crisis and some general disarmament proposals. (Refer to Document 88 for text.)

Premier Fidel Castro lifted a ban on sending food and clothing to the Cuban prisoners captured in the unsuccessful invasion of 1961. This was interpreted by some as a hopeful sign that the prisoners might be freed in the near future.

DECEMBER 23, 1962 — Cuban Premier Fidel Castro and New York attorney James B. Donovan concluded an agreement for the release of the Cuban prisoners held since the abortive "Bay of Pigs" invasion in April 1961.

The first few hundred of the 1,113 prisoners began arriving in Miami that night by Pan-American World Airways.

The prisoners were reportedly exchanged for some $54 million in drugs, medicine and baby food contributed by American companies.

DECEMBER 24, 1962 — All the Cuban prisoners captured in the unsuccessful "Bay of Pigs" invasion of Cuba in 1961 were released and flown to Miami, Florida. It was also intimated that Premier Castro might release about 1,000 close relatives for an additional sum.

DECEMBER 27, 1962 — Nearly 1,000 Cuban relatives of the prisoners who were released before Christmas arrived in Port Everglades, Florida.

The White House also revealed that a last minute demand by Premier Castro for $2.9 million in cash almost held up the release of the prisoners but that the money was raised.

DECEMBER 28, 1962 — President Kennedy replied to Chairman Khrushchev's letter of December 19th and discussed the larger question of disarmament. (Refer to Document 89 for text.)

DECEMBER 29, 1962 — President Kennedy reviewed the freed Cuban prisoners in the Orange Bowl at Miami and received their battalion flag as a token of appreciation. In accepting the flag the President expressed the hope that one day it would fly over a "free" Havana. This remark caused concern within Cuba, but satisfaction among the Cuban exiles. (Refer to Document 90 for text.)

JANUARY 2, 1963 — It was reported that President Kennedy believed the outcome of the Cuban Crisis had caused the Soviet leadership to reassess the opinion that socialism was steadily spreading throughout the world. The experience of the Cuban Crisis had apparently given the Kennedy administration greater confidence in both domestic and foreign policy.

On the fourth anniversary of the Castro revolution a large parade was held in Havana displaying anti-aircraft rockets, heavy artillery, tanks, anti-tank guns; and Soviet-built MIG jet fighter planes flew overhead.

In an hour and a half speech Premier Castro referred to President Kennedy as a "vulgar pirate chief" and said in reference to the Cuban prisoner exchange that "For the first time in history, imperialism has paid war indemnification."

JANUARY 7, 1963 — The United States and the Soviet Union issued a joint statement which formally ended the direct negotiations over the Cuban Crisis. The talks were reportedly terminated on the grounds that Cuba would not accept international inspection to verify that the Soviet weapons had been withdrawn. The significance was that the United States apparently would not be bound by its "no invasion" pledge. (Refer to Document 91 for text.)

Carlos Lechuga, the Cuban ambassador to the U.N., sent a letter to Secretary General U Thant on the termination of the Caribbean situation. (Refer to Document 92 for text.)

Soviet Ambassador Nicolai Fedorenko presented his credentials to Secretary General U Thant as the head of the Soviet delegation to the United Nations, replacing Valerian A. Zorin who was recalled the previous December.

JANUARY 8, 1963 — Secretary General U Thant sent a letter to U.S. Ambassador Adlai Stevenson and Soviet First Deputy Premier Vasily Kuznetsov separately on the disengagement of the Security Council from the Cuban situation. (Refer to Documents 93, 94 for texts.)

✧ ✧ ✧ SELECTED BIBLIOGRAPHY

Ruhl J Bartlett, Editor, *The Record of American Diplomacy*, Third Edition, (New York: Alfred A. Knopf, 1954).

Carleton Beals, *The Crime of Cuba* (Philadelphia: J. B. Lippincott Company, 1933)

Samuel Flagg Bemis, *A Diplomatic History of the United States*, Fourth Edition (New York: Henry Holt and Company, 1955).

James Daniel and John G Hubbell, *Strike in the West* (New York: Holt, Rinehart and Winston, 1963).

Theodore Draper, *Castro's Revolution: Myths and Realities* (New York: Frederick A. Praeger, 1962).

Russell H. Fitzgibbon, *Cuba and the United States, 1900–1935* (Menasha, Wis.. George Banta Publishing Company, 1935).

Harry F Guggenheim, *The United States and Cuba: A Study in International Relations* (New York: The Macmillan Company, 1934).

Albert B. Hart, *The Monroe Doctrine: An Interpretation* (Boston: Little, Brown and Company, 1916).

Leo Huberman, *Cuba: Anatomy of a Revolution*, 2nd ed. (New York: Monthly Review Press, 1961).

Leland H. Jenks, *Our Cuban Colony: A Study in Sugar* (New York: Vanguard Press, 1928).

Herbert L. Matthews, *The Cuban Story* (New York: G. Braziller, 1961).

Karl E. Meyer and Tad Szulc, *The Cuban Invasion* (New York: Frederick A. Praeger, 1963).

John Bassett Moore, *A Digest of International Law*, Eight Volumes (Washington: U.S. Government Printing Office, 1906).

Dexter Perkins, *A History of the Monroe Doctrine* (Boston: Little, Brown and Company, 1955).

Royal Institute of International Affairs, *Cuba: A Brief Political and Economic Survey* (London: Oxford University Press, 1958).

Robert Freeman Smith, *The United States and Cuba: Business and Diplomacy, 1917–1960* (New York: Bookman Associates, 1961).

Robert F. Smith, *What Happened in Cuba? A Documentary History* (New York: Twayne Publishers, Inc., 1963).

Richard P. Stebbins and Others, *The United States in World Affairs, 1946–1961*, 16 Volumes (New York: Harper and Brothers, 1947 ff.).

The Christian Science Monitor

The National Broadcasting Company, *Meet the Press*, with guest appearance by Professor Marshall D. Shulman, produced by Lawrence E. Spivak; Volume 6, No. 43, Sunday, November 25, 1962 (Washington: Merkle Press Inc., 1962).

The New York Times.

The Wall Street Journal.

U.N., *General Assembly* and *Security Council Documents* and *Press Releases.*

U.S., Congress, *American State Papers: Documents, Legislative and Executive, of the Congress of the United States*, Selected and Edited under the Authority of Congress by Asbury Dickins, Secretary of the Senate, and James C. Allen, Clerk of the House of Representatives, Second Series, Volume V, Foreign Relations (Washington: Gales and Seaton, 1858).

U.S., Congress, *Brazil and United States Policies,* Report of Senator Mike Mansfield to the Senate Committee on Foreign Relations, 87th Congress, 2nd Session, No. 79125 (Washington: U.S. Government Printing Office, 1962).

U.S., Congress, *Congressional Record,* 87th Congress, 2nd Session (1962), Volume 108, Numbers 1–187 (Washington: U S. Government Printing Office, 1962).

U.S., Congress, *Events in United States–Cuban Relations: A Chronology 1957–1963,* prepared by the Department of State for the Senate Committee on Foreign Relations, 88th Congress, 1st Session, No. 93338 (Washington: U.S. Government Printing Office, 1963).

U.S., Congress, *Latin America, November–December 1960,* Report of Senator Bourke B. Hickenlooper, to the Senate Committee on Foreign Relations, 87th Congress, 1st Session, No. 67147 (Washington: U.S. Government Printing Office, 1961).

U.S., Congress, *The Bogotá Conference, September 1960,* Report of Senators Wayne Morse and Bourke B. Hickenlooper to the Senate Committee on Foreign Relations, 87th Congress, 1st Session, No. 65774 (Washington: U.S. Government Printing Office, 1961).

U.S., Congress, *Punta del Este Conference: January, 1962,* Report of Senators Wayne Morse and Bourke B. Hickenlooper to the Senate Committee on Foreign Relations, 87th Congress, 2nd Session, No. 79749 (Washington: U.S. Government Printing Office, 1962).

U.S., Congress, *United States–Latin American Relations,* prepared by Northwestern University for the Subcommittee on American Republics Affairs of the Senate Committee on Foreign Relations, 86th Congress, 1st Session, No. 47753 (Washington: U.S. Government Printing Office, 1959).

U.S., Congress, *United States–Latin American Relations,* a study prepared by the University of Oregon for the Subcommittee on American Republics Affairs of the Senate Committee on Foreign Relations, 87th Congress, 2nd Session, No. 87299 (Washington: U.S. Government Printing Office, 1962).

U.S., Department of Defense, *Cuba: Questions and Answers* (Washington: U.S. Government Printing Office, 1962).

U.S., Department of State, *Bulletin,* Volumes I–XLVIII (1939–1963).

U.S., Department of State, *Memorandum on the Monroe Doctrine: December 17, 1928,* prepared by J. Reuben Clark, Undersecretary of State (Washington: U.S Government Printing Office, 1930).

U.S., Department of State, *Papers Relating to the Foreign Relations of the United States, 1900–1945* (Washington: U.S. Government Printing Office, 1925–1962).

U.S., Department of State, *The U.S. Response to Soviet Military Buildup in Cuba,* Department of State Publication 7449, Inter-American Series 80, Bureau of Public Affairs (Washington: U.S. Government Printing Office, 1962).

Richard W. VanAlstyne, *American Diplomacy in Action* (Stanford, California: Stanford University Press, 1944).

Philip G. Wright, *The Cuban Situation and Our Treaty Relations* (Washington: The Brookings Institution, 1931).